ON THE TRUTH
OF BEING

Studies in Phenomenology and Existential Philosophy

GENERAL EDITOR
JAMES M. EDIE

ON THE TRUTH OF
BEING

*Reflections on Heidegger's
Later Philosophy*

Joseph J. Kockelmans

Indiana University Press
Bloomington

*This book was brought to publication with the aid of a grant
from the Andrew W. Mellon Foundation.*

Library of Congress Cataloging in Publication Data

Kockelmans, Joseph J., 1923–
  On the truth of being.

  (Studies in phenomenology and existential philosophy)
  Bibliography: p.
  Includes index.
    1. Heidegger, Martin, 1889–1976. I. Title. II. Se-
ries.
B3279.H49K633 1984   193   83-49191
ISBN 0-253-34245-7
  1 2 3 4 5 88 87 86 85 84

CONTENTS

Chapter 7. On the Essence of Language 142

Chapter 8. On Art and Art Works 170

Chapter 9. Thinking and Poetizing 196

Chapter 10. Science and Metaphysics in the Modern Era 209

PREFACE

In this book I have made an effort to present some basic themes of Heidegger's later philosophy. The expression "Heidegger's later philosophy" refers to that period in Heidegger's thinking in which, in the relation between Being and *Dasein*, he gives the priority to Being, contrary to what had been the case in *Being and Time* and related works. It is difficult to specify this period in years, but generally speaking, one can say that it is the period between 1935 and 1965.

It appeared to be desirable to undertake this effort in view of the fact that many works on Heidegger's philosophy either focus on his magnum opus, *Being and Time,* or are concerned with his philosophical development, on the one hand (William J. Richardson, Otto Pöggeler, Walter Biemel, J. L. Mehta), or with an aspect of his philosophy, such as language, the holy, ethics, politics, art, literature, etc. (Arion L. Kelkel, Vincent Vycinas, Jean-Michel Palmier, Friedrich-Wilhelm von Herrmann, Werner Marx, Henri Birault).[1]

A "systematic" presentation of Heidegger's later philosophy is one of those tasks which at first sight are accomplished relatively easily. The reason is that in Heidegger's own view, every thinker has really only one single thought. Yet the matter is not so simple. For in one sense it is among the most difficult tasks to try to capture what is essential in the work of an author who has been as "prolific" as Heidegger has been. How is one to discover the "essence" of someone's thinking whose works involve more than eighty volumes? Furthermore, Heidegger himself has stressed time and again that each thinker has to relate his own efforts to those of the great thinkers who in his tradition preceded him. Thus an effort to explain the "essence" of Heidegger's later philosophy will lead us unavoidably into his reflections on the works of the great philosophers of our entire Western heritage, from Anaximander to Nietzsche. But how is one to accomplish such a task for which the author himself appeared to have needed the greater part of his life?

Furthermore, one should not forget how alien Heidegger's thinking really still is. Pöggeler once remarked correctly that this alien quality should not be too hastily concealed. Rather, it "must gape up at us out of its true depth before it can be 'bridged over.' Only if we do not overlook this alien quality can we properly ask: What is the actual point of departure for Heidegger's thinking? What is the midpoint of his thought? What is . . . Heidegger's main thought?"[2]

Then there is the problem that Heidegger's thinking continues to move on different levels, even though the main concern constantly remains the same. Thus if we wish to understand Heidegger's philosophy, we must grasp it as a thinking that is constantly "on the way." As a matter of fact, we must try to understand it as a way *(Tao)*, as a way of thinking, *ein Denkweg*.[3]

Many things could be said about Heidegger's use of language. Yet I wish to limit myself here to one basic remark. Heidegger is never concerned with beings or things, but with meaning and Being; never with stable entities, but with events. Thus his language is never ontic, but ontological; never scientific, but thoughtful. Heidegger's thought cannot even make use of the language of a "scientific philosophy" in the sense of Kant, Hegel, or Husserl. That explains perhaps somewhat why his style of writing sometimes gives the impression of being poetic. Yet as we shall see later, Heidegger has made a systematic effort to explain the difference between thinking and poetizing, and to maintain for thinking a rigor of its own.

Another difficulty is connected with the question of how we are to relate to his thinking. One could say that just as Heidegger had to relate his own thinking to that of those who preceded him, in the same way are we to take distance from his thought and relate to it in both a positive and negative manner, applying Heidegger's own "method" of destructive retrieve and re-collection. Yet one should realize that Heidegger is not really one of our predecessors. Heidegger and I, for instance, have been contemporaries for more than fifty years. In view of the fact that the necessary historical distance is still lacking, it is virtually impossible for us to relate critically to his work in the sense in which he himself "thinkingly" related to Anaximander, Aristotle, Leibniz, Kant, or Hegel. Also, it is not correct to try to relate to someone's thought in a "thinking" manner before one has made a serious effort to truly understand it. Obviously that does not mean that we should accept uncritically everything that Heidegger has said or written. Yet it does mean that we should first try to "think with him" rather than against him.[4]

In view of the preceding remarks, it should be clear that no effort has been made here to be complete. I admit that many similar introductory treatises could be written, most of which would perhaps be quite different from the one undertaken here. I have tried merely to go to the core of Heidegger's own concern along a path for which I am requiring no other criterion or characteristic than that it "stays on the way." I have taken my point of departure from Heidegger's own lecture on what philosophy has been taken to be; other points of departure could have been selected. In the second chapter, following Heidegger's own effort to learn to think, we shall be led to a number of issues, which then, in the subsequent chapters, will be taken up in a somewhat orderly fashion, even though I fully realize that the order suggested here does not flow from the very matter of thought itself, but rather is superimposed on it, and in part is the result of the pedagogical concern from which this book has been conceived. I have, therefore, made a special effort to write the chapters in such a manner that they can all be read independently, or in an order somewhat different from the one I have chosen.

The reader will notice that in some chapters I have used a simple paraphrase of some of Heidegger's basic texts, namely, where a theme was to be discussed to which Heidegger himself has devoted an important lecture or essay. In other chapters I have composed a survey of basic ideas developed in different essays, lectures, or works. Finally, in some chapters I had to follow Heidegger's development in its different phases. In each case I have given some reasons for the choice made.

Finally, I have tried to show that Heidegger's later philosophy is concerned with a wide range of issues, all of which are intimately connected with the manner in which the truth of Being has come-to-pass to our generation. In view of the fact that "the truth of Being" occupies a privileged position in Heidegger's thinking as a whole, I have focused on this basic idea in both the introduction and the epilogue of this book.

Where I have quoted Heidegger's works literally, I have indicated so in the usual manner. As a rule I have then made use of the "official" translations. Yet in some instances I had to adapt the existing translation to achieve uniformity in the terminology used in this book. As far as the translation of technical terms is concerned, generally speaking I have adopted the translations proposed by William J. Richardson, whose book on Heidegger's development I take to be truly outstanding and still consider to be the best available today. For matters which pertain to the development in Heidegger's thinking, I have therefore consulted it regularly and quoted it extensively.

If I have succeeded in bringing the reader to the point where he, too, begins to see Heidegger's way, even though this way may still appear to him to be some kind of forest trail, the efforts which went into writing this book will be more than rewarded.

Joseph J. Kockelmans

ABBREVIATIONS

ON THE TRUTH
OF BEING

CHAPTER 1:

Introduction: On the Essence of Truth

Article I: The Question of Truth in *Being and Time*

According to Walter Biemel, Heidegger's philosophy, taken as a whole, has clearly a double focal point: it centers around both the question of Being and the question of *alētheia*. It is obviously not possible to understand the real meaning of this claim as long as it is not carefully explained precisely how it is to be understood. That is the main goal of this book.[1]

Heidegger's interest in the relationship between Being and truth (*alētheia*) was aroused by Franz Brentano's book *On the Several Senses of Being in Aristotle*, which Father Conrad Gröber, then pastor of Trinity Church in Konstanz, later bishop of Meissen in Saxony, and still later archbishop of Freiburg, had given him in the summer of 1907.[2] In this book Brentano explained that according to Aristotle, being is said in various ways; one is being in the sense of "being true."[3] The question of what *on hōs alēthes, ens tamquam verum,* "being in the sense of true," precisely means and of how what-is is to be related to what-is-true occupied Heidegger thus from the very beginning.[4]

In 1925–1926 Heidegger gave a course in Marburg entitled *Logik: Die Frage nach der Wahrheit,*[5] in which he had planned to treat the question of truth both "historically" and "thematically." For reasons not known to me, Heidegger changed the outline of the course and eliminated the part which was to present us with a systematic explanation of the essence of truth,[6] in order to focus instead on the temporality of care and a retrieve of Kant's conception of time as found in the *Critique of Pure Reason.*[7] Yet the first part of the course deals with the relationship between logic and truth and contains a very detailed study of Aristotle's conception of truth

1

and Heidegger's retrieve of its basic ideas.⁸ We find here already a great number of insights, which Heidegger later would employ in section 44 of *Being and Time.*

It is perhaps interesting to note in passing that in *Prolegomena zur Geschichte des Zeitbegriffs,*⁹ which contains the lecture course of 1925 that preceded the course on logic, the question of truth is not discussed either, even though we find in this "first draft of *Being and Time*" the most important sections of this work.¹⁰ I have the impression that in 1925 Heidegger was not yet completely ready to communicate the results to which his "critical" and "historical" studies concerning truth had led him.

Be that as it may, the first systematic treatment of the question of truth which we now have is found in *Being and Time,* section 44. Here Heidegger states that from time immemorial philosophy has circled around the connection between Being and truth. That is particularly evident in Parmenides, but we find the same conviction also in Aristotle, who defined philosophy as *epistēmē, hē theōrei to on hēi on,* "the science which contemplates being as being," and equally as *epistēmē tēs alētheias,* "the science of the truth."¹¹ Heidegger then continues that in view of the fact that a fundamental ontology is to lay the foundation for ontology which is to concern itself with Being, fundamental ontology must try to establish the relationship between truth and man if we are to understand the reason why "Being necessarily goes together with truth and *vice versa.* . . ."¹²

Heidegger's investigation itself is divided into three sections: 1) the traditional conception of truth and its foundation, 2) the primordial phenomenon of truth and an account of the derivative character of the traditional conception of truth, and finally 3) the mode of Being of truth and its presuppositions.¹³

According to the traditional conception, truth is "the adequation of the intellect and the thing." This definition of truth, which is traditionally attributed to Aristotle but seems to have been formulated by Isaac Israeli on the basis of texts of Aristotle, can be summarized in two theses: (1) the place of truth is judgment, and (2) the essence of truth lies in the conformity of judgment and object. This conception has been maintained until the present without any serious opposition. It was accepted in the Middle Ages by most theologians and philosophers; and Descartes and Kant also subscribed to it, though with some modifications. In Heidegger's opinion, this conception of truth is undoubtedly correct; yet in his view, it is formal, "very general and empty." Furthermore, it is affected with difficulties which must be resolved; and even then it is still unfounded.¹⁴

The first issue to be raised is the question of what is meant here by agreement. For, in view of the fact that intellect and thing or object are in no way similar, we must ask the question of how intellect and thing can correspond to each other. The intellect must try to grasp the thing "as it is"; yet it cannot itself become identical with the thing. In each judgment we must distinguish between the act and its object. The act of judging is a real psychical process, whereas that which is judged is an ideal content. Furthermore, it is assumed that the ideal content is somehow related to the real thing. How are we to take ontologically the relation between an ideal thing and something that is real? "Such a relation indeed subsists; and in factical judgments it subsists not only as a relation between the content of judgment and the real object, but likewise as a relation between the ideal content and the real act of judgment."[15] But such a conception is affected with serious difficulties. The most important of these is the following: "Does not the actuality of knowing and judging get broken asunder into two ways of Being—two 'levels' which can never be pieced together in such a manner as to reach the kind of Being that belongs to knowing?"[16]

The answer to this question can be found only by making the relationship of agreement referred to here become visible in the "phenomenal context of demonstration."[17] Heidegger develops such a demonstration by means of a simple example. Someone makes a statement about a picture hanging on the wall without actually seeing the picture at that time: "The picture on the wall is hanging askew." He then turns around to see whether his statement is indeed actually correct. In this case the verification or falsification of the statement consists in the act of perception. When a statement becomes verified, a being becomes accessible in its Being; it becomes discovered. What is confirmed in this case is that the assertion uncovers the being toward which it is. "What gets demonstrated is the Being-uncovering of the assertion."[18] Thus, in carrying out such a demonstration, our knowing remains related solely to the known thing itself; this being itself, which one has in mind, shows itself just as it is in itself; it shows that it, in its selfsameness, is just as it is pointed out in the assertion as being—just as it is uncovered as being. Thus what is to be demonstrated is not an agreement between representations, an agreement between a representation and a real thing, or, still less, an agreement between knowing and object or between the psychical and the physical; but neither is it an agreement between contents of consciousness.

What is to be demonstrated is solely the Being-uncovered of the thing itself— that very being in the how of its uncoveredness. This uncoveredness is confirmed when that which is put forward in the assertion (namely the thing itself) shows itself as that very same thing. "Confirmation" signifies the being's showing itself in its selfsameness.[19]

Thus we accomplish the confirmation on the basis of the thing's showing itself. But that is possible only if the knowing which asserts and which gets confirmed is, in its ontological meaning, itself a Being toward real things, and a Being that uncovers. Thus to say that a statement is true means that this statement uncovers the thing as it is in itself. Such a statement lets the thing be seen *(apophansis)* in its uncoveredness. Thus the Being-true (= truth) of the statement must be understood as Being-uncovering. But Being-true as Being-uncovering is, in turn, ontologically possible only on the basis of *Dasein's* Being-in-the-world.[20]

Heidegger is aware of the fact that this interpretation of the meaning of truth seems to be arbitrary. Thus he points out first that at the very beginning of philosophy, in the first fragment of Heraclitus, *logos* is declared to be that which tells us how it is with things. In that fragment

> [t]hose who are lacking in understanding are contrasted with the *logos,* and also with him who speaks that *logos,* and understands it. The *logos* is *phrazōn hopōs echei:* it tells how beings comport themselves. But to those who are lacking in understanding, what they do remains hidden—*lanthanei.* They forget it . . . ; that is, for them it sinks back into hiddenness. Thus to the *logos* belongs unhiddenness—*a-lētheia.*[21]

By translating *alētheia* as "unhiddenness," Heidegger does not engage in etymology but rather tries to bring into view the experience which for the Greeks was associated with this phenomenon. In Aristotle, the statement, i.e., the *logos* as *apophansis,* is still an *alētheuein* in the sense of an *apophainesthai,* i.e., a letting-be-seen of the entities that are brought from hiddenness into unhiddenness. What is thus disclosed are the things themselves, "entities in the 'how' of their discoveredness."[22]

Heidegger then shows what the relationship between man as *Dasein* and truth precisely is and that *alētheuein,* "Being-true," is to be regarded primarily as a mode of Being of man as *Dasein,*[23] a mode in which *Dasein* acts in an uncovering manner. What is true in the primary sense is this mode of acting; that which becomes accessible through this acting is true only in a secondary sense. To indicate that man as *Dasein* is essentially in a position to disclose beings, Heidegger uses the expression "*Dasein* is in the truth."

> In so far as *Dasein* is its disclosedness essentially, and discloses and uncovers as something disclosed, to this extent is it essentially "true." *Dasein* is "in the truth." This assertion has meaning ontologically. It does not purport to say that

ontically *Dasein* is introduced "to all the truths," either always or just in each case, but rather that the disclosedness of its ownmost Being belongs to its essential constitution.[24]

Yet if the Being of *Dasein* is taken in its full eksistential-ontological meaning, it is clear at once that the statement that *"Dasein* is in the truth" states equiprimordially that *"Dasein* is in untruth." *Dasein* not only reveals things; sometimes man hides things, disguises them, allows them to show themselves in the mode of semblance, allows what was once uncovered to sink back again in hiddenness. Heidegger refers here to the goddess of truth, who guided Parmenides and put two pathways before him, one of uncovering and one of hiding.[25]

Article II: *On the Essence of Truth*

We must now turn to *On the Essence of Truth,*[26] in which Heidegger developed these ideas in a more systematic fashion. *On the Essence of Truth* marks the transition from Heidegger's earlier to his later philosophy. In his effort to lay the foundation for metaphysics in a fundamental ontology, Heidegger first tried to clarify the relation between the process of Being and the finitude of that being which understands Being, namely, *Dasein.* In *Being and Time* he analyzed the mode of Being of *Dasein* phenomenologically and hermeneutically in order to find access to the problem concerning the meaning of Being. Subsequently he focused more directly on Being itself and particularly on the problem of the truth of Being, in view of the fact that the meaning of Being is its truth. The growing importance of the problematic of truth, which can be discerned in the works that followed *Being and Time,* culminates in the essay on truth.[27]

The essay consists of ten sections. It can be divided into an introduction, in which Heidegger focuses on the tension between philosophy and common sense; two major parts (sections 1 through 3 and 4 through 7); a brief conclusion (section 8); and a note (section 9). In the introduction Heidegger discusses the question concerning the tension between philosophy and common sense, a tension which directly confronts us with the question of truth. In part 1 he takes his point of departure from the common conception of truth, namely, truth in the sense of correspondence, and inquires into its presuppositions and its ground. In part 2 Heidegger explains why the essence of man is to be rethought in light of the outcome of the analysis contained in part 1. It appears, namely, that the inquirer himself is changed because of the investigation. Thus part 2 provides us with an exposition of the essence of *Dasein,* inasmuch as it must be understood in terms of the essence of truth. This exposition finally leads to a new conception of philosophy, which concludes the essay. "The conclusion, however, does not constitute the end, in the sense of reaching the goal, but rather points forward to a beginning which remains to be made afresh."[28]

I. FROM TRUTH AS CORRESPONDENCE TO THE GROUND OF CORRESPONDENCE

In the introduction to the essay, Heidegger writes that he will make an effort here to determine the very essence of truth, i.e., that which characterizes every kind of truth *as* truth, the ground of its inner possibility. According to ordinary common sense, however, such an investigation is superfluous; it makes no sense to inquire into the essence of truth, since nobody is really interested in the *nature* of truth. What interests us is the "real" truth, which can give us a standard against the prevailing confusion of opinions and calculations. If a questioning concerning truth is necessary, what we then demand is an answer to the question of where we stand today. Yet, Heidegger observes, if we want to call for the "actual" truth, then we must realize that in calling for the actual "truth" we must already know what truth as such means.[29]

Section 1 begins with an analysis of the conventional conception of truth, according to which truth consists in the conformity between judgment and judged, *adaequatio intellectus et rei.* There is an ontological truth, in which the thing conforms to an intellect, and a logical truth, in which the intellect conforms to the thing. In the first case, the thing means every created thing, whereas the intellect referred to is the divine intellect. Thus this conception of the ontological truth "implies the Christian theological belief that, with respect to what is and whether it is, a thing, as created *(ens creatum), is* only insofar as it corresponds to the idea preconceived in the *intellectus divinus,* i.e., in the mind of God. . . ."[30] In the second case, the issue is about the human intellect, which must conform to the things which it shows. And it is claimed further that the proper place of truth in this case is the human intellect's act of judgment. It is important to realize that in this conception of truth, the measure of truth in both cases lies in the correctness *(Richtigkeit)* of the conformity mentioned; untruth simply is non-conformity, or incorrectness.[31]

In Heidegger's view, this traditional conception of truth is undoubtedly correct and even important. Yet we must ask about the conditions which must be fulfilled in order to make this conformity possible, because it is in these conditions that the *essence* of truth is to be found.[32]

In section 2, Heidegger explains the exact meaning of the term *conformity.* The answer to this question will open the perspective on the fundamental question of how such a conformity precisely is possible. In every statement there is a correspondence between the judgment and the judged things: *adaequatio intellectus ad rem*. That does not mean that the statement becomes the thing or is somehow identical with it. The correspondence is determined by the kind of relation that obtains between the statement and the thing. The statement "relates itself" to the thing in that it "places it before itself" *(vor-stellt)*; it puts it in front of itself and says of the thing so posited how, according to the particular perspective that guides it, it is disposed. Thus what is stated by the pro-posing statement is said of the posited thing in just such a manner as that thing, as so posited, indeed is. In other words, the statement lets the thing stand opposite to itself as an object. As thus posited, what stands opposite must traverse an open domain which is opposite to it, and must, in so doing, nevertheless continue to stand there as this thing and to manifest itself as something constant. This appearing of the thing in traversing a domain opposite to it takes place in an open region, whose openness is not first brought about by man's pro-posing but is rather taken over in each case as a matrix of relationships. The relationship *(Beziehung)* of the pro-posing proposition or statement to the thing is the actual execution *(Vollzug)* of that relation *(Verhältniss)* which originally and at any given time makes itself vibrate as a comportment *(Verhalten)*. But every comportment is characterized by the fact that, standing in the open region, it always adheres to something that is manifest as such. What is manifest in this way, and what in the strict sense is so manifest only, was experienced early in Western thinking as that which is present and has long been called "being."[33]

In this very difficult passage, which can be interpreted in more than one way, Heidegger seems to express the following: *Dasein*, as Being-in-the-world, relates understandingly to things, because its essence is transcendence (intentionality). In each judgment *Dasein* takes a stand in regard to certain things. In its assertion it gives expression to its judgment and thus completes the act of knowledge by which it has been made possible for the thing-to-be-known to reveal itself as opposed to *Dasein*. The expressed judgment makes the thing-to-be-known present, and lets it take up its position as the object of *Dasein's* knowledge. But there is still a third "element" involved here, in addition to *Dasein* and thing. Heidegger calls this element "the open." This open, in which *Dasein* encounters the thing-to-be-known that now is the object of *Dasein's* knowledge, must itself be considered to be an open region that is opposed to *Dasein*, across which the thing-to-be-known must pass in order for it to appear to *Dasein* and thus become the object of its "knowledge." But the openness of the open is not constituted by the fact that the thing-to-be-known appears to *Dasein* by passing through it. The open region must be conceived as the matrix of relations *(Verhältnis)* which constitutes the domain of potentialities for *Dasein;* one of these potentialities is materialized when an actual contact takes place and *Dasein* enters into comportment with the thing-to-be-known-and-judged. What characterizes this comportment is the fact that, while standing in the open, it refers to something-that-is-open, *das Offenbare.*[34]

All comportment is thus a standing open toward beings. Concretely, this standing open can take place in many ways, depending upon the kind of beings and the manner of comportment. All working and doing, and all acting and calculating, maintain themselves within an open region within which beings, with respect to what they are and how they are, can properly take their stand and become capable of being said. But that happens only if beings become pro-posed in a pro-posing statement, so that the latter submits to the directive that it speak of beings only *such as they are.* In following this directive, the statement conforms to the relevant beings. A statement that directs itself accordingly is correct, true. What is thus stated is what-is-correct,-true.

Thus the statement derives its correctness from the openness of the comportment that precedes the statement; for only through the latter can what is so opened up become the standard for the pro-posing correspondence; only because such a comportment precedes all statements does it become possible for statements to express what beings are and how they are. That means that the beings laid open in *Dasein's* comportment must become the measure of the correctness of the statement. But if the correctness (truth) of the statement becomes possible only through the openness of the comportment, then that which makes the correctness first possible must also, and with more original right, be taken as the essence of truth.

Thus the traditional custom of attributing truth exclusively to statements as the sole and essential place of the truth has no ground. Truth does not originally reside in statements, but is to be found somewhere prior to them. Does it then perhaps reside in the open character of *Dasein's* comportment as such? To answer this question, we must first try to discover the ground which makes this comportment possible.[35]

II. TRUTH AND THE ESSENCE OF FREEDOM

In section 3 Heidegger sets out to answer this question. What makes this comportment possible is the fact that *Dasein* is so completely open and free toward the open as to accept any being which it may encounter within the open for what it is. Thus the openness of comportment which is the inner condition of the possibility of correctness (truth) is grounded in freedom. The essence of truth is freedom.[36]

But to turn truth into freedom, is that not to abandon truth to arbitrariness and to human caprice? Can truth be more radically undermined? Is truth not driven back here to the subjectivity of the human subject? Furthermore, deceit and dissimilation, lie and deception, fraud and pretense must also be ascribed to man. According to the traditional conception, untruth is the opposite of truth; thus, as the non-essence of truth, it must be excluded from the domain of the question concerning the essence of truth. Genuine truths are imperishable and eternal; they can never be founded on the fragility which is inherent in man's essence. Only untruth has its origin and root in man. Thus it is foolishness to seek the ground of the essence of truth in human freedom.

Yet in Heidegger's view, this conception rests on several questionable assumptions. One assumes that freedom is a property only of man. Furthermore, one assumes that the essence of freedom neither needs nor allows for further questioning. Finally, it is assumed that everyone knows what man is.[37]

The second part of the essay begins with a discussion of freedom as the foundation of truth, a discussion which is to refute these preconceptions. Already at the very beginning Heidegger indicates the direction which the inquiry is to take: ". . . freedom is the ground of the inner possibility of correctness only because it receives its own essence from the more original essence of uniquely essential truth."[38]

Freedom was at first defined as freedom for the manifest, for something that is open; freedom itself was there thus exhibited as *man's* openness. The manifest to which the pro-posing statement as correct is to correspond is the being as it manifests itself in and through an open comportment of *Dasein*. Standing in the realm of the open, *Dasein* is able to subject itself to what is manifest and shows itself, and to commit itself to it.[39] This freedom lets in each case beings be what they are. Freedom thus reveals itself now as letting-beings-be. Letting-be does not mean that *Dasein* is indifferent in regard to beings, but rather that it lets itself in on them. To let beings be as the beings which they are means to concern oneself with the open region and its openness, into which each being in each case comes to stand. The Greeks thought of this open region as *ta alēthea,* "the unconcealed." If we thus translate *alētheia* as "non-concealment" rather than "truth," this translation not only is more "literal" but also implies the hint that we have to revise our ordinary conception of truth in the sense of the correctness of our statements and to trace it back to the still-uncomprehended disclosedness of beings. But to let oneself in on the disclosedness of beings is not to lose oneself in it; rather, it unfolds and develops into a withdrawal before the beings so that they themselves may reveal themselves as that which they are and how they are, and in order that the pro-posing correspondence may take its standard from them. As this letting-be, it ex-poses itself to the beings as such and transposes all comportment into the open region. Thus, as this letting-be, freedom is essentially ex-posing and ek-sistent. From the point of view of the essence of truth, the essence of freedom now shows itself as the ex-position into the disclosedness of beings.[40]

In other words, that which makes it possible for *Dasein* to let itself in on beings is the fact that by its very constitution *Dasein* itself lets itself in on the open and its openness,[41] within which all beings abide and comport themselves. This process by which *Dasein* lets itself in on the open is ek-static by its very essence, so that it is by this process that *Dasein* stands outside itself in the direction of the open. That is what is meant by *Dasein*'s ek-sistence, its transcendence by means of which it goes beyond the beings that are open to the open itself, to the world, to Being. Thus in its constitutional freedom, *Dasein* is on the one hand committed to attain the open only in and through beings; on the other hand, however, *Dasein* transcends these beings unto the open itself.[42]

Freedom is thus not only that which common sense calls freedom: the sometimes emerging, capricious ability to go this way or that in one's choice. Freedom is not just the absence of constraint in regard to what we do or do not do. Nor, on the other hand, is freedom the mere readiness to do something that is necessary. Over and above the negative and positive freedom, freedom itself is first the letting oneself in on the unveiling of beings as such.[43]

Unveiledness itself is preserved in *Dasein*'s ek-sistent engagement, through which the openness of the open, i.e., the *Da*, is what it is. In *this* *Da-sein* there is preserved for the human *Dasein* the essential ground which, for a long time unfounded, allows man to ek-sist. "Ek-sistence," thus, does not mean here the medieval *existentia* or the existential *Existenz;* rather, ek-sistence, as grounded in truth as freedom, is nothing less than the ex-position into the being-unveiled of beings as such. It is ek-sistence which constitutes the essence of *Dasein.* "Still uncomprehended, indeed, not even in need of an essential grounding, the ek-sistence of historical man begins at that moment when the first thinker takes a questioning stand with regard to the non-concealment of beings by asking: what are beings? In this question non-concealment is experienced for the first time."[44]

Genuine history begins only when the beings themselves are expressly drawn up into non-concealment and preserved in it, and only when this preservation is thought in terms of *Dasein*'s questioning of beings as such. Thus the primordial disclosure of beings as such and taken as a whole, the question concerning being as such *(on hēi on)*, and the beginning of Western history are one and the same. They occur together in a "time" which, itself not measurable, first opens up the open for every measure.[45]

Heidegger then concludes that man does not "possess" freedom as some kind of property. Rather, the converse is true: freedom, ek-sistent, revelatory *Da-sein*, possesses man; it possesses man in such an original manner that it alone preserves for humanity that distinctive relatedness to beings as such and taken as a whole, which first founds all history. Only ek-sistent man is historical.[46]

Freedom, taken as letting beings be, is the fulfillment of the essence of truth taken in the sense of the revealment of beings. "Truth" is thus primarily not a characteristic of correct statements which are asserted of an "object" by a human "subject." Truth is rather the unveiling of beings through which an openness comes-to-presence. But if the essence of truth is not exhausted by the correctness of our statements, then neither can untruth be identified with the incorrectness of our statements.[47] In view of the fact that the essence of truth consists in freedom, ek-sistence, and transcendence, non-truth seems to be somehow connected with the negativity that affects freedom. But if that is so, then non-truth must also permeate truth as profoundly as negativity permeates *Dasein*'s freedom. The question, therefore, is one of how this negativity is to be understood. Before we are able to answer this question, we must turn once more to the question concerning the essence of truth.[48]

III. NON-TRUTH

In section 5, Heidegger repeats that the essence of truth shows itself as freedom. Freedom is the ek-sistent, revealing letting-be of beings. *Dasein*'s open comportment is in each case related to a particular thing or group of things. Yet in view of the fact that each comportment is also an engagement in the disclosure of the beings as such and taken as a whole, freedom has also already attuned all comportment to the beings taken as a whole. Thus in every particular comportment there is a certain attunement, by reason of which the beings taken as a whole become manifest. Heidegger refers here to the ontological disposition or "moodness" which discloses *Dasein*'s essential reference to the world, which, taken in an ontic sense, may be called *Dasein*'s orientation toward the beings as such and taken as a whole.[49]

But in "moodness" this whole itself remains rather vague. For as a matter of fact, the more completely *Dasein* is involved in any particular comportment in which one particular being or group of beings becomes manifest, the more the whole itself appears undetermined and even undeterminable; and it is for the same reason that this whole is all the more easily forgotten. Looking at it from this point of view, we may thus conclude that in every comportment by means of which *Dasein* reveals a particular being or group of beings, letting it be manifest, it conceals the whole as such. To reveal this particular being is to fail to reveal the beings as such and taken as a whole; thus a certain concealment is intrinsic in every revealment. If now truth is essentially revealment, then concealment must be what Heidegger calls "untruth." That is the reason why the essence of non-truth is now to be investigated in greater detail.[50]

The next two sections are very difficult. Biemel correctly observes that the difficulty which we encounter here does not lie so much in the obscurity of Heidegger's thought or language as in the fact that "Heidegger is pushing forward into a domain with which we are unfamiliar. . . . Heidegger attempts here to lay open a basic experience underlying the fact that man's way of being is historical *(Geschichtlich)*."[51] In view of the fact that we shall have to return to this basic experience in several chapters of this book, we shall limit ourselves now to a brief summary of some of the most important issues which Heidegger addresses here.

In section 6 we find two very important theses of Heidegger's later philosophy which must be explained here briefly, namely, the "mystery" as the authentic non-essence of truth, and the "forgottenness of the mystery." In the preceding sections we have seen already that the essence of truth consists in revealment and that the non-essence of truth, i.e., the essence of non-truth, consists in non-revealment, i.e., concealment. It is evident then that only that can be revealed which hitherto was concealed. Thus concealment is ontologically prior to any form of revealment. That means that the letting-be which is called revealment must always take place within a horizon of hidden darkness, which Heidegger calls concealment. Since, furthermore, revealment is essentially connected with freedom, concealment, which is ontologically prior to revealment, must also be ontologically prior to the freedom that comes-to-pass in and through each particular comportment between *Dasein* and an individual being or group of beings.

Again, this comportment itself not only leaves concealed the beings as such and taken as a whole, it also enters into a special relationship with the concealing of what is so concealed. But that, in turn, means that the concealment of the whole of beings is of such a nature that the concealing of this whole itself also remains concealed as such. Thus that which is concealed in *Dasein*'s liberating comportment is not only the beings as such and taken as a whole but also the fact that this whole is concealed.

What Heidegger calls the mystery is this concealing of the concealment; as the primordial and unique obscurity, this mystery enshrouds not only the individual beings but also, and even especially, the entire *Dasein* of man.

According to Heidegger, this primal mystery is non-truth in the most authentic sense. As such it dominates man's *Dasein*, insofar as *Dasein* is what it is, i.e., ek-sistence. But that can be explained only if a certain negativity is essentially intrinsic in *Dasein* itself, i.e., if *Dasein* is essentially finite, temporal, and historical.[52]

In conclusion, we may therefore say that there is a certain priority of non-truth over truth, of concealment over revealment, and, consequently, that the mystery necessarily connected with concealment dominates man's *Dasein*. At the same time, however, we must also admit that there is a certain dependence of the mystery on man's *Dasein*. This aspect of the problem is still to be explained; only if we succeed in the attempt to do so shall we be able to fully understand what it means that non-truth is prior to truth.

Speaking about the forgottenness of the mystery, Heidegger briefly refers to an important chapter of *Being and Time*.[53] He points out that the mystery is easily forgotten in the superficiality of man's everyday life. To be sure, in the domain of everydayness, *Dasein* really lets be the beings with which it has to do. Yet most of the time *Dasein* becomes completely fascinated by them and "loses" itself in them; it wants to use and control them. And even if *Dasein* purposely broadens the horizon of its interest, even then it is still determined by its own ontic intentions and needs. In this manner, however, man "refuses," implicitly at least, to let the mystery dominate his very own *Dasein*. The consequence is that the mystery slips into forgottenness.

Yet the mystery does not disappear by the simple fact that man forgets it. It still abides by a presence of its own; it even dominates man; it abandons man to his imprisonment in the domain of the ontic. Man is allowed to fashion his own "world" in such a way that it corresponds to his intentions and needs. But in this way, the things themselves become the norm by which man measures himself. Forgetting the beings as such and taken as a whole, man neglects to reflect on the ground which makes every measuring possible, because it, itself, precisely is the very essence of measure. There is only one escape route possible here, and that is to re-collect the mystery which pervades everything.

If we call *Dasein*'s power to transcend beings toward Being itself "ek-sistence," then *Dasein*'s propensity to adhere ontically to beings, once the mystery is forgotten, may be called "in-sistence." In the next section, Heidegger continues, we must thus examine how the abiding mystery that in its forgottenness is the non-essence of truth is still exerting its influence on the in-sistent ek-sistence. There it will become evident why the forgottenness of the mystery must be called properly "errancy," *die Irre.*[54]

Despite the difficult problems which the text poses for any commentator, it is nevertheless evident immediately that section 7 is one of the most important sections of the whole essay. Let us therefore try again briefly at least to indicate the main lines of Heidegger's explanation.

First of all, exactly what is meant here by "errancy?" Heidegger articulates his answer to the question in the following manner: In his everyday life, man, because of his in-sistence, adheres to the beings which, at the same time, through his ek-sistent freedom he somehow reveals. As we have seen, in his everyday life, man reveals the beings in such a way that he turns away from the mystery, toward which he nevertheless possesses an essential orientation. Although man thus, in a hidden manner, remains oriented toward the mystery, he nevertheless "wanders from one being to another in a state of confusion, driven about hither and thither, looking for a satisfaction that no being can give, searching for a repose that no being, torn from the roots of ultimate meaning in mystery, can offer." Errancy now is this congenital wandering about of man in a condition that his equally congenital orientation toward the mystery belies. It, too, is therefore called non-truth.[55]

Errancy, as intrinsic in the very structure of man, is thus the ground of all error which man commits in his life. But error is to be understood here not as a single, concrete mistake but rather as the whole complex of ways by which man in his wandering about from being to being can take the wrong way. True, man can wander about in forgetfulness of the mystery in many ways, but all these ways of vitiating truth have their root and origin in the errancy which is intrinsic in man's structure as *Dasein.* Errancy is the range of every modality by means of which truth can be vitiated. If the mystery itself may be called "non-truth," then errancy is a still more profound negation of truth.[56]

But now a second question arises: What is the precise relation between the non-truth called the mystery and the non-truth called "errancy?" Seen from one point of view, one must say that errancy is the source of the mystery insofar as man's insistent adherence to the beings necessarily implies a turning away from the mystery. Seen from another point of view, however, a certain domination of the mystery still abides. That is the reason why man constantly oscillates between the two forms of non-truth, errancy on the one hand and the mystery on the other.[57] In other words, non-truth itself is the necessary interwovenness of errancy and mystery. We must even say that both, errancy and the mystery, together constitute the full essence of truth itself, insofar as the *full* essence of truth includes within itself its own proper non-essence.

But if in this way errancy and mystery are incorporated into truth itself, and if both errancy and mystery necessarily dominate man in all his concrete comportments, then we must come to the conclusion that now truth itself is somehow prior to the freedom which in the preceding pages was described as the very essence of truth *as correctness*. But that would mean that the coming-to-pass of the truth, although it occurs in man's *Dasein*, does not have its *origin* in man's *Dasein*, but rather in that which in the mystery itself hides itself, namely, Being.

The last question we must ask here is the following: Is there no escape possible for man from errancy and mystery in the coming-to-pass of the truth? Heidegger believes that a *certain* escape is always possible, insofar as man is always able to experience errancy itself for what it is and to refuse to overlook the mystery any longer. When man really comprehends errancy as such, he recognizes it as the necessary consequence, and even as the reverse side, of his own forgetfulness of the mystery. But that means *eo ipso* to re-collect the mystery. For when man by means of this re-collection recognizes and acknowledges the mystery, surrenders to the mystery in an authentic resolve, the scene changes completely. In his everyday life, man through his freedom, lets be the beings which he encounters in every concrete, open comportment. At that very moment, the beings as such and taken as a whole become concealed, and in this concealing of the concealment, mystery and errancy rule man's life. However, when man recognizes errancy for what it is, and opens himself up toward the mystery as such, he no longer lets be the individual beings of a particular comportment, but rather the whole of the beings as such. This surrender to the mystery in authentic resolve, however, which comes-to-pass as soon as man recognizes errancy for what it is, does not destroy the mystery. On the contrary, it permits man to meditate the mystery for itself, and thus to pose the supreme question concerning what beings as such are, taken as a whole. Such an interrogation thinks the question of the Being of beings as such; such a questioning thinks Being itself.[58]

IV. TRUTH AND PHILOSOPHY

In section 8, Heidegger describes the relation between the question of truth and philosophy. In his view, the investigation has gradually led us from the specific question concerning the essence of truth to the very center of philosophy itself, whose basic function is to ask the question concerning the meaning or truth of Being. For to ask this question has been the task of philosophy since Plato. Heidegger himself articulates the course taken in this investigation as follows:

> The present undertaking takes the question of the essence of truth beyond the confines of the ordinary definition provided in the usual concept of essence and helps us to consider whether the question of the essence of truth must not be, at the same time and even first of all, the question concerning the truth of essence. But in the concept of "essence" philosophy thinks Being. In tracing the inner possibility of the correctness of statements back to the ek-sistent freedom of letting-be as its "ground," likewise in pointing to the essential commencement of this ground in concealing and in errancy, we want to show that the essence of truth is not the empty "generality" of an "abstract" universality but rather that which, self-concealing, is unique in the unremitting history of the disclosure of the "meaning" of what we call Being—what we for a long time have been accustomed to considering only as being as a whole.[59]

In a note, Heidegger explains that already in the original project this lecture on the essence of truth was to have been completed by a second lecture on the truth of essence. In his own view, "the latter failed for reasons that are now indicated in the 'Letter on Humanism.' "[60] We shall return to this remark and to the others made in this final note in the pages to come.

Let us conclude this introduction by stating once more that in Heidegger's view, the traditional "correspondence theory of truth" is neither false nor trivial. The conception according to which truth is the correspondence between man's knowledge and its object is correct and important. And similar remarks can be made for the other theories about truth, namely, the coherence theory and the pragmatic conception of truth. Yet, Heidegger argues, these theories tell us relatively little about the very essence of truth, about that which makes correspondence, coherence, and correctness precisely possible as such. This essence is to be found first in *Dasein*'s openness, freedom, ek-sistence, and transcendence; primordially, however, that which makes correctness possible consists in Being itself, because Being itself is the ultimate condition of possibility of all discovering.

These reflections on the essence of truth obviously do not constitute the end of our thinking reflections. Rather, they refer to a beginning which remains to be made afresh. It is to this beginning that we must now turn.[61]

CHAPTER 2

The Thinking of Being

I would like to begin these reflections on Heidegger's later thinking with an attempt to explain what Heidegger understands by philosophy, how in his own view philosophy is to be related to the work of the great thinkers of the past, and with what philosophy should concern itself first and foremost, if not exclusively.

In view of the fact that these questions have been developed by Heidegger in a more or less systematic fashion, it seems advisable to turn to some of his essays and to follow his own exposition of these questions as closely as possible. I have thus decided to paraphrase a few relevant essays and to add explanatory remarks and pertinent interpretations where they seemed meaningful.

In the first section I shall make use of Heidegger's lecture *Was ist das— die Philosophie?* (1955).[1] Here Heidegger tries to explain the origin of Western philosophy, its basic concern from the very beginning, and its history from the Pre-Socratics to Marx and Nietzsche. Finally, he explains how he himself conceives of philosophy and how his thinking should be related to the thought that has preceded it in the West.

In the second section of this chapter, I hope to turn to some basic ideas developed in Heidegger's "Letter on Humanism" (1947).[2] Of the many ideas on which the lecture *What is Philosophy?* briefly touches, there are some which ask for an immediate further elucidation. In my view, these certainly include the following issues: What is the subject matter of philosophy, or as Heidegger calls it, the matter of thought? Assuming that the subject matter is Being, taken in the sense of the Being of beings, as our entire Western tradition suggests, how are Being and man, taken as *Dasein*, then to be related to one another, and, in this relation, to whom must the privileged position be granted? Assuming also, as the lecture on philosophy suggests, that this relation is thinking, precisely what then is to be understood by thinking? Finally, what is one to think of the historicity of Being, man, and thinking? Here, too, I plan to follow the same "method" as in the first section.

Finally, I hope to turn to the question of how Heidegger relates in his own thought to that of his predecessors. I hope to explain how he later came to conceive of what originally was called the *destructive retrieve*.[3]

Article I: What Is Philosophy?

In 1956, Heidegger published a lecture entitled *Was ist das—die Philosophie?* The lecture was presented at a meeting of French-speaking philosophers in Cérisy-la-Salle (Normandie) in August 1955, and it was meant as a general introduction to a discussion on the meaning of philosophy. The basic problem which he raised in this lecture was in Heidegger's own view of vital importance, and it was an issue which had occupied him regularly since the publication of *Being and Time* in 1927. The question concerning the meaning of philosophy is raised not only in the introductory sections of a number of lecture courses but also in such publications as *What Is Metaphysics?, An Introduction to Metaphysics, Letter on Humanism, Was heisst Denken?, Identity and Difference,* and many other publications.[4]

The lecture begins with a question which is first formulated in French and then repeated in German: "Qu'est-ce que la philosophie?" Heidegger does not translate this question as "Was ist Philosophie?" or even as "Was ist die Philosophie?" but rather literally as "Was ist das—die Philosophie?" This German rendition focuses obviously first on the manner in which the French people ask questions. They ask "What *(qu')* is *(est)* that *(ce [que])*—the philosophy *(la philosophie)?* Yet in addition, in German, the question suggests also: "What kind of 'thing' is that—*the* philosophy?" "What kind of 'thing' could that now be which one usually calls *the* philosophy?" In other words, taken by itself, the title *Was ist das—die Philosophie?* suggests that one commonly assumes that there is something which one calls philosophy, which is, always was, and always will be, and which, unimportant changes over time notwithstanding, remains basically unchanged and invariant. If one were to try to understand the meaning of the title in this manner, he would soon find out that Heidegger will argue that such an interpretation of the question not only is in conflict with the historical facts but also seems to run contrary to the undeniable fact of the historicity of all human thought. Thus it seems that

Heidegger, by translating the French question literally, will focus the reader's attention immediately upon an issue that has plagued many modern philosophers: How is the "scientific" character of philosophy to be combined with its intrinsic historicity?

It is clear that by looking at the title in this way, we are immediately confronted with the issues which in Heidegger's own view go to the heart of the matter: What does it mean to philosophize? Why should one engage in philosophy? In view of the fact that we are not the first ones to philosophize, how are we to relate our thinking to that of those who preceded us? In the past, and particularly since the time of Descartes, there have been philosophers who have stressed the scientific character of philosophy so one-sidedly that they believed it possible to eliminate its historical character altogether. To be sure, few of these authors have denied the pedagogical value of the knowledge known already in our rich heritage. Descartes, who decided to reject completely for once in his lifetime "the opinions which [he] had been receiving since [his] birth,"[5] nevertheless also wrote in the same treatise: "I did not, however, cease to value the disciplines of the schools. . . ." Yet for him, "conversing with the ancients is much like traveling. It is good to know something of the customs of various peoples, in order to judge our own more objectively. . . . But when one spends too much time traveling, one becomes at last a stranger at home. . . ."[6] Thus one day, Descartes brushed aside all opinions of past philosophers and decided "never to accept anything as true unless [he] recognized it to be certainly and evidently such. . . ."[7] Since Descartes, more and more thinkers, even though they may have still accepted the pedagogical value of past philosophies, have believed that philosophy is a question of method, principles, and indubitable starting points, or a question of dialogue and dialectic.

Heidegger does not share this opinion. As far as this issue is concerned, he sides with Aristotle and the Aristotelians, as well as with Hegel. Yet where Hegel was predominantly concerned with giving the great thoughts of the past a "place" within the system of absolute knowledge, Heidegger tries to relate to the great thinkers by means of re-collection, a re-collection that has the character of a destructive retrieve. In "The Onto-Theological Constitution of Metaphysics" (1957),[8] Heidegger explains his position by comparing it with Hegel's. In his opinion, the subject matter of philosophy is the same for both Hegel and himself; it is Being. Yet Hegel thinks Being with respect to beings which have been thought in absolute thinking and as absolute thinking. For Heidegger, on the other hand, it is Being with respect to its difference from beings. For Hegel, the matter of thought is the idea (of Being) as the absolute concept; for Heidegger, on the other hand, it is the difference as difference. Both Hegel and Heidegger also agree with Aristotle that in thinking Being one must enter into a conversation with the history of thinking. In so doing, both use the same criterion, namely, the force or power and the range or domain of what has been thought by earlier thinkers. Yet whereas Hegel uses this criterion in an effort to find something that has already been thought and from the perspective of the absolute knowledge appears to be true, Heidegger uses it to discover something that has not yet been thought.

In using the criterion in his way, Hegel finds something that is to be maintained and, thus, is to be given a definitive place in the absolute system so that the earlier thinking becomes part of the later systematization which surpasses it. Heidegger, on the other hand, uses the criterion in such a way that the thinking of the past can be set free in its having-been, so that the thinking of the past in each epoch can be kept in reserve as something to be re-collected time and again. Thus this having-been continues to prevail and govern throughout the entire subsequent tradition; it abides there as something that is constantly in advance of it, and yet is never explicitly thought in its own right and as that which was first in the beginning. However, our thinking today is not determined by the thinking that has been; rather, it is set free by it.

Finally, Heidegger then turns to the character of the conversation. For Hegel, the conversation with the thinkers of the past has the character of *Aufhebung;* in other words, it "negates," preserves, and overcomes what has been thought already so that only the truth will be maintained. For Heidegger, it has the character of a step backward, a step-in-reverse, which points to the domain which until now remained unnoticed and from which the essence of truth itself first becomes something that is worthy of thought. This step-in-reverse is not an attempt to return to the beginning, to the pre-Socratics or perhaps to Plato and Aristotle; the step-in-reverse is not to lead us back to the past; rather, it is to lead us forward, even though the concrete direction shows itself only in the actual execution of the step itself. Furthermore, the step-in-reverse is not one isolated, single step; rather, it is a way which time and again leads away from what has been thought already, to what remained unthought. Tentatively, Heidegger refers to what remained unthought with the term *the difference of Being and being;* what remained unthought again and again is the difference as such, the forgottenness of the difference, the concealment of the difference as such.[9]

We shall return to the issues raised here later in a more systematic manner. Let us now first turn to the text of the lecture: What is philosophy?

I. THE LECTURE

If we analyze the content of this lecture carefully, we will find it meaningful to distinguish at least six major parts: an introduction and five basic theses, the last of which harmoniously leads into a brief conclusion.

1. Introduction The question which is touched upon in this lecture is broad, and to some degree it is even indefinite. Thus there is the danger that our discussion of it will lack the necessary depth and systematic cohesion. We must therefore try to define the question more accurately, to steer our discussion in a more definite direction by bringing it on a more definite path, even though this path may not be the only one possible. Yet we must stipulate at least one condition, namely, that the path of our discussion must give us the guarantee that we are indeed moving within philosophy itself and not around it or outside of it.[10] That means that our discussion must be such that that of which philosophy speaks concerns us personally, affects us, and touches us in our very mode of Being.

Heidegger thus claims here first that philosophy is not just for an élite, for "professional" philosophers, or even for philosophy teachers. Rather, it is necessary for all human beings to philosophize. In other words, Heidegger joins Aristotle and many other thinkers of the past who have claimed that it is "natural" for man to seek wisdom through philosophical speculation. Furthermore, Heidegger also claims that philosophy does not just provide us with some kind of knowledge which it is very desirable to have, but rather that the engagement in philosophy will codetermine the self we shall be while standing in the heritage to which we belong.

One will obviously object here that by claiming that philosophy is to affect and touch us in our Being, we make philosophy a matter of affection, emotion, or sentiment. Yet philosophy is most certainly not something irrational; rather, since the time of the Pre-Socratics, philosophy has been called the guardian of reason itself. On closer investigation, however, it becomes clear that in making this kind of assertion, we have already made a decision a priori as to what philosophy is supposed to be: everyone assumes that philosophy is a matter of reason. Furthermore, we also assume that what moves us is intimately related to what is usually called emotions or feelings, and that the latter are inherently irrational. But is all of that indeed true? We shall return to this question shortly, but let us conclude here provisionally that if we wish to know what philosophy really is, greater care will be required than we have shown thus far. Thus the first thing to do is to lead the question to the proper path. This path lies directly before us, even though we do not immediately see it, because it is the nearest at hand: the word *philosophy* itself points to this path.[11]

Here it is obviously not Heidegger's intention to claim that philosophy is not a form of thought which as such can and should be called the work of "reason." What he does object to is the one-sided Enlightenment conception of reason which was dominant in Germany through the influence of Kant and German idealism, neo-Kantianism, and even to some degree Husserl. In Heidegger's view, reason is always interwoven with lack of reason, truth with untruth; revealing and hiding cannot be completely separated. He also tries to go beyond an analytic attitude which a priori distinguishes and often even separates man's cognitive from his emotional and volitive life. Here too, it is not his intention to claim that such distinctions are always meaningless; on the contrary, at the proper level of discourse they may very well be vital and essential. For instance, it is difficult to see how one could have meaningful psychological research if such distinctions could not be made. The point for Heidegger here merely is that it is not correct to begin philosophy with a number of assumptions in which a certain conception of what philosophy is supposed to be is already implied.

2. The Importance of the Greek World and the Greek Language Our English word *philosophy* comes from the Greek word *philosophia*. This word tells us that philosophy is something that first of all determines the mode of existence of the Greek world, as well as the innermost basic characteristic of our entire Western European history. Thus we shall find a meaningful answer to our question of what philosophy is only if we return to the heritage and tradition to which the Greek word *philosophia* refers. In so doing, we must realize that this heritage has become an integral part of Christendom and that it is also at the root of modern science and technology. Furthermore, one should note that a heritage and a tradition do not surrender us to a constraint by what is past, but that to hand a heritage down to someone means to deliver *(délivrer)* him into the freedom of a meaningful discourse *(logos,* dialogue) with what has been.[12]

Heidegger here thus states that our entire Western civilization or culture, the entire Western world, orginated in Greece, and that philosophy played an essential part in the coming-to-pass of this world. This Greek world was later "mediated" by Christianity, which undoubtedly also left its traces on the heritage which was so handed down. Finally, he claims that science and technology have their essential root in this very heritage. He concludes these reflections with some brief remarks on the meaning and function of heritage and tradition. Each of these claims can obviously not just be taken for granted, and some of them may even seem to be arbitrary. Heidegger was aware of that; thus he will return to these claims in what is to follow, and most certainly these issues did turn up time and again in his later work, as he here presupposes. Let us not forget that this lecture was meant to introduce a discussion which was to go on over a prolonged period of time. The provocative statements formulated here were meant to evoke a meaningful discussion in which Heidegger had a chance to clarify his position more carefully and present reasons for the position taken. We shall return to some of these issues in the chapters to come.

In Heidegger's view, not only what philosophy is, is Greek in origin, but also the manner in which we question is Greek. For when we ask what philosophy is we ask: *"Tí estin"*—"What is. . . ?" This question can be interpreted in different ways, and in the history of the West the question concerning the what, the *quid*, the quiddity has indeed been interpreted in different ways by Plato, Aristotle, Kant, Hegel, and so on. Yet even though that which is asked in each instance by means of the clue of the *tí estin* was to be determined each time in a new way, in every case one nevertheless asked an originally Greek question when one philosophically asked: "What is. . . ?"

It is also important to note here that the question of what philosophy is, thus is a *historical* question. And it is not *just* a historical question which tries to determine how that which we call philosophy really came to be and how it developed over time; rather, it is also a question that is full of destiny *(geschick-lich)*, a destiny which affects our entire Western mode of Being. It is a question which points to our origin as well as our future; through its historical origin, the question has helped us find a direction into a "historical" future which is full of destiny and yet does not determine and bind us. Heidegger concludes these reflections by saying that we thus have found a path, although we still have no guarantee at this point that we shall be capable of pursuing this path in the right way.[13]

The last remarks clearly indicate that Heidegger was aware of the ambiguity and seeming arbitrariness of some of the theses formulated here. In several lecture courses, individual lectures, and in essays, he had already given a detailed account of the origin of philosophy and its development between Heraclitus and Nietzsche.[14] Furthermore, from 1935 on he had time and again tried to explain how in his view in the history of the West the truth of Being comes-to-pass in various epochs and how in each of these epochs a certain conception of the meaning of Being becomes dominant.[15] Finally, on several occasions he had also tried to explain how in his opinion thinking today is to relate to the thinking of those who have preceded us.[16] Those who took part in the discussion in Cérisy-la-Salle were all aware of these lectures and publications, so that Heidegger must have thought that these brief and terse remarks were adequate to focus the discussion to follow and to evoke questions to be developed in the subsequent dialogue. It is impossible here to unfold these theses in detail; we shall return to them later in one of the subsequent chapters. Yet what is of immediate importance to understand Heidegger's conception of philosophy will be mentioned later in this chapter.

In Heidegger's opinion, the question of what philosophy is concerns first and foremost the very mode of Being of philosophy itself, the very manner in which philosophy now abides among us today, *das Wesen der Philosophie (wie die Philosophie heute west)*. But if this question originates from a genuine need, i.e., if we ask the question not because we have to talk about something but because we know that it is of vital importance that the question be asked now, philosophy itself must have become questionable and worthy of question for us. But that presupposes that we already somehow know what philosophy is. Thus we appear to find ourselves in a circle, and philosophy itself seems to be this circle. If we want to know how we are to look at this circle, we must turn again to the word *philosophy*, which here, too, will indicate for us the proper direction.

Heidegger here refers to his conception concerning the hermeneutic character of all genuine questioning, which he had described for the first time in the opening sections of *Being and Time*.[17] Speaking about the question concerning the meaning of Being, Heidegger had written already in the second section of the book:

> Inquiry, as a kind of seeking, must be guided beforehand by what is sought. So the meaning of Being must already be available to us in some way. As we have intimated, we always conduct our activities in an understanding of Being. Out of this understanding arise both the explicit question of the meaning of Being and the tendency that leads us towards its conception.[18]

Heidegger admitted there the "circular" character of this line of questioning, but he also explained why this "hermeneutic circle" is not a vicious circle in the logical sense of the term. We shall return to this issue in chapter 3.

Heidegger concludes this section of his lecture with the remark that the Greek language occupies a privileged position among the European languages. The Greek language, and it alone, is still *logos* in the proper sense of the term. That means that if we hear a Greek word properly, we are still directly in the presence of the thing named, and not first merely in the presence of the mere signification of the word.[19] For many people today, particularly in the Anglo-American world, these latter claims must look totally arbitrary. Is it really true that the Greek language occupies a privileged position as far as philosophy is concerned? And even if this assertion is so, does that mean that it is so precisely because the Greek words in antiquity still brought those who heard them into immediate presence with the things named? And finally, is it indeed true that today words bring us merely into the presence of the significations of these words? I do not think that anyone can easily answer these questions with the help of a few statements. They flow from Heidegger's interpretation of the concept of *logos* in Greek thought. I plan to return to this subject in the chapter on language. Suffice it to note here that philosophy as we conceive of it in the West indeed did originate in Greece, and that it certainly is not farfetched to assume that this fact is connected with the structure and the interpretation of the structure of the language of those who began to philosophize.[20]

3. Philosophia The Greek word *philosophia* is derived from the adjective *philosophos*. It is not impossible that this adjective was coined by Heraclitus; at any rate, he did not yet know the word *philosophia*. For Heraclitus an *anēr philosophos* was not a "philosophical man" or a philosopher but rather a man who loves *(philei) to sophon*, i.e., a man who speaks in the manner in which the *logos* speaks, a man who speaks in correspondence with the *logos*, in harmony with *to sophon*, according to which all is one *(Hen Panta)*. Thus, according to *to sophon*, all beings are gathered together in Being, because Being is the very gathering together, i.e., the *logos*.[21] For us it seems rather trivial to claim that all beings belong in Being and are in Being. Yet for the early Greek thinkers this idea became the most astonishing thing; the thinker must respond to Being taken as *logos*, which gathers all beings unto themselves and lets them be what they are.

Yet even the Greeks had to protect the astonishing character of this most astonishing truth against the views of the Sophists, who interpreted both appeal and response in a quite different way. At a later stage, the mystery of Being in beings disclosed itself again to genuine thinkers, whose authentic response tried to save Being from this fallen condition; a few thinkers then began again to strive for *to sophon*, beings in Being, and in this way also kept alive in others the yearning for and the love of *to sophon*. For Plato the fundamental drive had the character of *erōs*, whereas for Aristotle *to sophon* disclosed itself as *Beingness (= ousia)*. Because for them the loving of *to sophon* is no longer in original harmony with it, but rather a striving toward it, the loving of *to sophon* becomes *philosophia*.

Heraclitus and Parmenides were not yet called philosophers; they were not yet philosophers because they were still in harmony with the one-in-all. The step into philosophy was prepared by the Sophists and then first accomplished by Socrates and Plato. Almost two centuries after Heraclitus, Aristotle could therefore write: "And thus, as was in the past, is now too, and will be ever more, that towards which [philosophy] is on the way and to which it time and again does not find access, is what is being. . . ?"[22] Philosophy thus now begins to seek what being is insofar as it is, *on hēi on*. It seeks what the Beingness *(ousia)* of beings is. In the final analysis, *ousia* is for Plato *idea* and for Aristotle *energeia*.[23]

Heidegger claims here that what the Greeks called philosophy is the striving after Being, the Being of beings; in their opinion, this striving implies some form of transcendence. Plato interpreted this transcendence in terms of a passing beyond the sensible to the super-sensible and intelligible, whereas Aristotle interpreted it in terms of a passing beyond the physical toward the metaphysical. For them, as for most Western thinkers who followed them, philosophy became thus identical with metaphysics, which Aristotle in the first book of the *Metaphysics* defines as *epistēmē tōn prōtōn archōn kai aitiōn theōrētikē*. This phrase is usually translated as "the theoretical science of the first principles and causes." This translation is, however, very misleading: *epistēmē* does not mean "science" in the modern sense; *theōrētikē* had for the Greeks a different meaning from that of the word *theoretical* for us. Finally, it is not at all clear what the Being of beings *(ousia)* has to do with such things as "principles" and "causes." For Aristotle, philosophy is some kind of aptness or human competence which makes him capable of holding in his glance the Being of beings. Philosophy is some endowment in man by which he catches in view *(epistēmē theōrētikē)* the beings in that by which they are as beings *(archōn, aitiōn)*, namely, Being.[24]

4. The Question about Philosophy Is Really a Historical Question Thus it seems as if Aristotle has already answered the question which occupies us here in our discussion. If this were true, then our conversation would be superfluous. Why should we raise the question once more? One will say that Aristotle's conception is obviously only one answer among many; in the course of the centuries, many other definitions of what philosophy is have been proposed. Yet at the same time we must also note that philosophy from Aristotle to Nietzsche has remained the same, all of these changes notwithstanding.

At any rate, it is certainly not true that Aristotle's definition of philosophy is valid in an absolute sense. Even within the realm of Greek thought, it was only one interpretation of philosophy. It does not really characterize the thinking of Parmenides or Heraclitus, and one cannot even legitimately claim that Aristotle's conception of philosophy with necessity followed from their conceptions of thinking. Aristotle's definition is thus no more than a *free* consequence of earlier thinking. Hegel's thesis that individual philosophies and epochs of philosophy have emerged from one another with the necessity of a dialectic process is thus unacceptable.[25]

Heidegger's interpretation of this definition of philosophy rests thus on Aristotle's conception that metaphysics is concerned with *on hēi on*, with being *as* being, and particularly with *ousia*, Beingness. In his view, that was once a legitimate conception of what philosophy is, but it did not once and for all establish the meaning of philosophy; it is no more than Aristotle's authentic response to the address of Being. Yet it cannot be attributed to Heraclitus or Parmenides, any more than it can be imposed on Kant or Hegel. In Heidegger's opinion, Being remains forever "free" to address itself to man via some other type of "sending."

Richardson correctly observes here that in his later works, Heidegger uses the term *philosophy* sometimes in a narrow sense, according to which it is identical with metaphysics; sometimes he uses it in a very broad sense for any authentic response to Being's address. If it is taken in the narrow sense, philosophy is to be overcome; if it is taken in the broad sense, it means that for which every authentic thinker strives.[26]

We have mentioned already that over the past two thousand years, different conceptions of philosophy have been proposed. It will be clear at once that one cannot come to the "true" conception by means of a process of comparative abstraction which reduces the different conceptions to some kind of common denominator, because such a process would ultimately lead to an empty formula.

Without denying the importance of the historical methodology as it is now employed in the science "historiography," we must still maintain that the answer to the question of what philosophy is cannot be found by the sciences, but only by philosophy itself. The answer to our question must be a philosophical one which, as a response, "philosophizes" in itself, so to speak. Let us thus try to clarify how an answer, insofar as it is a genuine response, can itself be a "philosophizing" one.

Our own answer to the question of what philosophy is, is a "philosophizing" one only when we enter into a discussion with the great philosophers of the past and the present, and talk through with them that about which they speak, i.e., that which as the same concerns them always in a new manner. Thus the speaking *(legein)* of the philosophers is inherently a speaking in the form of a dialogue *(dialegesthai)*. That means that our answer is a philosophizing one not if it just describes the opinions of other philosophers but only if it *discusses with them* that of which they speak.

Let us now assume that the philosophers indeed try to state what being is insofar as it is *(on hēi on)* and, thus, that the Being of beings addresses itself to them; then our discussion with these philosophers is addressed by the Being of being, and it must try to co-respond to that which it addresses to us. If our co-responding succeeds, we are truly answering the question. Our answer will never be exhausted by a response that just has the form of a statement; rather, it is always a co-responding which responds to the Being of beings.[27]

Thus, the answer to the question of what philosophy is consists in our co-responding to that toward which philosophy itself is on its way: the Being of beings. It follows that we shall attain this correspondence only when we remain in conversation with that to which the tradition of philosophy delivers us, liberates us, makes us free. In other words, we shall find an answer to our question if we converse *with* that which has been handed down to us as the Being of beings.

This path toward the answer to our question is not a passive acceptance of our philosophical heritage; nor is it a break with or a repudiation of that historical tradition. Rather, it is an adoption and a transformation of what has been handed down, so that *this* adoption of that historical heritage implies what *Being and Time* calls a destructive retrieve. The destructive retrieve puts to one side the merely historical assertions about the history of philosophy and thus makes us free for what in the tradition speaks to us as the Being of being.[28]

Here we encounter a fundamental difficulty. One could say that man by his very nature is already in correspondence with the Being of beings; but if that is true, why should we make an additional effort to reach such a correspondence through philosophy? It is true that the correspondence to the Being of being is and remains man's abode. But only at times does it become an unfolding attitude specifically adopted by us. Philosophy is the actual corresponding to the Being of beings in which the correspondence comes to fulfillment and fully unfolds itself. Such a correspondence can occur in different ways, and we may wish to discuss them later. For now we must return to an issue touched upon earlier.[29]

5. Philosophy and Attunement (Stimmung) We have seen that philosophy is the expressly accomplished correspondence which speaks insofar as it considers the appeal of the Being of beings. The correspondence listens to the voice of this appeal; that presupposes that it is attuned to the

Being of beings. Only on the basis of this attunement does the language of correspondence obtain its precision, its tuning.[30]

This reference to the essential attunement of correspondence is not meant to surrender thinking to continually changing feelings or sentiments; for this reference is not a modern invention: already Plato and Aristotle called attention to this tuning and attunement. "For this is particularly the *pathos* of a philosopher, to be astonished; for there is no other beginning of *philosophia* than this."[31] The word *arche*, "beginning," indicates here not only the starting point but also that which governs, carries, and pervades the entire subsequent movement. Aristotle says the same thing in the *Met. A,2*: "Through astonishment men have reached now as well as at first the determining path of philosophizing."[32]

Both Plato and Aristotle were of the opinion that wonder is not just the "cause" of philosophy but something which governs and pervades it all the time. Furthermore, *pathos* is not emotion or feeling but disposition, tuning, attunement, determination. We refrain in astonishment and hold back from beings, from the fact that there is being and not nothing, that it is so and not otherwise.[33]

A completely new era in philosophy began with Descartes; it flowed from a different kind of tuning. In his *Meditations*, Descartes does not ask primarily *ti to on*, but rather what that being is that is true in the sense of the *ens certum*. In addition, the term *certitude* here no longer has the meaning of *essentia* (objective certitude), as was the case in the Middle Ages. Certitude is for Descartes that subjective certitude which is to remove the doubt and which for him becomes the tuning in philosophy. The tuning of confidence (which finally results from the unquestionability of the *cogito-sum*, and which thus is related to the absolute certainty of the knowledge of the *ego*, the distinctive *subjectum*, a certitude which is attainable at all times) becomes now the *pathos* and the *arche* of modern philosophy.[34]

It is difficult to say where the *telos* of this modern philosophizing lies: Hegel, Nietzsche, Marx? One thing is clear in asking these questions: we are not just posing historical questions but rather considering the future mode of Being of philosophy. We are trying to listen to the voice of Being and ask into what kind of tuning it puts contemporary thinking. We cannot answer this latter unequivocally; the tuning that prevails is still hidden from us. What we find today are various kinds of tuning, ranging from doubt and despair to a blind obsession with method and untested principles.[35]

6. Philosophy and Language. Conclusion   Philosophy is thus the expressly adopted and gradually unfolding correspondence which corresponds to the address of Being. This corresponding is a form of speaking and, thus, stands in the service of language. This statement is difficult to understand today, because language now appears mainly as an instrument of expression and communication. Today language is in the service of thinking, rather than thinking, as correspondence, being in the service of language.

For the Greeks, the essence of language was revealed as *logos.* In other words, the Greeks dwelt in the coming-to-presence of language, even though they never explicitly thought this coming-to-presence as such.[36] Thus, if we are ever capable of fully understanding what philosophy truly is, we must again try to come to some understanding of the Greek essence of language *(logos)*, without, however, passively returning to that conception and without passively adopting it. Instead, one must enter into a conversation with the Greek experience of *logos.*[37]

But that will lead us with necessity to a careful reflection on the relation between thinking and poetizing.[38] A secret kinship exists between these two, although they are separated by an abyss, in view of the fact that they dwell on mountains which are separated as far as possible.[39]

Whoever asks the question concerning the meaning of philosophy can thus not limit himself to philosophy as such, nor can a discussion about philosophy set itself the task of just winding up a fixed program. It belongs to the essence of thinking to be preparatory, so that the genuine thinker must prepare himself time and again to be seized by Being. Thus the discussion must prepare those engaged in it for a gathering in what is called the Being of beings and which as such addresses itself to them. Beingness appears in many ways: *to on legetai polachōs; hē ousia legetai polachōs.*[40]

II. QUESTIONS AND ISSUES TO BE DISCUSSED FURTHER

In this lecture Heidegger touches on a number of issues which may appear to be strange or even simply unacceptable. Some of them we have mentioned already. Let us now list them in a more systematic fashion. Is it true that philosophy must touch us humans in the very mode of our Being? Is it true that our entire Western culture is essentially related to Greek culture? Is philosophy inherently a Greek "phenomenon?" Is it true that what-is questions, i.e., questions which ask about the essence of all that is, are intrinsically Greek, flowing from a typically Greek way of questioning? Is it true that every question presupposes some form of pre-understanding concerning that which the question is about? Thus is it true that the hermeneutic circle affects all forms of questioning? More specifically, is philosophical questioning indeed hermeneutical in essence? Does the Greek language occupy a privileged position among all European languages, and is that so because in the Greek language and in the Greek language alone there is not yet a gap between word and thing?

What is one to say about Heidegger's view of the etymology of the word *philosophy,* and about his interpretation of Aristotle's definition of philosophy? Assuming that it is correct that the adjective *philosophos* appears for the first time in the writings of Heraclitus, is it indeed true that for Heraclitus the term meant to refer to the person who strives after *to sophon,* the *Hen—Panta?* And is it correct to claim that the latter expression says that all beings are in Being? And above all, is it indeed true that in Plato and Aristotle the question concerning the Being of beings was changed into a question concerning being insofar as it is?

A third set of problems is connected with Heidegger's claim that the question concerning philosophy is inherently a historical question, that no definitive answer can be given to this question which would make all further questioning concerning the essence of philosophy superfluous, and that this question thus is to be raised time and again. Historically, it is indeed true that in the course of the centuries many answers to this question have been given. It is true also that every philosopher who asks the question must try to do justice to all of his predecessors, either by explaining that and why they were mistaken basically, or by somehow giving their conception a place in his own conception. Yet is it true that Aristotle was mistaken in considering his predecessors merely from his own point of view; is Descartes to be criticized for "rejecting" the philosophical tradition altogether; was Kant incorrect when he called all metaphysics a mere random groping; is Hegel to be reproached for having "incorporated" all previous philosophical systems within his own philosophical system? Is Heidegger correct when he claims that every subsequent philosophical view is no more than a *free* consequence of one or more earlier philosophical views? Is Heidegger indeed on the right track when he states that a genuine answer to the question of what philosophy is can be found only if the one who asks the question remains in a lively dialogue with the great philosophers of the past to the degree that they, too, were addressed by Being? Also, is it correct to argue that such a dialogue with one's predecessors necessarily implies a destruction, so that the authentic attitude in regard to a philosopher of the past is to be characterized by the expression "destructive retrieve?"

Assuming that philosophy indeed is the consciously and reflectively executed response to the address of the Being of beings, which constantly attempts to be properly tuned to the Being of beings, is Heidegger indeed correct in distinguishing different epochs in the history of philosophy, in characterizing these epochs in the manner in which he does, and in expressing concern over the current epoch?

Finally, what is one to say about Heidegger's remarks about the essence of language and about the "place" of reflections on language in a discussion about what philosophy is, about the relationship between thinking and poetizing, and about the need in a discussion about philosophy to engage in a discussion of no more than just one issue?

In the chapters to follow, I plan to return to the most important issues and questions raised here. Yet for the balance of this chapter, I would like to focus immediately on the theses which appear to underlie all other claims made here, namely, that philosophy basically is concerned with the Being of beings, with the meaning of Being, with the question of Being, and that in his response to the address of Being, the philosopher has to realize that Being's address is different in different epochs, so that his own response must include a dialogue with the thinkers of the past, and that it is never a definitive response, yet one which nevertheless is in harmony with the demands of his own epoch. Heidegger discussed these issues regularly in his later works. Let us see how he tries to explain and justify them in his "Letter on Humanism" and in other works of the same period.

Article II: The Relation between Being and Man—
The Meaning of Thinking

Everyone who is familiar with Heidegger's thinking knows that there is an apparent difference between Heidegger's original view on the relationship between Being and man and the one which we find in his later works. In *Being and Time*, Heidegger suggests that man plays the leading role in this relationship, whereas in the later works it is clearly Being itself which holds the primacy in its own self-disclosure. Furthermore, Being itself, which in *Being and Time* was described as the total-meaningfulness of the world which is projected by *Dasein*, is later described as that which gives itself to man, determines him, and even dominates him as its *Da* among beings. In *Being and Time*, Heidegger had stated that only as long as *Dasein* is, "is there" Being, and only as long as *Dasein* is, "is there" truth; in the later works, however, it is made clear that the *Da* itself is thrown, and that it is thrown by Being itself. Finally, whereas in *Being and Time* the coming-to-pass of Being is said to take place in and through *Dasein*'s care, in the later works we find that it is *Dasein*'s thinking which is to occupy this important place.[41]

Yet however great, in this regard, the difference between Heidegger's original view and his later conception may seem to be at first sight, on closer consideration it becomes clear that this difference is the necessary consequence of the complexity of the relationship between Being and man, a relationship which can be brought to light adequately only by approaching it from more than one perspective. That is obviously not to say that there is no development in Heidegger's thinking. On the contrary, we have already pointed out that Heidegger's thinking remained in a continuous development and that in his thinking he was constantly "on the way."[42] Thus it is undoubtedly the case as far as this issue is concerned, too, that in his later works Heidegger moves on a "higher" dimension than he did in the earlier works. Yet we should keep in mind that the latter phase of his thinking is not in contradiction with the former and that the one cannot be fully understood without the other.

From the outset, Heidegger had seen clearly that the relationship between Being and man cannot be thought of in terms of the subject-object relation. From the very beginning it was also clear that man's relationship to Being is constitutive for man's essence. But whereas in the earlier treatises, as far as the discourse about this relationship is concerned, the focus was primarily on man's *Da* as transcendence, in the later treatises the focus shifted for the most part to that toward which *Dasein* transcends beings, i.e., Being itself. It is then explicitly claimed that Being as coming-to-presence is always a coming-to-presence for *Dasein*, insofar as this coming-to-presence is a demand which summons and hails *Dasein* to its essence. Thus the very essence of *Dasein* is such that it implies that it is continuously in a state of listening, because its essence belongs to the summoning and evoking hail of Being, i.e., because it belongs to its coming-to-presence itself. It is in this context that Heidegger sometimes relates *Dasein*'s thinking to thanking.[43] Let us now see how Heidegger tries to relate Being and man in the "Letter on Humanism."

As we shall see in the next chapter, for Heidegger, Being is not God; nor is it the totality of all beings. Rather, it is the totality of all meaning. Taken as such, Being *is* not; rather, it continuously comes-to-pass as the process of non-concealment *(alētheia)*. Being comes-to-pass in its *Da*, i.e., in *Dasein*. Furthermore, it is the lighting-process in and by which beings are illuminated as what they are.

Being is that which "is" above all else. Thinking establishes the relation between Being and man. It does not cause this relation to be. It merely offers this relation back to Being as something that was first handed over to it by Being. This offering consists in that in man's thinking Being comes to language. Thus language is the house of Being, in whose home man dwells. Those who think and those who poetize are the guardians of this home. As guardians they must accomplish the manifestation of Being, in that in and through their speaking they bring this manifestation to language and preserve it in language.

Thinking is thus indeed an action, but it is not an action because some effect issues from it. Thinking acts only insofar as it thinks. It is the simplest, as well as the highest, form of action, because it establishes the relation between Being and man. But in this establishing, all effecting lies in Being and is directed toward beings. Thus thinking lets itself be claimed by Being in order to say the truth of Being. Thinking lets itself be claimed by Being and for Being.

In order to learn to have a genuine experience with the essence of thinking and bring it to completion, we must free ourselves from all technical interpretations of thinking and from all grammatical and logical interpretations of language. The origin of these interpretations goes back as far as Plato and Aristotle. They took thinking to be a *technē*, the method of a consideration which stands in the service of doing and making. Thinking is thus determined here from the perspective of *praxis* and *poiēsis*, and it itself is determined as *theōria*. From the very beginning, thus, thinking had to try to preserve its autonomy over against all acting and doing. Since that time, thinking has also tried to justify its existence before all "other" sciences. One has attempted to do that by showing that thinking itself is a form of science. But this attempt is really the abandonment of the essence of thinking. For the effort on the part of thinking to become scientific led to the abandonment of Being as the element of thinking; from then onward, thinking was judged by a standard that does not measure up to it, and this standard was set by logic. [44]

But thinking is not without all standard and measure. Yet the rigor of thinking, in contrast to that of the sciences, does not consist in a theoretical and technical exactness of concepts and notions. Rather, it consists in that its speaking remains purely and completely in the element of Being and lets the simplicity of its multiple dimensions rule. [45]

When thinking leaves its element, it comes to an end, just as a fish will die when it leaves the water. The element is that which enables *(vermögen)* thinking to be a thinking. It concerns itself with thinking and brings it into its essence. Thinking therefore is the thinking *of* Being. That means first that thinking belongs to Being, insofar as it comes-to-pass in the happening of the appropriation through Being itself. Secondly, thinking is *of* Being, insofar as thinking, belonging to Being, listens to Being. Thinking is what it is according to its essential origin if and only if it continues to belong to Being and listens to it.

Thinking "is" insofar as Being, time and again committing itself to thinking, favors it by bestowing itself upon it as a gift. Such favoring is the genuine essence of enabling, which lets something be what it is. It is on the basis of this enabling which favors that thinking is properly able to be *(vermögen, mögen, Mögliche)*. In its favoring, Being presides over thinking and, thus, over man's relation to Being. To enable something here means to preserve it in its essence and to maintain it in its element.[46]

When thinking leaves its element and thus comes to an end, it tries to replace what was so lost by securing a validity for itself as a *technē*, as an instrument of education, a cultural concern, a matter for the classroom, etc. Gradually, thinking becomes a philosophy which develops into a technique for the explanation of everything by means of highest and ultimate causes. Then one no longer thinks but begins to *occupy* oneself with philosophy. One can occupy oneself with philosophy in different ways. These ways are usually in competition with one another, so that such occupations offer themselves publicly as "-isms." The dominance of these terms in the modern age rests above all on the peculiar dictatorship of the public realm, which also is the reason why language has fallen into the service of an effective communication along routes where objectification (= the uniform accessibility of everything to everyone) continues to branch out indefinitely and disregards all limits. It is the public domain which decides in advance what is intelligible and what must be rejected as unintelligible.

To think means to move into the proximity of Being and to let oneself be addressed by Being itself. By responding properly to Being's address, man will be able to bring to light the truth of Being, discover the true essence of language, recognize the seductions of public opinion, and re-discover the genuine humanity of man.[47]

In the past, people have tried to determine the humanity of man in many ways. Every form of humanism which resulted from these efforts was either grounded in a metaphysics or was itself made to be the ground of a metaphysics. For every determination of the essence of man which presupposes an interpretation of beings without explicitly asking about the truth of Being, is inherently metaphysical. But in defining the human-ity of man in this manner, humanism not only does not ask about the relation of Being to the essence of man, it even impedes the question. Metaphysics obviously presents beings in their Being, and thus it does indeed think the Being of beings. Yet it does not think the difference between both, and it does not ask about the truth of Being itself. Thus it does not ask, either, in what manner the essence of man belongs to the truth of Being. And metaphysics until now not only has failed to ask the question, it is even totally incapable of asking this question. Being is still waiting for the time when it will again become thought-provoking to man. But until now, metaphysics has closed itself to the simple fact that man essentially comes-to-pass as what he is in essence, where he has been claimed by the address of Being. For only from that claim does he find that wherein his essence dwells. And only from this dwelling has he language as the house of Being, and the home that preserves the ek-static character of his essence. Heidegger calls this standing in the clearing of Being man's ek-sistence.[48]

It is thus understandable that ek-sistence can be said only in connection with the essence of man. As far as our experience shows, only man is admitted to the destiny of ek-sistence. What man is consists in his ek-sistence. This statement means that man comes-to-pass essentially in such a way that he is the *Da*, the clearing of Being. The Being of the *Da*, the clearing of Being, has the fundamental character of ek-sistence, of an ek-static inherence in the truth of Being. In terms of content, ek-sistence means to stand out into the truth of Being. Ek-sistence localizes the determination of what man is in essence, in the destiny of the truth of Being. As ek-sisting, man takes the *Da*, the clearing of Being, into his "care." But *Da-sein* comes to pass essentially as thrown *(geworfen)*. Essentially it abides in the throw *(Wurf)* of Being, which sends and, thus, apportions the proper sending.[49]

In order that we today may attain to the domain of the truth of Being and ponder it, we must first of all make clear precisely how Being concerns man and how it claims and hails him. Such an essential experience happens to us when we realize that man is in that he ek-sists, that ek-sistence is man's true substance.[50] Man's standing out into the truth of Being does not mean that man is the ruler over Being. Rather, man is thrown by Being itself[51] into the truth of Being so that, ek-sisting in this way, he may guard the truth of Being in order that beings may appear in the light of Being as the beings which they are. Thus man does not decide whether and how beings appear, whether and how God or the gods, history, and nature come forth into the clearing of Being, come-to-presence, or depart. Rather, the advent of all beings lies in the destiny of Being's sending. For man, the basic question is time and again to discover what in his essence is fitting and proper such that his essence continues to correspond in each case to such destiny. For it is in harmony with such destiny that man as ek-sisting must guard the truth of Being. Man is the shepherd of Being. But what then is Being? It is it itself.[52]

The new thinking which is still to come must learn to have an experience with the fact that Being is it itself, and to say it. Being is neither God nor some cosmic ground; it is farther than all beings and yet nearer to man than every being. Man usually concerns himself with beings. When he begins to think and presents beings as beings, he undoubtedly relates to Being. But in truth he usually thinks of beings as such, but never of Being itself. Even in its critical phase, philosophy thought from beings back to other beings, and in passing had only a glimpse of Being. Classical philosophy recognized the clearing of Being either just as the look *(eidos)* of what is present in outward appearance *(idea)* or perhaps critically as that which is seen as the result of the categorial representation of a transcendental subject. That means that in Greek and medieval philosophy as well as in modern thinking, the truth of Being remained concealed for philosophy.

Yet this concealment of the truth of Being is not a defect on the part of philosophy but rather a treasure which, withheld from it, is nonetheless continuously held before it. In Greek and medieval philosophy, it was the destiny of Being that Being's clearing first afforded a view by which what was present came into contact with man, who thus was present to it, so that man himself in his understanding *(Vernehmen)* could first touch *(thigein)* upon Being.[53] This view-at drew a view-to toward itself and abandoned itself to it only when in modern philosophy understanding had become a positing, a setting-before-itself in the *perceptio* of the *res cogitans* taken as the *subjectum* of the *certitudo.*[54]

But how does Being now relate to ek-sistence? Being itself must be this relation, insofar as it gathers to itself ek-sistence in its ek-static essence as that which makes room for the truth of Being among beings. It is in view of the fact that man in this way comes to stand in this relation that Being has destined for itself and in care takes it upon himself, that at first he fails to recognize the nearest, and thus does not realize that nearer than the nearest is nearness itself, i.e., the truth of Being.[55]

In the history of Being, the truth of Being was forgotten; thinking focused then primarily on beings. At the same time, the essence of man remained veiled, and a metaphysical explanation of language covered up the essence of language. We have seen already that in its essence, language is the house of Being, which comes-to-pass through Being and is structured by Being. Thus, we must try to think the essence of language from its correspondence to Being and indeed as this correspondence, i.e., as the home of man's essence. Language is the house of Being in which man dwells and ek-sists insofar as he belongs to the truth of Being which he is to guard. Thus, when we think about the humanity of man and try to understand it as ek-sistence, the genuine issue at stake is not man himself but Being, which is the dimension of the ek-stasis of ek-sistence. This dimension is obviously not something spatial in the common sense, because everything spatial and the entire space-time abide in the dimensionality which Being itself is.[56] Thinking attends to these simple relations and tries to find the proper word for them. Thinking cautiously says: "There is Being," *Il y a l'être, Es gibt Sein.* The German expression says literally: "It gives Being." And that which gives is again Being itself. Furthermore, the words *gives* and *grants* name again the essence of Being, which is granting its truth. Thus the self-giving into the open together with the open region itself is Being itself.[57]

Thinking avoids the expression "Being is." For the word *is* is commonly said of a being which is; but Being is precisely not a being. And yet Parmenides, in the early age of thinking, did say: *Estin gar einai,* "For there *is* Being." In this phrase the primal *(anfänglich)* mystery for all thinking is concealed; Parmenides' phrase is still unthought today. That suggests that philosophy does not really make progress. When philosophy attends to its own essence, it does not make forward strides at all. It remains where it is, and it constantly tries to think the same. The "there is" and the "it gives" rule the destiny of Being, which is apportioned by Being itself. Its history comes-to-pass in the words of essential thinkers. Thus, the thinking which thinks the truth of Being is, as thinking, inherently historical.[58]

It is thus not correct to assume that "systematic" philosophy and history of philosophy just stand next to one another, and that the latter is merely an illustration in which one can explain "modern" ideas with the help of past opinions. Nor is it correct to assume with Hegel that there is only a systematic philosophy, which can make the law of its own thinking the law of philosophy's history and at the same time subsume history into its system. If we think about these matters in a more primordial manner, we will come to the conclusion that Being grants the history of Being to which thinking belongs as the re-collection of this history that unfolds of itself. This re-collection differs essentially from the subsequent presentation of an evanescent past. The happening of the history of thinking occurs essentially as the destiny of the truth of Being.[59]

In Heidegger's view, thus, everyone who tries to philosophize tries to think the meaning of Being, whose history comes-to-pass in the words of the great thinkers of our Western heritage. That is the reason why each person who philosophizes has to relate in a positive manner to the thinking of those who preceded him in our tradition. All genuine thinking is therefore re-collection. The question of how one is to relate to our philosophical tradition is one which, like the problem of Being, concerned Heidegger almost from the beginning of his career. In view of the fact that it is an issue which is often misunderstood, I shall discuss it in the third article of this chapter.

Article III: Destructive Retrieve and Re-collection

After *Being and Time,* Heidegger was convinced that as a thinker he had to take a stand in regard to the philosophical tradition to which he belonged. He was also aware of the various options which in this regard had been proposed in our Western tradition since the time of the Pre-Socratics, i.e., the views of Plato and Aristotle, the Stoa, the entire scholastic tradition, the opinions of Descartes, Hume, Kant, Hegel, Marx, and many others. Heidegger always tried to avoid two extremes; it cannot be correct to assume that in the past some philosopher or tradition has already thought whatever there is to be thought, so that our own efforts can be reduced to a commentary or to the formulation of some footnotes on the works of the master(s); on the other hand, it will not do to shove the entire philosophical tradition aside as a mere random groping. But even if one remains within the broad course between these two extremes, historically there are still different options to be considered: are the works of the great thinkers of the past merely relevant from the perspective of an aporetic (Aristotle), are they to be taken as efforts which were on the way toward the true and definitive philosophy (Husserl), or are they to be given a place within the all-encompassing system which describes the self-realization of the absolute in absolute knowledge (Hegel)?

Heidegger did not subscribe to any of these views. From the very beginning, he realized that he had to relate his own thinking to that of the Western tradition in a positive manner, without having to make his own thought subservient to that of one of his ancestors in philosophy. In *Being and Time* he formulated his own position for the first time in a "systematic" fashion and characterized it by the label *destructive retrieve*.[60]

It seems to me that in unfolding this basic position, Heidegger never changed his mind as far as essential elements are concerned. Yet he certainly articulated this view in different ways during the period between 1927 and 1976. That is quite understandable. First of all, every thinker matures over time and often finds "better" ways to articulate his deep-seated convictions. But more importantly, the relation between the thinker and his tradition can and must be articulated from different perspectives: from the perspective of the thinker, from the perspective of the tradition, and above all from the perspective of that which both the thinker and his tradition try to think, namely, the Being of beings.

In the pages to come, I shall try to describe first how Heidegger has tried to articulate the relation between the philosopher and the tradition to which he belongs from the perspective of the one who begins to think. I shall also indicate the objections which one can offer against such an approach to the tradition and the answers which from Heidegger's point of view can be given to such objections. Finally, I hope to indicate how Heidegger in his later writings tried to articulate the same relation, par-

ticularly from the perspective of the thinking *of* Being. I shall be employing here again ideas from the "Letter on Humanism," Heidegger's
lectures on Greek and modern philosophy, and some other lectures and
essays. The issue is obviously too broad to be adequately dealt with in
this section; I thus plan to return to it in some of the chapters to follow.

In his earlier works, and notably in *Being and Time*, Heidegger had
already defended the view that temporality constitutes the meaning of
man's mode of Being. Temporality is also the condition which makes
historicity possible as a temporal mode of Being which is constitutive for
man's coming-to-pass as such. Taken as *Dasein*, man is *as* he already was,
and he is *what* he already was. *Dasein* is its own past, not only in the
sense that it possesses its own past as a kind of property which is still
present-at-hand; *Dasein* is its past particularly in the way of its own
Being, which comes-to-pass out of its future on each occasion. Regardless of how *Dasein* is at a given time or how it may conceive of Being, it
has grown up both into and in a traditional way of interpreting itself. Its
past, which includes the past of its generation, is thus not something that
just follows along after *Dasein* but something which already goes ahead
of it. But if *Dasein* itself as well as its own understanding is intrinsically
historical, then the inquiry into the meaning of Being is to be characterized by historicity as well.[61]

When a philosopher turns to philosophy's own history, he must realize
that this tradition constitutes that from which he thinks as well as that
from which he, to some degree at least, must try to get away. Yet *Dasein*
is inclined to fall prey to its tradition. This tradition often keeps it from
providing its own guidance, whether in inquiring or in choosing. When a
tradition overpowers one's own thinking, it often conceals what it really
tried to transmit.

Thus, in the inquiry of the question concerning the meaning of Being,
one has to have a ground of one's own, and yet one's thought must
carefully heed its own philosophical tradition. Both these demands are
met in the "destructive retrieve." One must "destroy" in the tradition
what is philosophically unjustifiable and maintain those primordial experiences from which any genuine philosophical insights ultimately flow.
The meaning of the retrieve is not to shake off the philosophical tradition
but to stake out the positive possibilities of a tradition and keep it within
its proper limits.[62] To retrieve an important philosophical problem is to
disclose the potentialities that are still hidden in it. But that means that the
problem, while it is being so preserved, will also be changed and transformed.[63]

It is obvious that in these reflections Heidegger takes a critical stance
with respect to Descartes, Kant, and Husserl, whose positions in regard

to the philosophical tradition are too negative. In this regard Heidegger's position is closer to that adopted by Hegel. The only point in which he does not follow Hegel in this respect consists in the fact that Hegel saw the various philosophical perspectives developed in the past as elements of an organic unity or system, and that, thus, some form of necessity is constitutive for "the life of the Whole." In Heidegger's view, philosophy's history does not bind the philosopher who lives today with the necessity of the unbreakable laws of the Hegelian dialectic; rather, the philosophical tradition, like every other form of tradition, delivers and liberates man. The answer to a philosophically relevant question consists in man's authentic response to what in philosophy's history is already on the way to him. Such a response implies, at the same time, his willingness to listen to what is already said and the courage to take distance from what he has heard. That makes a *certain* criticism of the past necessary in philosophy.

Heidegger, thus, does not deny the necessity to re-think every "experience," to mediate it, and to transcend it. Yet he does deny that that should be done from the perspective of the absolute knowledge of the Absolute. In his opinion, each "experience" is to be mediated from the perspective of Being. It is in this finite perspective that man understands his own Being in its full potentialities. Furthermore, it is within this finite perspective also that one can "let things be seen from themselves and in themselves," because within this perspective, one can show them in their full potentialities.[64]

Heidegger obviously maintains that the philosophical reflection should be methodical and critical. Although he rejects presuppositionlessness (Husserl) and absoluteness (Hegel), he does not reject method and rigor. The first, last, and constant task of our philosophical reflection is never to allow our prejudgments to be dominated by merely arbitrary conceptions but rather to make the relevant themes secure *scientifically* by working out our anticipatory conceptions in terms of "the things themselves."[65] In other words, the destructive retrieve is guided by a hermeneutic phenomenology which in each case allows for a careful comparison of the claims made by thinkers of the past with the "things" to be reflected upon.[66]

In the "Letter on Humanism," Heidegger returned to the question of how the thinker today must relate to the works of those who preceded him. We have seen already that he there rejected Hegel's answer to this question and tried to determine this relationship in terms of re-collection, as which man's thinking belongs to Being and its history. Thus for Heidegger, to think authentically means to re-collect Being's history. History does not come-to-pass primarily as a mere happening. Furthermore, to happen does not mean primarily to pass or to cease. The coming-to-pass of history comes-to-presence as the sending of the truth of Being from Being itself. Being sends itself by giving itself, i.e., by granting itself and refusing itself at the same time. Nevertheless, Hegel's determination of history as the development of the Spirit is not untrue. Neither is it partly true and partly false. It is just as true as metaphysics is true, which in his system for the first time brings to language its own essence, thought in an absolute manner, through Hegel himself. Absolute metaphysics, just as much as its inversions by Nietzsche and Marx, belongs to history of the truth of Being. What originates from it cannot be countered by refutations and arguments. It can be taken up only in such a manner that its truth is sheltered in Being itself in a more primordial way and, thus, removed from the domain of mere human opinion.[67]

Only as long as man is as *Dasein* does Being grant itself.[68] In light of what has just been said, that means that only as long as the clearing of Being comes-to-pass does Being grant itself to man. But the very fact that this clearing, the *Da*, the lighting of the truth of Being itself, comes-to-pass at all is due to the sending and apportionment of Being itself *(Schickung)*. The phrase does not mean to say that Being is just the product of man.[69] Instead, Being itself is the *transcendens* pure and simple.[70] Being itself is here still thought on the basis of beings and thus from within metaphysics, which even here is still dominant; for only from the perspective of metaphysics does Being show itself as transcending. Yet the statement that Being is the *transcendens* pure and simple does indeed articulate in one statement the manner in which the essence of Being hitherto has illuminated man. This conception of the essence of Being is indispensable for the prospective approach of thinking toward the question concerning the truth of Being. In this way thinking attests to its essential articulation or unfolding as destiny.[71]

Thus this thinking does not presume in arrogance that it can begin anew with a clean slate, so to speak, and declare all past philosophy simply false, or irrelevant. The question of whether or not the characterization of Being as the *transcendens* pure and simple understands Being from the truth of Being and adequately expresses the essence of Being, is still to be considered. And that is to be done in and by a thinking that listens to Being's address and hail.[72]

In dealing with the thoughts of a philosopher of the past, one must thus adopt a dual attitude: on the one hand, one must examine his thoughts critically and take distance from them to the degree that they apparently went astray or were so bound up with the world which they addressed that they are no longer relevant to our present condition; on the other hand, one must make these thoughts into one's own to the degree that they appear to reveal a truth which is to be accepted. In these efforts one is thus directly concerned not with philology or history but rather with the matter of thought. Yet it is assumed that the one who tries to retrieve someone's thoughts has familiarized himself with the results of competent philological and historical research. The retrieve of someone's thoughts has a positive and a negative aspect: through *critical* reflection one has to *bring to light* what is universally worthy of being thought about. Thus by retrieving a fundamental problem that is worthy of being thought about, we understand here the disclosure of those original possibilities of a problem which up to the present have lain hidden.

Philologists and historians have the greatest difficulties with such an approach, in that they understand it usually as a criticism of their own research and research methods. That is a mistaken attitude to adopt: how could one ever meaningfully speak about someone's thoughts that are to be retrieved if one does not first make a responsible effort to discover what these thoughts really have been? Still, the philologist will argue that any attempt to retrieve someone's thoughts inherently implies that one does violence to the text. In some sense, that is indeed the case, because one makes a text say what explicitly it did not claim; yet it is certainly not correct to assume that a retrieving reading of a philosophical text tries to change the philologically correct way of reading the text. It is of the greatest importance to realize that both the historico-philological concern with the text and the thoughtful dialogue with a text have their own legitimacy, their own aim, their own standards, their own principles, and that the one cannot possibly make the other superfluous.

Thus, the process of retrieve means something more than a mere exposition of what an author has said already. Rather, it means bringing to light what he did not say and could not say yet nevertheless laid before our eyes as unsaid in the expressions which he actually used. That, however, he himself was no longer able to say. Thus what must become decisive for us in every type of philosophical knowledge is not "what is expressed in explicit formulae, but what is laid before our eyes as still unsaid through the formulae that are used."[73] It cannot be denied that such an interpretation does violence to the text. "Obviously in order to wring from what the words say that which they want to say, every interpretation inevitably must do violence. . . ."[74] We must keep reminding ourselves of the "violence" of the process of retrieve if we are to establish a thoughtful dialogue with the thinkers of the past.

That is of the greatest importance, because we must constantly connect the idea of retrieving with the idea of destruction.

If . . . [a philosophical problem] is to have its own history made transparent, then this hardened tradition must be loosened up, and the concealments which it has brought about must be dissolved. We understand this task as one in which by taking . . . [the genuine matter of thought] as our clue, we are to destroy the traditional content of ancient ontology until we arrive at those primordial experiences in which we achieved our first ways of determining the nature of Being—the ways which have guided us ever since.[75]

Yet we must stress the point that this destruction does not have "the *negative* sense of shaking off the ontological tradition. We must, on the contrary, stake out the positive possibilities of that tradition, and this always means keeping it within its limits. . . ."[76] Furthermore, the destruction is aimed not at the past but at the present, i.e., "at the prevalent way of treating the history of ontology, whether it is headed towards doxography, towards intellectual history, or towards a history of problems."[77] The task of the destruction, then, is not to eliminate metaphysics but to justify it through thinking the ontological process as such which gave rise to its birth. Foundational thinking does not tear out the roots of philosophy, but dresses the ground and tills the soil from which it draws its strength.[78]

In the re-trieve which must come about in a thoughtful dialogue with the thinkers of the past, the thinker must think upon what is as having been (past) and receive it as still coming (future) with perennial freshness. Our efforts must limit themselves to abiding close to the words of the thinkers. That can perhaps help us "to direct a coming *(künftiges)* thought into a whole domain of intimations to which we have not yet attended."[79] Having attended to such intimations, the thinker must render them present by formulating them in language, as the thinkers of the past have done. That means that the thinker may be hearing more in the words of past philosophers than they really say. But that is precisely the function of ad-ventive thinking, to let that which past philosophers brought into words continue to come now to the one who thinks and who again expresses it in language. No one thinker can express by what he says the inexhaustible abundance which the truth imports to him in the moment of experience. Parmenides and Heraclitus, Plato and Aristotle, Kant and Hegel were forced to express thoughts as they disclosed themselves *geschicklich* to them. There remains hidden in what a thinker says the entire wealth of thoughts that he does not say and could not say yet which somehow remain present in what he does say, in a mysterious and submerged fashion. It is the unsaid that is present in the past philosophers' utterances which we must try to express in our own dialogue with them. Such a dialogue often uses the interrogative method as especially adapted to this type of thinking.[80]

Those who have difficulty accepting this conception should realize that Heidegger's basic intention here is to do full justice to what was great in the great works of great thinkers of the past.

CHAPTER 3

What Then Is Being?

Article I: The Being-Question in the Early Works

It has been said time and again that Heidegger tried to think only one thought: the meaning and truth of Being. Like Henri Bergson, Heidegger kept insisting that his thought was oriented toward one basic issue only. Every thinker thinks only one single thought. That essentially distinguishes him from the scientist. For Heidegger, this basic and focal point was the question concerning the meaning of Being.[1]

It has also been said many times that it is a truism to say that the subject matter of Heidegger's philosophy is the question concerning the meaning of Being and that this statement, although true, is also very misleading.[2] Theodore J. Kisiel observes that after decades of exegesis of his own attempt to revive the famous question, one is often still tempted to turn the quote from Plato's *Sophist* with which *Being and Time* begins against Heidegger himself: "You obviously know what you mean when you use the word 'being.' But we, who once thought we knew, have now fallen into perplexity."[3] Kisiel immediately adds that the confusion is much greater for the English reader, who often is "alienated" from Heidegger because of ugly neologisms, clumsy phrases, and other esoteric expressions which are part and parcel of the Teutonic English to which many translators have had recourse. That is true in Kisiel's view particularly with respect to the translations of both *Seiendes* and *Sein*. He is especially opposed to Richardson's suggestion to translate *Seiendes* as "being" and *Sein* as "Being." In his view, this convention not only calls too much attention to being as a concept, it also promotes a dangerous mystique of the capital *B*, "which thereby becomes the key shibboleth of a latter-day gnostic cultism."[4] Kisiel suggests sparing use of the term,[5] and Thomas

Sheehan thinks it might "enhance the explanation of Heidegger's subject matter by retiring the terms 'Being' and 'the question of Being' from the discussion."[6]

As for the latter expression, Sheehan explains that the expression is really a condensation for "the question concerning the meaning of Being," and that futhermore the full form of the phrase changed from the question concerning the *meaning* of Being, via the question concerning the *truth* of Being, to the question of the *place* of Being. In addition, according to Sheehan, the word *Being* in Heidegger has two distinct but easily confused meanings, with the result that Heidegger, to specify his interpretation of the meaning of the term, had to resort to spelling it archaically or crossing it out, in order to finally drop it from his lexicon altogether. Finally, Sheehan focuses on the fact that expressions such as "Being hides itself," "Being sends itself," "Being withdraws," etc. suggest that Heidegger has lapsed into theology or some form of metaphysical anthropomorphism.[7]

Another difficulty is connected with the fact that Heidegger from beginning to end keeps repeating that the question of Being has been forgotten by the great thinkers of the West at least since the time of the Pre-Socratics. This claim is obviously difficult to accept for many philosophers familiar with our Western tradition and particularly for those who defend some form of Aristotelianism, Thomism, or Hegelianism.[8]

I tend to agree with these authors that the difficulties and dangers to which they have pointed indeed exist. I also readily grant that these difficulties and dangers are even much greater when, as is the case here, an effort is being made to unfold what Heidegger understands by Being itself while "cutting it off," so to speak, from the place where the process of Being comes-to-pass, namely, language, and by systematically eliminating all references to the so-called ontological difference, i.e., the basic difference between Being and beings. Yet, on the other hand, there is the undeniable fact that Heidegger time and again in virtually every work and lecture course has tried to explain what he understands by Being and what he thought the basic problem of philosophy to be. Furthermore, the reason I have decided to isolate this question from the other two mentioned is simply the fact that it appeared desirable to discuss them elsewhere in this book. I shall mention these issues in this chapter only where Heidegger himself explicitly raises them in connection with his effort to "state" what he means by the meaning of Being.

The main goal of this chapter is thus to present a survey of some of the most important characteristics which Heidegger attributes to Being. In harmony with the scope of this book as a whole, the focus will be on Heidegger's later works. Yet in order to be able to place these reflections in their proper perspective, a few words must be said about Heidegger's conception of Being as found in the early works.

In *Being and Time*, the question concerning the meaning of Being is raised but not explicitly treated as such. Heidegger states there that it is the function of *ontology* to concern itself with this question, whereas *fundamental ontology* must focus on the mode of Being of the one who asks the question, i.e., the mode of Being of *Dasein*. Because the book was published in an incomplete form, the being queston itself was never explicitly discussed in *Being and Time*. In *Kant and the Problem of Metaphysics* (1929), where the basic perspective of *Being and Time* is maintained, it becomes clear that for Heidegger Being is the pure horizon of meaning, within which beings appear and by reason of which they can reveal themselves for what they are. That suggests that in his early works Heidegger was of the opinion that "Being" and "world" to some degree are equivalent. For in these works, Heidegger constantly maintains that Being is that which in the final analysis makes the comprehension of beings possible, while on the other hand it is argued that beings become understood as what they are to the degree that they are projected upon the horizon of the world. World is that toward which *Dasein* transcends beings; thus world is the concrete form in which every being encounters Being.[9]

In *Vom Wesen des Grundes* (1929), Heidegger stresses the point that Being is clearly related to truth as unveiledness,[10] an important idea that was mentioned earlier both in *Being and Time* and in the Kant book.[11] In the same essay Heidegger also states that Being is the Being *of* beings and nothing else; when one understands Being, one never understands it just as such, but always as the Being *of* beings. Yet, although Being and beings are thus inseparable, they are nevertheless also different.[12]

Already in the analytic of *Dasein*, as found in *Being and Time*, Being was described as Non-being or Nothing.[13] Particularly in the analysis of the mood of anxiety, Non-being emerges as that which is not a being within the world but rather the world itself in its lack of determination.[14] The question of how it really is with this Non-being is then taken up systematically in Heidegger's inaugural address, *What Is Metaphysics?* (1930). It is argued there that Non-being reveals itself as belonging to the Being of beings.[15]

Thus, during the years immediately following the publication of *Being and Time*, Heidegger tried to eliminate part of the ambiguity which originally had affected his claims about Being by explaining some of its fundamental characteristics. In so doing, he could maintain his original view that Being in some sense is the ground in which all significations of Being are to be grounded and from which all understanding of Being must nourish itself. On the other hand, however, the meaning of Being cannot be understood in terms of an eternal standard of Being (Plato's Ideas, Aristotle's First Mover, the Christian God, the God of the philosophers, etc.). Rather, it itself must be conceived of as an abysmal ground. For *the fact* that an understanding of Being emerges in the way we actually find it, no one can indicate a ground, because each process of grounding already presupposes the meaning of Being. When the meaning of Being lets a determinate signification of Being become the standard signification for a certain epoch, it "groundlessly" bars all other significations and even itself *as* the ground of the manifold possible other significations. It is in this sense that Being shows and hides itself at the same time in each case, and that is why the meaning of Being is to be called "truth," non-concealment, whose coming-to-pass is and remains a mystery and whose happening is historical in a sense which cannot be understood on the basis of what we usually call history.[16]

In *Vom Wesen des Grundes* (1930, 1943), Heidegger constantly uses the expression *das Seiende im Ganzen*, "the beings as such and taken as a whole," and then speaks of Being to refer to this whole. Yet in the same text Being is also taken in a sense which is quite different from beings taken as a whole. It is then said that Being is the one and only one which conceals itself. "This self-concealing one-and-only . . . is what . . . we call Being and for a long time have been accustomed to consider only as beings-in-their-totality."[17] From then on we begin to see a more clearly drawn distinction gradually appear between the Being of beings taken in a more categorial sense and the Being of beings taken in a more transcendental sense. It is the latter to which Heidegger later often refers with the expression "Being itself." It is then immediately distinguished from, but equally intimately related to, becoming, seeming-to-be, thinking, and ought or obligation.[18] Furthermore, it is then explicitly set apart from the concept of beings; thus it is also separated from what scholastic philosophy used to call *ipsum esse subsistence* or *actus purus*, from Descartes's or Leibniz's God, from Hegel's absolute Spirit, and from Nietzsche's will to power. Therefore, what Heidegger calls Being itself is then neither *ens commune* nor God taken as *causa sui.* But what then is Being? It is itself. It is that which hides itself when it grants itself such that beings may be what they are in truth. It is that which grants itself in different ways during different epochs of Being's own history, because it is inherently temporal and historical. It can be called legitimately time, language, abyss, mystery, the open, the fourfold, the holy, the simple, the source, the aboriginal saying, the advent, the fullness, the expanse, the time-play-space, etc.[19]

In the pages to come, I have brought together *some* of the more important characterizations of what Heidegger in his later works understands by Being itself. There I hope to return also to the meaning of the expressions "the Being of beings" and "Being as the beings as such and taken as a whole." Yet one final note is necessary before we can turn to the question of how Heidegger describes Being in its various "aspects" in the works published after 1943. As far as the translation of key terms is concerned, I have systematically followed the suggestions made by William J. Richardson, whose study on Heidegger I still regard as the best available to date; I thus have decided to use it very extensively and to quote it repeatedly. Yet I shall not use capitals for these key terms in order to avoid suggesting hypostatization or even divinization.[20]

Article II: The Meaning of Being in the Later Works

1. NEGATIVE AND POSITIVE ASPECTS OF BEING. THEIR UNITY

In the later works, Heidegger continues to stress the negativity of Being; and it is in this connection that he states that the ontological meaning of Non-being implies that it can also be called Being. In his inaugural address (1930), Heidegger had stated that "in the clear night of the Non-being of anxiety the original openness of beings as such arises, namely that they are beings and not nothing."[21] In the postscript to the same lecture (1943), he clarifies this assertion by stating that a careful study of the lecture might focus on the question "of whether Non-being, which corresponds to anxiety, in its essence, is exhausted in a mere denial of every being, or whether perhaps what is never and nowhere a being unveils itself as that which we call Being as distinguishing itself from all beings."[22] But why does Non-being show itself as Being? The answer is that Being, in the process of distinguishing itself from beings, grants itself to beings as that which allows them to be. Thus the Non-being which lets beings be unveils itself as Being itself, insofar as it reveals the Being of beings.

From then on, Heidegger begins therefore to stress more and more that Being is not just the Being *of* beings, but that it first and foremost is *itself*, the "other of beings," somehow antecedent (a priori) to all beings.[23] And that is unfolded with ever greater clarity with respect to the manner in which Heidegger from then on more carefully articulates the ontological difference, i.e., the difference between beings and Being.[24] To avoid misunderstanding, Heidegger adds again immediately that what is now called Being itself is not to be identified with God, regardless of how one conceives of God; nor is it to be identified with some cosmic ground.

Furthermore, Heidegger also adds here that as far as man is concerned, Being itself is farther away than all beings; yet it is also nearer to him than every being. Man usually concerns himself only with beings; when he presents beings *as* beings, he does indeed relate to Being itself, but even then he thinks only of beings as such and not of Being itself as such.[25] Being is thus not a being; rather, it is that which enables beings to be present to man and to each other. It is nearest to man, insofar as it is that which lets him be what he is and makes it possible for him to enter into comportment with beings. On the other hand, Being is farthest from man, insofar as it is itself not a being and insofar as man is structured in such a way that he can deal directly only with beings.[26] Thus, Being is the mystery.

As we have seen, the term *mystery* was first introduced in 1930.[27] Heidegger there again describes uncovering, i.e., revealment, as the essence of truth. He then calls non-revealment i.e., concealment, the non-essence of truth. Since now only that can be revealed which was before concealed, concealment is ontologically prior to revealment. Thus revealment, the letting-be-manifest, must take place within a horizon of darkness, i.e., concealment. In every comportment between *Dasein* and individual beings, we encounter concealment. Each comportment leaves concealed not only all other beings found in beings taken as a whole but also the fact that the totality of beings remains concealed here. This concealing of Being's being concealed is then called *the mystery*. "The authentic non-essence of truth is the mystery . . ."[28] This mystery is furthermore forgotten in *Dasein's* everyday ek-sistence; this forgottenness of the mystery itself is called the errancy *(die Irre)*.[29]

In "The Origin of the Work of Art" (1935), it is said that errancy and mystery, which together constitute the full non-essence of truth, are to be called the dissimulation *(das Verstellen)*. In the art work, truth is at work; it is always a truth which is affected by negativity, in view of the fact that the clearing process by which beings emerge is at the same time a concealing as well. When this concealment does not just pertain to the surface of the shining forth, so to speak, but permeates the whole of it, it is to be called dissimulation.[30]

In "Nietzsche's Word 'God is Dead' " (1940), Heidegger uses the term *mystery* for the first time for the negativity which is intrinsic to each concrete sending of Being. This negativity is said to be due to the essence of Being itself; in each case it remains unthought, because it simply withdraws into its own truth.[31] Thus, Being hides itself in each concrete disclosure and conceals itself as thus hiding.[32] Metaphysics is a particular epoch of Being; it is in its essence the still-withheld and thus unthought mystery of Being itself.[33] We find similar ideas developed in Heidegger's elucidations of Friedrich Hölderlin's poems "Homecoming"[34] and "Recollection,"[35] which were both written in 1943. It is stated there also that it is the role of the poet to guard and preserve the mystery. Thus he is not to unveil it[36] but rather to respect it while articulating it as such in words.[37]

In his reflections on the fragment of Anaximander (1946), Heidegger explains that the mystery of Being is closely related to the ambiguity of the word by which, in most Indo-European languages, Being is named, because this word is in each case at once a noun and a verbal adjective *(eon* or *on, ens, être, seiend, being)*. The ambivalence of Being itself consists in the correlation of that which is manifest *(being* as a noun) and the process by which it becomes manifest *(being* as a verbal adjective). This correlation obviously presupposes that we have already experienced some difference between the two "elements" so correlated. Thus, the ambivalence in Being names the difference between Being and beings, the ontological difference. Every concrete form of metaphysics was rooted in this ambivalence. The Being whose meaning or truth Heidegger is seeking in order to give a solid "ground" to metaphysics is nothing but the emergence or issuance of the ontological difference itself. What Heidegger calls the forgottenness of Being in the era of metaphysics is thus really the forgottenness of the ontological difference.[38] Heidegger has discussed these ideas also in connection with his interpretation of different fragments of Parmenides.[39]

In *Aus der Erfahrung des Denkens* (1947), Heidegger regularly uses the old German spelling *Seyn* ("Beon") instead of *Sein* ("Being"). He does not explain the significance of the old German spelling. Yet in 1949, in a note added to the second edition of *On the Essence of Truth*, Heidegger writes that the old German spelling signifies "the difference which holds sway between Being and beings," i.e., the ontological difference as such, as it emerges from the process of unconcealment *(a-lētheia)*.[40] In *Aus des Erfahrung des Denkens,* Beon *(Seyn),* which thus refers to the ontological difference, is described as a process of light and as the aboriginal saying. It is said there that it never *is* in the manner in which beings are. Thus it can never be adequately expressed in human language. For the same reason, it remains necessarily within the domain of the unsaid. It shines forth in beings with the greatest simplicity; it is the one, the only one, worthy of being thought. It holds sway over thought and even evokes it. It gathers thought into a unity within itself. Thus Beon is inherently affected by negativity; taken in its negativity, Being is mystery as well as errancy.[41]

From the very beginning, Heidegger has always stressed the negativity of the Being process. Being lets finite beings emerge from concealment, and in so doing it hides itself. In his earlier works, Heidegger immediately attaches finitude to negativity and thus claims that Being itself is also inherently finite. In the later works the issue is more complex.

Heidegger states there usually that each individual "process" in and through which Being sends itself is necessarily finite. Being itself, on the other hand, i.e., that which hides itself, the mystery, and the *lēthē*, is then said to be the wealth, the treasure, the hidden fullness, the inexhaustible wellspring, the simple, the all, the only, the one and only, etc. One might be inclined to draw the conclusion that in the later works Heidegger rejects the intrinsic finitude of the Being process itself. It seems to me, however, that such a conclusion is unwarranted. If Heidegger indeed had rejected the intrinsic finitude of the Being process, he would have returned in his thinking to a metaphysical position. But in his latest publications we still find the claim that thinking must try to overcome all metaphysics. Secondly, if Heidegger had changed his view on such an important matter, he certainly would have raised the issue explicitly and given us some reasons why such a change seemed necessary. It will not do to say that Heidegger has changed his position in regard to other important issues without explicitly making an issue of this change. The best-known change in this regard is the one related to the postscript of his inaugural address, to which I shall return later. Yet it seems to me that in the latter case there may just have been a printing error; furthermore, by explicitly correcting the error, Heidegger made it quite clear that a change was made. As for the question concerning the inherent finitude of Being, on the other hand, which pertains to the very core of Heidegger's thinking, there is no such explicit evidence. Let us not forget that Being indeed is the wealth, the fullness, the inexhaustible wellspring, the one and only, etc., even if it is intrinsically finite.[42]

At any rate, for Heidegger, Being is obviously not just negativity. It also has its positive dimension. It is this latter dimension which is often called the "holy."

In his elucidations of Hölderlin's poems, Heidegger often calls Being *das Heitere*, "the gladsome." Richardson correctly observes that if Being may be called light, then it is not inappropriate to call it by a name which directly refers to light's brightness, serenity, and even lightheartedness. Being as the source of all joy is the gladsome, the supremely joyous.[43]

In the light and the warmth of the gladsome, the "nature" of all beings (including man) is maintained in wholesome integrity *(heil)*. Thus, Being is also called the holy, the ultimate source of the conserving power that guards beings in the integrity of their Being. It is neither God nor the gods; it is "beyond" both gods and men, granting to both the integrity of their Being in the sense that it opens up the domain in which both gods and men may come-to-presence as what they are. It is the overflowing source which gives rise to all beings.[44] As such, Being is also ground.

Being is called the holy because it is "older" than the gods; for it is that by which they too are. Holiness is not a property borrowed from one single god. The holy is not holy because it is divine, but the divine is divine because it is holy in a way proper to itself.[45] Being is not only that by which the gods are, it is also that by which they are holy. Being is the holy because it is completely wholesome. Finally, it is the holy insofar as it, because of its very immediacy, is unapproachable.[46] Because Being is the holy, it is also the awesome; by its very coming it dislodges and deranges every experience from the patterns of everydayness.[47] It is also the eternal heart of things, because it is the innermost source of their presence, and because it is the perpetual Being that lets all abiding be.[48] It is the omnipresent and the undefiled.[49]

In his thought, Heidegger is thus concerned with Being itself, taken in both its negative and its positive aspects. His entire philosophical effort is oriented toward an attempt at understanding the strange paradox (hidden for all metaphysics) that Being conceals itself in the beings which it makes manifest, that it hides by the very fact that it reveals.[50] When Heidegger thus speaks about Being as the process of non-concealment, he takes both the positive and negative aspects of this process as a unity. Richardson has described this process in the following statements: "Being as the process of non-concealment is that which permits beings to become non-concealed (positivity), although the process is so permeated by 'not' that Being itself remains concealed (negativity). To think Being in its truth, then is to think it in terms of both positivity and negativity at once."[51]

II. BEING AND BEINGS. BEING AND MAN

Yet Heidegger's preoccupation with Being itself never focuses on Being in isolation from all beings, and certainly not in isolation from man as *Dasein.* The Being of beings is not something that is just "out there" all by itself, or even "out there" in beings; rather, it implies the meaningful relatedness and the intelligible presentness of things to and for man taken as *Dasein.* That is the reason why Heidegger, when he asks about Being, immediately asks questions about "thinking."[52] In *Being and Time,* Heidegger had tried to approach the relationship between man and Being from the perspective of man. In his later works he tried to think the same relationship from the perspective of Being. This change in approach explains why in *Being and Time, Dasein* was called a *lumen naturale,* whereas in the later works Being itself is described as illumination or the clearing process. This change in approach also explains why truth is described in *Being and Time* from the perspective of *Dasein's* Being as uncovering, whereas in the later works the self-manifestation of any being comes-to-pass only if it can show itself as a being out of Non-being in which Being itself hides. Thus, Being itself does indeed show itself; *it is* revealedness, *a-lētheia*, even though that still implies the disclosure by man's thought. In the later works, therefore, Being can correctly be spoken of as the *original* illumination, which allows itself and all beings to be seen. Being itself emerges in the diffuse clarity of its own light. Light is now the primordial characteristic of Being itself. Thus Heidegger can write in the "Letter on Humanism": "But the clearing process *(Lichtung)* is Being itself."[53]

As the clearing process which sheds light on itself and on beings by the very fact that it illuminates everything, Being may thus be correctly called truth. Yet the term *truth* here obviously does not mean "agreement"; rather, it means clearing, illumination, original self-manifestation, the emergence of Being and of all beings. But truth here also includes concealment; thus the rise of the light of Being essentially includes concealment and withdrawal. That means first that the self-illuminating rise of Being comes-to-pass in such a way that Being itself actually hides in the background. It also means that this self-lighting rise can open up the understanding of Being and beings, as well as close it off. The ascent of Being and beings is always from hiddenness, and it keeps something of hiddenness always in it. Finally, it means that truth is not something manageable and fixed; rather, it is to be achieved, and it comes-to-pass little by little.[54]

When Heidegger uses the expression "the meaning of Being," the word *meaning* (*Sinn*, "sense") means the non-concealment by which Being appears as itself. We have seen, however, that "non-concealment" is the "literal" meaning of *a-lētheia*, which we usually translate as "truth." Thus the expression "the meaning of Being" and the expression "the truth of Being" have the same meaning.[55]

Before we continue with our analysis of the manner in which in his later works Heidegger tries to specify the precise meaning of Being, we must first focus our attention on two expressions which regularly occur in Heidegger's works and in regard to which there is certainly "progress" in his thinking, namely, the expression "Being as beings taken as a whole" and the expression "the Being *of* beings."

With respect to the former, in *On the Essence of Truth* Heidegger takes the term *Being* usually to mean the beings as such taken as a totality *(das Seiende im Ganzen)*. Insofar as this totality is affected by negativity, it is called mystery.[56] But already in the first edition of this work (1930), it is quite clear that for Heidegger Being is more than just this totality. It is then referred to with the expression *Wesen*, which is to be taken in a verbal sense; thus it has the meaning of emerging into presence and abiding as such. It too is inherently affected by negativity.[57] Being is then said to be the one and only which conceals itself. "This self-concealing one and only is what we call Being."[58]

In the second edition of the same work (1949), Heidegger explains how these two meanings of Being are to be related to one another. There he writes that the essence of truth is the truth of Being: "das Wesen der Wahrheit ist die Wahrheit des Wesens." In the first part of the statement, the German word *Wesen* has the meaning of essence and then refers to the mode of Being characteristic of truth. As for the second term *Wesen*, Heidegger says again that it is to be taken in a verbal sense; thus it has the meaning of Being but refers to a characteristic of Being not yet stressed in *Being and Time* and other works of the same period. In the concept of *Wesen*, taken in a verbal sense, philosophy thinks Being. Being has for a long time been considered only as beings as such taken as a whole. To refer to all beings taken as such and in their totality, the Greeks used the term *phusis; phusis* is *the whole ensemble of beings* taken in the sense of *the process of emerging into presence.*[59] Thus Being, taken in the sense of *Wesen,* means the whole ensemble of beings as coming-to-presence, as emerging into presence, which as such abides and holds sway.[60]

In the later works, on the other hand, the expression *das Seiende im Ganzen,* i.e., "the beings as such taken as a whole," is used by Heidegger to refer to the manner in which *classical metaphysics* speaks about Being. Metaphysics is concerned not with Being itself as such but rather with beings *as* beings. When metaphysics speaks about Being, it always takes Being in the sense of the totality of beings, or also in the sense of their beingness *(ousia).*

In the introduction to *What is Metaphysics?* (1949) Heidegger explains this issue in detail. There he writes that metaphysics states what beings are as beings. It moves in the domain of the *on hēi on* and deals with beings as beings. It tries to present beings as such in their totality; it deals with the beingness *(ousia)* of beings *(tou ontos).* But metaphysics represents the beingness of beings in a twofold and thus ambiguous manner. First it attempts to present the totality of beings as such by describing their most universal traits *(on katholon; to koinon).* Yet at the same time it also presents the totality of beings as such with an eye on the highest being, the divine *(on katholou, akrotaton, theion).*[61] Because metaphysics presents beings as beings, it is really two in one; it is concerned with the truth of beings in their universality and with the highest being; thus, at the same time it is ontology and theology, and it is so according to its nature. In other words, the theological character of metaphysics is not due to the incorporation of Greek metaphysics into Christian theology. Rather, it is due to the manner in which beings as beings have been disclosed from the very beginning. By its very nature, metaphysics is the presentation of beings as beings. As such it is excluded from the experience of Being; in presenting beings as beings, it cannot pay attention to what conceals itself in this very *on* insofar as it becomes unconcealed.[62] Let us now turn to the second expression mentioned earlier.

The expression "the Being *of* beings" already occurs regularly in Heidegger's early works.[63] Yet the expression was affected from the beginning by several ambiguities, which were created in part by the fact that *Being and Time* was published in an incomplete form and in part by the fact that Heidegger changed a sentence in the second edition of the epilogue to his inaugural address. In *Being and Time* Heidegger focused mainly on the relation between Being and one particular kind of being, namely, *Dasein;* and it is often suggested there that the primacy in this interaction belongs to *Dasein.* Heidegger described the relationship between man and Being here in terms of transcendence; and in view of the fact that Being concretely always has the structure of world, the term *world* is often used instead of *Being.* In Heidegger's original view, the projection of world is brought about by a being which is immersed among other beings and beyond which it must go in the process of transcendence. Now, that which is transcended (beings) belongs as essentially to the process of transcendence as that whereunto the transcendence is oriented (world, Being), so that already in *Being and Time* Being appears as the Being *of* beings.[64]

In the later works, Heidegger begins to place the stress on the coming-to-pass of the truth. He then maintains that Being is the Being *of* beings, in that Being is that by which beings are, and Being is drawn toward beings in which it must emerge in order that it be itself.[65] Yet a shift in Heidegger's thinking seems to have taken place. For in the earlier works, the correlation analyzed by thinking is that between thought and Being, although it is said that Being is the Being *of* beings. After 1941, as we shall see in chapter 4, Heidegger began to focus more directly on the ontological difference as such, so that the correlation analyzed is then one between thought and the Being *of* beings; in this expression, the *of* must now be taken to point in two directions, expressing that Being means the Being of beings and that being means the being in terms of its Being.[66]

In the epilogue to his inaugural address, Heidegger describes how he tries to overcome metaphysics by meditating Being as truth, as the coming-to-pass of *a-lētheia.* Heidegger suggests here that Being can and even must be thought by itself, independent of the beings. "It pertains to the truth of Being that Being indeed comes-to-presence without beings . . ." even though beings are never without Being.[67] Yet in most other later works, we constantly find the claim that Being is nothing but the Being of beings, and in 1949 Heidegger corrected the statement of the epilogue to read "Being never comes-to-presence without beings."[68]

Richardson has discussed the implications of all of that in detail. Although I tend to agree with him in most instances, it nonetheless seems to me that by now much of the ambiguity has been eliminated, because of the publication of Heidegger's early lecture courses, and *The Basic Problems of Phenomenology* in particular. For these publications have given us a clearer idea of how Heidegger at that time thought about the ontological difference.[69]

After these lengthy digressions, which nonetheless appeared to be necessary in order to avoid misunderstanding, let us now return to the question concerning the meaning of Being. If we approach Being itself from the perspective of beings, then Being appears as somehow encompassing them, just as a domain of openness encompasses what is found within it. This domain is not space, however, but rather that openness out of which even space and time themselves come-to-presence. Furthermore, Being must not be understood as something static; it is a process, the clearing process by which beings are lighted up. When man enters into a comportment with beings, this light is neither man nor the beings; rather, it is the "between" that is between them as that which makes the encounter take place.[70]

The expression "an open region" or "the open" is found first in *On the Essence of Truth*, where Heidegger states that each true judgment comes to expression in an open region. *Dasein* when it judges forms its judgment after having encountered the beings to be judged in some open space, in the open.[71] The term *the open* appears to refer to what in *Being and Time* was called *world* and in *Kant and the Problem of Metaphysics* was called *horizon* or *domain (Spielraum)*. Richardson explains what is meant here as follows:

The openness of the open is not constituted by the fact that the being to be known appears to *Dasein* by traversing the open region. On the contrary, the open must be conceived as a matrix of relations which constitute the sphere of potentiatlities of *Dasein*, one of which potentialities is actualized in the actual contact with one or more beings. It is in this sense that Heidegger then can say that the encounter takes place *in* the open. While standing in the open, *Dasein*'s comportment refers itself to something that is open, something manifest, *das Offenbare*, and the latter was experienced in the earliest phase of Western thought as that which comes-to-presence *(das Anwesende);* later it was called that which is, being. The being and that which is open, both of which are to be distinguished from the open itself, are intimately correlated here, as they were already in *Being and Time*.[72] Later Heidegger adds that the open which lets be is the same as that which originally was called Non-concealment and which, at the beginning of Western thought, was designated as *a-lētheia*, truth.[73]

Be that as it may, Heidegger later returns to the term *the open* to refer to Being, namely, in his essay on release (1955). Being is understood there as the open domain, the broad region of expanse *(Gegnet)* which is completely open and free, wherein all beings may while, and which gathers together every being to itself and all beings unto one another in the "process" which whiles and rests within itself.[74] Being is here understood primarily as the gathering process, *logos;* yet it is also called *die Gegnet,* "the expanse," because it is the open domain which, in gathering beings together, opens itself up in such a way as to establish and maintain the open which permits every being to emerge and rest within itself.[75]

In the same essay Heidegger also points out that if Being is called the open in the same sense in which it is the horizon of *Dasein's* transcendence, then *Dasein* is taken to be the center of reference and the horizon as man's field of vision, within which beings appear as objects to man taken as the subject. What is called Being as horizon, however, is no more than the side of the encompassing open that is turned toward *Dasein.* Thus revealing itself as the horizon, Being conceals itself as the open. What interests Heidegger in his later works is primarily the open as such.[76]

In *Was heisst Denken?* (1952) Heidegger often describes the attitude which man in his thinking adopts in regard to Being. It is said in this essay that thinking is not an act of conquest but rather one of surrender. It is not a dictating but rather a listening. It is an opening oneself up for, a committing oneself to, Being's demand. Thus, it truly is an act of freedom by which man as *Dasein* acquiesces to Being's address. Being's call to thought solicits but does not necessitate; it invites but does not compel. It leaves *Dasein* free to refuse its call; it is the address of Being which makes man first free. Thus that which is free in the most original sense is not *Dasein* but Being itself. As *a-lētheia*, Being is liberation which frees from concealment. As such it is the open, the "domain of the free."[77]

From the preceding reflections, it is clear that Being establishes among beings their mutual relationships. Thus one can also say that the beings are mediated by Being. Being itself, however, taken as the open and as the source of this mediation, is itself not mediated; it is not made present by something else, not even *Dasein.* Thus it may be called the *immediate* in the strict sense of this term. Being, as the source of presence by which all beings become present to *Dasein* and to each other, is absolutely *ultimate;* there is nothing that mediates between Being and the beings which it makes present. Richardson calls it therefore the immediate mediation between beings. Insofar as Being is the immediate, it is also the *inaccessible*.[78]

III. APPROPRIATING EVENT, ISSUANCE, SENDING. THE HISTORY OF BEING

We must now turn to another important aspect of Being, to which Heidegger usually refers with the term *Ereignis*, "event." In his commentary on Hölderlin's poem "As When upon a Day of Rest" (1939), Heidegger describes Being as *phusis* and then states that Being as *phusis* is essentially presence; yet the manner of its presence is that it is a coming.[79] From the context, it is clear that Being is to be understood here as advancing to the poet and the thinker. Thus, to the extent that Being can be said to be as abiding, it must not be understood to simply endure; rather, its abiding is a coming that is always new and original. In "The Time of the World as Picture" (1938), Heidegger therefore calls Being that which is still in advent.[80]

Being is thus essentially temporal. And because it is a continual coming to beings, it is said to be "older" than the intervals of time *(die Zeiten)* that can be measured by beings. Yet it is not "older" than time itself, because Being *is time* in its origin. In other words, Being is neither beyond time, if time is understood in the usual metaphysical sense, nor eternal, if eternal is defined as it usually is in Christian theology.[81]

That Being has the character of a happening, an event that comes-to-pass, was already suggested in 1930.[82] Heidegger refers there to Being with the word *Wesen*, which is to be taken in a verbal sense. He refers to this event character of Being for the first time with the technical term *Ereignis* in 1946.[83] Richardson notes that Lessing still wrote the verb *ereignen* as *eräugnen*, which suggests that its original meaning, as a reflexive verb, must have been "to eye one another." Taken in that sense, the term *Ereignis* expresses the correlation between Being and thinking in terms of a mutual eyeing: Being casts its eye on man (appeal), and *Dasein* catches Being's eye in turn (response). Yet the word *Ereignis* also refers to the verb *eignen*, "to be suited for, to be characteristic of, to be the property of." *Ereignis* thus also expresses the process in which Being appropriates to man his essence in order to appropriate him thus to itself.[84]

In the *"Logos"* essay (1944), Heidegger describes how the ontological difference, the difference of Being and beings, issues forth from the appropriating event. He says there also that there is a middle-point between Being and *Dasein* which somehow gives rise to both.[85] In *Was heisst Denken?* (1952) this middle-point is spoken of as if it were a third thing, prior to both *einai* and *noein*.[86] Finally, in *Identity and Difference*, the *Ereignis* is understood as an origin that lies deeper than Being and man.

As such it is called an ultimate simplicity and a *singulare tantum.* This
absolute ultimate is then also called *the event of the truth.*[87] If one limits
himself to these and similar texts, he may be inclined to assume that
Heidegger, in articulating his conception of Being taken as the ontological
difference, is reaching here beyond the difference toward some ultimate
unity (the differentiating one), out of which the duality of Being and
beings (as the two which are differentiated) derives.

Yet there are other texts which make us believe that the appropriating
event is only Being itself, taken from a certain "perspective." Thus the
Being which arises out of the event is simply Being, insofar as it sends
itself in any given epoch. In other words, the event means Being as such,
insofar as it is the process through which the ontological difference issues
forth.[88] Thus, the appropriating event signifies nothing more than the
process of *a-lētheia,* by which Being in each case sends itself to man. The
term *event* is thus just another word for "sending"; its advantage is that it
suggests the ontological difference as such. "That which brings about the
event is the event itself, and nothing else besides."[89]

In the "Letter on Humanism," Heidegger states again that Being is the
clearing process by which beings are lit up so that they can emerge as
what they are. The domain where this clearing process takes place is
Dasein. Yet Heidegger stresses the point here that in the coming-to-pass
of this process, Being occupies the privileged position: Being itself grants
itself to *Dasein* and "dominates" it. That is what is meant by the sending
of Being, *die Schickung des Seins.*[90] This sending, which in each case is full
of destiny, takes place for the sake of Being; *Dasein,* which itself is
brought-to-pass by the sending, must sustain the process and guard it, so
that in the light of Being the beings can appear as what they are.

Thus, although Being is still in need of *Dasein,* it is nevertheless not for
Dasein to decide whether the clearing process will take place and how it
will take place. It is still the case that only insofar as *Dasein* is, is there
Being; yet that now means that only insofar as the clearing process
comes-to-pass by Being in *Dasein* does it come-to-pass at all. Thus it is
no longer said here that Being's coming-to-pass depends on *Dasein. Dasein* itself is thrown, and it is thrown by Being. Being sends and grants
itself; it is the sending of Being in its truth that constitutes the process of
the history of thought and of history as such.

Heidegger furthermore stresses again that the coming-to-pass of truth
in different ways at different times has a positive and a negative aspect;
that is why he calls Being itself the contentious.[91] Every sending of Being
is affected by negativity insofar as Being, giving rise to beings, must
withdraw at the very moment that it reveals itself. In the process of truth,
one can distinguish different epochs; the era of metaphysics is one of

these epochs, even though one can distinguish different moments in it, such as neo-Platonism, scholasticism, rationalism, dialectic materialism, nihilism, etc. Each of these is in its own way a sending of Being in its truth; in each case Being reveals itself and hides at the same time, and in each case the self-concealment founds a typical form of errancy, whose essence in each case is the forgottenness of Being.[92] This forgottenness is due to Being itself and not necessarily to any error on the part of man.[93]

Heidegger makes a special effort to show that all individual forms of the sending of Being, each of which is an event which has the character of a *singulare tantum*, nevertheless have also something in common, even though it is very difficult to articulate and name this common "element." In *Identity and Difference* (1957), Heidegger writes:

> Perhaps, indeed, through this analysis of the difference between Being and beings something perduring appears . . . which passes through the sending of Being from the beginning to its consummation. But it remains difficult to say how this perdurance is to be thought, in view of the fact that it is neither a generality that is valid for all cases nor a law which the necessity of a process, in the sense of a dialectic, certifies.[94]

I shall return in chapter 4 to the question of how Heidegger conceives of the third alternative to which he refers here, in addition to an abstract generality and a dialectic necessity.[95]

Already in "Nietzsche's Word 'God is Dead' " (1940), Heidegger had explained that by sending he understands any special way in which the ontological difference issues forth. The comportment of man to beings in any given epoch is thus grounded in the difference between Being and beings, insofar as this comportment is determined by man's relation to Being itself. The precise relationship between difference, issue, and difference *(Unterschied, Austrag, Differenz)* will be discussed later in the chapter on language.[96] Suffice it here to note that the entire era of metaphysics arose out of the fact that Being sent itself to man in such a way that man tried to comprehend beings *as* beings. It is thus understandable why Heidegger can say that the entire history of metaphysics is an event in which the difference issued forth in a particular manner.[97]

Yet the differentiation is not the result of an explicit and extrinsic "act" which divides Being from beings. In its origin, the differentiation is the coming-to-presence of Being itself, the originating power of which consists in the fact that the event just takes place.[98] Heidegger can thus conclude that "Being-as-history is neither the history of man and of humanity nor the history of man's relationship to beings or Being. Being-as-history is Being itself and nothing else. . . ."[99]

We may thus conclude here that in Heidegger's view, the truth of Being comes-to-pass in singular ways. Each self-manifestation of Being and beings has the character of an *Ereignis,* an appropriating event. In each concrete case, the appropriating event binds together Being and beings; it weaves Being, man, things, and world together into an articulated and textured whole. It is the appropriating event which in each case lets man come into what he most properly is; it is what first launches man into his essence. At the same time, it constitutes his destiny. Out of this destiny history grows, in the sense that history is shaped from the way Being presents itself and all beings to man in each case. The appropriating event, thus, in each case "determines" the way and form in which Being and beings arise for man or are closed off to him. Finally, the appropriating event also "determines" the free spaces, the possibilities of human life, and the historical forms of human *Dasein* on earth. All of that is "determined" in the final analysis from the manner in which Being illuminates itself and beings, or closes itself off and withdraws. Heidegger therefore can say in *Identity and Difference* that the manner in which it, Being itself, gives itself is itself "determined" by the way in which it illuminates itself.[100] Concerning the way in which Being gives itself in each case, Heidegger says in the same passage that it is full of destiny and that it has an epochal character.[101] In other words, the fact that in the history of thought we encounter epochs is due to "epochal turns" which are originally founded and made possible by the change in the way in which Being illuminates itself, gives itself.[102]

Our entire Western history, as far as thinking in particular is concerned, must be interpreted from this perspective. In Heidegger's view, the destiny of Being in the West began in such a way that Being had no sooner arisen among the pre-Socratic Greeks than it was again submerged, so that later on Being addressed man only from the distance of its withdrawal. The fact that Being became forgotten and that this forgottenness increased and grew in the course of the ages is not just a consequence of a neglect on man's part or on the part of its thinkers but rather a "fateful twist" of Being itself. Thus Heidegger writes in "The Anaximander Fragment" (1946) that the history of Being begins with the forgottenness of Being and that this concealing of its essence and of its essential origin is yet characteristic of Being's primordial self-illumination, so much so that thinking simply does not pursue it further. [103]

The consequence of this withdrawal of Being at the very beginning of its destiny in the West is that from Anaximander to Nietzsche, in the words of the great thinkers, beings took precedence over Being, so that Being itself as such became forgotten. Furthermore, man's thinking in the form of rational and scientific thought took precedence over both beings and Being. Man's thinking becomes more and more a representational form of thought which secures beings as objects over against itself and for itself as the subject. Furthermore, the subjectivity of the subject is then born along with the objectivity of the objects. In Heidegger's view, in the West thinking has gradually become a mere representational and calculating thinking of objects, and the subject more and more posits in advance how the beings are to manifest themselves. We see this development most clearly in modern philosophy since Descartes and notably in our contemporary world, which is preoccupied with science and technology.[104]

IV. LANGUAGE. LANGUAGE AND THE APPROPRIATING EVENT

We must now finally turn our attention to a last characteristic of Being to be discussed here. In his later works, Heidegger progressively stresses the narrow relation between Being and language. He even uses an expression which runs parallel to the one used earlier to describe the intimate relationship between Being and truth: the essence of language is the language of Being. To understand Heidegger's position in this regard, it is helpful to begin with a few general remarks.

For Heidegger, the primary meaning of language is not to be simply an instrument of communication but "to bring beings as such for the first time into the Open."[105] Language thus *is* Being insofar as Being lets beings be manifest as what they are in an *articulated* form. Being taken as language gives beings their name; its authentic saying projects the light "by reason of which it is declared what kind of beings they appear to be as they come into the open."[106]

As we shall see later, *logos,* which is usually translated as "word" or "speech," is for Heidegger "collection, gathering." In gathering we must then distinguish the process of gathering (*Dasein*'s understanding, *noein*), the gathered-togetherness of Being, and the things gathered together or the beings.[107] The emergence of Being and the origin of language are so profoundly identified by Heidegger that the one in truth cannot be without the other; both come-to-pass in *Dasein*'s understanding of Being, which in truth is no more than a response to Being's aboriginal saying. Thus as long as *Dasein* is, language comes-to-presence, for in *Dasein*'s irruption into beings, language is simply Being itself formed in and articulated by its word. Yet it should be stressed again here that in both the emergence of *Dasein* and the rise of language, Being retains its primacy.[108]

In the essay *"Logos"* (1944), Heidegger writes that the sense of *legein,* "to lay," which also means "to speak" or "to say," does nonetheless not go from one meaning ("the letting-lie-forth of thought") to another (to speak"); rather, the original meaning of *saying,* too, is nothing less than "to-let-lie-forth."[109] *Logos* taken in its primary sense is the aboriginal saying *(Sage),* the saying of Being; it is Being-as-saying. Yet language does not come-to-pass as such without *Dasein;* for as we have just seen, language comes-to-pass when *Dasein* acquiesces to Being-as-saying. Thus *legein* occurs only when human language concurs completely with the aboriginal saying of Being, i.e., with the Being of beings taken as aboriginal saying.[110] Language, insofar as it proceeds from *Dasein,* is basically an attending to the still more original saying of *Logos* (= Being itself) as articulated in the beings that now come-to-presence, insofar as the human concurrence lets them be.[111] That is the reason Heidegger can say that the essence of language is the language of Being.[112]

Sometimes language, too, is called an event of appropriation. In the "Letter on Humanism" (1947), Heidegger writes that language is the "house of Being,"[113] yet, on the other hand, language is also "the illuminating and concealing arrival of Being itself"[114] and "the coming-to-presence of nearness."[115] Language is thus described here as an event which has Being as its final origin. In his lecture "Language" (1950), Heidegger specifies this idea by explaining that language brings man into his own, so that he remains appropriated to the essence of language. "Such an appropriating takes place in that the very essence, the coming-to-presence, of language needs and uses the speaking of mortals in order to sound as the peal of stillness for the hearing of the mortals."[116] Being is always on the way to language and "uses" *Dasein* for this "purpose." Once it has arrived in words, "language is the language of Being in the same way that the clouds are the clouds of the sky."[117]

Heidegger again explicitly thematizes Being as the aboriginal saying in the lecture series *The Essence of Language* (1957–1958). The claims made here about Being as language run remarkably parallel to the appeal-response claims made about Being and thinking in *Was heisst Denken?*[118] Being withdraws into the beings which it reveals and behind the words by which they are brought to the fore. There is thus a "not" in every word, behind which Being, its inexhaustible wealth notwithstanding, must withdraw. That constitutes the domain of the unsaid, which is immanent in everything that is said. That which remains unsaid is the hidden wealth of what was said. What remains unsaid is the noiseless voice of Being, which "speaks" in every word to which we attend. "Every original and authentic naming brings into language something unsaid and, indeed, in such a way that it remains unsaid. . . ."[119] But this topic need not occupy us here further, in view of the fact that we plan to return to the issues raised here in some of the chapters to follow.

In the last section of this chapter, I wish to focus on the manner in which in the later works Heidegger conceives of the relationship between Being and time. It is well known that the problem of the relationship between Being and time occupied Heidegger from the very beginning.

Already in *Being and Time* he was guided by the idea that in the ontological tradition, Being had always been understood as continuous presence and, thus, from only one of the dimensions of time, namely, the present. Heidegger wished to bring the one-sidedly accentuated "continuous present" back into the full, pluridimensional time, in order then to try to understand the meaning of Being from the thus originally experienced time. In his attempt to materialize this goal, Heidegger was at first guided by a second basic idea, namely, that each being can become manifest with respect to its Being in many ways, so that one has to ask just what is the pervasive, simple, unified determination of Being that permeates all of its multiple meanings. But this latter question raises others: What then does Being itself mean? How can these various modes be brought into a comprehensible harmony? Whence does Being as such receive its ultimate meaning?[120]

In the later works, Heidegger no longer pursues this way of questioning. Yet there too he tries, time and again, to unfold the primordial relation between Being and time, particularly where he speaks about the aboriginal event of appropriation.[121] It is this latter approach to the issues which is at the root of Heidegger's concern with time and Being in the lecture "Time and Being" of 1962, to which we must now turn.[122]

Article III: Time and Being

In the "Zeit und Sein" lecture, Heidegger makes an effort to say something about the attempt "which thinks Being without any reference to a foundation of Being from the side of beings."[123] Thus in this lecture there will be no reference to a *summum ens* taken as *causa sui* which could be conceived of as the foundation of all that is; nor is Being to be understood here within the perspective of the metaphysical interpretation of the ontological difference, according to which Being is thought merely for the sake of beings.[124] Heidegger believed such an attempt to be necessary for at least two reasons. First of all, without such an attempt it will be impossible to bring to light in a genuine way the Being of all that which we today encounter in the world as beings and which is fundamentally determined by the essence of technicity *(Ge-stell)*.[125] Secondly, such an attempt is necessary if one is adequately to determine the relationship between man and that which until now has been called "Being."[126]

What is contained in the lecture, Heidegger says, is no more than an attempt and a venture. The venture consists in the fact that the essay is formulated in propositions, whereas its theme is such that this way of "saying" is incongruous.[127] What is important in the essay, therefore, is not so much the propositions of which it consists but rather that which is pointed to *(zeigen)* by the questions and answers by means of which we try to approach that theme. These questions and answers presuppose an experience of "the thing itself," and it is for this experience on the part of the reader that Heidegger's essay tries to prepare.[128]

I. BEING AND TIME

In the first part of the lecture, Heidegger states that Being and time are mentioned together here because from the very origin of Western thought, Being has always been interpreted as Being-present *(Anwesen),*[129] while Being-present and presence *(Anwesenheit)* refer to the present *(Gegenwart)*, which, in turn, together with the past and the future constitutes what is characteristic of time. Thus, as Being-present, Being is determined by time. But in how far and in what respect is Being determined by time? Why, in what way, and from what is it that time resounds in Being? It is obvious that any attempt to think about this relationship with the help of our everyday conceptions of Being and time is doomed to failure.

It is thus essential that we maintain first that Being is not a thing. As such it is not in time, either. Thus it is not something temporal, although as Being-present it is determined by time. And on the other hand, time is not a thing, either, and thus not something-which-is, and yet in elapsing it permanently remains, without it itself's being something temporal. Therefore, Being and time determine one another in such a way that Being is not something temporal and time is not something-which-is.

One could try here to overcome this seeming contradiction by transcending Being and time toward a higher and more encompassing unity. But such an approach would certainly lead away from the "things themselves" and their mutual relations; for such a procedure would certainly no longer deal with time as such, with Being as such, or with their mutual relationship. The genuine problem with which we are confronted here seems precisely to consist in the question of whether the relationship between Being and time is a relationship which results from a certain combination of Being and time, or whether perhaps this relationship itself is primary, so that Being and time result from it. In order to find an answer for this question, we must try to think cautiously about these "things themselves," that is, about Being and time, which are perhaps the two main themes of thought.[130]

Being is a theme of thought, but it is not a thing; time is also a theme of thought, but it is nothing temporal. Of a thing we say: "It is." With respect to Being and time, we are more careful; here we say: "There is Being, and there is time."[131] "There is," this English expression, stands for the German *Es gibt.* It can be understood to mean "It gives" in the sense of "There is something which grants."[132] If we follow this suggestion, then the question is one of what this "it" is which grants Being and time. And also: What is Being which is granted here? What is time which is given here? Let us first try to think about Being in order to grasp it in what is characteristic of it.

Being marks each being by coming-to-presence (Anwesen), insofar as it, by coming-to-presence, lets beings be present, unveils them, and brings them into the open. In the process of unveiling, there is a kind of granting at work which grants Being-present, while it lets-be-present that which is present, namely, beings. In this process we come again upon a granting, and thus upon an "it" which grants.[133] We do not yet know precisely what this granting means, nor do we know what this "it" refers to. One thing is clear, however: if one wishes to think about what is characteristic of Being as such, he must focus his attention on this typical granting and that mysterious "it" which grants. Being somehow belongs to this granting; it is the gift of the "it" which grants. Being is not something which is found outside the granting, as is the case with a common gift. In the granting, Being as Being-present becomes changed. As letting-be-present, it belongs to the unveiling itself, and as gift it remains contained in the granting. For Being is not. Being as the unveiling of Being-present is granted by a mysterious "it."[134]

In the different epochs of our Western thinking, Being has been granted in different ways; the different modes in which Being has been granted reflect themselves in the changes which have taken place in the various conceptions of Being.

The unfolding of the fullness which shows itself in these changes manifests itself at first sight as a history of Being. However, Being has no history in the way a city or a nation has its history. The historylike character of the history of Being is determined only and exclusively from the way Being comes-to-pass, that is, from the way in which "it" grants Being.[135]

According to Heidegger, the kind of granting which grants only its gift but which itself withdraws can perhaps be called "sending" (Schicken). That becomes immediately clear when one compares the case in which someone gives someone else a present with the case in which he sends it to him. Viewing it from this perspective, one may say that Being which is granted is that which has been sent and which (as sent) remains in each one of the modifications which we find in history. Thus the historical character of the history of Being must be determined from that which is characteristic of this sending and not from an undetermined coming-to-pass.

History of Being, therefore, means the sending of Being. And in the various ways of sending, the sending itself, as well as that mysterious "it" which sends, holds itself back in the various manifestations in which Being "shows" itself. To hold oneself back means in Greek *epochē*. That is why we speak of epochs of Being's sending. Epoch does not mean primarily a certain period of time in the coming-to-pass of Being's truth; it means the basic characteristic of the sending itself, that is to say, this holding-itself-back in favor of the various manifestations of the gift, namely, Being with respect to the discovery of beings. The sequence of the epochs in Being's sending neither is arbitrary nor can be predicted with necessity. And yet what is appropriate shows itself in each sending, just as what is appropriate shows itself in the belonging-together of the epochs. These epochs overlap in their sequence, so that the original sending of Being as presence is more and more concealed in the various modifications of the unveiling. Only the "demolition" of these concealments (destruction) will grant to thought a provisional insight into what then manifests itself as the sending of Being.

When Plato represents Being as *idea*, when Aristotle represents it as *energeia*, Kant as *positing*, Hegel as absolute concept, and Nietzsche as will to power, these are doctrines which are not just accidentally brought forth. They are rather the "words" of Being itself as answers to an address which speaks in the sending but which also hides itself therein, that is to say, in that mysterious "It grants Being." But how are we to conceive of this "it" which grants Being? From the preceding pages as well as the title of this essay, Heidegger says that one might expect it to be found in time.[136]

We all know what time is, and just as was the case with Being, we have a common-sense conception of it. It will be clear that this common-sense conception is of no help here. We do not yet know what is characteristic of time as such. We have just seen that if one tries to understand what Being is, one is led away from Being toward the sending which grants Being as a gift. We may expect that the same thing will be true for time, and that is why our common-sense conception will be of no avail here. And yet the titles *Being and Time* and "Time and Being" suggest that we try to understand what is characteristic of time the moment we try to understand what is characteristic of Being. For, as we have seen, Being means Being-present, and letting-something-be present.

Presence is not the present, although the former almost immediately leads to the latter. Present *(Gegenwart)* suggests past and future, the earlier and the later in regard to the "now." Usually we describe time in terms of the "now," assuming that time itself is the "sum" of present, past, and future. We seldom think of time in terms of presence. The conception of time in terms of the "now," as a series of "nows" which succeed one another, of a one-dimensional continuum, was suggested by Aristotle and has since been defended by many thinkers. It is this time which we refer to when we measure time, when a "temporal interval" is to be measured.[137]

But obviously all of that does not answer the question of precisely what time is. Is time, and does time have a place? Time is obviously not nothing. If we wish to express ourselves more carefully, we should say here again: "There is time" *(Es gibt Zeit)*. Time must be understood from the "present," which must be taken not as "now" but as presence.

But what is to be understood by presence *(Anwesenheit)*? Presence means the continuous lingering-dwelling-abiding *(verweilen)* which concerns man, reaches him, and is granted to him. But from where does this granting reaching come? We must realize here, Heidegger continues, that 1) man is always concerned with the presence of something which is present, and that he never immediately heeds presence itself; 2) that which is no longer present often still concerns man, and as such it is still present to him; in what has been, presence is still granted in some sense; and 3) that which is not yet present is present in the sense that it approaches man; in that which approaches man, presence is already granted to him. It follows then that presence does not always have the character of the present.[138]

But how are we to determine this granting of the presence in the present, past, and future? Does this granting consist in the fact that it reaches us, or does it reach us because it is in itself a granting? There is no doubt that the future grants and adduces the past, whereas the past grants the future. And this mutual granting gives the present at the same time. They thus grant themselves to each other, and in so doing they make it possible that coming-to-presence is granted to them.

That which comes to light in the mutual granting of one another to each other of present, past, and future is the open, or also the time-space. This time-space precedes what we commonly call space and time. It is a three-dimensional open, in that it comes to light by means of a threefold granting of present, past, and future.[139]

But from what are we to determine the unity of the three dimensions of this time-space? We know already that a presence is at work in the coming of what is not-yet-present and in the having-been of what is no-longer-present, as well as in what we usually call the present. This presence does not belong to one of these three dimensions to the exclusion of the others. While the three dimensions give themselves over to one another, and precisely in the interplay of the one to the other *(Zuspiel)*, still another granting manifests itself, which opens up a fourth dimension. It is this latter granting which is characteristic of time itself and which brings about the presence which is typical in each case for the coming, the having-been, and the present. It keeps these latter dimensions separated, and nevertheless it keeps them in each other's proximity, also, so that these three dimensions can remain close to one another. That is why one can call the primordial granting in which literally everything begins (*anfängt*) and in which the unity of genuine time precisely consists a "proximity which brings near" (*nähernde Nähe*). It brings close to one another the coming, the having-been, and the present by keeping them apart. For it keeps open the having-been by denying it its coming as present, just as it keeps open the coming (future) by witholding the present in this coming, that is, by denying it its being present. Thus, the proximity which brings near has the character of a denial and withholding.[140]

Time *is* not. "It" gives time. The granting which gives time is to be determined from the proximity which denies and withholds. "It" grants the open of time-space and guards that which is denied in the having-been and that which is withheld in the coming. This granting thus is revealing and concealing at the same time; while granting the open of time-space, it hides itself as granting.

But where now is this mysterious "it" which grants time and time-space? Since the beginning of Western thought, people have asked this question, and many of them have said with Aristotle and Augustine that "time is in the soul." Thus, time cannot be without man. The question, however, is whether or not it is man who gives time, or whether it is man to whom time is granted. In the latter case, the question is still who or what "it" is which gives time. One thing is clear, however: man is what he is only and exclusively because he stands within the threefold granting and "endures" the proximity which denies and withholds, and which determines this granting. Man does not make time, and time does not make man. Expressions such as "making," "producing," and "creating" do not make sense here.[141]

II. "IT" GRANTS BEING AND TIME

We have seen that we must say: "There is something which grants Being as well as time." But what now is this "it?" In answering this question, Heideger suggests, we must not think of this "it" as a "power" or a "God." We must try to determine it from Being as coming-to-presence and from time as the transcendental domain in which the clearing of the multiform coming-to-presence is granted.

From what we have said about Being and time thus far, one might expect that genuine time, the manifold granting of the open, constitutes that mysterious "it" which grants Being as coming-to-presence. Genuine time would then be the "it" we have in mind when we say "It grants Being." The sending in which Being is granted would than consist in the granting of time. But is it really true that time is that mysterious "it" which grants Being? By no means, for time itself, too, is the gift of an "it grants." Thus, this mysterious "it" is still undetermined.[142]

Heidegger points out that perhaps we find ourselves in a very difficult situation here, in that we have to use sentences of Indo-European languages which do not have a clear theory about "impersonal propositions." He invites the reader, therefore, to pay attention not so much to the propositions as to the "thing itself" to which they refer. What is meant by the "it" must be determined from that granting process which belongs to it, that is, the granting which at the same time is a sending *(Geschick)* and a lighting presenting *(lichtendes Reichen)*.

In the sending of Being and the presenting of time, an ap-propriation manifests itself making Being (as coming-to-presence) and time (as the open) that which they properly are. That which makes both, namely, Being and time, what they properly are *(Eigenes)* and makes them belong together is what Heidegger calls *Ereignis*, aboriginal and ap-propriating event. In other words, that mysterious "it" about which we have spoken is the *Ereignis*. And this *Ereignis* is ontologically prior to Being as well as to time, because it is that which grants to both what they properly are. This expression is correct, and yet it is not completely true, because it hides the original relationship between Being, time, and the event.

What then is this ap-propriating event? It is very difficult to answer this question, because the event with which we are concerned here cannot be captured in propositions, and because we can obviously not presuppose here what Being and time are in essence.[143]

That is why it is perhaps better to say first what event does not mean. The word *event* does not have its common meaning here. It usually means "occurrence," whereas in this case it means "the ap-propriation taken both as a presenting and a sending." Furthermore, event is not a *summum genus* under which one must distinguish Being as well as time. As we have seen, Being has manifested itself as the gift of the sending of the coming-to-presence which is granted through the presenting of time. As such Being remains a property *(Eigentum)* of the ap-propriating event; Being vanishes in the event. And the same is true for time. In the appropriating event, Being as letting-be-present is sent just as time is presented there. In the event, Being as well as time is appropriated *(ereignet im Ereignis)*. But what about the event itself? Is there anything more we can say about it? Heidegger is of the opinion that one could indeed say

more about it. In his view, that implies that we say something more about
the withdrawal which is essential to the event as well as about its relation
to man.[144]

We have seen that the sending of Being was determined as granting.
That which grants was said to hold to itself, to adhere to itself, to with-
hold itself; it withdraws from the revealment. A similar statement was
made in regard to the presenting characteristic of time. But if it is true that
the event withdraws from revealment, we may say that the event ex-
propriates itself from itself and that a certain ex-propriation is characteristic for the ap-propriating event. That means not that the event gives up
itself but precisely that it preserves its own property.

We have seen also that in Being as coming-to-presence, a process manifests itself which is going-on and which concerns us humans in such a
way that the vital characteristic of our humanity is to be found in becoming aware of this procedure and thus taking it over. But the acceptance of
this coming-to-presence which goes-on rests on the fact that we stand in
the domain of presenting which the four-dimensional time has passed on
to us.

Insofar as Being and time are found only and exclusively in the appropriation *(das Ereignen)*, appropriation is characterized by the fact that it
brings man who receives Being to that which is typical of him as he stands
within the domain of genuine time. This belonging-to rests on the complete ap-propriation, characteristic of the ap-propriating event. It is this
complete ap-propriation which lets man enter this event. That is why we
cannot conceive of the event as something opposite to us or as something
which encompasses everything. Re-presentational thought has as little
access to the event as does a speaking in propositions.

Finally, by going from Being to the sending of Being, and from time to
the presenting of the time-space, we have gained some access to the event.
It is of importance, however, to repeat once again: The event is not a
thing. The event *is* not; nor is there something which gives the event. The
only thing we can say is: *Das Ereignis ereignet.* This tautology points to
what hides itself in the truth as *a-letheia.*[145]

CHAPTER 4

Reflections on the Ontological Difference

Article I: The Ontological Difference in Heidegger's Early Works (1923–1935)

The issues to be discussed in this chapter could have been incorporated into the preceding chapter, but after careful reflection I decided to separate the question concerning the meaning of Being from the problem about the ontological difference because of the complexity of the issues involved, as we shall see when we proceed.

In this chapter I shall give the reader an idea of how Heidegger's own thinking about the ontological difference developed gradually. Particularly, I plan to focus on the following questions: 1) How is one to relate the different ways in which Heidegger appears to articulate the ontological difference (the difference between a being and its Being, the difference between beings and Being itself, the difference between thing and world)? 2) Is Being itself or is the ontological difference as such the very matter of thought? 3) What is the precise meaning of the distinction between naming the difference and thinking the ontological difference as such, a distinction which Heidegger often makes in his reflections on the thought of great thinkers of the past? 4) How is the ontological difference to be related to the connection between Being and thinking, and does the latter indeed imply some "third thing," as Heidegger sometimes seems to suggest? 5) Did Heidegger perhaps eventually eliminate the issue of the ontological difference altogether?

But before I turn to these questions, I wish first to describe briefly how Heidegger introduced the issue of the ontological difference and how it seemed to grow in importance, especially after 1935, the year in which he

delivered the lecture course *An Introduction to Metaphysics.* I shall then
present Heidegger's "final" conception of the ontological difference in its
various aspects and modalities. Yet let us first briefly indicate what is
meant by the ontological difference and "show" its origin and its
manifold implications for philosophy and its history. In so doing, I shall
summarize some important ideas which William J. Richardson, following
Heidegger himself, has developed in the introduction to his book on
Heidegger's philosophy.[1]

Heidegger often said that "the forgottenness of Being is the forgottenness of the difference between Being and beings."[2] The difference between Being and beings was forgotten because of an ambiguity intrinsic in
the expression commonly used in Indo-European languages to refer to
beings as the subject matter of metaphysics. "Being as being," *to on hēi
on,* is ambiguous in more than one respect. The expression "being as
being" was used to refer to the whole of beings considered in terms of
what makes them be, their "beingness" *(ousia).* The beingness of the
whole of beings can mean just the common denominator of all beings,
"being in general," *ens commune.* But the beingness of beings can also
refer to the ultimate ground which lets the totality of beings be. Therefore, metaphysics, as the study of beings as beings, has from the very
beginning been conceived either as the study of being in general or as the
study of a supreme, divine, being, or both.[3] The ambiguity of the expression *on hēi on* is connected with an equally fundamental ambiguity of the
word *on* itself.

Grammatically, this word is a participle that may be used as either a
noun or an adjective with a verbal meaning. Thus, it either means "that
which is, a being," or it designates that by which a being "is," namely, its
Being. Heidegger wished to overcome classical metaphysics by thinking
Being itself as a process through which this ambiguity and ambivalence
can be overcome. In so doing, he gradually became aware of the necessity
of thinking Being neither as being in general nor as supreme being, but
rather as the process of unveiling.[4]

When Heidegger uses the term *ontological difference* in this context to
refer to the basic theme for thought, it is not his intention to refer to the
ambivalence that has been the source of all confusion in metaphysics for
so many centuries. He intends, rather, to refer to a more fundamental
difference between *Being* taken as the original process of unconcealment
and *beings* taken as things that have their proper modes of Being and,
thus, their proper meaning. The original proposal to ground metaphysics
by examining the meaning of Being as the process of non-concealment
through which the ontological difference between Being and beings,
taken here in the sense just indicated, comes about, has been Heidegger's
concern from the first page of *Being and Time* (1927). To ground

metaphysics in this way necessarily implies overcoming metaphysics, transcending it, and passing beyond it. Classical metaphysics, by reason of its forgottenness of the genuine meaning of the ontological difference and, thus, because of the ambiguity connected with it, is unable to meditate the Being process which is its ground.[5]

In *Being and Time*, the term *ontological difference* does not occur, although the issue to which the term refers is clearly present, particularly in the introductory section of the book.[6] The expression itself appears for the first time in Heidegger's published works in *The Essence of Reason* (1929),[7] and it was alluded to also in *Kant and the Problem of Metaphysics* (1929).[8] Yet Heidegger had used the expression explicitly already in a lecture course of 1927, namely, *The Basic Problems of Phenomenology.*[9] From the manner in which Heidegger in these works speaks about the ontological difference, it is clear that in his opinion this issue is one of the greatest importance, insofar as "the possibility of ontology, of philosophy as a science, stands and falls with the possibility of a sufficiently clear accomplishment of this differentiation between Being and beings, and accordingly with the possibility of negotiating the passage from the ontic consideration of beings to the ontological thematization of Being."[10]

If we take together all the elements concerning the ontological difference as found in Heidegger's earlier works, we can perhaps express Heidegger's first conception of the ontological difference in the following theses: 1) In the works and lecture courses written between *Being and Time* and *Vom Wesen des Grundes*, the Being question is formulated in terms of the ontological difference, and the identity of Being and truth as a process of unveiling is maintained. 2) The ontological difference comes about only by reason of *Dasein*'s power to differentiate between Being and being; this power is to be found in *Dasein*'s transcendence. 3) The final term toward which *Dasein* transcends beings is not the beingness of beings *(Seiendheit)* but rather Being itself, taken as the emergence of the difference between Being and beings *(das Sein).*[11]

To understand the implications of the third thesis, a few additional reflections will be necessary. In my opinion, it is undoubtedly true that in *Being and Time* and related works and lecture courses, Heidegger was at least in part concerned with showing that the temporality of *Dasein* is the principle of the division of *Dasein*'s own modes of Being, and that time as temporalized by *Dasein* is also the principle of the division of the meaning of Being into the possible significations of Being (ek-sistence, ready-to-hand, present-at-hand), so that the interplay of the three dimensions of temporalness in its different modalities can be taken as the guiding clue for the division of the different significations of Being.[12] Yet it is clear also that all of that does not constitute Heidegger's basic concern. Toward the end of *Being and Time*, Heidegger explicitly says that the distinction between the various modes of Being is only the point of departure for the genuinely ontological problematic: the question concerning the meaning of Being and the question of whether primordial time indeed manifests itself as the transcendental horizon of Being.[13]

That which constitutes the unity of the multiplicity of the various modes of Being must be determined "critically," and it cannot just be postulated. There must be some final "ground" which as *identity of difference* can be taken as the foundation of the difference. This ground can be revealed only after a naive realism as well as every form of dogmatic idealism has been given up in favor of a transcendental form of philosophy. As *The Basic Problems of Phenomenology* and *Kant and the Problem of Metaphysics* clearly show, Heidegger's main concern was to substitute a "transcendental *ontology*" for the Kantian transcendental *logic;* and that implies a fundamental reinterpretation of Kant's conception of the transcendental and the a priori.[14]

The transcendental problematic also plays an important role in the manner in which Heidegger conceives of the ontological difference. We can see that already in *Being and Time,* where the problematic hinted at by this expression constitutes an essential part of the work's basic aim, even though (as we have mentioned already) the expression itself is not yet found there.[15] Sometimes Heidegger specifies the difference in this work by means of the distinction between a being and its Being. But that cannot be all. For the *identity* presupposed by the ontological difference is not just the categorial identity of those beings which have the same mode of Being, because *this* identity presupposes the transcendental identity of an a priori synthesis as its necessary condition. Heidegger alludes to this dual principle of identity in both *The Basic Problems* and *The Essence of Reasons,* as we have seen already.

The categorial-ontological difference is the difference between a being *(on)* and its Beingness *(ousia).* On the other hand, the transcendental-ontological difference refers to the distinction between the meaning of Being, the truth of Being, Being itself *(der Sinn von Sein, einai),* on the one hand, and the Beingness of a being *(die Seiendheit eines Seienden),* on the other.

Already in the second section of *Being and Time,* Heidegger speaks of his attempt to examine *the meaning of Being* by investigating *a being,* namely *Dasein,* in *its Being.*[16] In Heidegger's original thought, these two differences are often taken in combination. The basic point to realize here is then that the categorial-ontological difference is to be founded upon the transcendental-ontological difference.[17]

One final remark is in order here. We shall see later that in Heidegger's reflections on the ontological difference in his later works, considerations about language begin to play an ever more important part. At first sight it is thus amazing that in dealing with the ontological difference in his earlier works, Heidegger does not mention language at all, especially if one considers that in *Being and Time* he had pointed to the intrinsic relationship between the apophantic *as* structure of the assertion and the hermeneutic *as* which is characteristic of man's understanding as found in his concerned dealing with things. For it can be shown that this relationship intermediates between the ontological difference and the apophantic *as* structure of the assertion.[18] Upon closer consideration, however, it becomes quite clear why Heidegger did not succeed at this point in making the necessary links.

Although he had already concluded that Being must be conceived of as being identical with truth taken as the process of unveiling, and that the ontological difference comes about only by reason of man's transcendence, at that time Heidegger did not yet understand how that toward which man transcends, namely, the world, can be brought into contact with Being taken as truth. Furthermore, there can be no doubt that the analysis in *Being and Time* of *logos* as an ek-sistential of *Dasein* and as the ontological foundation of language is completely inadequate for giving a justified answer to the question concerning the relationships among the ontological difference, the hermeneutic structure of man's understanding, and language.[19] There are no texts establishing these relationships, and, furthermore, Heidegger himself admitted the impossibility of answering these questions on the basis of the language conception found in *Being and Time.* "I know only this one thing: it is precisely because the reflection on language and Being has determined the course of my thought that the explanation of them has remained as far as possible in the background. Perhaps the basic weakness of my book *Being and Time* is that I dared too early to go too far ahead."[20]

So many serious problems concerning the relationship between Being and world, Being and time, Being and thought, Being and language, were involved here that even in 1954 Heidegger was convinced that the "adequate word" to express the relationship of language to Being was still lacking.[21] Yet it is not impossible that in 1929 Heidegger was already aware of the need to admit that the ontological difference might very well have a certain primacy over *Dasein.*[22]

Article II: The Ontological Difference in the Later Works (1935–1962)

I. HEIDEGGER'S FIRST ATTEMPTS TO FORMULATE THE ISSUE

We must now turn to the question of how Heidegger finally came to conceive of the ontological difference and its relation to language. In treating this complex issue, we shall also try to examine his answer to the other questions mentioned at the beginning of this chapter, namely: 1) Is the ontological difference indeed the true subject matter of thought? 2) What is the precise meaning of the difference between naming the ontological difference and thinking it? 3) What is the precise relation between the ontological difference, on the one hand, and the correlation between thinking and Being, on the other? 4) Did Heidegger perhaps eventually change his view on the importance of the ontological difference for thought? In view of the fact that Heidegger does not always seem to speak in the same manner about these issues, it is important to follow his "development" from *An Introduction to Metaphysics* (1935), via the *"Logos"* article (1944), the "Letter on Humanism" (1947), *What Evokes Thinking?* (1951–1952), and *Identity and Difference* (1957), to *On the Way to Language* (1950–1959).

In the later works we see that Heidegger, when he tries to determine the genuine matter of thought, gradually shifts his attention from the question concerning the meaning of Being as such to the ontological difference. Already in *An Introduction to Metaphysics,* he took his point of departure from the question of the ontological difference.[23] Yet in that work he still focused primarily on the problem concerning the meaning of Being as such, as he had done in *Being and Time* and the other works of the early period. Thus, the correlation examined there was still one *between thought and Being,* even though it was clearly understood at that time that Being is the Being *of* beings, such that the word *of* names the ontological difference. In other words, the expression "the Being *of* beings" signifies that Being never comes-to-presence without beings and that beings are to be taken in terms of their Being.[24] The difference between the conception found in *An Introduction to Metaphysics* and that of, for instance, *What Evokes Thinking?* appears thus to be that in the former work the ontological difference is merely named but not yet explicitly thought as such, whereas in the latter work an effort is made to think the difference itself and to think it as such.

> When we say Being, it means the Being of beings. When we say beings, it means beings with respect to their Being. We always speak *from out of* the ambivalence *(Zwiefalt).* The ambivalence is always pre-given, for Parmenides as much as for Plato, for Kant as much as for Nietzsche. The ambivalence has always already unfolded the domain within which the relation between beings and Being can be presented. This relation can obviously be interpreted and explained in various ways.[25]

But let us not yet immediately jump to any definite conclusion. We must once more look more carefully at how Heidegger's thought moves from the one point of view to the other.

In the essay "European Nihilism" (1940), Heidegger discusses the ontological difference extensively, and there he develops in detail what in the lecture "Nietzsche's Word 'God is Dead'" (1940) already was indicated, and where it was stated that each individual sending of Being is a special way in which the ontological difference issues forth. The section entitled "The Comportment toward Beings and the Relation to Being"[26] has as a subtitle "The Ontological Difference." Heidegger explains here that in every epoch of Being's history, man comports himself in a special way toward beings, *because of* his relationship to Being. Thus, in each case man's comportment with beings is grounded in the manner in which the difference between Being and beings issues forth in that epoch. The epoch of metaphysics is that epoch in which Being sends itself to man in such a way that he tries to understand beings *as* beings. The entire history of metaphysics is thus an "event" in which the difference issued forth in this particular manner.[27]

> The relation of man to Being is obscure. And yet we stand everywhere and continually in this relation wherever and whenever we comport ourselves toward beings. When and where did we, who are also beings, *not* comport ourselves toward beings? We comport ourselves toward beings, and maintain ourselves above all in the relation to Being. Only in this way is the totality of beings our stay and abode. That means that we stand in the difference of beings and Being. This difference supports our relation to Being and our comportment toward beings. It holds sway without our paying attention to it. It seems to be a difference which is such that what is distinguished here is not really distinguished by anyone; thus it is a difference for which no one is there to make the distinction, and for which no domain of difference is established, let alone experienced.[28]

In the same essay Heidegger explains the relationship between the technical terms *Unterscheidung* (distinction), *Differenz* (difference), and *Austrag* (issuance), to which he later returns in his lectures on language.[29]

> Ontology is grounded upon the distinction between Being and beings. It is more appropriate to name this distinction with the name difference, which indicates that being and Being somehow are carried away from one another, are separated from one another, and yet are also related to each other; and that occurs from themselves and not on the ground of some act of distinction *(Unterscheidung)*. Distinction in the sense of difference implies that there is an issuance between Being and beings. From where and how this issuance comes-to-be is not said. . . . But the ontological difference is introduced here not in order to solve the question of ontology but merely in order to name that which, as something that remained unquestioned until now, makes all ontology, i.e., metaphysics, questionable.[30]

Thus the term *ontological difference* merely names the ground or foundation of all ontology and metaphysics. The explicit naming of the difference in this context indicates that it now has become necessary to
question this ground and fundament.[31]

II. THE ONTOLOGICAL DIFFERENCE IN "LOGOS" AND "THE SAYING OF ANAXIMANDER"

Richardson is of the opinion that Heidegger tried to think the ontological
difference as such for the first time in the *"Logos"* essay of 1944. In his
view, in *An Introduction to Metaphysics* (1935) Heidegger had already
stated that his concern with the question concerning the meaning of Being
was a necessary but preliminary study to interrogate the ontological difference.[32] Up to 1944, the search for the meaning of Being had thus been
an attempt to understand Being's meaning as the process of the truth, out
of which the ontological difference was to arise. Yet in the *"Logos"* essay,
Heidegger speaks about a middle-point between beings and Being. He
then asks whether human thought is capable of finding a way to reach this
point. For Richardson this question presupposes the complete correlation
of Being and beings and thus their interdependence; it also means that the
middle-point to which Heidegger refers here is the ontological difference
as such, which now emerges clearly as the main theme of thought.
Richardson sees a confirmation of this thesis in the following sentence:
"What happens when the Being of beings, the beings in their Being, the
difference between the two *as* difference is brought into language?"[33]
From the context it is clear, however, that the question of whether or not
the ontological difference as such can indeed be thought is only posed
here but not yet answered. Finally, it appears that Heidegger wished to
suggest that asking this question is typical for his own way of thinking
and "bears testimony to his relentless pursuit of an always more fundamental, always receding source."[34]

At any rate, Heidegger continued to concentrate on the issue. In "The
Saying of Anaximander" (1946), he stated that the only fragment which
we still have consists of two clauses; the first is concerned with Being, and
the second focuses on beings. But in both cases the issue is really the
same, namely, the process by which beings come-to-presence in non-
concealment. The distinction and the relation between the two clauses
suggest the distinction and the relation between Being and beings, i.e.,
the ontological difference.[35]

In Heidegger's view, Anaximander names Being as such and, implicitly,
also its relationship to beings, but the ontological difference as such
remains forgotten. "The oblivion of Being is the oblivion of the difference
between Being and beings."[36] But this oblivion of the distinction was by

no means the consequence of a forgetfulness, and hence a weakness, on the part of Anaximander's thinking. The true origin of this forgottenness is Being itself, which, in disclosing itself to him in his epoch of history, concealed itself at the same time. "Oblivion of Being belongs to the self-concealing essence of Being. . . . That means that the history of Being begins with the oblivion of Being, since Being—together with its essence, its distinction from beings—keeps to itself."[37] Furthermore, the oblivion of the distinction should not be understood as something totally negative. For "[the] oblivion of the distinction, with which the destiny of Being begins and which it will carry through to completion, is all the same not a lack, but rather the richest and most prodigious event: in it the history of the Western world comes to be borne out. It is the event of metaphysics."[38]

Richardson has focused our attention here on two important statements which seem to refer to a paradox, which perhaps can clarify the important change in the second edition of the epilogue to *What is Metaphysics?* In the first statement, taken from "The Saying of Anaximander," Heidegger speaks about the meaning of the Greek word *chreō* in connection with the expression *kata to chreōn*, which appears in the fragment of Anaximander. Heidegger claims that we should think of this word as referring to the Being of beings. Thus in *chreō*, somehow or other the relationship between Being and beings is thought, "especially if the relation of Being to beings can come only from Being, can rest only in the essence of Being."[39] A few pages further in the same essay, Heidegger adds that Being hands out the beings in such a way that it antecedently contains within itself the beings that are so handed out, gathers them into itself, and guards them as beings in their Being.[40] In both these texts, the primacy of Being over beings is stressed, but in both cases the ontological difference is not named explicitly as such, even though it is hinted at. Thus these texts seem to suggest that Being can come-to-presence without beings.[41]

Yet on another page of the same essay, Heidegger states explicitly that it is the matter and the business of Being to be the Being *of* beings.[42] This statement seems to imply that Being, its full primacy notwithstanding, cannot come-to-presence without beings.[43] And this implication is confirmed by other similar texts, which also suggest that the ontological difference is to be thought as such.[44] What are we to think about this seeming contradiction?

III. THE CASE OF THE EPILOGUE TO *WHAT IS METAPHYSICS?*

I think that it cannot be denied that between 1935 and 1943 Heidegger was indeed of the opinion that it is possible, and perhaps even necessary, to think Being without beings. Thus, in the epilogue to *What Is Metaphysics?* of 1943, Heidegger still could write: "It pertains to the truth of Being that Being indeed *(wohl)* comes-to-presence without beings, but that a being never is without Being. . . ."[45] The expression "coming-to-presence" in this case does not refer to the manner in which Being "is" by itself, so to speak, but rather to the manner in which it comes-to-pass in thought, in *Dasein*. Yet it is already understood here that *Dasein* no longer has the privileged position in the process of the coming-to-pass of the truth of Being, a position which *Dasein* undoubtedly had enjoyed in the earlier works.

In the same epilogue, Heidegger for the first time states unequivocally that it is the basic intention of his thinking to overcome metaphysics. Whereas Heidegger in his earlier works had tried to "overcome" metaphysics from the inside, as it were, beginning within the domain of metaphysics and attempting to move on beyond the entire metaphysical movement, in his later works he leaves classical metaphysics behind and resolutely goes on the way in a new direction. A thinking which is on the way in this direction tries to think Being as truth, as non-concealment, *a-lētheia*. It seems that in 1943 Heidegger still was of the opinion that Being as non-concealment has a meaning in itself and that it can and should be thought for itself.[46]

Yet that does not necessarily imply that Being can *be* by itself, or that the ontological difference as such is less important here. For Heidegger still maintains that the ontological difference arises out of the coming-to-pass of the truth of Being. According to Richardson, both here and in *An Introduction to Metaphysics*, Heidegger speaks about thinking Being itself as if this thinking merely is a *preliminary* approach to the interrogation of the ontological difference. Just as in the Hölderlin essays, here, too, Being is described as the source of all beings; it encompasses them all; thus it includes and gives rise to the ontological difference.[47]

Six years later, in 1949, Heidegger added an introduction to *What Is Metaphysics?* He used the occasion to make an important change in the epilogue of 1943. The statement "Being indeed *(wohl)* comes-to-presence without beings. . . ." is now changed to "Being *never* . . . comes-to-presence without beings. . . ."[48] In Richardson's opinion, the first text, if taken in its context, states the primacy of the Being-process in the emergence of beings; it names the ontological difference, but not yet *as such*. The second text, if taken within the same context, states that although Being is to be thought for itself, if the ontological difference is to be understood, Being can nonetheless never *be* by itself. Thus it is true to claim that beings cannot be without Being as well as that Being cannot be without beings. That names the ontological difference *as such*.

Richardson then presents some intrinsic and some extrinsic arguments for the correctness of his view that in 1949 the focus of Heidegger's thought was on the ontological difference as such. In particular, the arguments taken from two other texts which appeared in 1949 are very convincing, indeed.[49] For in 1949, Heidegger added a brief introduction to the third edition of *The Essence of Reasons.* There he writes that the essay *The Essence of Reasons* and the lecture *What Is Metaphysics?* were both written in 1928. The latter is concerned with Non-being, whereas the former is concerned with the ontological difference. In *What Is Metaphysics?*, Non-being describes the Not which is characteristic of Being when it is seen from the perspective of beings; the ontological difference, too, is the Not which separates beings and Being. Just as Being, taken as the Not in regard to beings, is not simply a negative nothing, so is the ontological difference not just an *ens rationis.* As a matter of fact, the Not of Non-beings and the Not of the ontological difference are the same, they are one, even though they are not identical. They are one in the sense that, in the coming-to-presence of the Being of beings, they belong together. This sameness is the only problem that merits thought and which both treatises, which were purposely kept separate, attempted to consider more closely, without really being up to the task.[50]

A note which was added to *On the Essence of Truth* in 1949 expresses this idea even more clearly. There Heidegger states that the essence of truth is the truth of Being *(Wesen).* In his explanation of this phrase, which is not meant to be a strict proposition or statement, Heidegger writes that "because a hiding *(Bergen)* that lightens belongs to it, Beon *(Seyn)* appears primordially in the light of the concealing withdrawal."[51] Thus Beon is the process that lights up beings, and in so doing it conceals itself in these beings. With respect to the expression "Beon," Heidegger remarks *that it is the difference* that holds sway between Being and beings, i.e., the ontological difference *as such.* Thus, it cannot be doubted that in 1949 Heidegger was certainly preoccupied with the ontological difference as such.[52]

IV. THE ONTOLOGICAL DIFFERENCE IN *IDENTITY AND DIFFERENCE*

In *Identity and Difference* (1957) we find the most comprehensive treatment of the ontological difference as such. In this work Heidegger tried to think *the relation between identity and difference,* which he finally came to understand as *the* task of thinking. "That identity and difference belong together is shown in the present publication as that which is to be thought." He also suggests there that the difference stems from the manner in which the identity comes-to-presence and abides. In his view, the reader will learn to understand that when he listens carefully to the harmony between the appropriating event *(Ereignis)* and the issuance *(Austrag)*.[53]

In Heidegger's view, Western thinking originated from the ontological difference, i.e., the difference between Being and beings. Each being has its Being in light of Being itself. The difference thus implies the being, its Being, and Being itself. Although Western metaphysics originated from this difference, in Western thought this difference is never thought *as difference.* Heidegger tries to think the difference as difference, i.e., the coming-to-presence and abidance of the difference as such. And Heidegger tries to think the difference as difference by showing that it originates, or perhaps better stems, from the manner in which the identity comes-to-presence and abides *(Wesen).* It is important to stress here the point that for Heidegger all other differences which one encounters in philosophical thought are rooted in the ontological difference between Being and beings.

It is Heidegger's main task in the lecture on the onto-theo-logical conception of metaphysics to show that there is a difference which is intrinsic in the being itself, i.e., the difference between the being and its Being, as well as a difference in Being, insofar as Being itself, to the degree that in each case it shows itself, differs from itself, to the degree that at the same time it hides itself.

In the lecture "The Onto-Theo-Logical Constitution of Metaphysics," with which Heidegger in 1957 concluded a seminar on Hegel's *Logic*,[54] Heidegger explains his position in this regard in the following way. In his view, Western metaphysics, since its very beginning, has tried to think the matter of thought under the name of "Being." That means always and everywhere the Being *of* beings. Yet classical metaphysics left the difference between Being and beings unthought. We think about Being rigorously only when we think of it in its difference from beings and of beings in their difference from Being. Usually, the difference which in this way comes into view is reduced to a distinction, i.e., something made up by our understanding. That is totally inadequate in this case, because any time our understanding brings difference about anywhere, we find that Being and beings in their difference are already "there." One could still try with Kant to explain this phenomenon by stating that our understanding is structured in such a way that it always must insert the difference between Being and beings a priori.[55] One could perhaps also say that the difference between Being and beings is somehow connected with the structure of the Indo-European languages in which Western metaphysics has been articulated.[56] In Heidegger's view, much can perhaps be said about that, and much more must even be asked about these explanations.

Yet for one thing, these explanations *do not give an account* of the "be-tween" into which the difference so to speak is inserted.[57]

Heidegger decides at this point not to enter into a discussion of these views; instead, he notes first that we encounter the difference always and everywhere unquestioningly. Usually we do not notice the difference, and there does not seem to be anything that compels us to notice the difference. Yet upon closer inspection, it becomes clear that one has to ask the question concerning the difference because Being shows itself as the Being of . . . , and beings show themselves as the beings of. . . . Thus we must ask the question of what one is to make of the difference as such, *if* Being as well as beings appear only from the difference. But in order to be able to deal meaningfully with this question, we must first take a step back and bring ourselves in the proper position in regard to the differ-ence. By taking distance from the difference which is so near to us, we shall be able to let the difference for the first time come to the fore as such.[58]

If we take a step back and then focus on the difference, releasing it into what is to be thought, we can say that the expression "the Being of the being" really means the Being which the being *is*. The "is" is to be taken here in a transitive sense; note that here "transitive" means "going-over." Thus Being comes-to-presence and abides in the sense that it goes over to the being. In going-over to the being, Being, however, does not leave its own place, as if the being first would be without Being and only later would be approached by Being. In a manner that is revealing, Being goes over to and goes beyond that which first comes to the fore as something non-concealed, of and by itself, only by such a coming-over *(Überkommnis)*. For the being, arrival *(Ankunft)* means to shelter itself in non-concealment and, thus, to endure and wear on as so sheltered, i.e., to be the being that is.

Being shows itself here as the revealing coming-over, whereas the being as such appears in the manner of the arrival that shelters itself in non-concealment. Being and the being, both taken in the sense just ar-ticulated, come-to-presence and abide as the ones thus differentiated, from out of the selfsame, the dif-ference or inter-scission *(Unter-Schied)*. It is the inter-scission which first yields and holds apart the "between" in which the coming-over of Being and the arrival of the being are held toward each other, i.e., are borne apart from one another and, thus, held apart, borne toward each other. The difference of Being and the being, taken as the inter-scission of the coming-over and the arrival, is the issuance *(Austrag)* of the two, which both shelters and reveals. In the issuance there governs a clearing of what veils and closes itself, and whose governing grants both the growing apart and the coming-together of Being's coming-over and the being's arrival.

By trying to think about the difference as such, we thus do not make it disappear, but rather we follow it to the point where its coming-to-presence originates. And on the way to that point we must try to think the issuance of Being's coming-over and the being's arrival. Being, thought from out of the difference, is the genuine matter of thought.[59]

Heidegger then inserts a brief note about Being to the effect that any time we speak about Being in a general manner, we present it in a way in which it never presents itself and gives itself. For Being always appears in a particular historical form, as *phusis, logos, hen, idea, energeia*, substance, subject, objectivity, will, will to power, etc. The manner in which Being gives itself is itself determined by the way in which it itself clears and sends itself. As such, Being endures and abides for us only insofar as we let it be free in genuine re-collection. And the same is true also for our experience of the characterization of the difference of Being and the beings as such which is typical for each epoch, and to which in each case a given interpretation of beings corresponds. And that holds true above all for our own attempt to think the difference and the issuance *(Austrag)*. And yet it may be that this discussion which assigns the difference of Being and beings to issuance as the provisional place *(Vorort)* of its coming-to-presence and abidance, brings to light something that is all-pervading, i.e., that pervades the sending of Being itself from its beginning to its completion.[60] We shall have to return to *Identity and Difference* later on, where we must focus briefly on the first lecture contained in this work. But first we must turn to the question of how the difference relates to language.

We have seen already that in his later works, Heidegger gradually began to realize that the relationship between Being and language is much closer than he had assumed at first. Since I plan to deal with the relation between Being and language in one of the chapters to follow, I shall limit myself here to a few remarks which may be helpful in understanding the implications of this development for the formulation of the ontological difference.

V. LANGUAGE AND THE COMING-TO-PRESENCE
OF THE ONTOLOGICAL DIFFERENCE

In *An Introduction to Metaphysics*, Heidegger touches on the issue where he attributes to *logos* characteristics which elsewhere he attributes to Being. *Logos*, it is said there, is the gathered-togetherness of beings which lets them be what they are by constantly gathering them together and dominating them.[61] In the *"Logos"* essay of 1944, these ideas are developed in much greater detail in a context that attempts to elucidate the relationship between Being and *Dasein* in terms of the aboriginal saying of language and *Dasein*'s authentic response to Being's address. There Heidegger says, among other things, that the word *logos* led Heraclitus's thought to that which gathers all present beings into becoming present and so lets them lie before us. Thus the *logos* names that in which the becoming present of beings comes-to-pass. The Greeks called this *to eon*, "the Being of beings." Thus in the word *logos,* the Being of beings emerges as that which alone is worthy of thought. In other words, in Heraclitus's fragments, Being sometimes comes-to-presence as the *logos*, as the laying-down that gathers beings. Yet this lightning flash of Being remained forgotten, even in Heraclitus's own thinking.

Toward the end of the essay, Heidegger muses about what happens if the Being of beings and the beings in their Being, i.e., the difference between them as the difference, are brought to language? Then the Being of beings is secured and sheltered in the essence of language. It seems that this event was prepared when the *logos* became the guiding word in Heraclitus's thought. The *logos* is the laying that gathers; but it is, equally speaking, saying; it even *is* language. The *logos* is thus also the essence of the saying as thought by the Greeks. In its essence, language is then saying, the gathering letting-lie-before-us of what is present in its coming-to-presence. The Greeks dwelt within the essence of language understood in this way, but they never thought it in this manner, not even Heraclitus.

But what would have happened if Heraclitus and others at that time had thought the essence of language explicitly as *logos?* Then the Greeks would have thought the essence of language from the essence of Being, *indeed as Being itself.* For the *logos* is really Heraclitus's name for the Being of beings. Yet none of that happened.[62]

From these remarks, it is understandable that in his later works Heidegger often attempts to think the essence of language from the essence of Being, and even as Being itself. The relationship between Being and man is then usually articulated in terms of the relationship between the aboriginal saying of language and man's authentic response to Being's address. The *logos* as the aboriginal language hails, evokes, summons, solicits, invites *Dasein* to respond in an authentic manner to its gift, and to think what is truly thought-worthy.[63] What is hailed in the aboriginal saying of language is in some sense obviously *Dasein.* In another sense it is Being and beings, world and things.[64]

Thus in his later works, Heidegger often suggests that man's thought and his speaking are a response to the saying of language as *logos.* Originally it is language *(logos)* which summons beings and Being, things and world. Language summons things to give a bearing to the world, and the world is summoned to "yield" things in their being things. By summoning things and world in this way, language sets world and things, Being and beings, apart without separating them; in this way it brings about the ontological difference. That obviously does not mean that before language's summoning, both Being and beings are already separated or distinct from one another. The ontological difference that comes-to-pass in language must be understood as a process, a *dif-ferre,* a bearing each other out, as if both Being and beings shared a common center that remains interior to both, a common measure that serves as the single dimension of both, a primal unity by reason of which each adheres to the other and out of which both "issue forth." The ontological difference is a scission *(Schied)* between *(Unter)* Being and beings that relates them to each other by the very fact that it cleaves them apart. [65]

In other words, what is summoned in the coming-to-pass of language as *logos* is the correlation between Being and beings, and both are summoned toward the unifying scission of the difference that prevails between them. "In the bidding that summons things and world [beings and Being], what, properly speaking, is called is their scission."[66] Finally, that which calls itself is again the scission. "It is the scission that calls." Heidegger explains the latter as follows: "The unifying scission gathers together the two [differentiated elements] out of itself, insofar as it calls them into the fissure *(Riss)* which it itself is."[67] But that means that the difference is described here as being at the same time unity and twoness, calling and called, differentiating and differentiated, and the scission as such is nothing but the tension and mutual adhesion of unity and duality.[68]

Language, originally seen, is thus this scission as the coming-to-pass of the ontological difference out of original *logos.* Language comes-to-presence as the scission that takes place between world and thing, Being and beings, totality of meaning and concrete structure of meaning.[69] Language shows a unity, but it shows this unity by taking it apart in mutually opposed "elements." But in order for *logos* as scission to come about, there is need for man as *Dasein.* The differentiating cannot give issue to the differentiated except in, through, and for that being whose nature it is to be open to the *logos* as scission. We shall return to this aspect of the issue, where we shall explicitly focus on Heidegger's conception of language. (Cf. chapter 7.)

VI. THE ONTOLOGICAL DIFFERENCE AND
THE RELATION BETWEEN BEING AND THINKING

We must now turn to the question of precisely how Heidegger relates the ontological difference between Being and beings to the correlation between Being and thinking. Between 1935 and 1962, it became more and more clear to Heidegger that there must be a very close connection between the ontological difference and the relation between Being's address and man's response to it. We have seen already in chapters 2 and 3 that he had become convinced that in the process of unveiling the privileged position is to be granted not to man's thinking but to Being itself. But Being can then no longer be taken as "beings as such taken as a whole"; rather it must be understood as the process of non-concealment and as the coming-to-pass of the ontological difference.

Speaking about the relationship between Being and man's thinking, Heidegger suggests in *What Evokes Thinking?* (1952) that there must be a unity involved here which as a "third" element constitutes the connection between man's thought, on the one hand, and the Being of beings, on the other.[70] This third element is then said to be the "first" one in the sense that out of it the two members of the complex relation arise. "But it is just in their difference that they belong together. Where and how? What is the element in which they belong together? Is it the *noein*, or the *einai*, or neither? Is it, then, a third thing which in truth is the first for both—the first not as their synthesis, but still more primary and more originary than any thesis?"[71]

In the essay *"Moira"* which is an undelivered portion of the same lecture course, Heidegger speaks about the ontological difference in terms of the "duality of Being and beings" and then states that thinking comes-to-presence because of this still unspoken duality.[72] Parmenides names this duality, but he did not yet explicitly think it.[73] The mysterious third element appears here as *to auto* in Parmenides' third fragment: *to gar auto noein estin te kai einai.* It allows both the Being of beings and thought to arise. Finally, it is even said to be the process of truth itself. "Truth, characterized as the disclosure of the duality, lets thinking, from out of this duality, belong to Being. What is silently concealed in the enigmatic key word *to auto* is the revealing bestowal of the belonging together of the duality and the thinking that comes forward into view within it."[74]

In *What Evokes Thinking?* the middle-point between Being and thinking is thus spoken of as a "third" thing, which for *einai* (Being) and *noein* (man's thought) is a "first" thing, prior to both. This middle-point was mentioned for the first time in the *"Logos"* essay, and it was explicitly said there that this middle-point gives rise to both Being and *Dasein.* In *Identity and Difference* (1957), it is understood as an origin that lies deeper than both Being and man and permits them to belong to each other; it is an ultimate simplicity that is called a *singulare tantum.* This absolutely ultimate thing is called there again the event of the truth.[75] To explain these claims we can perhaps proceed as follows.

Man is obviously a being. He belongs to the totality of beings *(das Ganze des Seins)*. To belong means here to have been given a place in the order of Being. But man's distinctive feature is that, as the being that thinks, he is open to Being and stands face to face with Being; he remains related to Being and so answers to it. Man is essentially this very relationship of responding to Being, and as such he is only that. Thus the belonging to Being prevails in man; in man we encounter a belonging to Being which makes man listen to Being because he and his thinking are appropriated to Being. On the other hand, Being means originally coming-to-presence. But Being comes-to-presence only in regard to man. Being comes-to-presence and abides only as it concerns man through the claim which it makes on him. Only man is open to Being, and only man lets Being come-to-presence. Such coming-to-presence needs the openness of a clearing, and by this need Being remains appropriated to man. That does not mean that Being is just posited by man. Rather, Being and man are appropriated to each other; they belong to each other such that the one "is" not without the other; from their belonging together, both man and Being receive those essential determinations by which metaphysics has tried to grasp both man and Being. But one misunderstands the belonging together of man and Being as long as one represents everything only by means of traditional classifications and mediations.

If we are to enter the domain of the belonging together, we must move away from representational thinking, take a leap away from the idea of man as a rational animal or a thinking substance, from man as the subject that posits objects. We must also take a leap away from Being as the ground in which everything is grounded. Instead, we must learn to think the belonging together of man and Being in terms of the appropriating event *(Er-eignis)*.[76]

We must now finally return to a statement that is contained in the preface to *Identity and Difference* and in which Heidegger says that the reader is to discover for himself in how far the difference stems from the coming-to-presence and abidance of the identity, and that he can do so by carefully listening to the harmony that reigns between appropriating event and issuance, between *Ereignis* and *Austrag*. There Heidegger states that even though somehow identity may stem from the difference, it nevertheless is the case that in a more fundamental sense the coming-to-presence of the difference stems from the coming-to-presence of the identity and the selfsame. Heidegger furthermore claims there that we can derive this conclusion from the fact that there is a harmony between issuance and appropriating event. Now, in view of the fact that the issuance presupposes that the appropriating event already has come-to-pass, it follows that in some sense at least the coming-to-presence of the difference must stem from the coming-to-presence of the identity.[77]

To show that, Heidegger first explains in what sense the principle of identity speaks of the Being of the beings. To every being belongs identity and unity with itself. This unity of identity constitutes a basic trait in the Being of the being. Yet even more fundamental than the identity which belongs to Being is the identity of Being with thinking. Thinking and Being belong together into the selfsame and out of this selfsame.[78] For in man there holds sway a belonging to Being, a belonging which listens to Being because it is given over to Being and appropriated to it. Yet on the other hand, Being itself belongs to man, insofar as it needs the openness of a clearing, and thus, because of this needing, it remains given over to the coming-to-presence of man and remains appropriated to him; for only with man and in man can it come-to-presence and abide as Being.[79]

Finally, Heidegger claims there that Being belongs with thinking in an identity whose coming-to-presence and abidance stem from the appropriating event that ultimately lets them belong together. Identity comes-to-presence and abides as the domain which is the property of the appropriating event which lets Being and man be what they properly are.[80] For Heidegger, thus, the selfsame, taken as the appropriating event, is the origin and the domain of the coming-to-presence of identity.

We must now finally turn to the question of whether Heidegger eventually eliminated the ontological difference from his thinking altogether. In light of the preceding reflections, the question almost seems superfluous. What prompted me to ask this question is Biemel's claim that as Heidegger's own thought matured, he no longer needed to focus on the ontological difference.[81]

VII. DID HEIDEGGER ULTIMATELY ELIMINATE
THE ONTOLOGICAL DIFFERENCE ISSUE?

Biemel admits that originally the ontological difference occupied a central place in Heidegger's philosophy, and that the dimension in which his questioning moved was first opened up through the discovery of the ontological difference. But this concern with the ontological difference was connected with the fact that Heidegger originally had to take his point of departure in traditional philosophy. The more he succeeded in overcoming metaphysics, the more he could move away from the problematic of the ontological difference. In Biemel's view, we find a parallel movement in Heidegger's thought with respect to the concept of transcendence, which is essential in the earlier works and then gradually disappears completely.

I have explained elsewhere that I agree with Biemel that the term *transcendence* is no longer used after 1947 and that in *Zur Sache des Denkens* Heidegger explicitly says that he will make an effort to think Being without regard for the foundation of Being from the part of beings.[82] I also admit that between 1935 and 1946 Heidegger often suggests that the ontological difference is intimately connected with metaphysics. "Thus confined to what is metaphysical, man is caught in the difference of beings and Being which he never experiences."[83] I finally wish to mention here once more the first edition of the epilogue to Heidegger's inaugural address.

Yet all of that does not mean that the question hidden in the ontological difference can be eliminated. For first of all, the issue is discussed regularly in many works which appeared after 1947. It appears in these works that even though the technical term no longer has the meaning which Heidegger originally attributed to it, it still refers to the basic problem which Heidegger tried to "solve" in *Being and Time*. Secondly, the text of the epilogue was changed in 1949. Thirdly, in several instances Heidegger explains the precise link between the ontological difference and metaphysics. It is thus not the case that the ontological difference refers to an issue discussed in and by metaphysics and to be overcome in "genuine" thought. Rather, it is the case that metaphysics failed precisely because it was unable to experience and think the ontological difference.

> Metaphysics is a fate *(Verhängnis)* in the strict sense of the term. . . .It lets mankind be suspended in each case in the middle of beings. . . . without the Being of beings ever being able to be experienced, questioned, and structured in its truth as the twofoldness of both. . . .[84]
> Together with the beginning of the completion of metaphysics, the preparation begins, unrecognized by metaphysics and essentially inaccessible to it, for a first appearance of the twofoldness of Being and beings. In this appearance the first resonance of the truth of Being still lingers, which takes back into itself the precedence of Being in regard to its dominance.[85]

And speaking about the world of modern technicity and similar epochs dominated by the will to power, Heidegger writes that the power which is intrinsic in this kind of metaphysics

> expropriates from man the possibility of ever escaping from the oblivion of Being. This struggle is . . . as such undecidable . . . because it has nothing to decide, since it remains excluded from all differentiation, from the difference [of Being from beings], and thus from the truth *(Wahr-heit)*. Through its own force it is driven . . . into the abandonment of Being.[86]

Finally, with respect to the passage from *Zur Sache des Denkens* referred to above, Heidegger later wrote that the expression "to think Being without beings," like the expression "without any reference of Being to beings,"[87] should be understood as an abbreviated expression for "to think Being without any reference to a *foundation* of Being from beings."

Thus, "to think Being without beings" does *not* mean that the relationship of Being to beings is not essential and that one can leave this relationship one day out of consideration. It says, rather, that Being must not be conceived of in the way in which it has been in metaphysics. Thus, what Heidegger later rejects is not the ontological difference as such but rather "the metaphysical characterization of the ontological difference," in part still found in Heidegger's own earlier works.[88] Furthermore, one cannot identify the ontological difference between Being and the beings with the coming-to-presence and abidance of the difference as such. The ontological difference itself is an essential structure of all metaphysical thinking; Heidegger tries to think it in its coming-to-presence and to relate it to the coming-to-presence of identity, which itself is to be situated in the domain of the appropriating event.

CHAPTER 5

Reflections on the Fourfold

The basic issues to which Heidegger refers with the technical term *das Geviert* ("the fourfold, the quadrate, the foursome") emerged in all likelihood from Heidegger's concern with the poetry of Friedrich Hölderlin. In his poems, Hölderlin often speaks about the gods and the mortals, about heaven and earth.

The term itself appears for the first time in the published works in the lecture "The Thing" of 1950.[1] In this lecture Heidegger describes Being as a fourfold polyvalence, the four basic dimensions of which he specifies there with the help of an analysis showing the four basic aspects of a pitcher, which are intimately related to the dimensions of the fourfold, heaven and earth, gods and mortals. Heidegger adds there that these four dimensions are complementary; to think one of them thoroughly is to think all of them as a unity. They are said to mirror each other, and in this mutual mirroring each becomes properly itself. The event of mirroring each other appropriates and liberates each unto its proper self; yet it also binds what is so liberated in the oneness of their essential belonging together.[2]

Although the term appeared for the first time in 1950, the themes which are implied in it had already been discussed earlier in *Erläuterungen zu Hölderlins Dichtung* (1943) and *Der Feldweg*(1949).[3] Otto Pöggeler points out that the fourfold theme refers to a virtually universal mythological tradition.[4] William J. Richardson explains that by earth and heaven Heidegger means the entire "world" of "physical" nature, the whole of all inanimate and animate beings; if we thus think these two together and then add the domain of the divine as well as the mortals, we "are reminded of the trilogy that characterizes classical metaphysics:

God, man, and the physical universe. This is a hierarchy of beings, of course, and we are dealing here clearly with Being."[5] At any rate, Being taken as the polyvalent one is what Heidegger understands by world.[6]

The term *fourfold,* as well as the four terms *heaven, earth, gods,* and *mortals,* must be understood as being ontological in character; thus all semblance notwithstanding, they do not refer to ontic things, nor do they divide the totality of all ontic things into four basic sets of things. They express the fact that whatever has meaning ultimately means whatever it means, with respect to these four basic dimensions of Being, which—as we have seen—in a concrete form always manifests itself as world. Heidegger thus wishes to express that world, even though it is one, is nonetheless also structured; and the structure of all structures is the four-fold of heaven and earth, gods and mortals. This concept is to be under-stood in the following way: Whatever world one encounters, and however that world in each case may be structured, it can always be understood in terms of these four basic ontological regions.

In the different epochs of Being's long history, this structure of the world has been materialized in different ways. Furthermore, there has also been a strife, a tension between these four dimensions: sometimes the "divine" dimension was dominant; sometimes the "human" dimension held sway; sometimes even the dimensions of heaven or earth dominated. Today we live in the era of the *Gestell;* the fourfold is now materialized in such a manner that the gods have universally withdrawn. The mortals have demanded all their prerogatives for themselves, and they no longer wish to be reminded of death. Yet the positing and calculating way of thinking which is characteristic of the modern epoch (subject-ism) has led to a universal technologization of human life so that humans are no longer mortals but just raw materials for the all-consuming technological process. The heaven as such has completely disappeared; there is nothing mysterious about the heaven and the sky; there is no basic difference between the infra-lunar and the supra-lunar; the heaven has meaning only in poetry or mythology. Finally, the earth is so radically abused that as the abode of the mortals it has become endangered.

With respect to the terminology, I have decided to translate *Himmel* not as "sky" but as "heaven." First of all, that is common practice in almost all myths in which these four dimensions are mentioned. Sec-ondly, the word *sky* originally had the same meaning as *cloud;* it is only by using this word of a part for the relevant whole (synecdoche) that it also came to mean heaven or the heavens. Thirdly, Heidegger explicitly states that the term refers to the expanse in which the sun, the moon, and the stars are seen; it is also the region of the atmosphere in which the clouds float, the winds blow, the birds fly, and the bees hum and zoom;

then it is also the region of "space" beyond the visible sky, so that the expression "heaven and earth" taken together refers to the entire universe; finally, it is said to be the celestial abode of the immortals, the divines, and the gods. But to refer to *all* of that, the English word *heaven* seems more appropriate than the word *sky.*

The issues referred to by the technical term *the fourfold* have drawn relatively little attention in the literature thus far. Vincent Vycinas has discussed these issues in his book *Earth and Gods;* Pöggeler has devoted a section to the same problem in his *Der Denkweg Martin Heideggers.*[7] Richardson discusses some of the issues in great detail but has written little about the fourfold as such, as well as about heaven and earth, gods and mortals.[8] Yet these issues are of great importance, as we shall see, and they are raised in many later essays which bring the ontological difference in relation to both world and language.

In this chapter I plan to proceed as follows: In a first section I shall present the reader with a general description of the fourfold and its basic dimensions; the second section will focus on the dimensions of heaven and earth, whereas in the next chapter I shall be concerned with the mortals and the gods. There I hope to describe Heidegger's conception of God and explain why in his opinion God is absent in this ungodly world.

Article I: The Fourfold in Heidegger's Later Philosophy[9]

In each epoch of history, Being always appears concretely in the form of world; the world is the domain of what in each case is proper.[10] In Heidegger's view, the world is to be thought of as the fourfold of heaven and earth, gods and mortals. The earth is what carries and builds, nourishes and bears fruit, guards waters and rocks, plants and animals. On the other hand, the heaven is the path of the sun, the course of the moon, the splendor of the stars, the seasons of the year, the light and dusk of day as well as the darkness and the brightness of night, the favorableness or inclemency of the weather, the clouds, and the blue depth of the ether. The gods are the messengers of the true God who give us mortals hints; God himself appears in His essence from out of the region in which they hold sway. It is this essence which makes it impossible to compare Him with whatever else comes-to-presence. The mortals are the humans; they are called mortals because they can die. We call humans mortals not because their life on earth will one day come to an end but because they can know death as death. Mortals are what they are as mortals when they abide within the sheltering openness of Being that gathers everything. But when we say mortals, we are also already thinking of the other three. Heaven and earth, gods and mortals, which of their own accord are at one with one another, belong together by way of the simpleness of the united fourfold.[11] "They are together in the simpleness, in the dance and the roundelay of the four, in the world play."[12]

In conceiving of the world in terms of the fourfold of heaven and earth, gods and mortals, Heidegger attempted to retrieve ancient thoughts. As long as man is capable of living in a mythical conception of world, he experiences the world as a wedding of heaven and earth, and he experiences himself as the mortal upon whom the gods make legitimate claims. In the *Gorgias,* Plato writes that wise men say that heaven and earth, gods and men are held together by the principle of sharing, by friendship and order, by self-control and justice; that is the reason they call the universe *kosmos* and not disorder.[13] Many other examples could be quoted here, and there are even passages in the Chinese literature which are immediately relevant in this context. Richardson[14] cites a passage from Laotse in which a primordial being is mentioned that was self-contained, undifferentiated, and yet complete, and which existed before heaven and the earth; it was formless, soundless, and mateless, and therefore also changeless; it may be considered to be the mother of all that is; there can be no name for it. Laotse called it the way, *Tao,* because there is nothing that does not go through it. If forced to give it still another name, he would call it great, because it is immeasurable, far-reaching, but inapproachably far away, completely self-contained. Therefore one could say that *Tao* is great, the earth is great, the heaven is great, and a fit man is great. Thus there are four great ones in the universe, and man is one of them. Man models himself after earth, earth models itself after heaven, heaven models itself after tao, and tao or the way models itself after itself or after nature *(Tzu-jan).*[15]

Heidegger himself admits explicitly that his own way of thinking about the fourfold was inspired by the mythical conception of world held by Hölderlin and, through his poems, by the great myths of the past which Hölderlin tried to retrieve. In his own attempt to think the fourfold, Heidegger, like Hölderlin, does not passively repeat the myths, but in genuine thought he tries to retrieve the "wisdom" hinted at by the myths. In other words, he attempts to think authentically what the myths have merely named.[16]

With Hölderlin, Heidegger is convinced that the time has come to attempt to incorporate the wisdom of the ancient myths into thought. Let us not forget that myth originally meant the telling word.[17] For the Greeks, *mutheomai* meant "to speak, to tell"; and "to tell" meant "to lay bare, to make something appear." *Muthos* is that which has its essence in this telling. The *muthos* taken as that which is apparent and manifest in the unconcealedness of its address is an appeal of foremost concern to all human beings, which makes each man think of what appears and is in an abiding manner. *Logos* says the same, so that *muthos* and *logos* are not to be placed in opposition to one another, as many philologists and historians of philosophy claim; on the contrary, the early Greek thinkers, such as Parmenides and Heraclitus, used *muthos* and *logos* in the same sense. *Muthos* and *logos* became separated from one another and then opposed to each other in the work of Plato, where neither *logos* nor *muthos* can keep to its original essence. Historians and philologists, because of a prejudice which modern rationalism adopted from Platonism, imagine that *muthos* has been destroyed by *logos.* Yet nothing religious is ever destroyed by logic; it is destroyed only by God's withdrawal.[18]

When thought attempts to think these myths, it must unfold the wisdom that they name, in an independent manner. For as long as thought wishes to maintain its independence, it cannot just accept answers that flow from sources other than itself. Yet such an effort immediately encounters great difficulties. For, first of all, it is not at all clear how one can "translate" the mythical conception of heaven and earth into claims that are meaningful for people in our scientific and technological world. Heidegger's own characterizations of heaven and earth seem completely inadequate. What is really gained by claiming that the earth carries and builds, and by describing the heaven by means of sun, moon, stars, seasons, and the weather? Furthermore, the myths claim to have knowledge of gods and mortals. Yet in *Gelassenheit,* Heidegger himself has stated that if we do not deceive ourselves, we have to admit that we no longer know who we are.[19] And a similar contradiction appears to exist between the manner in which, in connection with the fourfold, he speaks about God, and his claims in *Identity and Difference* to the effect that those who have made a serious study of philosophy and sacred theology prefer to keep silent about God.[20]

But how is one then to think about the world as fourfold, and precisely why should one try to engage in the effort. Pöggeler suggests that we must try to come to an experience with the world which is similar to the experience which appears to be at the root of Heidegger's own conception of the fourfold. Now, Heidegger himself apparently encountered this experience on the road which begins with the question concerning the meaning of Being.

We have seen that Being is the openness of beings. A being comes to its own Being when it is taken in the proper manner as that which it genuinely is; that occurs when we let it show itself in the clearing of Being. If one takes a being *as* a being, then in it a fissure comes to be so that it becomes distinguished from itself, from its own Being. The fissure, in turn, tears open the difference between Being and beings; it brings about the "between" through which beings arrive in the openness of Being. Thinking, which takes beings *as* beings, is thus employed on behalf of the openness insofar as the "between" makes it possible for Being to be the Being *of* beings. This "between" is that which in Being itself reigns as its "ground" and its "truth." How do the "between" and the "truth" precisely come-to-presence? They come-to-presence as the belonging-together of revealment and concealment, i.e., as the event of non-concealment; and it is in this event that Being reveals itself as world.

Heidegger tries to think non-concealment in many ways. It is the free *(das Freie)*of the clearing process, which nonetheless abides in self-concealment.[21] It is also the nearness which brings close, while it preserves farness.[22] It is called the dimension of all dimensions, the "between" that is opened up for every measure-taking.[23] It is the region which as the open expanse *(die Gegnet)* lets beings be encountered in its openness.[24] As region and open expanse, unconcealment is also the aboriginal movement, which for the first time opens up all the ways of thought and speaking; it is the way, *Tao.*[25] This movement along the way originates from rest, which here is to be thought of not as rigid motionlessness but rather as a resting in itself which gathers all movement in itself and lets it flow from itself.[26] As the stillness, the rest stills that which is in the intimacy of its own resting in itself.[27]

Of all the names which Heidegger uses for non-concealment, the name "world" occupies a privileged place. This word names the building-structure in which non-concealment establishes itself. Thus that which holds sway in the world is the revealing concealing of non-concealment; it is happening and event. When we say of non-concealment that it "is," we obviously speak rather freely. For Being itself and its own essence, i.e., non-concealment and world, obviously "are" not in the manner in which a being and a thing are; for Being, non-concealment, and world are not beings among other beings. They abide and hold sway. To abide and to hold sway must be taken here as that happening which, as the appropriating event, hides itself in its coming-to-presence. For Being, non-concealment, and world hide themselves, in order that beings may be. In view of the fact that concealment permanently belongs to revealment, this event cannot be understood in a teleological sense such that concealment ultimately could ever be overcome in a complete revealment. Such a happening in which revealment and concealment remain inextricably intertwined is called a sending *(Geschick).*

In sending as such, the essence of time holds sway. By time we do not understand here that time with the help of which we measure movement, and which is derived from beings, but rather the temporality which belongs to the transcendental horizon of the meaning of Being. It is merely

the *mode* in which non-concealment comes-to-pass. In the entire metaphysical tradition, time has never been adequately unfolded or even discussed. That was the reason that the Being of beings has always been
taken from the perspective of presence *(Anwesenheit)* and time has been
thought as a series of now-moments, of which one is present only in the
strict sense and the others are no longer or not yet present. In this way,
one of the ek-stases of time began to occupy the privileged position over
the other ek-stases, and, thus, the present was taken to be the core of
time; the other ek-stases were then interpreted from that point of view.
But in all of that the entire horizon which stands behind all presence was
never examined. Heidegger, in an effort to overcome the dominance of
presence and the present, tries to think time as the simultaneity of past,
present, and future, or, as he often says, the oneness of having-been-ness,
presence, and the present that is waiting for our encounter and is usually
called the future.[28] "Simultaneity" is the playing into one another of the
three dimensions, but it itself is not something like a fourth dimension.
Rather, it is that out of which the three dimensions originate. Furthermore, in Heidegger's view the three dimensions are equally important; it
is not possible for one of them to hold sway over the other two. Having-
been-ness, which goes away and nonetheless remains, just as well as the
future, which arrives and yet is still outstanding, cannot be thought from
the perspective of the constancy of the present, as something that is not
yet or no longer present. Furthermore, the present is not at all that which
is constant; rather, the authentic present comes-to-pass in each case if and
when having-been-ness and future play together and mesh. It will be clear
also that the "simultaneity" referred to here cannot be thought of as the
"in itself" of time; rather, it can be experienced only in the differentiation
which nonetheless also joins by holding back having-been-ness, letting
the future arrive, and accommodating itself in what is proper in the
genuine present.[29]

Furthermore, time, taken as simultaneity, and space hold sway together. And the unity of the two must be taken not to refer to the totality
of all the "places" which are exterior to one another in terms of both
space and time but rather as that which makes such an exteriority of
"places" possible in the first place. Simultaneity and space, understood in
the sense intended here, constitute together the scope of the time-space
(Zeit-Spiel-Raum), the moved and articulated domain of non-
concealment, which opens itself as sending and at the same time withdraws in concealment, in order that beings may be.

Time as the measurable set of now-moments and space as the measurable exteriority of points come to the fore only after the original scope of
the time-space has been masked and the withdrawing and hiding of Being

have been forgotten in favor of something that is present as measurable. We see that already in Aristotle's treatise on time.[30] And all subsequent conceptions of time (including those of Augustine, Leibniz, Kant, Hegel, and Schelling) have their roots in this basic, Aristotelian idea of time, which was already implicit in Greek thought at the time.[31] But this objectified conception of space and time does not exhaust the possibilities hidden in the essence of the scope of the time-space. It is also obvious that the nearness and farness of God, and the being-opposite-to-one-another of God and man, cannot be experienced from the perspective of such an objective space and time. Once space and time are posited as that which can be measured, the world taken as the scope of the time-space is distorted.[32] On the other hand, when Heidegger focuses on the scope of the time-space and then speaks about the original meaning of space and time, it is not his intention to reject the conceptions of space and time proposed by the objectifying sciences. On the contrary, he explicitly states that these conceptions, too, are correct; he merely indicates and circumscribes the domain within which such conceptions hold, and then adds that the essence of both time and space is as inexhaustible as that of Being itself.[33]

Non-concealment as the sending of the scope of the time-space organizes itself and forms the building-structure of the world, as it develops into the fourfold of earth and heaven, gods and mortals. The concealing, which is one of the basic characteristics of non-concealment, shows itself as earth, which emerges only as it closes itself. The other basic characteristic, namely, revealment, manifests itself in the heaven which as unavailable extends above the earth, and thus elevates the earth into the open. As such, world is the battle or strife between earth and heaven, strife taken here as the intimate toward-each-other in which the one can never be without the other. But world is never just a world in itself; rather, it is the happening of the openness of the beings in *Dasein*. In his essence man is employed for the coming-to-pass of non-concealment, but he is so employed as the mortal, to whom the holding-sway of truth and world is being given only to the degree that this holding-sway is gathered toward the appeal of that which is wholly other, namely, the divine.

The world as the fourfold of heaven and earth, gods and mortals cannot be explained from the perspective of a ground that lies outside it; but it cannot be explained either by one of the structural moments which one can take from the fourfold itself, in order then to declare it to be the ground of the others. The concealing revealment which holds sway in the world is and remains an abysmal "grounding" for which no one can secure an ultimate ground. The world is a play, in regard to which every attempt at grounding founders. The world is the fourfold; and that is a mirror-play in which each dimension, gods and mortals just as well as heaven and earth, mirrors the essence of the others and so mirrors itself back into what is proper for itself. This mirroring should not be taken in a Platonic sense; it means here not the presentation of an image which merely mirrors that which in truth is, but rather the lighting concealing which as the appropriating event brings everything to what is proper for it. This mirroring is thus a clearing process only on the basis of concealment; in other words, it comes-to-pass as sending *(Geschick).*[34]

The world taken as the fourfold of heaven and earth, gods and mortals, and thus taken as the appropriating event, brings all that is to what is proper for it, and so lets it be. But precisely how does world appropriate each being to that which is proper for it, and how does it free each being toward itself? How does the world shelter each being in non-concealment? This process of sheltering does not come-to-pass in such a way that a being (standing by and for itself) and non-concealment (standing by and for itself) are just brought together. Rather, truth and world hide in the beings which find shelter in them. The world grants things, while things gather the world by holding it back and hiding it.[35] Let us see, therefore, how in Heidegger's opinion the world shelters each being in non-concealment by focusing on his conception of the four dimensions of the world, on heaven and earth, gods and mortals.[36]

Article II: Heaven and Earth. The Richness of Heidegger's Reflections on Earth

I. HEAVEN AND EARTH. DESCRIPTION OF A PROBLEM

Although Heidegger sometimes speaks about the earth without referring to heaven, on many occasions he speaks about both in their intimate relation to each other. The heaven is discussed in order to open up the domain in which the earth stands out. Yet it is quite clear that it is not so much the heaven which is problematic for Heidegger as the earth. The heaven is the domain of the sun, the moon, and the stars, of the weather and the winds; it also is the abode of the divines, the gods, and even God himself. Obviously, one can ask meaningful philosophical questions about the heaven, and we shall see soon how Heidegger tries to deal with them. Yet these problems are minor if compared to those raised by the earth. That is the reason that I shall focus first on the earth, in order then to discuss Heidegger's conception concerning the function of the heaven within the fourfold of the world.

Reflections on earth appeared in Heidegger's thought for the first time in "The Origin of the Work of Art" (1935). Heaven and earth then became a relatively common theme in his meditations on Hölderlin's poetry (1936–1943), and finally they appeared again in his own way of thinking in several essays published in *Vorträge und Aufsätze* (1950–1951) and *Unterwegs zur Sprache* (1950–1959).[37]

In the secondary literature, these reflections on heaven and earth have received little attention, as is the case with the fourfold as a whole. The best-known commentaries are those developed by Vycinas and Pöggeler.[38] One might be inclined to conclude that Heidegger's concern with heaven and earth as a theme for thoughtful reflection is one of little importance. This view, however, is not shared by these commentators. As far as the earth in particular is concerned, in his memorial address, presented in Freiburg on 16 December 1977, Hans-Georg Gadamer stressed that the fact that Heidegger made the earth a theme of philosophical reflection has the character of a genuine breakthrough in his thought, as well as in modern philosophy as a whole. The earth is no longer given a privative and limited function but for the first time begins to play an ontological and constitutive part.[39]

To appreciate this opinion fully, one should realize that all of us obviously "know" the earth very well in our everyday lives. We receive from the earth everything to maintain ourselves: food, clothing, shelter, and protection. In some sense, we come from the earth and eventually will return to it. We also know the earth through the great works of art. In addition, we have learned about the earth through a number of empirical sciences. And we have had our own experiences with the earth through the great myths of the past. Finally, in the Judeo-Christian tradition, we have heard time and again that "in the beginning God created the heaven and the earth," that He "created man in His own image," and that man nevertheless will die and return to the earth. And yet in the entire philosophical tradition since the days of Plato, the earth has never constituted an *essential* element of the great philosophies developed in the West. In this tradition, the earth has always been taken for granted as something which contains nothing worthy of being thought about. In Heidegger's thinking, that is no longer the case.

The commentators who have touched on Heidegger's conception of earth correctly state that his reflections on earth are closely related to other basic themes of his later thought: the truth of Being, the world, the thing, the appropriating event *(Ereignis)*, language, and the fourfold, the dangers inherent in our one-sided calculating and technological way of thinking in modern and post-modern times, the necessity of overcoming classical metaphysics, etc.[40]

If I understand these commentators correctly, they seem to believe that it is possible (although not easy) to develop one, homogeneous conception of earth, in which all references to the earth made in Heidegger's later works can find a harmonious place. Vycinas is of the opinion that such a homogeneous conception of earth can be derived from the realization that after Heidegger had described man as that being whose essence is to be in the world, and that man therefore is to be characterized as that being who stands out into the openness of Being which is the world, he finally came to conceive of dwelling as the specifically human way of being.

> Dwelling is disclosed there as the preservation of the foursome, as letting earth and sky, mortals and gods bring up the structural world in which things can become what they are and in which man can live his life as placed in his history in the sense of befalling. . . . Earth and sky together with gods and mortals are the phenomena whose play bestirs a world, or rather whose play *is* world.[41]

Vycinas then explains this interpretation by subsequently focusing on world, *phusis, logos,* language, and truth in their relation to earth.[42] On several occasions he states that there is some ambiguity in Heidegger's later works as far as the relationship between earth and world is concerned. He resolves this ambiguity by claiming that world as the openness or truth of Being and world as the strife of world and earth are the same.[43] On another occasion he states that both world and earth are world in the same manner, that truth and untruth are truth. World taken in the strict sense is the strife between revealment and concealment, i.e., between world and earth. *Phusis* taken in the sense of revealment is world; taken as concealment, it is earth. Vycinas again remarks here that there is still some ambiguity in the interrelation of earth and world, but that this ambiguity will be diminished in the investigation of the foursome.[44]

Pöggeler, too, discusses Heidegger's conception of earth in connection with the latter's reflections on the world as fourfold.[45] He briefly describes how Heidegger originally conceived of Being and world and then explains how he gradually began to realize that both are to be understood in a "dynamic" sense; both come-to-pass, and this coming-to-pass continuously conceals itself while it reveals beings as what they properly are. Yet the event in which revealment and concealment are thus connected inseparably is not governed by our common conceptions of time and space. Time and space are to be taken here in their most basic senses, and the interplay of time and space as we encounter it concretely in each epoch is what we call world; it unfolds itself in the fourfold of earth and heaven, mortals and gods.[46] But this interplay, too, is marked by revealment and concealment. Concealing as a characteristic of all non-concealment shows itself as earth. Referring to an unpublished manuscript (written in 1936–1938),[47] Pöggeler clarifies this last remark by pointing out that for Heidegger earth is earth only in its battle with the heaven, a battle which man must wage. If one no longer identifies nature *(phusis)* with what is available for use and control, and conceives of earth from the perspective of its own battle with the heaven, a battle in which the earth, as that which bears, continuously turns in unto itself, while the heaven keeps lifting it up into the open, then nature *(phusis)* becomes earth. In some sense earth is even more primordial than *phusis,* because the former is immediately related to history.[48]

As far as I can see, neither Vycinas nor Pöggeler takes the position that in his later works Heidegger developed two different, but related, conceptions of earth. Pöggeler uses elements from the lecture on the work of art and from an unpublished manuscript of the same period (1936–1938) to explain the function of earth *within the fourfold.* Vycinas does the same, but he seems to have felt that there are serious problems connected with this approach; he explicitly admits that in his interpretation there is an ambiguity concerning the relationship between world and earth. Richardson speaks about earth in two different contexts but does not attempt to relate these two sets of reflections explicitly.[49] Finally, von Herrmann limits his investigation to the concept of earth as developed in the lecture on the origin of the work of art and, thus, does not make an effort to relate this conception to that proposed in Heidegger's reflections on the fourfold.[50] At any rate, it seems to me that the interpretations of Vycinas and Pöggeler do not account for all aspects of the problematic of earth, whereas Richardson and von Herrmann (for very understandable reasons) do not explicitly attempt to relate the various elements of the problem to each other. Before returning to the difficulties inherent in these interpretations, I wish briefly to summarize how Heidegger characterizes earth in "The Origin of the Work of Art" (1936) and in "The Thing" (1950). As we shall see, what is said in "The Thing" is in complete harmony with what is claimed about the earth in several other lectures of the same period; but the insights gained in the later lectures cannot be immediately integrated into the conception of earth proposed in the lecture on the work of art. As far as the latter is concerned, I plan to discuss the content of the entire lecture in detail in chapter 8; thus I shall limit myself here to a brief reflection on some points that seem particularly relevant to the issue under discussion.

II. EARTH AND WORLD IN "THE ORIGIN OF THE WORK OF ART"

In "The Origin of the Work of Art," Heidegger tries to show that the origin of both the artist and the work of art is to be found in art itself. To elucidate this thesis, he first explains what the work of art is as a work. Thus, he turns to the question of what is characteristic of a work as distinct from a thing. Our philosophical tradition has suggested three different answers for the question of what a thing in truth is. According to Heidegger, none of these answers is completely satisfactory. A thing is more than the composition of substance and accidents; it is closer to us than the sum of the sensations which announce it, and matter and form do not explain the thing-character of the thing, but they articulate rather the mode of Being of a piece of equipment.

Equipment is more similar to a work of art than things are, inasmuch as both are brought forth by man, albeit in a distinctly different manner in each case. A piece of equipment can be characterized by its adaptability, reliability, and serviceability. We experience these characteristics when we use tools for their respective purposes. The work of art as such does not have these characteristics, and yet it too is capable of revealing to man beings as they are. In its own way, the art work opens up the Being of beings, and this revealing opening-up or truth comes-to-pass *in* the work. Thus, in the art work the truth of beings has established itself in the work, and art itself is truth establishing itself in the work.

To clarify these claims Heidegger tries to make visible the happening of truth in the work with the help of an example. He deliberately selects a work that cannot possibly be called an example of representational art. He selects a Greek temple and briefly describes its reference to the historical people who built it, to the figure of the god whom it encloses and whose presence in it opens up and delineates the surrounding region as holy. In addition, Heidegger indicates how the temple affects the lives of the mortals worshipping the god. Standing there, the temple rests on the rocky ground; it holds its ground against the raging storm, the luster of its stones brings to radiance the light of the day and the darkness of the night, and its steadfastness contrasts with its surroundings: the sea, the plants, the animals, which in this manner all emerge as what they are. This emerging of all things was once called *phusis;* it brings to light also that in which man bases his dwelling. This latter ground, so brought to light by *phusis,* we call the earth.[51]

Earth does not mean here a certain mass of matter or a planet. Earth is that toward which the emerging brings back and shelters everything that emerges. In everything that emerges, the earth co-emerges as that which abides and gives shelter.

To be a work of art thus means first to set up a world, to open a world and maintain it as something that abides and governs. The world is not a collection of things; nor is it a framework to be added to the sum of such things. The world "functions as world" *(weltet)* by letting things be what they are. Once a world is opened up, things, mortals, and gods appear as what they are. When a world emerges and functions as such, that spaciousness is gathered out of which all beings are granted to be what they are. A work of art, by being a work, makes room for this spaciousness, liberates this open region, and articulates it in its basic structure.[52]

Secondly, every work of art has in common with a piece of equipment that it is made "out of" some material. In a piece of equipment, the material totally disappears into the tool's serviceability. By contrast, the work of art, in setting up a world, does not cause the material to disappear but rather makes it come forth for the first time as what it is. Now, that into which the work in this way sets itself back and which it thus makes come forth we call the earth. It comes forth as that which gives shelter. Historical man grounds his dwelling in the world upon and into the earth. In setting up a world, the work sets forth the earth and lets the earth be earth.

The earth which in this manner comes into non-concealment resists any further understanding penetration; scientific knowledge and technical know-how are also of no avail. The earth manifests itself here as that which in principle is undisclosable. To set the earth forth means to bring it into the open as that which is self-secluding. It is true that all things constituting the earth and the earth itself as a whole appear to flow together into a reciprocal accord, and yet in each thing there is the same non-knowing of one another. Yet in the work, the self-seclusion of the earth is not a uniform, inflexible staying-under-cover; it unfolds itself in an inexhaustible variety of simple modes and shapes, in which the "materials" are not being used up but precisely become and remain what they truly are.[53]

The world is the totality of meaning taken in its most basic structures, into which in a given community each member finds himself thrown and in which, in cooperation with his fellowmen, he tries to find his own self. The earth, on the other hand, is the spontaneous forthcoming of that which continuously is self-secluding and to that extent is as that which gives shelter and conceals. World and earth are essentially different from one another, and yet they cannot be separated. The world grounds itself upon the earth, and the earth towers up in and through the world. The world is resting upon the earth and strives to surmount it. The earth as sheltering and concealing tends to draw the world into itself and keep it there. The opposition between the two has the character of a striving. This striving is to be understood not as discord, disorder, or destruction but rather as that which makes the opponents raise each other into the self-assertion of their proper mode of Being. In the struggle, each opponent carries the other beyond itself.

In setting up a world and setting forth the earth, the work is an instigation of this striving. The work-being of a work of art precisely consists in the fighting of the battle between world and earth, and it is this fighting of the battle which establishes the truth in the work of art.[54] Truth should be understood here as the process of non-concealment, which is Being itself. Being is that which allows beings to become non-concealed, although the very process is so permeated by negativity that Being itself remains concealed. Truth understood in this way thus implies a basic opposition between clearing and concealing. Truth itself is the *primal* conflict in which that open center is won within which what is, stands and from which it sets itself back into itself. This open region comes-to-pass in the midst of beings, and it implies both a world and the earth. But the world is *not* the open region itself that corresponds to the clearing, and the earth is *not* the closed region that corresponds to the concealing. Rather, earth towers up through the world, and the world grounds itself on the earth, only insofar as the truth of Being comes-to-pass as the primal strife between clearing and concealing. The coming-to-pass of the truth of Being occurs only in a few basic ways. One of these ways is the working of the work of art as such.[55]

From the preceding paraphrase of a few sections of the lecture on the art work, it is clear that the fourfold as such is never mentioned; the term *fourfold* is not used there, either. Furthermore, there is no explicit reference to the heaven as such, even though it is true that some elements of the sky have been mentioned; yet these are said to be "parts" of the earth, and the whole of earth and sky is described in terms of *phusis*. It seems that the god is mentioned mainly because of the fact that Heidegger takes a Greek temple as an example of a work of art; in his description of the peasant's shoes by van Gogh, the "divines" are not mentioned at all. Heidegger also refers to the "mortals"; yet most of what he has to say about the humans is related to the Greeks as a historical people who have both a native homeland and a world; at any rate, the Greeks taken as mortals are nowhere opposed to the god. Finally, earth, which is described in a twofold manner (namely, as the foundation on which the world rests and as the material out of which the work has been made), is never described as one of the four regions of the world; rather, it is always placed opposite to the world, and both are described as being in a constant battle with each other. Let us now see how the earth has been described in the lecture "The Thing."

III. EARTH AND WORLD IN "THE THING"[56]

If we now turn to the lecture "The Thing" (1950), it will be clear at once that we find here a different context, which will lead to a different problematic. The lecture "The Thing" begins with a reflection on the fact that today all distances in space and time are shrinking, although this elimination of distance has brought us no real nearness. Science and modern technology may be necessary, and to some degree they may even contribute to progress; yet it is true also that both imply grave dangers which demand careful and thoughtful reflection. Heidegger attempts to say something about nearness by focusing on what is near to us, namely, things. He develops his ideas using the example of a jug, and in so doing he sharply contrasts a scientific conception of the jug-thing with the thing as it appears in thoughtful reflection. The analysis shows that the jug's jug-character consists in the gift of what is poured out; it may be water or wine, and both may be poured out for a drink or for a libation. Both water and wine remind us of the earth and the sky. In the water of the spring dwells the marriage of earth and heaven, and in the fruit of the vine the earth's nourishment and the sky's sun are betrothed to one another. Thus, in the jug's jugness, heaven and earth dwell as well.[57]

If the gift is a drink for mortals, it quenches their thirst, refreshes their leisure, or enlivens their conviviality. If the gift of the pouring is given for consecration, it is the libation poured out for the immortal gods. And just as in the drink mortals come-to-presence in their own way, so in the libation the gods come-to-presence in their own manner. Earth, heaven, mortals, and gods dwell together all at once in the gift of the pouring. In the gift of the pouring dwells the simple singlefoldedness of these four. And the outpouring is a gift, because it lets earth and heaven, mortals and gods dwell. This dwelling in turn appropriates the fourfold, in the sense that it brings the four to light as mutually belonging together; it entrusts them to one another. And at one in thus being betrothed to one another, they are unconcealed. That which appropriates the fourfold is the thing. Appropriating the fourfold, it gathers *(dingt)* the fourfold's dwelling and its while into something which stays for some time, namely, into this very thing. In so gathering, it lets earth, heaven, gods, and mortals dwell. It brings these four, in their remoteness, near to one another while preserving their farness.[58] Let us now see how Heidegger articulates these ideas in another essay of the same time.

In the lecture "Building, Dwelling, Thinking" (1951),[59] Heidegger comes to the same view via a different route. In it he says that human beings as mortals *are* in the sense that they dwell on earth. But "on the earth" implies "under the heaven." And both of these together imply that mortals remain before the gods. By a primary openness, these four, earth and heaven, mortals and gods, belong together in one. Earth is that which serves and bears, which blossoms and bears fruits, spreads out in rock and water, rising up into plant and animal. The heaven is the vaulting path of the sun, the course of the moon which constantly changes its phases, the wandering glitter of the stars, the year's seasons and their regular succession, the light and dusk of day, the glow of night, the clemency and inclemency of the weather, the drifting clouds and the blue depth of the ether. The gods are the hinting messengers of the godhead; and out of the holy sway of the godhead, God Himself appears in His presence and withdraws into concealment. Finally, the mortals are the human beings; they are called mortals because they can die; they are those beings for whom death is the most proper, exclusive, and ultimate potentiality. Only man dies, and indeed continuously, as long as he remains on earth, under the heaven, and before the God. When we think and speak of any one of the four, we are already thinking of the other three along with it, but usually we give no thought to the simple oneness of the four, the fourfold *(Geviert)*.

The mortals are what they are *in* the fourfold *by* dwelling. The basic characteristic of dwelling is to treat with care *(schonen)*. The mortals dwell in the fourfold in such a way that they treat with care the fourfold in its abiding coming-to-presence *(Wesen)*. Mortals dwell in that they save the earth and set it forth as what it really is. Mortals dwell in that they receive the heaven as heaven and leave the sun, moon, stars, seasons, night, and day to be what they are. Mortals dwell in that they await the gods as gods, and they hold up to them in hope of what is unhoped for; they wait for intimations of their coming and do not misinterpret the signs of their absence. Finally, mortals dwell in that they guide their own and proper abiding coming-to-presence *(Wesen)*, according to which death is the most proper, exclusive, and ultimate potentiality, into a positive employment of this potentiality, so that there may be a good death. Taken in a concrete sense, dwelling is always a staying with things, so that dwelling preserves the fourfold by bringing its Being *(Wesen)* into things. In turn, things secure the fourfold to the degree that they themselves as things are let be in their proper mode of Being by it. That occurs when mortals nurse things that grow and construct things that do not grow.[60]

Earth and heaven, mortals and gods, being at one with one another of their own accord, belong together by way of the simpleness of the united fourfold. Each of the four mirrors in its own manner the presence of the others and herewith reflects itself in its own way into its own. This appropriating mirroring does not imply that the four portray likeness to one another; rather, it sets each of them free into its own, while binding these free ones into the simplicity of their essential belonging together and being toward one another. The appropriating mirroring is the play that betroths each of the four to each other. In view of the fact that none of the four insists on its own separate particularity, the mutual appropriation implies for each some form of expropriation into its own being. The expropriating appropriation is the mirror-play *(Spiegel-Spiel)* of the fourfold, in which the latter comes forth as the simple onefold. This appropriating mirror-play of the simple onefold of earth, heaven, mortals, and gods is what we call the world. It is out of the round-dance of the mirror-play that the gathering *(dingen)* of the things comes-to-pass. The gathering of the things gathers the fourfold, i.e., the world, by letting the fourfold dwell and abide as the happening of the simple onehood of the world. On the other hand, the world lets things be what they are by functioning as world *(welten)*.[61]

IV. EARTH AND WORLD VS. EARTH AND HEAVEN

If we now carefully compare what Heidegger has to say about earth in the lecture on the origin of the work of art with what he claims with respect to earth in the lectures, "The Thing," "Building, Dwelling, and Thinking," and other lectures of the same period, it will be extremely difficult to derive one homogeneous conception of earth from all of these ideas. In the first essay, Heidegger is concerned with the manner in which in a given world the earth functions in the process of the coming-to-pass of the truth of Being. He attempts to describe the original strife between earth and world and the function which the art work has to play in this strife. In the later essays Heidegger is concerned with the relationship between thing and world, the inner structure of the world itself, and the process of appropriation which in each case takes place in the coming-to-pass of the truth of Being. Here the earth is no longer in a strife with the world, but rather it is one of the four basic regions of the world. Furthermore, the earth is explicitly opposed here to the heaven with which it finds itself again in a permanent and continuous strife of its own. Finally, in the reflections on the work of art, Heidegger makes an explicit reference to his own interpretation of the Greek conception of *phusis*, which is lacking in the later essays. It is difficult to understand how earth taken as intimately related to *phusis* could be one and only one region of the fourfold, given the fact that the other three regions are constituted by heaven, mortals, and gods. On the other hand, it is equally difficult to understand how earth taken as one of the four regions of world (= the fourfold) and as distinct from heaven could be said to be in an original strife with the world.

Thus it seems that one must distinguish here between two distinct, but related, concerns as far as earth is concerned. In 1936, Heidegger attempted to say something about the relationship between the totality of meaning (= world) as it historically comes-to-pass for a community *and* that of which this totality is the totality of meaning (= earth). It is in this context that he used his own "retrieved" conception of *phusis* to explain this relationship in a manner which is not realistic, idealistic, or critical. On the other hand, in the fifties Heidegger was concerned with showing that world as the totality of meaning which in each case is concretely erected in the process of the coming-to-pass of the truth of Being is not a totally homogeneous unity but has a structure of its own. Following hints taken from Hölderlin and inspired by a very old religious and mythical tradition, Heidegger characterized this structure by means of the regions: heaven and earth, gods and mortals.

This difference in concern is the reason why in the lecture on the work of art Heidegger specified the earth by the following characteristics: it is that in which man bases his dwelling; it is not a certain mass of matter or a planet; it is that toward which the original emerging brings back and shelters everything that emerges; in particular, it is that into which the work of art sets itself back as that which shelters; in everything that emerges, the earth co-emerges as that which gives shelter and conceals; it resists any form of further understanding penetration; it is in principle undisclosable because it is self-secluding; it is what grounds by towering up in and through world. On the other hand, in the later lectures we find the following characteristics of earth: it is that which serves, which blossoms and bears fruit, spreads out in rock and water, and rises up into plants and animals; it is that which is in a constant strife with the heaven above it.

If this view is correct in principle, we must still explain precisely: 1) what is meant by earth taken in the sense of that which is undisclosable in principle, 2) what is meant by earth taken as that which serves and bears, and 3) how these two ways of conceiving of earth can be related to one another.

In order to find an answer to the first question, let us recall first that in trying to say what a work of art is as a work, Heidegger discussed three conceptions of the thing, all of which in his opinion are not satisfactory. He particularly rejected the matter-form conception on the ground that it is valid primarily for artifacts. Instead of conceiving of a work of art in terms of matter and form, he tried to understand it in terms of earth and world. Secondly, it should be noted that the relationship between earth and world is intimately connected with Heidegger's interpretation of the original meaning of *phusis*. In light of these two reflections, it seems reasonable to assume that the historical analogue for the basic problem with which Heidegger was concerned here is to be found in the problem concerning the relationship between what Kant in his first *Critique* calls "nature" and "world."[62] Obviously that does not mean that Heidegger shares Kant's view in this regard. When he says that the earth is that which is undisclosable, if taken as such, he does not mean to repeat, but rather to retrieve, Kant's view. Earth is that of which the world is the totality of meaning. As such it cannot be determined, except through the particular interpretations which it continuously receives in each given world. Thus earth taken as such is not a planet, because that would be "earth" taken in a scientific interpretation, "earth" as co-emerging in a scientific world. It is not the totality of all that is *phusei* (Aristotle), either, because that again would be "earth" taken in a certain metaphysical interpretation.

From this perspective, it will be clear why Heidegger could take the strife between earth and world as intimately related to *phusis*, taken in the sense of his own interpretation and retrieve of Greek thought. He says in the lecture on the art work that the Greeks called the emergence in itself and in all things *phusis*. *Phusis also* illuminates that on which and in which man bases his dwelling. And this ground we call earth. In *An Introduction to Metaphysics*, retrieving basic elements of the thought of Heraclitus, Heidegger explains that for the early Greeks, Being was *phusis*, emergent-abiding-presence; for them *phusis* was closely related to *a-lētheia, logos,* and *dikē*.[63] It is to this conception that Heidegger refers in the lecture on the art work. In Heidegger's view, world is the total meaningfulness into which a man with his contemporaries finds himself thrown in each epoch of history. World is the concrete totality of meaning as which Being's truth comes-to-pass to him as the *Da* of Being in a given epoch and which has its own destination, common to all living in that epoch. What is called earth here is the totality of all that *of* which the totality of meaning is the meaning. It is in this sense that the *aboriginal* emerging can *also* illuminate that *on* which and *in* which man grounds his dwelling. According to the original Greek conception, *phusis*, as the emergent-abiding-presence, is also the overwhelming power, the inscrutable union of movement and rest which for Heraclitus is the aboriginal strife *(polemos)*. This aboriginal strife is not identical with the strife between world and earth, but the latter merely "mirrors" this original discord. That is why in the lecture on the work of art, Heidegger states explicitly that the world is not simply the open region itself that corresponds to the clearing of the aboriginal coming-to-pass of the truth of Being, and that the earth is not simply the closed region that corresponds to this emergent-abiding-presence's concealment. Rather, earth towers up through the world and the world grounds itself on the earth, only insofar as the truth of Being happens as the primal strife between revealing and concealing.

In the lectures written in the fifties, Heidegger described a third strife, namely, that between heaven and earth. The strife between the heaven's calling-out and the earth's resounding, a strife which takes place *within* the world taken as fourfold, should thus not be identified with the strife in which the earth towers up through the world and the world grounds itself on the earth. To explain the relationship between heaven and earth, we must now turn to Heidegger's own retrieve of Hölderlin's conception of the same relation. In the lecture "Hölderlin's Earth and Heaven," Heidegger tries to establish the nature of this relationship by means of a reflection on Hölderlin's poem "Greece." In Heidegger's interpretation, Hölderlin conceives of heaven and earth as the structure of the heavenly ones which shelters and supports the holy, i.e., the sphere of the God. The earth is the earth only as the earth of the heaven, and the heaven is heaven only insofar as it works down upon the earth. Earth and heaven as well as the God who is concealed within the holy are all present *within* the whole of primordial, emerging nature. In other words, the relationship between heaven and earth is part of a more complex relationship which also includes man, the latter taken as mortal, and God.[64] The four regions of this basic relation do not stand by themselves, but freed from one-sidedness and finitude, they belong in-finitely[65] to one another in the relation which "thoroughly" holds them together from its center. The center itself, which as center mediates, is neither earth nor heaven, neither man nor God. The in-finity that is to be thought here is abysmally different from that which is merely without end, for the latter does not allow for spontaneous growth.

Hölderlin describes the heaven as that which rings out. Its voice is the clouds' serene mood, the thunderstorm's extreme appearance, the lightning flash, the thunder, the arrows of rain. In all of that, the presence of the God is concealed. The earth is another voice; it resounds from the claps of the lightning and the showers of arrows. The ringing out of the earth is the echo of the heaven's ringing. In resounding, the earth replies to the heaven. In so doing, heaven and earth pursue great laws. Hölderlin refers here to the great destiny which points and sends everything and everyone where they are needed according to their own mode of Being. These laws thus determine the in-finite cohesion of the relation as a whole. The earth fully reconciles itself to these great laws.[66]

Heidegger then explains how in Hölderlin's view the mortals and the God are intimately related to the ringing of the heaven and the resounding of the earth. He also stresses the point that both thinkers and poets have an important task with respect to the great laws just mentioned, in that they must hold the earth open to the heaven through "knowledge and tenderness." The calling of thinkers and singers is a looking out for immortality and for the divinity which is sheltered in the holy. And they are called to do so.[67]

Thus there are really four voices which ring out: heaven and earth, God and man. Destiny gathers the whole in-finite relation in these four voices. Yet no one of the four stays and goes one-sidedly by itself. In this sense,

no one is finite; no one is without the others. In-finite, they hold themselves to each other; they are what they are from the in-finite relation;
they are this whole itself.[68]

According to Hölderlin, then, heaven and earth and their inter-
relatedness belong in the much richer relation of the four. "Four" there
does not name an arithmetical number; rather, it names the self-unifying
form of the in-finite relation of the voices of destiny. Destiny sends the
four to each other by holding them gathered to itself in the relation taken
as a whole. Destiny centers and mediates, insofar as it determines the
manner in which the four belong together in any given epoch of history.
As the center of the whole relation, destiny is the all-gathering beginning;
it is the great beginning. The word *beginning* is here to be taken in the
sense of what is present as continuously coming. Thus the beginning
taken in this sense *remains* as continuous advent. The great beginning
remains all the more, the closer it keeps itself within the basic possibility
of its own Being and the more, in its own coming, it sends what it must
keep to itself, namely, the in-finite relation. In principle, something great
must correspond to the coming of the great beginning, something which
can await it greatly and can grasp it greatly. Hölderlin admits that that is
factually not yet the case. The in-finite relation still waits for the time
when it may stand great in the poor place, a time which will genuinely
correspond to the great beginning.[69]

After elaborating upon Hölderlin's conception of these basic ideas,
Heidegger turns to the question of whether this great beginning still can
come to us today. In his view, that has been made extremely difficult by
the scientific and technological conception of world. The earth has become a planet, and as such it has been included in the interstellar cosmic
space; it has been put at man's disposal. Hölderlin's heaven and earth
have vanished. The un-ending relation of heaven and earth, God and
mortals seems to have been destroyed. Perhaps this relation has not yet
appeared within our own epoch as the un-ending relation. In that case, it
is not destroyed but merely displaced and denied its appearance. Then it
would be up to us to think about this denial of the in-finite relation. To
think about a matter means to let it be said, to listen to it where something is still said about it, namely, in the works of great thinkers and
poets.[70]

Toward the end of his reflections, Heidegger suggests that we still have
a chance to re-think the great beginning, although obviously one cannot
just return to it. He admits that we perhaps are not yet in the proper
disposition and so are unable to hear the "need" from which the four of
the in-finite relation call to each other. Its need consists in that the mortals
do not heed how what may possibly come, comes to us all the more, the

further we step back from it. We must step back into an awaiting reserve. Such reserve anticipates what is coming and tries to experience what is coming. Today the appearing of the in-finite relation as a unified whole remains denied to us; and yet what denies itself to us actually approaches us in its own way. Today the men of the earth are provoked by the absolute domination of the essence of modern technicity into developing a world formula which would once and for all secure the world as uniform sameness and, thus, make it available to us as a calculable fund. The togetherness of the four voices of destiny no longer rings out; our calculating making-available of everything that is and can be displaces the in-finite relation. The provocation which reigns in the domination of modern technology holds sway within the realm of what no longer can be experienced as that from which the ordering power of the provocation itself receives its very mission. That is pure destiny itself.

Destiny approaches man silently in a mysterious kind of stillness. Man will presumably ignore this stillness for a long time to come. Thus he will remain unable to respond to this destiny in a positive manner. Rather, he will avoid it through his more and more hopeless attempts to master technology with his mortal will. And yet, the ordering of a jointing (*Harmonia*) may still hold sway within the power of that provocation, i.e., within the absolute domination of modern technology. Only with the greatest of difficulty can we hear the silent voice of this jointing. Yet it is important that we try to listen to this voice; for "the jointing that denies its appearance is of a higher ruling than one that comes to appearance."[71]

In "Overcoming Metaphysics," which is a set of notes written down between 1936 and 1946, Heidegger elaborates on these ideas. There he explains how in the modern era Being usually shows itself as will to will, and that will to will wards off every new sending of Being, every granting of a new openness of the Being of beings. The will to will rigidifies everything, so that there is no longer any destiny. Thus we now live in an unhistorical era which is dominated by scientific historiography, which, in turn, implies historicism. Furthermore, the will to will allows only calculation and technical arrangement as the basic forms of its own appearance. Thus the basic form of appearance in which the will to will arranges and calculates everything in the unhistorical world of modern metaphysics can be called concisely "technicity."[72] In this epoch Being itself remains unquestioned, and thus it remains unthought. It holds itself in a truth which has long since been forgotten, in a truth which is also without ground.[73]

In virtue of the fact that the will is sometimes personified in individual "men of will," it obviously looks *as if* the will to will originates from these persons. Thus the opinion rises that the human will is the true origin of the will to will; yet in truth, man himself is willed by the will to will, without experiencing the essence of this willing and without knowing that he is always already outwitted by this will.[74]

Modern man is obsessed by the desire for power. He does not understand that his struggle for power is always in the service of the power of the will to will. The will to will alone empowers numberless struggles for power. Power overpowers man today to such a degree that it completely expropriates from him the possibility of ever escaping from the oblivion of Being. But in this way, the struggle for power which we now find everywhere on earth is as such undecidable; there is nothing that could decide it, because it itself remains excluded from the difference between Being and beings and, thus, from the truth. Through its own immanent force it is driven to the abandonment of Being, to nihilism.[75]

A sign that the ultimate abandonment of Being has been reached can be found in the cries about great ideas and about values. All of that is really no more than an element of the vacuum which the abandonment of Being has left behind; in this vacuum, the consumption of beings for the manufacturing of modern technicity is now the only way out for man. The complete consumption of all beings is determined by the mobilization through which man tries to make himself the "master" of what is "elemental." Even world wars and their character of being total are also a consequence of the abandonment of Being. They, too, press toward a guarantee of the stability of a constant form of employing things in such a way that they become used up.

> Man, who no longer conceals his character of being the most important raw material, is also drawn into this process. Man is the "most important raw material" because he remains the subject of all consumption. He does this in such a way that he lets his will be unconditionally equated with this process.[76]

As a consequence of the abandonment of beings by Being's truth, the world has become an unworld.[77]

The consumption of all materials, including the raw material "man," for the unconditioned possibility of the production of everything is determined in a concealed way by the complete and utter emptiness in which beings, the materials of what is real, are suspended. This emptiness is obviously to be filled up somehow. But since the emptiness of Being can never be filled up by the fullness of beings, the only way to escape it seems to be incessantly to rearrange beings. Seen from this point of view, technicity is the organization of a lack, because, contrary to its knowledge, it is intimately related to the emptiness of Being. Wherever there are not enough things, technology has to jump in, create substitutes, and exhaust all raw materials. But the mass production of substitute things is not just a temporary device; it is the only possible form in which the will to will keeps itself going. The increase in the number of masses of human beings is also planned, so that one can always continue to claim more "room to live" for the ever increasing masses of people, whose size then in turn demands correspondingly ever larger masses of human beings for their arrangement. This circularity of consumption for the sake of consumption is the sole procedure which characterizes the world which really has become an unworld.[78] Our earth now appears as the unworld of erring. From the perspective of the history of Being, it has become the erring star *(der Irrstern)*.[79]

The earth itself has always been governed by an unnoticeable law which preserves the earth so that always enough things emerge and enough things perish "within the allotted sphere of the possible." It is first the will to will which arranges itself everywhere in modern technicity that literally devours the earth, exhausts its resources, and so consumes everything. Technicity drives the earth beyond the limits of what is possible into the impossible. It is one thing to use and abuse the earth; it is quite another thing to receive the blessing of the earth and to be at home in the law of this reception in order to shepherd the mystery of Being and watch over the inviolability of the possible.[80] The desolation of the earth begins as a process that was willed, although it was not known as such; it was not even knowable at the time when the essence of truth became defined as certainty. Yet it can be known, and there is a way back, provided the coming-to-pass of Being calls the humans as mortals to return to the path of thinking, poetizing, and building.[81]

V. SUMMARY AND CONCLUSION

In his reflections on the origin of the work of art, Heidegger tried to retrieve an important problem discussed in philosophy between Plato and Hegel. How does a being's appearance relate to that which so appears? A number of different solutions for this problem have been proposed, ranging from naive realism to absolute idealism. Heidegger's answer to the question is inspired by Kant, as is clear from what was argued in this regard in *Being and Time* and *Kant and the Problem of Metaphysics*. The "thing in itself" is unknowable. What we call "the thing in itself" is merely the totality of the potentialities which in each case concretely become actualized only in part. It, taken in and by itself, never appears as such; it always appears *as* this or *as* that. The process of the coming-to-pass of the truth of Being, taken concretely as world, lets the beings be things and, thus, lets them appear as what they (now) have come to be. No world could possibly actualize all potentialities of meaning, because each world is inherently finite, temporal, and historical. Nor can finite understanding grasp a being other than either *as* this or *as* that, depending on the a priori synthesis upon which it is projected. Heidegger disagreed with Kant only on one basic point: he was convinced that Kant underestimated the fact that in each appearance it is obviously the "thing itself" which so appears.[22]

In the fifties Heidegger tried to retrieve thoughtfully what certain great myths of the past had hinted at. He took his point of departure from Hölderlin's attempt to retrieve certain Greek myths, but he later made that which was pointed to there an element of his own way of thinking. Richardson has pointed out correctly that Heidegger does not take heaven and earth, God and mortals in an ontic sense. Thus he is not concerned with the basic problems of classical metaphysics; rather, he takes these expressions ontologically and, hence, as referring to basic regions of the world.[83] Furthermore, the number four should not be taken literally, but rather as an indication of the complex structure of the world which each generation has to accept as its destiny.

Those who are confronted with these ideas for the first time will wonder what the meaning of such suggestions really could be. From the viewpoint of literary criticism, one could argue that Heidegger's reflections do not represent a legitimate form of text interpretation vis-à-vis Hölderlin and the Greek authors. From the viewpoint of classical philosophy, one could say that Heidegger violates all "rules" developed for the direction of the mind. From the viewpoint of modern science, one could argue that his later work suggests itself as a form of primitive myth. *To some degree* all of these remarks are correct. Indeed, Heidegger does not intend to give a text interpretation along the lines of classical exegesis or scientific hermeneutics. He is not concerned with thinking metaphysically; his entire philosophy is dominated by the sincere effort to overcome classical metaphysics. Finally, he does turn to mythical thinking in many instances; yet his intention is not to repeat myths but rather to receive a hint concerning something which is still worthy of being thought about.

Basic for Heidegger's later philosophy is the idea that classical metaphysics is to be overcome because it is inherently nihilistic. Furthermore, for Heidegger the genuine fruit of classical metaphysics is modern science; modern science itself is the full realization of what classical metaphysics intended to become. One should realize that for science the calculating way of thinking is the only genuine form of thought, so that "genuine" thought is now replaced by theoretical, scientific thinking. Thus it is necessary again to make room for thought, taken in a more original sense of the term.[84]

When we now turn to the question of what Heidegger really means by earth, it should be noted first that in his view earth belongs together essentially with the other regions of the fourfold and, thus, that it is incorrect to try to say what earth is and means except in relation to the other three regions of the relation which constitutes the fourfold. Secondly, it should be stressed once more that Heidegger attempts to retrieve certain myths, not to repeat them. Thus it is incorrect to take his speaking about the fourfold in a literal sense and interpret it in a mythical or pantheistic manner. That would be tantamount to making two grave errors. First of all, it is obviously not Heidegger's intention to suggest that myth is and remains the only way of genuine thought. Secondly, such an interpretation would again be metaphysical in the classical sense. Heidegger is concerned not with beings, their origin, and their relationships but with the coming-to-pass of the truth of Being, which in the final analysis lets beings be what they are in each given world.

Heidegger's appeal to poetic language is fully justified by the fact that our Western languages have become so scientific that most words of our languages, and certainly the technical vocabularies of them, have become totally inadequate for the formulation of important "philosophical" problems. From the time of *Being and Time*, Heidegger has consistently tried to avoid all metaphysical and all scientific concepts and expressions, because using such concepts and expressions would undoubtedly lead back to that way of thinking which precisely is to be overcome.

To understand Heidegger's real concern, it is perhaps good to approach the basic issue from a negative point of view. Let us assume that Heidegger's thinking about the fourfold indeed is irrelevant. One must then face the questions of how he is to think and speak about heaven and earth, God and mortals. It obviously will not do to argue that either science or classical metaphysics is able in principle to answer all relevant questions. But if it is true that there are questions which are accessible neither to philosophy as metaphysics nor, and even less so, to the sciences which stem from philosophy, then there is still a task reserved for thinking. It is to this thinking that Heidegger's reflections are pointing the way.[85]

In Heidegger's view, mortals no longer dwell "poetically" on the earth. The earth is no longer heeded in its own Being as that which serves, bears, and sustains. Instead, it is exploited. Under the dominion of the essence of modern technicity, it is positioned for its energy and raw materials. It is provoked into delivering all available energy for industry. Under the dominion of science and technology, it is forced to yield the impossible. Yet it is one thing to use the earth; it is quite another thing to receive the blessings of the earth and to begin to feel at home again under the "law" of this reception, in order so to guard the "mystery of Being" and to watch over the invulnerability of the *possible.*[86]

To dwell on the earth also means to dwell under the heaven in the presence of the pointing messengers of God. Modern man no longer dwells "poetically" under the heaven, and he can no longer await the hints of the messengers' advent. In our technological world, the very trace which leads to the holy has long been lost. Finally, modern man no longer lives as mortal, because he has forgotten to relate to death *as death,* forgotten what it means to experience his own Being as Being-unto-death.[87] Yet all of that does not mean that there is no hope for we who live in this "dangerous" situation. For there always was and still is the possibility of genuine and serious thought, a thought which listens to and heeds the great wisdom hidden in our own tradition since the days of "the great beginning." True, the menace is real, and many of us have already completely surrendered; but it is true also that we still have some of those who as poets or thinkers are able to point to what can and will bring salvation.

CHAPTER 6

The Fourfold:
Gods and Mortals

Article I: Some Reflections on the Place of God
in Heidegger's Thought

I. INTRODUCTION: GODS AND MORTALS

When Heidegger speaks about man, he never focuses his attention explicitly on those characteristics which set man apart from the rest of nature. True, ontically man is a being among other beings, and thus it is always possible to consider him in his difference from other inanimate and animate beings. For Heidegger, however, man is the place in which Being, truth, and world come-to-pass in order that the beings can show themselves as such and as that which they in truth are. What is mainly characteristic of man is not the fact that he has certain ontic properties which other beings do not have but rather the fact that he has understanding of Being. In the "Letter on Humanism," Heidegger asks whether one really is on the right track toward the essence of man as long as one sets man off as one living creature among others, in contrast to plants, animals, and even God. One can proceed in that way, and one can locate man in this fashion within beings as one being among others. In so doing, one will always be able to state something correct about man, but one will not say anything about his true essence. Man essentially occurs only where he is claimed by Being. Only from this claim has man found that wherein his essence truly dwells. Only from this dwelling has he language as the home that preserves the ek-static dimension for his essence. This standing in the light of Being is what Heidegger calls the ek-sistence of man. This way of Being is proper only to man. Ek-sistence means here nothing but the human way to be.[1]

Thus for Heidegger man is not so much that being which through certain characteristics can be distinguished from all other beings; rather, he considers man as that being whose essence is employed in order that beings can appear in their Being, in order that Being can come-to-pass and, as unconcealment, can "articulate" itself into its building-structure which we call the world. If Heidegger incidentally touches on typical characteristics of man which indeed set him apart from other things, he always does so in a context in which he is concerned primarily with the question concerning the truth of Being.[2] Heidegger often speaks about man as the one who produces art, who concerns himself with technology, and, generally, as the one who in different epochs stands in different ways in regard to his heritage and its history. But even then Heidegger's intention is not to oppose man to "nature" and to unfold his mode of Being in its manifold possibilities but rather to come closer to an experience with the truth of Being. It should be noted, however, that when Heidegger conceives of man as the place and the "Da" of Being and attempts to show that man's true essence is to be found in his relation to Being, he obviously is not suggesting that one could not pose other meaningful questions in regard to man; yet it is his intention to show the genuine "foundation" from which such questions should be asked and ideally also can be solved.[3]

When man freely accepts his own death and in the face of death resolutely projects himself authentically toward death, it becomes clear at once that man's unbridgeable and abysmal character has its last ground in his having to die; it is man's death which, in the final analysis, lets man be the temporary place for the unconcealment of Being, whose coming-to-pass cannot be reduced to an ultimate ground. Man often misunderstands the meaning of his own death, and he even often deliberately tries to avoid realizing its true implications. Also, it is indeed not at all inappropriate to consider death theologically and to conceive of dying as the transition to another, better, and "eternal" life; yet if death is experienced as it is in essence for man, then death is that which brings man to his own genuine essence, according to which he has to be the place where Being can come-to-pass in a finite way. Death appropriates to man the appropriating event of both truth and world and transforms him in such a way that he now, as the one who can die, belongs within the fourfold of heaven and earth, gods and mortals.

As the mortal, man stands before the divines. The world to which he and the gods belong is the "between" that lies between the gods and the humans; this between is also the event which appropriates the divines and the mortals to each other. But truth and world do not grant themselves to man immediately and suddenly; rather, they give themselves in the form of a claim, which creates obligation and responsibility. It is depending upon whether this claim brings about a being-at-home or lets a being-uncanny be experienced as such that the claim is one which grants the saving grace *(Heil)* or one that withdraws it; it is the claim of what is holy which either arrives or departs. In what is holy, the divine hides that which grants the saving grace or withdraws it. Thus the divine shows itself in each case as a claim, i.e., as God or the gods.[4]

II. HEIDEGGER'S EXPERIENCE WITH CHRISTIAN THEOLOGY

Questions about God have concerned Heidegger in his thought from the very beginning. He encountered these questions first in Christian theology, which at that time was still deeply influenced by metaphysics and, thus, conceived of God as the ultimate ground of all beings.

From the time in 1907 when he moved from the Gymnasium in Konstanz to the Bertholds Gymnasium in Frieburg, Heidegger had a very special interest in theology. When he entered the University of Freiburg in 1909, he devoted himself first to the study of theology for two years.[5] In an inaugural address given at the Heidelberg Academy of Science in 1957, he described these years in the following terms:

> In 1909 I began my studies by reading theology at the University of Freiburg in Breisgau, for four semesters. . . . The decisive, and therefore ineffable, influence on my later academic career came from two men who should be expressly mentioned here in memory and gratitude; the one was Karl Braig, professor of systematic theology, and the last in the tradition of the speculative school of Tübingen which gave significance and scope to Catholic theology through its dialogue with Hegel and Schelling; the other was the art historian Wilhelm Vöge. The impact of each lecture by these two teachers lasted through the long semester breaks which I always spent at my parents' house in my hometown of Messkirch, working uninterruptedly. . . .[6]

Between 1911 and 1924, Heidegger was mainly occupied with philosophy, but even in these busy years he devoted a considerable amount of his time to the study of theological problems. That is evidenced not only by his special interests in the writings of Kierkegaard, Pascal, and Meister Eckhart but also by an explicit testimony dating from 1953. In the early fifties Heidegger was visited by Professor Tezuka from the University of Tokyo. Both philosophers discussed a number of issues of mutual interest. In 1953–1954, Heidegger wrote a dialogue in which he touched upon the most important topics from these discussions. This dialogue was subsequently published in *On the Way to Language* in 1959. In this dialogue, Heidegger explicitly states 1) that his interest in hermeneutics originated from his interest in and knowledge of theology, 2) that without this knowledge of theology he would never have found the way to his hermeneutic phenomenology, and 3) that in 1923 he was particularly preoccupied with the question concerning the relationship between the Word of the Bible and the way of thinking found in speculative theology.[7]

Already in the lectures which he gave in Freiburg, immediately after World War I, Heidegger tried to object to metaphysical theology. The God which metaphysics tries to grasp and comprehend and which it tries to employ as the foundation of all thought is not the living God of the faith, nor is it the God of genuine freedom and the God of true history.[8]

In 1923, Heidegger came in contact with Rudolph Bultmann in Marburg. There he would later also meet Paul Tillich. Bultmann introduced Heidegger to the works of Karl Barth, and both Bultmann and Barth directed Heidegger for a second time to Kierkegaard's theological writings, as well as to Luther, whose works he then studied thoroughly. It is well known that Heidegger had a great influence on Bultmann's later ideas on the meaning and function of theology and its relationship to philosophy. Heidegger also influenced Tillich's later thought; yet the question as to whether Tillich's work had a notable influence on Heidegger cannot easily be answered in a few statements.[9]

In *Being and Time*, Heidegger no longer tries to found philosophy on specuative theology; on the contrary he makes a deliberate effort to get rid of all "remnants" of Christian theology within the domain of philosophy proper. Let me give one example. In the section on truth he writes: "Both the contention that there are 'eternal truths' and the jumbling together of Dasein's phenomenally grounded 'ideality' with an idealized absolute subject, belong to those residues of Christian theology within philosophical problematics which have not as yet been radically extruded."[10] In these instances Heidegger's intention is obviously not to deny the relationship between God and man, or to declare that all theology is impossible and meaningless, but rather to make room for philosophy as well as for a renewed kind of theology.

> Theology is seeking a more primordial interpretation of man's Being towards God, prescribed by the meaning of faith itself and remaining within it. It is slowly beginning to understand once more Luther's insight that the "foundation" on which its system of dogma rests has not arisen from an inquiry in which faith is primary, and that conceptually this "foundation" not only is inadequate for the problematic of theology, but conceals and distorts it.[11]

In 1927 Heidegger received an invitation from the theological faculty of the University of Tübingen to present his views on the relationship between hermeneutic phenomenology and theology. As he explicitly testified at a later date, in writing these lectures he was deeply influenced by Nietzsche's *Unzeitgemässe Betrachtungen* and Franz Overbeck's book *Über die Christlichkeit unserer heutigen Theologie.*[12] But to the sources which are explicitly mentioned here, we obviously must add Heidegger's contact with Catholic theology at the University of Freiburg, his study of the works of Luther and Kierkegaard, and his immediate and personal contact with Bultmann and through him with the Lutheran theology of his time.

In this lecture, "Phänomenologie und Theologie" (1927), Heidegger resolutely rejects the idea of trying to reduce the Christianness of the Christian faith to a general principle that can be derived from the philosophy of religion or reduced to a religious a priori or some immanent spiritual value; for the believer, God manifests Himself in Christ in history, thus in the Crucified. Now, it is obvious that a revelation which is inherently historical cannot be made evident, nor can it be reduced to or founded upon a universal principle. It is a *positum,* something laid down before man which he has to accept, even though it does not make the philosophical questioning completely superfluous. Even the possibility of a thinking toward the essence of God is left open in *Being and Time,* and the part of the book which was not published in 1927 was to have had a section on the distinction between the ontological and the theological "difference."[13]

Yet Heidegger makes it perfectly clear everywhere that he is making a deliberate effort to separate philosophy completely from religion and theology. In a course on the history of the concept of time of 1925 in which he tried to determine his own position in regard to Husserl's phenomenology, he does not hesitate to state that in his view philosophy is inherently "atheistic," provided one understands this concept correctly. Philosophy does not and cannot deny the reality of God; yet neither does it make the existence of God a condition for the possibility of philosophy.[14] These ideas, as well as the relationship between philosophy and theology, are then discussed more systematically in the lecture "Phänomenologie und Theologie" and in *An Introduction to Metaphysics* (1935), to which I shall return shortly.

Between 1927 and 1970, Heidegger was repeatedly confronted with the problem of theology and with particular theological issues. Not only was he in close contact with several leading Lutheran and Catholic theologians, he also discussed with some of these authors the degree to which hermeneutic phenomenology might be *indirectly* of some importance to contemporary theology. However, in his own publications covering this period, there is little direct evidence of this interest in and concern for theology. In the 1970 edition of the lecture on phenomenology and theology, Heidegger mentions only the following essays as immediately relevant to the problematic: "Nietzsche's Word 'God is Dead,'" "European Nihilism," and "Nihilism As Determined by the History of Being."[15]

III. THINKING ABOUT GOD. ITS INTRINSIC LIMITS

Over the past thirty years or so, a great number of books and essays have been written about the place of God in Heidegger's thought.[16] It is not my intention here to discuss at length the numerous stimulating ideas that have been proposed in these publications or to reflect on the implication of these ideas for contemporary philosophy and theology. Rather, I shall try to reflect on some passages in which Heidegger himself has formulated his position. In so doing, I shall repeat an effort first made by Bernard Welte, and I shall make use of many ideas which were first formulated in his article "God in Heidegger's Thought."[17] The reason for this decision is that Heidegger, in a letter dated 23 August 1974, wrote to Welte that his careful and painstaking thinking along with him was as gratifying as it was rare.[18] In formulating his view, Welte carefully follows a single thread of Heidegger's thought in its most important stages. Yet, in Heidegger's view, the effort could still be enriched by a discussion of two important themes not mentioned by Welte, namely, the essence of modern technology and the still-unconsidered foundation of present-day science. Heidegger recommends that the reader begin with the last part of the article and try to understand the rest in light of what is said there; in his view, that will keep the reader from looking for fixed theses and help him stay on the path of inquiry.[19]

In the final sections of the essay, Welte states that Heidegger's claims about God should be understood as conjectures. There are no proofs for these claims; yet they are justified by beckonings of the gods, which poets and thinkers must interpret for modern man. These interpretations are necessary, for in our contemporary Western world, dominated by the essence of technology and "guided" by sciences which have not yet discovered their genuine foundations, God is no longer found; He has withdrawn, and nothing is left except some traces and hints which very few understand. If it were not for "the somber nod of death," contemporary Western man would not even be interested in listening to possible interpretations of these traces and hints. God has withdrawn from this world; the few messages which He has left us speak of two things only: wait and hope. Welte finally summarizes his interpretation with the following sentences: "What happens in this way is hearkening and waiting, entrusting oneself to obscure pointers, so that in a Being-forgetful and God-forgetful time one may pick up some stirrings of the hidden divine God in a region beyond metaphysics. . . ."[20]

In the first six sections which follow the introduction, Welte does not explicity speak about God, but he rather focuses on basic characteristics of Heidegger's thinking. I take these reflections to be of prime importance, in that in these sections the place is staked out within which Heidegger's fragmentary remarks about God are to be understood. It makes little sense to place labels on Heidegger's thought about God and call it pantheistic, theistic, or atheistic; in most cases these characterizations tell us more about the view of the one who uses them than about the thought they are meant to characterize. Anyone who wishes to understand Heidegger's position in regard to God must first make a careful study of what it means for Heidegger to think, and what the limits are that are to be put on this thinking.[21]

First of all we must mention that Heidegger uses a phenomenological approach, the nature of which he has articulated in his earlier works under this very title and later under the general heading of thinking. We need not enter into these characterizations here; suffice it to state that, as I have argued elsewhere, after the turn *(Kehre)*, too, Heidegger's method is still phenomenological, even though it is no longer hermeneutical.[22] For the phenomenological approach as Heidegger conceives of it, two "principles" are of great importance: 1) one must go to the things themselves, and 2) one must let be seen that which shows itself, as it shows itself in itself and from itself. What shows itself in this manner must be brought into language in a manner which is adequate to what showed itself in this way. It is clear that in this manner Heidegger tried to overcome all the distortions of the things themselves by concepts, notions, images, and representations which stem from a tradition that cannot be justified, as well as from all reductionist conceptions of the things which flow from an attitude in which the subject posits the conditions under which a thing is to show itself.

For one who adopts this attitude, it may very well happen that with respect to God he has to keep silent, and for several reasons. First of all, it could be the case that God no longer shows Himself in our world, and in the world of the philosopher in particular. Secondly, it could be the case that by God we really mean that which cannot show itself in the manner in which "the things" show themselves. Thirdly, it could be the case that all the words one has to describe what shows itself are either inadequate to what shows itself (directly or indirectly in traces and beckonings) or have lost their original meaning because of a reductionist and positivist attitude promoted by the sciences that concern themselves with religious phenomena.

Secondly, one must realize the full implications of the radical finitude, temporality, and historicity of both man and Being, and above all the fact that for Heidegger the ontological difference is the very matter of philosophical thought and the only such matter. A philosophy which employs the phenomenological method should focus on only one thing, the Being *of* beings. That means that here considerations about God do not occupy the same place as they once had in traditional philosophy between Saint Augustine and Hegel. The Being of beings is at first mostly hidden and forgotten. It is *in need* of being brought to light and into language; but it also *can* be brought to light and into language, because it is that which lets the "things" which show themselves immediately be what they are. But that means that the coming-to-pass of the truth of Being is essentially and thus necessarily affected by negativity and that Being and Non-being inherently belong together. That explains that on his way Heidegger had to focus time and again on Not-being and nothingness.[23]

This fact obviously had important consequences for the manner in which his thinking would be received. Many people have rejected his thought as nihilistic; others have misinterpreted it and placed it on a par with atheistic existentialism. But furthermore, many philosophers who had given an important place to the *concept* of God in their own philosophical *systems* thought that adopting Heidegger's point of view would entail atheism or at least agnosticism. This idea was suggested all the more clearly when Heidegger began to stress the so-called ontological difference in a more radical way; according to this conception, Being is not a being but rather that which in a finite manner, temporally and historically, lets beings be what they are. But if that is so, then Heidegger's Being can be neither the God of the modern philosophers *(causa sui)* nor the *ipsum esse* of Aquinas and the entire scholastic tradition.[24] But then, is Heidegger's philosophy not inherently nihilistic, and does it thus not reject all religion? It is thus understandable that on various occasions Heidegger had to clarify his position to prevent misunderstanding. He has said more than once that what he understands by Being is neither God nor some cosmic ground. But saying that does not commit one to either theism or atheism.[25]

IV. NIETZSCHE AND HEIDEGGER ON GOD

During the thirties, Nietzsche's experience that God is dead became in many respects decisive for Heidegger's later thought. Regardless of what Nietzsche himself may have meant to express, Heidegger interprets his statement not to mean that God Himself is dead but rather that the god has died which had been determined metaphysically and was then experienced in the epoch of history which was influenced by metaphysics.[26]

We all know the passage of *The Gay Science* in which Nietzsche speaks about a madman who went into the marketplace in the morning with a burning lantern, crying incessantly: "I am looking for God! I am searching for God! Where has God gone? I shall tell you. We have killed Him—you and I."[27] We are also familiar with the common interpretation of this story according to which the madman represents Nietzsche himself, the people in the marketplace are his contemporaries, and the message of the story is that God indeed is dead in the hearts of men, because scientific knowledge and rationalism have shown beyond a shadow of a doubt that man's belief in God is without any foundation. But without God the world has lost its meaning, even though we all still behave as if the disappearance of God left everything where it once stood. For Nietzsche himself, however, the opposite is the case; the death of God means the disappearance of everything for which the conception of God was capable of accounting. The truth of the matter is that with God's death, the basis for all moral judgment, for all values, for all notions of right and wrong, of good and evil, has been removed, so that our world indeed has become completely meaningless. For Nietzsche such a world is unlivable, so that he devoted his entire life's work to an attempt to find a new meaning for what is valuable in a purely human existence. Thus the aim of Nietzsche's work as a whole is to elevate man to a position from which he can permanently assume the place in the world formerly occupied by God.[28]

There obviously have been philosophers who were convinced that this commonly held interpretation is simplistic and that the genuine attitude for a thinker to adopt in regard to Nietzsche's work is not one of passive acceptance or radical criticism but rather one which calls for thought. That is true particularly for Heidegger's interpretation of Nietzsche's work. Since it is impossible and not necessary to follow Heidegger's interpretation in detail, let me at least recall some of the basic ideas which guided Heidegger in his concern with Nietzsche's work.

First of all, he warns us not to take the matter of God's death too easily. Nietzsche understood his own thought as belonging under the heading of "nihilism." That is the term for a historical movement which already has ruled throughout the preceding centuries and now determines our own era. Nietzsche sums up his interpretation of this movement in the statement that God is dead. One could assume that this statement merely expresses the opinion of Nietzsche, the atheist, and that it can easily be refuted by the observation that today everywhere numberless people still go to church and often endure hardships because of their trust in God as defined by Christianity.[29]

Secondly, one cannot identify what Nietzsche calls nihilism with the negation of Christianity. For nihilism does not rule primarily where the Christian God is disavowed or where Christianity is combatted, nor does it rule exclusively where atheism is preached. Thus nihilism in Nietzsche's sense in no way coincides with the situation in which the Christian God of biblical revelation can no longer be believed in. For Nietzsche did not consider the Christian life which once existed for a short time before the Gospels were written down, and before the missionary work of St. Paul, to belong to Christendom. In other words, one must make a distinction here between Christendom and genuine Christianity. Christendom for Nietzsche is the historical, world-political movement of the Church and its claim to power, so that Christendom in this sense and the genuine Christianity of the New Testament are not the same. Even a non-Christian life can affirm Christendom and use it as a means of power, just as, conversely, a Christian life does not necessarily require Christendom. Therefore, a confrontation with historical Christendom is absolutely not in any way an attack against what is genuinely Christian, any more than a critique of theology is necessarily a critique of the Christian faith. Thus unbelief in the sense of falling away from the Christian doctrine as upheld by historical Christendom is never the essence or the ground but always only a consequence of nihilism; for it may well be that historical Christendom itself represents a consequence of modern nihilism.[30]

Thirdly, one should realize that a thoughtful concern with a philosophical text cannot limit itself to what the text literally claims; every thoughtful interpretation must give to the text something of its own. The part that in this way is added to the text is what the layman, judging on the basis of what he holds to be the content of the text, constantly perceives as the meaning read into the text. Still, while the right elucidation never understands the text better than the author understood it himself, it does certainly understand the text differently. Yet this difference must be of such a kind as to touch on the same as that toward which the elucidated text itself is pointing.[31]

Fourthly, one should also realize that in diagnosing the actual historical situation, Nietzsche remains within the nihilism of Western metaphysics, and that in proposing a remedy for the situation, he remains basically in that same tradition, even though he puts it on its head, so to speak; thus he proposed a transvaluation of all values, not realizing that thinking in terms of values precisely is nihilism.[32]

Also, for the thinker who does not limit himself to a philological interpretation of the text, but adds to it the retrieve of the thoughts which remained unsaid in the text, it is simplistic to assume that the genuine meaning of Nietzsche's claim is that dominion over all that is must pass from God to man, or that man is to be put into God's place. For whoever believes that does not think in a very godly way about God. Man can never put himself in God's place, because the mode of Being of man can never reach up to the realm which essentially belongs to God. Compared with this impossibility, something far more uncanny can happen. The place which *Western metaphysics* attributes to God is the place of that being which in a causal manner brings about and then preserves whatever is as something created. The fatal blow against God consists in the fact that God, as the being of all beings, is degraded to the highest value. The heaviest blow against God is not that God is held to be unknowable, or that His existence is demonstrated to be unprovable, but rather that the God held to be real is elevated to a value, i.e., the highest value. For this blow comes not from the unbelievers who are standing about but from the believers and their theologians who discourse on the being that of all beings is most being.[33]

Finally, one should not forget that the madman which Nietzsche describes in *The Gay Science* cries incessantly: "I seek God!" The man who is de-ranged *(ver-rückt)* is dis-lodged *(ausgerückt)* from the level of modern man and carried out *(hinausgerückt)* beyond modern man. A man who is de-ranged in this way has nothing in common with the kind of men who just stand about in the marketplace and who do not believe in God. For these men are unbelievers not because God as God has to them become unworthy of belief but rather because they themselves have given up the possibility of belief and faith, insofar as they are no longer able to seek God. They can no longer seek because they no longer are able to think. The madman, on the other hand, is the one who seeks God. Has a thinking man perhaps here really cried out *de profundis?* And the ear of our own thinking, does it still not hear the cry? We shall refuse to hear the cry as long as we do not begin to think. But thinking begins only when we have come to know that reason, glorified for centuries in the form of calculating thinking, is the most stiff-necked adversary of genuine thought.[34]

In his "Aufzeichnungen aus der Werkstatt," which appeared in the *Neue Zürcher Zeitung* in 1959, Heidegger notes that Nietzsche himself in 1886 admitted that he did not try to refute God, but he tried rather to get rid of the "moral God." A God who is taken to be a value, even the highest value, is no God at all. God himself is not dead; His godhead is alive and well. As a matter of fact, today the godhead is even closer to thought than it is to faith, insofar as the godhead as the one who comes-to-presence, and so abides, receives His origin from the truth of Being, and Being itself taken as the appropriating beginning is different from a ground and certainly from the ultimate cause of all beings. The "moral God" represents the failure of a people which adopts a negative attitude toward itself and toward life.[35] Should one ever overcome this conception of man, this form of humanity, then the moral God would be refuted at the same time. Heidegger obviously goes here beyond Nietzsche and, furthermore, leads the entire problematic of a moralizing conception of God to an essentially deeper dimension. Only when one succeeds in genuinely overcoming metaphysics, and only when one abandons the metaphysical conception of God, will thought become free again for the divine God. For metaphysics God is *causa sui.*

> This is the right name for the god of philosophy. Man can neither pray nor sacrifice to this god. Before the *causa sui,* man can neither fall to his knees in awe nor can he play music and dance before this god. The godless thinking which must abandon the god of philosophy, god as *causa sui,* is thus perhaps closer to the divine God . . . more open to Him than onto-theo-logy would like to admit.[36]

Thus Heidegger feels that he can pose the question about God in a new way, because according to his own experience, it is not the godhead of the true God that has been refuted by Nietzsche but merely the essence of God insofar as it has been thought metaphysically. Hölderlin, who tried to retrieve the pre-metaphysical conception of God as one still finds it in the great Greek tragedies, can thus perhaps warrant the possibility for a theology which knows itself to be claimed by the divine in a time in which God himself has withdrawn.[37]

Article II: The Question about God in Heidegger's Later Works[38]

In the late twenties and early thirties, Heidegger had thus come to the following conclusions: 1) Classical metaphysics is to be overcome in a radical manner; 2) its conceptions of God are totally inadequate; a philosophical theology does not speak about a God with whom any human being could ever establish a personal relationship; 3) most forms of sacred theology are equally to be overcome, in view of the fact that since the time of Augustine they have mixed together ideas about God which go back to Revelation with notions about God that have their origin in philosophical theology. In the thirties Heidegger began to concern himself seriously with Nietzsche's philosophy, and as far as the problem of God is concerned, he saw himself confronted with Nietzsche's claim that God is dead. In his attempt to determine both the meaning and the implications of this claim, he did not interpret it to imply that there is no God; rather, he tried to understand why so many people today think that they can live without God and how it came to be that our world has changed into a godless world.

In his criticism of philosophical theology, Heidegger had come to realize that analogy is not really applicable to our speaking about God, because of the infinite distance that is implied when one tries to apply concepts relevant to "created" things to the divine. Thus, in his attempt to speak about God, he was left with only one viable alternative, namely, "symbolic" language, in view of the fact that "symbols" refer to a "surplus" of meaning without having to articulate this meaning conceptually. That explains Heidegger's interest in the poetic language about God and in Hölderlin's poetry in particular. Yet this appeal to "symbolic" language presupposes that the thinker, after rejecting every classical form of theology, still is convinced that as a thinker he can say something meaningful about God. But how is one to justify this conviction, and precisely how is one to think about God? In the late thirties, Heidegger tried to answer these questions by employing ideas derived from Meister Eckhart, Hölderlin, and (indirectly) Nietzsche.[39]

Between 1936 and 1939, Heidegger wrote his *Beiträge zur Philosophie*, which until now has remained unpublished.[40] In the first part of these reflections he had tried to think Being as it itself is, i.e., as the appropriating event of non-concealment. Toward the end of these reflections he turned again to the questions about God. For the coming-to-pass of the truth of Being appears to be oriented in such a way that in it claims speak which determine and change everything and, therefore, also affect man and his thought. Thus everyone who inquires into the essence of Being will find that in the manner in which Being shows and hides itself in his epoch, "divine things" are hidden. These can be discovered, but only from the manner in which Being in that epoch first lets gods and mortals become distinguished and separated, and then lets them come-to-pass as what they properly are, so that they can relate to each other. The mortals who think and thus know that they are being employed for the coming-to-pass of non-concealment itself also know that they are at the disposal of the gods. But that means, among other things, that from then on they stand outside the domain of common things, because they are those to whom the gods remain closest. In other words, Being as the coming-to-pass of non-concealment grants God to man, while it appropriates man to God.[41]

In view of the fact that the decision as to whether and how God addresses man does not at all depend upon man himself but on Being, and in view of the fact that a thinker who tries to think in the direction of the coming-to-pass of the truth of Being must leave such decisions open, Heidegger usually speaks in an undetermined manner about both gods and God. Furthermore, he denies that God is Being but equally claims that God cannot be thought as either being or non-being. Heidegger denies that God is Being in order to avoid that, as has been the case in classical metaphysics, God ultimately would be thought of as that being which is most in being, the highest being, so that His true essence would be completely misapprehended, not to mention the fact that Being itself, too, would so be completely misunderstood. When Heidegger says that one cannot attribute Being to God, he merely means to say that Being does not stand "over and above" God; yet God obviously does not stand "over and above" Being, either. However, it is and remains the case that even God Himself "needs" Being in order to become manifest. God does not need Being as His property, in which He, so to speak, can have his "place." Yet He "needs" Being in order that He, through that which does not belong to Him at all, may belong to Himself and manifest Himself to man. The fact that even God "needs" Being, which He did not create or even condition, shows us the true essence of Being. That even God needs Being also shows us that it makes no sense to try to prove the existence of God.[42]

Furthermore, if one tries to experience the divine from the perspective of the coming-to-pass of non-concealment, the coming-to-presence of the divine becomes in each concrete case elevated to being the highest and the last; the human being, who experiences God in the coming-to-pass of non-concealment, is always the one who-is-to-come *(Zukünftiger)* for the passing-by *(Vorbeigang)* of the last God. By the last God, Heidegger does not mean the one who constitutes the final end in which everything ceases. The God who is experienced here as being the last announces in each case the beginning of a history that is to come. Also, the last God is not another God as compared to the gods who have been already; rather, the last God gathers everything divine that has been already and elevates it into the last and highest essence of what is divine. In what sense God in each case is the last becomes clear to those humans who know that they themselves stand out toward their own death as to that which is last, extreme, and final.[43]

Finally, God, who from the perspective of the appropriating event is experienced as the last, is only as the one who passes-by; it is impossible to bring Him to a standstill and make Him be a stable ground of all that is. He comes-to-presence and abides in and through hints, in and through the sudden arrival or the failure to appear, as well as in and through the flight of the gods that have been and their hidden transformations. In the manner in which the hint thus comes-to-pass, Being itself also comes to its full ripeness. Ripeness here means the willingness and readiness to become gift. It is in this hint that we find what is last, the essential and abiding end which is required by the beginning but was never added to it from the outside. Here the most inner finitude of Being manifests itself, i.e., in the hint of the last God. Yet Being itself and its coming-to-presence as the happening of non-concealment are themselves not God, although they are the "element" which God "needs" in order to appear and become manifest as God. The appropriating event and its articulation in the abyss of the openness of the time-space are the net in which the last God catches Himself, in order then to destroy the net and let it end in His singleness in a manner that is unique: divine, strange, and most unfamiliar among all that is.[44]

We just mentioned that the divine who is experienced from the perspective of the coming-to-pass of non-concealment cannot be posited as the ground which gives a ground to everything else. It withdraws in the abyss. It shows itself in each case in the relevant sending but always remains that which is completely other from that which is human. Thus, to the manner in which God abides belongs historicity, provided the latter be understood from the perspective of the appropriating event, which reveals and conceals at the same time. But it would also follow that each address of the divine has its own, proper time *(kairos)*. If this address was "true" for one epoch, it need not necessarily remain the non-concealment for another epoch. It is thus understandable why Heidegger can say with Nietzsche that even gods can die. For the divine, to die means not to end up in empty nothingness but merely to withdraw and to take itself back in its uniqueness and solitariness. It should be noted that in the coming-to-pass of the truth of Being, Heidegger attributes to man a function which even the gods, taken as such, do not have, even though in another sense they obviously are "infinitely" superior to the humans.

At any rate, if time and history are experienced from the perspective of the coming-to-pass of non-concealment, then one cannot think God as the one who is without time and history, as the one who stands above time and history. He can be inquired into only from the tragic movement of history and in each case from the genuinely relevant "moment." Perhaps one must even say that God is never manifest except as the one into whom man *must* inquire, in view of the fact that He is experienced as somehow absent. Furthermore, one might even ask whether God is not more truly divine in the question of those who search for Him than He is in the certainty of those who are absolutely certain about Him and in that certainty can dispose of Him when they do not need Him, and dispose over Him when they do.[45]

But if the divine shows itself only in historical appeals, how can one then still think the divine as a unity? Can the "eternity" of God then still be thought as infinite temporality, a position which Heidegger seemed to have doubted already in *Being and Time?*[46] Also, can one comprise the fullness of the divine in the idea of a "last God," or does such comprising completely pass over the historical experience of the divine? Is the thought of a "last God," a God of all gods, not totally inconceivable insofar as it tries to think the historical coming-to-pass of the divine as something that is highest and last and, thus, as no longer historical? These questions can be answered only after one has more carefully articulated what is meant by the lastness of the "last God" and how His passing is to be understood.

In his later works, Heidegger no longer employs the idea of the passing of the last God in the manner in which it was unfolded in his *Beiträge zur Philosophie*. There his speaking about the divine is much more reserved, and he calls the divines the hinting messengers of the godhead from whose hidden holding-sway God will appear in His true essence.[47] Heidegger also calls the divines the angels, and in so doing he again follows Hölderlin. The divines are now said to be the messengers who place man under the commanding appeal of what is holy and divine and in this way bring the abysmal coming-to-pass of non-concealment in each case to a peaceful stillness, which consists in being whole and wholesome. As these messengers, the divines are then said to belong to the world, the building-structure of non-concealment. In that case these divines can no longer be taken as "proof" for the existence of God, but rather they must be taken as attempts to respond to the appeal of the divine, which in each case is historical.[48]

Be that as it may, it is clear that the question about God is unavoidable for a thought which asks about the basic unity of truth and world, because such thinking asks how the coming-to-pass of truth and world can be related to a binding appeal. This thinking cannot say much *about* God, yet it realizes that it must leave ample room for the divine appeal which gives grace; and it even must make an effort to open up this domain in an epoch for which this domain has been closed off for a long time. Yet this thinking is never capable of deciding how such an appeal of God is to affect man; thinking is neither a theological nor a mythological response to this appeal.[49]

From the preceding reflections, it becomes understandable that (as Pöggeler has correctly observed) Heidegger's thought has been received by different theologians in different ways. It is undeniable that in Heidegger's earlier works we find traces of questions which pertain to speculative theology and that these questions are often still found in his later works. One could say that *Der Satz vom Grund*, which criticizes the concept of *causa sui*, is still a contribution to speculative theology; and a similar remark could perhaps be made in regard to *Identity and Difference*. Catholic theologians tend to pursue this dimension of Heidegger's thought. Lutheran theologians, on the other hand (Bultmann and the later Gogarten), place the stress on Heidegger's critique of classical

metaphysics, insofar as it has become an "essential" element of speculative theology. If metaphysics is to be overcome, then systematic theology,
which is essentially affected by metaphysics, is to be overcome as well.
One must then ask whether the ideas which Heidegger later derives from
Hölderlin and Nietzsche can still find a place within Christian theology
or whether they should be understood as a radical critique of Christian
theology.

There are also a number of theologians who have tried to relate the
history of grace *(Heilsgeschichte)* about which the prophets of the Old
Testament speak to what Heidegger calls the history of the lighting-
process (Rendtorff, Wilckens, Robinson). It is true that Heidegger's
thought was influenced by our entire Christian tradition, which includes
the Old Testament. Yet the identification or even close relationship of the
history of man's salvation through grace with the happening of the truth
of Being merely shows the helplessness and embarrassment of modern
theology. One should ask here whether Heidegger does not oppose himself to the Old Testament tradition and, following Hegel and Nietzsche,
whether he perhaps turns rather to Greek tragedy. But such an issue
cannot be discussed meaningfully if one does not first make a careful
comparison of the conception of God as found in the Old Testament and
the conception of God implicit in Greek tragedy.[50]

The question of God is one which is found in Heidegger's thinking
from beginning to end. His thinking tries to bring to a conclusion what
the Western experience of God has encountered on its long road; thus, it
must include reflections on Nietzsche's experience of the death of God.
Heidegger's thought had to make long detours before it was able to find
its own way in this respect. It even had to pass through a thought which
tries to prepare the preparedness for the divines or gods, a thought which
is still obsessed by the desire to make and bring about, obsessed by the
will to will.[51] Contemporary thought, which looks like a new beginning
but really and in truth is the destruction of the original coming-to-pass of
non-concealment and world, always lies there ready as a snare. In a time
of extreme confusion, the questioning about God must be maintained and
kept alive, because these are times for which it is true, as Sophocles wrote
in *Oedipus Rex:* "Irr aber geht die Gottheit der Götter" ("Things divine
are going down in ruin").[52] This thought must eliminate in itself what
hinders the preparation for the preparedness for the gods. This thinking is
thus on a tragic road, and it is called to enter that decline which is not
sheer annihilation but the entrance into the coming-to-pass of non-
concealment, the entrance into a happening which comes to completion
in that it separates from one another and appropriates to each other God
and man, heaven and earth, and thus becomes the structure of the world.

A thinking which becomes free for this happening can no longer attribute the right and the wrong way, nearness and distance of the divine to good or bad times or to human good or bad fortune. For this thinking continues to stand under the word of Sophocles, i.e., the last word of the last poetic work of the last poet of original Greece, namely: for everywhere and in every direction, that which has come-to-pass keeps secure a decision concerning its own completion, *pantōs gar echei tade kuros.* . . .[53]

CONCLUDING REFLECTIONS

From what we have said about Heidegger's conception of Being, about his interpretation of the destiny of Western thought in general, and of its contemporary consummation in particular, it will be clear that this destiny has very important implications for the question concerning God today.

The first consequence of this destiny is that in this epoch God cannot be understood except as a supreme being, of which man can form for himself some representation and whose existence can be made certain by means of arguments; once God has been secured in this manner, it is then possible to secure all beings in turn by showing how God is the ground of all other beings. God is here shown to be the ultimate cause and thus the self-cause.[54] About this God of our modern Western metaphysics, Heidegger writes: "Man can neither pray nor sacrifice to this god." And referring to his own thinking, he adds that this "god-less thinking which must abandon the god of philosophy . . . is thus perhaps closer to the divine God."[55]

A second consequence is that God more and more becomes a mere creature of man's thought, so that in the final analysis thought is more important and more powerful than the God of metaphysics. It is human thought which determines all beings, including the highest being, God. It is then understandable why at a certain moment in time thought raises its hand against this God and "kills Him." Nietzsche's cry that God is dead is only a description of the final episode in the modern destiny of Being in the West. But even if one were not to go so far as to "kill God," even then the destiny of Being still implies today that the God of metaphysics has lost its power of awakening, binding, and building. Contemporary man usually still has a name for God, but God is no longer permitted to shine forth in His own name as the most High, the Sovereign, the Mystery of Majesty, and the Holy. But this "default of God," as Hölderlin called it, too, was not something that happened simply because of a fault or neglect on man's part alone; its happening was necessary, because it is inherent in the current sending of Being.

The present era in the West is completely dominated by technology, and that has brought the "spirit" of Western metaphysics to its extreme with its representational and dominating form of thought. What is Heidegger's thought on the God question in light of all of that? Heidegger first suggests that thought must endure this destiny and endure its privation. The God question is obviously still a question today, but it has reached an impasse, and the search for an answer has come up against an impassable barrier. Furthermore, Heidegger says, thought today can be no more theistic than atheistic. "Not, however, because of an indifferent attitude, but out of respect for the boundaries that have been set for thinking as such, indeed set by what gives itself to thinking as that which is to be thought, by the truth of Being."[56] That in turn implies that the thinker no longer can name God, i.e., he no longer can speak the name in such a way that the God so named would indeed emerge of Himself into the light of His own presence.[57]

Yet Heidegger's thinking does not stop at this point, even though it admits to having reached the limits imposed on it. He still takes a few very cautious steps. The first and most important of these steps is to recognize and accept the limits as such. It is an important step, because it lets the "default of God" appear as a privation, as something that should not be. In the essay on "Nietzsche's Word 'God is Dead,'" Heidegger remarks that the madman of *The Gay Science* not only announces God's death but also incessantly cries: "I seek God!" The madman is not one of those who do not believe in God. Rather, he is the one who seeks God, "since he cries after God."[58] The "default of God" is seen here as a privation; the thinker experiences it here as a privation, and so it forces him to cry out. It stirs the quest for God, not the God of Western metaphysics but rather the God who arises of Himself.

Secondly, in a letter to a young student added as a postscript to the lecture "The Thing," Heidegger writes that the "default of God" is not nothing but the first appropriate presence of the hidden fullness of what has been and is of the divine in the Greeks, in prophetic Judaism, and in the preaching of Jesus.[59] Heidegger seems to refer here to the experiences of numerous "mystics" who have described their experience of God as experiences concerning the One who is absent and Whose absence was so sorely felt. Welte correctly adds that anyone who wishes to have more insight into the nature of this peculiar claim is referred to the historical experiences of the epiphany of God and the divine.[60]

But there is still another step to be taken, namely, the one in which a deliberate effort is made to overcome metaphysics. Today it is not yet possible to say in what direction thought is to go; yet a new direction can and must be prepared. The preparation of a thought which tries to overcome metaphysics is also a preparation for overcoming the God of metaphysics and, thus, also the preparation for the long-awaited coming of the still-hidden God.

In his "Letter on Humanism," Heidegger even gives us a list of conditions which must be fulfilled if God is again to be experienced as the divine. There he states that only from the essence of the holy is the essence of divinity to be thought; only in the light of the essence of divinity can it be thought and said what the word *God* is to signify. If one is to experience a relation of man to God, these words must first regain their true meaning. "How can man at the present stage of world history ask at all seriously and rigorously whether God nears or withdraws, when he has above all neglected to think into the dimension in which alone that question can be asked?"[61]

Heidegger finally takes a last step, in which he joins the poets, and especially the poet of poets, Hölderlin. In his reflections on Hölderlin's poems, Heidegger finds the proper words to describe Being as the holy. In "What Are Poets For?" Heidegger then explains in what sense the holy can be called the trace of God.[62] This clue points to the divinity and even bears witness to it; but God does not show Himself yet. The holy appears already, but God still remains afar.[63]

Welte observes here that if the holy appears as the pointer to the divinity, then one may assume perhaps that God "dwells" in the vastness of the holy, though without showing Himself. Thus Heidegger can say in the same essay that the All-High dwells in the highest, i.e., what is holy. But to dwell here still means to hold Himself back, to hide. Holding Himself back in the vastness of the holy (i.e., Being as what is whole), God waits there and sends holiness out before Him as his trace. He waits there to appear again, at the proper time. . . .[64]

CHAPTER 7

On the Essence of Language

Article I: Introductory Reflections

The question of how language and Being are to be related to one another is one which drew Heidegger's attention from the very beginning. Even before he had completed his doctoral dissertation, he wrote in a survey of new publications on logic that he wished to discover why language and logic are necessary in order that a being *(ens)* can be something that is true *(verum)*.[1]

Heidegger began to concern himself with language more systematically in his doctoral dissertation, *Die Lehre vom Urteil im Psychologismus* (1914), and particularly in his *Habilitationsschrift, Die Kategorien- und Bedeutungslehre des Duns Scotus* (1916). Although in 1972 Heidegger had a rather negative opinion about the value of these early investigations and then claimed that at that time he did not yet have any idea of what later would move his thought,[2] his road from logic to onto-logic is nonetheless essential for a proper understanding of his later thinking, because (as Heidegger himself admitted in 1972) his concern with the problem of the categories anticipated his later conception of the Being question, whereas his research into the medieval doctrine of signification led him to the question concerning language.

In his dissertation, Heidegger tried to come to grips with the basic problems of logic via a historico-critical study of the logical treatises of Wilhelm Wundt, Heinrich Maier, Franz Brentano, Anton Marty, and Theodor Lipps. In the second work Heidegger attempted to make a positive contribution to philosophical logic and to defend medieval logic against undue criticism on the part of certain modern logicians. Arion L.

Kelkel has shown in great detail how Heidegger's concern with the doctrine of the categories and the theory of signification gradually led him to a grammato-logic, in which questions about meaning and language begin to occupy a privileged position. Kelkel has also shown how Heidegger, particularly in 1916, was influenced by Husserl's *Logical Investigations,* even though Heidegger's conception of such a grammato-logic differs from Husserl's pure grammar in several important respects.[3]

In his *Habilitationsschrift* Heidegger made a historico-critical study of the medieval *grammatica speculativa* with the intention of developing an a priori speculative grammar, which he then attempted to relate to Husserl's pure logical grammar, on the one hand, and the purely empirical grammar of a given natural language, on the other. But Heidegger's own theory concerning forms of signification remains closer to the classical "scholastic" grammar than to Husserl's pure, logical grammar. For Heidegger maintains here the traditional classification of the grammatical forms according to the parts of the discourse, which rests on the distinction between substance and accident, and also tries to justify the validity of this classification by means of the principal syntactic function of words. Later Heidegger explicitly rejected this approach on the ground that it still begins with unjustified metaphysical assumptions.[4] Yet it remains true that Heidegger's concern with the medieval speculative grammar constitutes a prelude to some of the onto-logical, categorial problems which Heidegger would take up later in *Being and Time.*[5]

During 1920 Heidegger gave a course entitled *Phenomenology of Intuition and Expression,* to which he later sometimes refers with the title *Expression and Appearing.* In these lectures it becomes quite clear that at that time the question concerning the relationship between Being and language had already become central to his thought.[6]

In 1954, speaking about his original interest in hermeneutics, Heidegger wrote in *On the Way to Language:*

> At that time, I was particularly agitated over the question of the relation between the word of Holy Scripture and theological-speculative thinking. This relation, between language and Being, was the same one, if you will, only it was veiled and inaccessible to me, so that through many deviations and false starts I sought in vain for a guiding thread.[7]

Otto Pöggeler, commenting on this passage, points out that if speculative thinking is related to the word of Holy Scripture, then it must unfold an address that has the character of a claim which in addition is inherently historical. This hailing and claiming address is not something that can be established scientifically by historiographic means. It is not something that just lies there present-at-hand, that stands there in changeless permanence and can be established as such; rather, it is a happening that never is completed. In such a hailing address, truth gives itself while it holds itself back; it remains a mystery which continues to refer to a future revelation. In other words, the hailing address grants a new Being, but it does so in a historical manner and at the proper time. Now speculative thinking tries to unfold this Being as the Being of beings. But in such an effort, classical metaphysics had to fail, because in this case Being is to be thought no longer as permanent presence but as event which addresses itself to man while it withdraws. If language is thought with respect to Being, taken as a historical address, it itself can no longer be comprehended from the perspective of a *verum* which is convertible with an *ens* taken as permanent presence.[8]

One of the basic insights underlying *Being and Time*, therefore, is the realization that what was just said about the Word of Holy Scripture is true for Being as such. Being itself is inherently historical; thus, to ask about the meaning of Being is to ask about the relationship between Being and time, and that entails that one cannot analyze the relevant phenomena with the help of the means made available by traditional logic. "That even the traditional logic fails us when confronted with these phenomena, is not surprising if we bear in mind that it has its foundation in an ontology of the present-at-hand—an ontology which, moreover is still a rough one."[9]

It is thus understandable that when Heidegger began to teach, he tried to understand classical logic "ontologically" and to determine very precisely the domain within which classical logic can be applied meaningfully. As for the latter, it appears to be the domain of what is present-at-hand, as permanently present, so that classical logic is incapable of dealing with the problem of Being insofar as it is inherently temporal and historical. This effort is clear particularly in Heidegger's early concern with the works of Aristotle, which were to have a deep influence on his hermeneutic approach in *Being and Time*. The *logos* which Heidegger follows in his hermeneutic phenomenology tries to unfold the manner in which that being understands itself whose Being constantly changes; accordingly, he understands the mode of Being *(Wesen)* of this being as a being-able-to-be which is inherently both temporal and historical. The hermeneutic *logos* maintains the ek-sistential and hermeneutic *as* and does not allow it to degenerate into a merely apophantic *as*, which lets something be presented merely with respect to that which in it is merely present-at-hand.[10]

In this manner, Heidegger found a new approach to the entire problematic of language and logic, insofar as in *Being and Time* both logic and language are thought from the perspective of human discourse *(Rede)*, and the latter itself, in turn, is understood there as the articulation of a Being-in-the-world which finds itself in a mood and as such understands and, therefore, is essentially temporal and historical. In this way, language becomes the articulation of a world which in each case breaks open anew. But although *Being and Time* shows us this hermeneutic logic in operation, it failed in its effort to fully unfold such a logic with all of its implications. In *On the Way to Language,* Heidegger therefore could later write that "because reflection on language, and on Being, has determined my path of thinking from early on, therefore their discussion has stayed as far as possible in the background. The fundamental flaw of the book *Being and Time* is perhaps that I ventured forth too far too early."[11]

In *Being and Time,* Heidegger focuses on language in several contexts. First of all, he speaks about language in a rather indirect manner in the section in which he explains the "original" meaning of the word *logos,* as a constitutive element of the word *phenomenology,*[12] and also in the section in which he explains why in fundamental ontology phenomenology is inherently hermeneutic.[13] In both instances the proper *locus* of language is to be found in the ek-sistentiality of *Dasein*'s own *logos.* Later Heidegger focuses on the worldliness of language and its equipmental character; it is in this context that he treats the relationship between sign and signification in order then to explain the signification structure of language and its function in the everyday Being of *Dasein* and its concern with others.[14] Yet the most important places where Heidegger concerns himself with language in *Being and Time* are the sections which deal with the ek-sistential constitution of the "Da" of *Dasein* itself, which attempts to establish a relationship between understanding, interpretation, and assertion and, thus, to explain how the hermeneutic is to be related to the apophantic.[15] In these sections Heidegger describes original mood *(Befindlichkeit)* and original understanding *(Verstehen)* and states that they are fundamental ek-sistentials of the mode of Being which is characteristic of *Dasein* as Being-in-the-world. Original understanding as such contains in itself the possibility of explanation *(Auslegung),* in which consists the explicit articulating appropriation of what is understood. What we call enunciation *(Aussage)* is there shown to be only a derivative mode of explanation. Enunciating means first pointing out, showing; then it means attributing something to something else; finally it means communicating something. Only when one focuses on the last meaning of enunciation does one come across speech and language. But even though language is only to be mentioned there, it is nonetheless true also that it, via mood and original understanding, is ultimately rooted in the essential openness which is characteristic of the mode of Being of *Dasein,* taken as Being-in-the-world. Yet analyses which concern themselves with enunciation do not yet deal explicitly with the discursive, articulating *logos, (Rede),* which is the immediate and ontologic-ek-sistential fundament of language.[16]

Discursive and articulating *logos,* taken ek-sistentially, is as original as mood and understanding.[17] Its essential function is to articulate discursively the intelligibility of something. Only when the intelligibility is explicitly articulated can the appropriating explanation come about, so that discursive *logos,* in the final analysis, constitutes the basis for explanation and enunciation. Now, what can be articulated in explanation is meaning. It appears then that one ought to say that meaning is that which can be articulated in and through *logos.* Furthermore, what becomes articulated in discursive articulation as such can be called the total meaning, which can be disclosed as a whole in various particular significations. Thus these significations, taken as articulation of the total meaning, always carry meaning.[18]

However, if *logos,* as the discursive articulation of the intelligibility of all that is implicitly contained in man's concerned dealing with things in the world, is a primordial ek-sistential of disclosedness, which itself is primarily constituted by Being-in-the-world, then *logos,* too, must essentially have a specifically mundane mode of Being. This mode of Being consists in the fact that the totality of meaning of what is intelligible can be put into words in and through *logos.* It is in *logos* that words can be attributed to significations; thus it becomes immediately clear that the view according to which significations are to be attributed to "word-things" must be unacceptable.[19]

The "enunciatedness" of *logos* is what we call language.[20] Taken as that in which language has its mundane Being, the totality of the words and of the other language structures that are systematically built up from them are, once they are constituted, something which one encounters as an intramundane reality, ready-to-hand for anyone who wants to speak. It is true that language indeed can be conceived of also as the totality of all word-things that are present-at-hand, those which can be brought together in a dictionary and whose usage can be described in grammar and syntax. Ek-sistentially seen, however, language is the enunciatedness of the *logos,* because that being whose disclosedness is articulated by *logos* has the mode of Being of a Being-in-the-world that is entirely committed to the world. Discursive *logos* is therefore the "signifying" articulation of the intelligibility of man's Being-in-the-world and of everything that is essentially contained in it.[21]

In discursive *logos* this intelligibility, which has its root in primordial understanding and mood, becomes articulated in significations. The constitutive elements of this articulation are: that which our speaking is about, what receives its shape and form through it, communication itself taken in a very broad sense, and making known to others. However, these are not properties empirically found in each language. They are, rather, the essential characteristics of the *logos* rooted in original understanding and primordial mood which make language precisely possible as such. It is likely that in many actual linguistic forms, some of these elements remain implicit. The fact that not all of them always receive verbal expression is merely an indication that in concrete cases we always deal with one of many possibilities.[22]

Kelkel has shown that in the conception of language proposed in *Being and Time*, there is a contradiction which Heidegger himself later would realize. The resolution of the contradiction became one of the major factors that would help Heidegger "overcome" this way of thinking, which at bottom is still metaphysical.[23]

In *Being and Time* Heidegger describes *Dasein* as the *locus* and the true subject of all discourse about Being; authentic discourse is described as being inherently apophantic: it lets something be seen and makes us understand it independently of the structures of the significations of the words of the language which it must employ in so doing, and independently of the community which engages in discourse on the basis of the logico-semantic system which constitutes its language. Yet on the other hand, the basic theme running through the work as a whole assumes that all speaking and discourse ultimately rest on the language of Being. On the one hand, Heidegger defends the view that discourse can "produce" meaning only to the degree that it is already expressed by words and thus is constituted in language. On the other hand, he describes language as being merely the enunciatedness of *Dasein's logos;* it is the totality of meaning in which *logos* has a "worldly" Being of its own, after it has been put into words when "to significations words accrue."[24] Thus Heidegger here still maintains a totality of meaning which in itself and taken as such lies outside the domain of language and as such, therefore, is intemporal and invariant. In his effort to overcome the conception of meaning defended by transcendental philosophy, Heidegger, in *Being and Time*, succeeded only in part. When he later realized this inconsistency and admitted that in *Being and Time* he had merely succeeded in advancing to the threshold of the question, without being able to penetrate into its full depths, he immediately gave up the idea that *Dasein* "has" language and defended the view that *Dasein* is merely the place where language speaks. Language is no longer just a tool, but it itself speaks, and man's speaking is merely a response to its speaking, a response which presupposes that *Dasein* must learn to hear and listen to what the language of Being has to say.[25]

Article II: From *Being and Time* to *On the Way to Language*

In *Being and Time,* Heidegger uses the German word *Rede* to translate *logos*. *Rede* is that ek-sistential component of *Dasein* by means of which *Dasein* is capable of bringing to expression that which it understands. Thus it is said here that it is the ontological constitution of *Dasein* which makes spoken language possible.[26] Now, in the same work Heidegger states that the Greek word *logos* originally meant a process of making manifest, a letting-be-seen.[27] What is it then that *Rede (logos)* attempts to show? According to Richardson, in *Being and Time* (as well as in *Vom Wesen des Grundes*), Heidegger is quite obscure about the answer to this question. Section 34 is probably the least satisfying section of the entire book, and the reason seems to be that Heidegger at that time was still very much in the dark about these matters, and that the full sense of *logos* had not yet crystallized for him. In the later works *logos* will begin to play an essential role, where it will be used to explain why any effort to think the problem of Being must involve reflections on the essence of language and why, therefore, reflections on language are the principal way which a thought that tries to think Being has to follow.[28]

A first indication that for Heidegger there is a close relation between the interrogation of Being and the origin of language is found in *An Introduction to Metaphysics* (1935), where Heidegger states that to ask the question of Being is to try "to bring Being into word" *(zum Wort zu bringen).* To understand that, one must realize that *logos,* which usually is translated as "word" or "speech," originally meant "gathering-together." In the relation between Being and *Dasein,* the process of gathering consists in *Dasein's noein,* i.e., man's accepting containment which forces Being into disclosure,[29] whereas the gathered-together-ness is Being itself. Thus the process of *Dasein,* which as *logos* reveals the Being of a being, expresses that being in its Being and does so as a word. "A word, the forming of a name . . . [establishes] a being which is opening itself up in its Being and preserves it in this open-ness. . . ."[30] That means that for Heidegger the giving of a name is no longer a purely arbitrary procedure which makes some conventional sign available; thus it is not a second process which occurs subsequently to the discovering of a being by thought. "In original saying, the Being of a being, in its original collectedness, is opened-up. . . ."[31] Furthermore, the original word which expresses a being does not only play an essential part in the process in which this being is discovered; its name also preserves this being in its discovered openness. "In words, in language, things become and are. . . ."[32]

Heidegger thus relates the emergence of Being and the origin of language as closely as possible to each other. Language simply *is* Being itself formed into word. But this assertion entails that in the relation between Being as language and *Dasein*'s speaking, the language of Being retains full primacy. Man's authentic speaking is a responding to "the silent voice of Being." Yet the dominating power of Being as language is disclosed to *Dasein* only in a coming-to-presence which is inherently finite; Being dominates as that which conceals itself. The result is that language seems to be at the disposal of *Dasein*, when actually the reverse is the case. It seems as if *Dasein* invented language, whereas in fact it discovers itself only in and with language. It also follows that *Dasein* in its speaking can come to the truth only when its own listening and speaking are directed toward the saying of Being.[33]

Later, in *On the Way to Language*, Heidegger explains this view by saying that the earliest theme on which Western thinking focused was the relation between thing and word.[34] It was thought originally in the form of the relation between Being and original saying. Yet this relation overwhelmed thought so completely that it was articulated in one single word: *logos*. This word thus says at once the name for Being and the name for the original saying.[35] It is important to note here at once that if Being withdraws in the beings which it reveals, then it also withdraws in the words with which beings are brought to language. In other words, there is a "not" hidden in every word, behind which Being withdraws. This "not" constitutes the domain of the unsaid, which is the hidden wealth of what is said. It is as it were a noiseless voice which speaks within the words to which we attend in thought.[36] In *What Evokes Thought?* Heidegger stresses two aspects of this basic phenomenon: 1) Every original and proper naming says something unspoken, and it says it in such a way that it remains unspoken; thus Being is intrinsically mystery.[37] 2) The negativity of Being in language tricks even *Dasein* into disregarding it completely; language plays with our speaking; it likes to let our language wander astray in the more obvious meanings of words. It is as if man has difficulty in dwelling authentically in language; it is as if his dwelling in language is especially prone to succumbing to the danger of what is common.[38] Thus in the coming-to-pass of language, Being has the primacy, not only in its positivity but also in its negativity. By nature man is "thrown" into language, and, thus thrown, he is the plaything of Being-as-saying.[39]

Let us now see how in his later works Heidegger gradually unfolds these new insights.

In *An Introduction to Metaphysics* (1935), Heidegger describes Being as language *(logos)* in terms of what comes into the open to which *Dasein* must attend. It is only by a docile attending to *logos* that *Dasein* can be authentically itself as the place *(Da)* of Being as language *(logos)*. Further-more, it is only the docility to the *logos* which gives ground to the authentic use of words. True thinkers and true poets achieve such docil-ity.[40]

Richardson draws two important conclusions from this conception concerning the origin of language. First of all, *Dasein*, by properly dis-cerning the original meaning of words, can often interrogate Being, pro-vided that there is never a question of engaging in mere philology, and provided an effort be made to retrieve the primal freshness of language more originally than before, which obviously entails some form of "vio-lence" to the words. Secondly, if language in its essence is the coming of Being into words, then *Dasein*'s "orchestration of these words enjoys a privileged affinity with Being." Heidegger calls this the "primordial poetizing," whereby a people tries to capture Being in its songs.[41]

Heidegger discusses this new conception of language more systemati-cally in his paper "*Logos* (Heraclitus, Fragment B 50)," which was part of a lecture series delivered in 1944.[42] Here Heidegger points out that the essence of language is not to be sought by focusing on voice and vocaliza-tion, or on sign and signification. True, signification and expression are indeed characteristics of language, but they do not reach into the domain of what, as far as language itself is concerned, is primordial and essential. In his view, one way to get to the essence of language consists in a careful listening to the original meaning of the Greek words *logos* and *legein*. As we have seen already, *legein* unquestionably means "to say" and "to speak." Yet its original meaning is "to let something lie forth." It does not make much sense to ask how one gets from the one meaning to the other. In realizing these two meanings of the word *legein*, we stumble upon an event whose immensity is still concealed to us in its sheer simplicity. From the very "beginning," the saying and speaking of mortals has come-to-pass as letting-lie-forth and laying, *legein*. Yet already very early *legein* also unfolded itself as saying and speaking. Soon it let itself be over-powered by the latter meaning, which from then on became predomi-nant. This mysterious event refers to the earliest and most consequential decisions about the essence of language. Like the letting-lie-forth that gathers and shelters, the saying receives its essential form also from the non-concealment of that which lies together before us. Now, the un-concealing of the concealed into non-concealment is the very coming-to-presence of what is present, and that we call the Being of beings. Yet human thought was never perplexed by this great event which led from the one meaning of *legein* to the other; it did not even discern a genuine mystery in it, a mystery which actually concealed an essential dispensa-tion of Being in regard to man.[43]

The fact that *legein* means both "to let-lie-forth" and "to say or speak" implies that saying and speaking come-to-presence as the process of letting-lie-forth in collectedness everything that comes-to-presence precisely insofar as it is so laid out in non-concealment.[44] That means that *logos* for Heidegger originally means the aboriginal saying of Being, Being-as-saying, Being-as-language. Man's speaking, if it is to be authentic, must be a response to Being's original saying. Thus authentic language comes-to-pass when *Dasein* "acquiesces to Being-as-saying and, true to its commitment, achieves its own authenticity."[45] In other words, authentic speaking comes-to-pass when men's language concurs *(homolegein)* completely with the aboriginal saying of Being. By letting beings lie forth in the open as what they are, *Dasein* "concurs with the process of *logos,* which is the process that gathers these beings at once unto themselves and unto itself as aboriginal saying."[46] Authentic language comes-to-pass only in such concurrence. Language, insofar as it proceeds from *Dasein* authentically, is basically an attending to the still more original saying of *logos,* of Being-as-language, which itself is articulated in the beings that now come-to-presence precisely insofar as this *homolegein* lets them be.[47] One should note here that in this essay Heidegger for the first time tries to think the essence of language from the essence of Being and indeed as this essence itself.[48]

In the "Letter on Humanism" (1947), Heidegger describes again how the relation between Being and man is brought to completion by means of thought. Being is by its own nature non-concealment; yet it is through thought that the manifestation of Being comes-to-pass. But this manifestation comes-to-pass only insofar as ". . . through thought Being comes [to expression in] language." Thus it is said here again that man's language, like *Dasein*'s thought, "must be considered in terms of a response to Being and *as* this response."[49] As for philosophical speech in particular, in the history of Being, the event by which Being reveals itself to man and in *Dasein* comes to expression in the words of the great thinkers who give utterance to Being. It is in this manner that *Dasein* "takes up its lodging in the house of Being."[50] It is obviously not *Dasein*'s task to construct this house; it merely brings it to completion by its thought, which also is the thought of Being. For Being itself is already on the way to language; *Dasein*'s thought, for its part, brings Being, which thus comes toward it through utterance into language.[51] In other words, *Dasein*'s thought provides Being with the words it needs to disclose itself. "Thinking pays attention to the clearing of Being, in that it puts its saying of Being into language as the lodging of ek-sistence. . . ."[52]

In its own saying, thinking merely brings the unspoken word of Being to language. The expression "to bring to language" must be taken quite literally. Being comes, illuminating itself, to language. It is constantly on the way to language. In this way, language itself is raised into the clearing of Being. Language *is* only in this mysterious manner. And it is to the extent that language, which has thus been brought fully into its essence, is historical that Being itself is entrusted to re-collection. Ek-sistence thoughtfully dwells in the house of Being.[53] The expression according to which language is the house of Being was introduced for the first time in "What Are Poets For?" (1946). There Heidegger describes language as the domain which Being itself cuts out *(temnein)*. In view of the relationship between *temnein* and *templum,* one can thus say that language is the "place cut out," the temple, the house of Being. And it is because language is the house of Being that we reach what is by constantly going through this house.[54]

Yet it was not until 1950 that Heidegger would finally be ready to unfold his conception of the relationship between Being and language in a systematic fashion. Of the series of lectures in which Heidegger formulated his final view on this issue, I shall discuss the first one very briefly in order then in the next section to follow the series of lectures on the essence of language in greater detail.[55]

In October 1950 Heidegger delivered a lecture entitled "Language," in which he employed Trakl's poem "Winter Evening" as an occasion to explain the manner in which Being as language, by addressing and hailing *Dasein,* lets the difference come forth which in turn makes it possible for world and thing to come-to-pass.[56]

For our present purposes it is not necessary to paraphrase the entire lecture. Instead, I shall focus only on some ideas which Heidegger developed in the first part of the lecture, in order then to turn at once to the question of how in this lecture the ontological difference between being and Being is now determined from the perspective of Being-as-language as the distinction between thing and world.

The lecture begins with the observation that man speaks from a language which is already constituted and which man merely employs. In his speaking, man usually listens to what his language "has to say." It is important to note here the significant distinction between speaking and saying-something. It is possible for one to speak much and say nothing; it is also possible to say much by keeping silent. Etymologically, it seems that both the English *to say* and the German *sagen* mean "to point out, to show, to let something appear, to let it be seen or heard." Thus to say something means to show one another what one wants to talk about, to let it appear of itself. The essence of language now is to be sought not so much in speaking as in a primordial saying, taken as showing *(sagen— zeigen).*[57]

The one who speaks listens first to what his language has to say. A first indication of the exactness of this claim can perhaps be seen in the fact that speaking always implies a hearing or a listening. Not only are speaking and listening always found together in every genuine dialogue, but also taken in themselves they belong together intimately. Speaking is initially a listening to the language which one speaks. In this case, listening thus even precedes one's speaking. We do not so much speak a language as we speak *from* a language. And we are able to do so only because we have first listened to that language. What we hear and listen to in this way is the saying of that language.[58]

Although one could say that a language cannot speak unless man has first made it sound by means of his speech organs, it is nevertheless true also that language itself "speaks." It "speaks" insofar as it says something to us, points something out to us, shows us something. To be sure, its "speaking" originated once in a saying that was first spoken by man but until now remained undiscussed, a saying in which the fundamental difference, which seems to constitute the very essence of language, was enacted. And yet language itself, too, speaks, insofar as it points out and shows, insofar as it, penetrating all the domains of what can come-to-presence, lets what is already present manifest itself or hide itself. We must listen to language and let its saying speak itself out to us. This willingness to let language speak itself out to us precedes all other hearing and listening. In our own speaking we "say after" what somehow we have heard before. We let "the soundless voice" of language come over us and evoke the sound that is still locked up in us.

We must thus allow language to speak itself out to us; that presupposes that our own mode of Being is already open to its saying. We hear the "speaking" of a language only to the extent that we belong within the domain which it discloses for us in its "speaking." And since that is true for all languages, we may say thus that only to those who "belong" to language does language grant the possibility of listening to it and, therefore, the possibility of speaking. This granting, which goes on continuously in every act of man's speaking, is what ultimately lets us attain the possibility of speaking. As Heidegger sees it, the essence of language is to be found in the granting of this primordial saying.[59]

"To say" means "to point out, to show, to let appear, to offer, to hand over." That which is shown and handed over by language's saying is, in the final analysis, the world. Language's saying frees the world, and it does so in a manner which is intrinsically both finite and temporal. That is what we must now try to explain.[60]

In the lecture, Heidegger uses Trakl's poem to elucidate the way language lets the world be. In his view, the first stanza of the poem calls forth things; the second bids the world to come. The third stanza calls the difference of world and things, without, however, specifically thinking it. For our purposes, as we have said already, it is not necessary to follow Heidegger's interpretation in every detail. Instead let us focus only on what in his opinion all of that can tell us about the essence of language in general and about the difference brought about by language's saying in particular.[61]

EIN WINTERABEND	A WINTER EVENING
Wenn der Schnee ans Fenster fällt,	Window with falling snow is arrayed,
Lang die Abendglocke läutet,	Long tolls the vesper bell,
Vielen ist der Tisch bereite	The house is provided well,
Und das Haus ist wohlbestellt.	The table is for many laid.
Mancher auf der Wanderschaft	Wandering ones, more than a few,
Kommt ans Tor auf dunklen Pfaden.	Come to the door on darksome courses.
Golden blüht der Baum der Gnaden	Golden blooms the tree of graces
Aus der Erde kühlem Saft.	Drawing up the earth's cool dew.
Wanderer tritt still herein;	Wanderer quietly steps within;
Schmertz versteinerte die Schwelle.	Pain has turned the threshold to stone.
Da erglänzt in reiner Helle	There lie, in limpid brightness shown,
Auf dem Tische Brot und Wein.	Upon the table bread and wine.
(G. Trakl)	(trans. A. Hofstadter)

According to Heidegger, language bids things to come, not to be present among things present already but rather to come to a presence that is sheltered in absence. Language invites things to come so that they may bear upon men as things. The things which language calls and names gather to themselves heaven and earth, mortals and gods. Since time immemorial these four are united in being primally toward one another; they constitute the original fourfold. Thus the things called by language let the fourfold dwell among men. This gathering and assembling letting-dwell Heidegger calls *das Dingen der Dinge*,[62] "the begging of the things." Now the unitary fourfold of heaven and earth, mortals and gods, which is so made to dwell by the "begging" of the things, is called the world. When things are named, they are called into their "begging" as things, through which they unfold the world in which they themselves can then dwell and abide. Doing what as things they are supposed to do, namely, "begging," they can bear the world *(bern, bären, gebären, gebärden)*.[63]

Thus in Heidegger's view, the first stanza of Trakl's poem invites things to come and to "act as things." It calls things to come here and commands them to the world out of which they appear. The first stanza thus names really both things and world. The second stanza first calls the mortals in order then in the last two verses to name the earth. But since earth relates to heaven and mortals to gods, the second stanza really calls the world, the fourfold. World no longer has a metaphysical meaning here. It does not mean nature or the unity of nature and history; nor does it mean the creation (theological meaning). Finally, it does not mean, either, the totality of all things that are present *(kosmos)*.[64]

Just as the calling which names things calls them hither and thither, so also the saying that names the world calls in itself hither and thither. It entrusts world to things, and, at the same time, it keeps the things in the splendor of the world. The world grants to things their presence. World grants things, and things bear world.[65]

The first stanza bids things to come to world; the second calls world to things. The two modes of bidding are different, and yet they are also closely related to each other. For world and things penetrate one another. And in so doing they traverse a middle in which they are one. Yet world and things are not fused in this middle; in their mutual closeness *(Innigkeit)* they remain cleanly separated. Thus in the midst of the two, in the "between" of world and things, division prevails; Heidegger calls this division the dif-ference *(Unter-Schied)*. In this dif-ference, the closeness and intimacy of the things and the world are present. What is called here the dif-ference is a single and unitary phenomenon, so that the word *dif-ference* cannot be taken here as a generic concept. The dif-ference is unique; it holds apart the middle in and through which world and things are at one with each other. The dif-ference carries world toward things and things toward world. The dif-ference is not some third "thing" which after the fact, so to speak, must be added to world and things. Being the middle, the dif-ference determines world and things in their presence, in their being toward one another. The dif-ference is not a distinction between two objects which has been established by our proposing presentation; nor is it just a relation between world and things which actually happens to hold between them and, thus, by our proposing presentation can be so established. Rather, the dif-ference discloses world and things by appropriating things such that they bear a world and by appropriating world such that it grants things.[66] The dif-ference measures out and apportions world and things by bringing each to its own *(Moira)*. It opens up both the separateness and the towardness of world and things. The dif-ference, as the middle for world and things, metes out the measures of their abiding mode of Being *(Wesen)*.

The first stanza bids the things to come and to bear a world; the second bids the world to come and to grant things; the third stanza bids the middle for world and things to come and bids them to come into the stillness. The poem's last stanza calls the dif-ference, but it does not think it; nor does it call its essence by its name. Rather, it calls the *separation* of the gathering middle of the "between," in whose closeness and intimacy the things' bearing and the world's granting pervade each other.[67]

The third stanza gathers the bidding of things and the bidding of world together. In so doing it calls the dif-ference, but as we said it leaves it unspoken. The primal calling which first bids the intimacy of world and things is the authentic hailing. This hailing or bidding is the essence of speaking. The speaking that occurs in what is spoken in the poem is the speaking *of* language. Thus language indeed speaks. It speaks by hailing the bidden thing-world and the bidden world-thing to come to the between of the dif-ference. What is so hailed is commanded to arrive from out of the dif-ference into the dif-ference. The dif-ference lets the "begging" of the things rest in the "governing" of the world.[68] In this way the dif-ference ex-propriates the things into the rest of the fourfold. This expropriation does not take anything away from the things. It only frees each thing into its own; i.e., it frees it in such a way that it now can stay the world. To shelter something into repose is to "still" it. Thus the dif-ference stills the things as things into the world. It even stills in a twofold manner: it lets things rest in the "favor" of the world, and it lets the world "content" itself with the things. In this double stilling of the dif-ference *stillness* comes-to-pass.[69]

Richardson explains that what is hailed in the coming-to-pass of *logos* as language is the correlation of Being and beings in the form of world and things. World and things are hailed unto the unifying dif-ference of the issuance *(Austrag)* prevailing between them.[70] That would not be very complicated if it were not for the fact that a few pages later[71] Heidegger explicitly states that the dif-ference is also that which hails. But how can the same issuance be at the same time both hailing and hailed? Richardson suggests the following solution: Difference means differentiation, and that implies both differentiating and differentiated. The differentiation as it were begins with the moment of differentiating and as it were comes to rest in the moment when the differentiated issue forth as such. Heidegger conceives of the differentiating as a unity, whereas the differentiated are seen as necessarily two. The whole process of issuance consists in the tension and the mutual adhesion between this unity and duality, which is the dif-ference as such. Insofar as it is a unity, it is difference-as-hailing; insofar as it is a duality, it is a difference-as-hailed. "The [unifying] difference gathers together the two [differentiated] out of itself, insofar as it hails them into the dif-ference which it itself is. . . ."[72]

Furthermore, we should note also that Heidegger here states that language in its ultimate origin is the coming-to-pass of the ontological difference out of Being as *logos*. Languages comes-to-presence as the difference which takes place between world and things.[73] Thus the hailing of the dif-ference is not anything human. On the contrary, the human has been brought into its own by language; it comes-to-pass out of the speaking of language. Yet this appropriation comes-to-pass only insofar as the essence of language needs the speaking of mortal men. Richardson interprets this thesis to mean that

> the differentiat*ing* cannot give issue to the differentiat*ed* except in, through and for that being whose nature it is to be open unto *logos*-as-scission. The dynamic tension between differentiat*ing* and differentiat*ed* would be what constitutes the need for man which hails him to be himself. The ek-static open-ness to the aboriginal *logos* is the emerging of human language, which therefore does not have human activity alone as its source but rather ". . . reposes in [man's] relationship to language in its origin."[74]

Thus man's speaking is indeed also a hailing that names; it too is a calling which, out of the simple onefold of the dif-ference, bids things and world to come. But even in his most authentic speaking, and precisely then, is man's speaking really a response to the command by which the stillness of the dif-ference calls world and things into the issuance of its simple onefold. Mortals speak only authentically insofar as they listen to the hailing call of the stillness of the dif-ference.[75] Man uses language authentically when he freely responds to the hail addressed to him when the dif-ference comes-to-pass, when the differentiating shows its need of man in order that it may issue forth the differentiated, namely, world and things. When man responds authentically, he gives voice to the differentiated, to Being versus beings. This response implies attending and docility. In his response, man must remain unobtrusive without being totally passive; he must advance to the hail of the dif-ference, but he must do so with reticence.[76]

In his later reflections on language, Heidegger thus understands the ontological difference to mean that "process" in which Being (taken as equiprimordially comprising truth as the process of unveiling, world as the total-meaningfulness, and language as the aboriginal saying) and beings (taken as concrete beings or as the totality of all beings) become differentiated as world and things. This process comes about primarily in thought, but it is equally to be taken as coming-to-pass in language. It is to be noted that thought is equiprimordially the thought *of* Being and the thought *of* man, even though Being occupies the privileged position in this process; correspondingly, the speaking is equally the saying of language and the responding speaking of man. Thus it is understood that the thought *of* Being is found nowhere but in Being's language as it is listened to by man.

Now, in view of the fact that Being sends itself in different epochs in different ways and, thus, the original saying of the language of Being addresses man in each epoch in a different way, it should be added that in a given epoch of Being's sending, the ontological difference comes-to-pass effectively in all realms of meaning characteristic of that epoch (man's concerned dealing with things, science, technology, art, social practice, religion, etc.). All of these realms of meaning or worlds, which respond to different forms of man's experience, are articulated in the various "languages" which people use in that epoch. The expression "the aboriginal saying of the language of Being" refers to *the whole of meaning* that so comes to light in that epoch. That is to say, it refers not only to the meaning found in an explicitly articulated form characteristic of the various concrete "languages" but also (and even predominantly) to the meaning which shows itself in the way these people live, concernedly deal with things, care for one another, actively involve themselves in science and technology, bring about works of art, and dedicate themselves to God. It is in this "saying," which thus comprises all of these activities, that the totality of meaning as such, i.e., Being, partly shows and partly hides itself.

> Thought receives the materials and tools for this self-vibrating structure from language. For language is the most delicate, but also the most susceptible, all-encompassing vibration in the vibrating structure of the appropriation. We dwell in the appropriation inasmuch as our Being is given over to the appropriating event.[77]

Article III: The Essence of Language: The Language of Being

We must now finally turn to the question of why Heidegger believes that the essence of language is adequately specified by saying that it is the language of Being. To that end, we shall briefly paraphrase an essay entitled *Das Wesen der Sprache*. The essay contains the text of three lectures which Heidegger delivered in the studium generale of the University of Freiburg on 4 and 18 December 1957 and on 7 February 1958. At the beginning of the second lecture, Heidegger directly turns to his audience, which for the most part appears to consist of science majors, not philosophy majors. We may thus expect that he tried to be as clear as possible.[78]

Heidegger begins this series of lectures by stating that the aim of the three lectures is to bring us face to face with the possibility of having an experience with language.[79] The first lecture tries to give ear to a poetic experience with language; in so doing, it moves within the neighborhood of thinking and poetizing. The second lecture reflects on the way of this movement and tries to differentiate way and method. Finally, the third lecture attempts to enable us actually to have an experience with language.[80]

Heidegger then briefly explains what he means by having an experience with something *(mit einer Sache eine Erfahrung machen)*.[81] In his view, we have an experience with a thing when that thing befalls us, strikes us, comes over us, overwhelms us, and transforms us. An experience is not of one's own making; one submits to it, receives it as it strikes him, endures it when it comes-to-pass. Heidegger wishes to make that possible here with respect to language.

Now, if man finds the proper abode of his Being in language, then a genuine experience with language will obviously touch the very core of his Being; it may very well be the case that he will be transformed by this experience.

For we who live in the twentieth century, it may be very difficult to have a genuine experience with language, even if that experience were to strike us only to the extent that for once it would merely draw our attention to our relation to language, and to urge us from now on to keep this relation in mind. Suppose someone were to ask us: "In what relation do you live to the language you speak?" Probably we would answer by saying that that is a simple question: we speak it. Although that is obviously true, this answer is nonetheless inadequate, in that it leaves our relation to language vague, obscure, and almost speechless.[82] Furthermore, to undergo an experience with language is something else than to gather information about language. That is done today in the various sciences which concern themselves with language (linguistics, philology, psychology, etc.) but also in the so-called philosophy of language and in metalinguistics.[83] Although these investigations have their own justification and remain important, it is nonetheless true also that trying to have an experience with language is something quite different from gathering scientific or "philosophic" information about language.[84]

We must now ask the question of what way will bring us then to the point where we shall be able to have an experience with language. Such a way has long existed, but it was seldom used to lead people to articulate the experience with language which they can have because of it. In the experience which we undergo with language, we usually immediately focus on the thing, the event, the issue, or the question, but not on language's speaking, or on language itself. In our everyday speaking, we encounter language's speaking when we cannot find the right word for something that happens to concern us. Then we leave unspoken what we have in mind and undergo moments in which language itself fleetingly touches us with its own essence.

When one tries to put into language something which has never yet been said, everything depends on whether language itself gives or withholds the proper words. One of the cases in which language may give the proper words is that of the poet. A poet may come to the point where he feels compelled poetically to put into language the experience he underwent with language. A good example is Stefan George's poem "The Word." The last verse of the last stanza of this poem reads: "Where word breaks off no thing may be." In this line, language says something about the relation between word and thing; no thing can be where the proper word is lacking.[85]

DAS WORT	THE WORD
Wunder von ferne oder traum	Wonder or dream from distant land
Bracht ich an meines landes saum	I carried to my country's strand
Und harrte bis die graue norn	And waited till the twilit norn
Den namen fand in ihrem born—	Had found the name within her bourn—
Drauf konnt ichs greifen dicht und stark	Then I could grasp it close and strong
Nun blüht und glänzt es durch die mark . . .	It blooms and shines now the front along . . .
Einst langt ich an nach guter fahrt	Once I returned from happy sail,
Mit einem kleinod reich und zart	I had a prize so rich and frail,
Sie suchte lang und gab mir kund:	She sought for long and tidings told:
"So schläft hier nichts auf tiefem grund"	"No like of this these depths enfold."
Worauf es meiner hand entrann	And straight it vanished from my hand,
Und nie mein land den schatz gewann . . .	The treasure never graced my land . . .
So lernt ich traurig den verzicht:	So I renounced and sadly see:
Kein ding sei wo das wort gebricht.	Where word breaks off no thing may be.
(Stefan George)	(trans. Peter D. Hertz)

George uses the words *name* and *word* not in the sense of a sign, marker, token, or signal. Rather, he uses these words very thoughtfully. Also, the word *thing* is used here thoughtfully for everything that is, including God. Only where the word for a thing is found is the thing truly a thing. George seems to claim that the word alone gives Being to a thing.

Yet one should realize here that George is not a thinker but a poet; furthermore, Heidegger quotes the poem to prepare us for having an experience with language. Thus let us not hurriedly jump to unwarranted conclusions when it comes to the point of establishing a relation between thing and word.[86] Yet on the other hand, poetizing and thinking must be closely related to one another. What the poet comes to know from his experience with language is that he has learned that only the word makes a thing appear as the thing it is and thus lets it be present. The word presents itself to the poet as that which holds and sustains a thing in its Being.[87] Before he had this experience, the poet stood in a quite different relation to language and word. This relationship is described in the first part of the poem.[88]

Heidegger points out that *erfahren* means "to go along a way," *eundo assequi* "to obtain or reach something by means of a way."[89] The poet had originally assumed that he could bring the wonders that enthrall him and also the dreams that enrapture him to the wellspring of language; in language there are already all the words one needs to name the things. All things are already there standing within Being; the poet merely has to present them by naming them. One day, however, he experiences that poetic things are not, as long as they have not yet been named.[90]

Heidegger wonders whether we are here not thinking things into the poem. In his view, the greatest danger is rather that we think too little into a poem. He also explicitly rejects the idea that a true experience with language can be only a thinking experience. He warns us that the lofty poetry of all great poetic works vibrates within the realm of thinking. Furthermore, one should not forget that thinking obviously goes its own way in the neighborhood of genuine poetry.[91]

Poetizing and thinking need each other, and the one needs the other in its own neighborhood. This neighborhood has its domain in a region which poetizing and thinking define in a different way, although they find themselves always within the same domain. One will understand these claims only if one understands thinking not as calculating ratiocination or a means to gain knowledge but rather as that which cuts furrows in the soil of Being.[92]

We are engaged at the moment in reflections on "the essence of language." It is important to note that it is not at all clear how the word *essence* is to be understood here. Furthermore, anyone who asks questions about the essence of language assumes that he already has some pre-understanding of what language and essence are supposed to mean: That means that both language and essence must already have been granted to us; every posing of a question takes place within the granting address of what is put into question in it. Finally, we should note that the most authentic attitude of thinking is not posing questions but rather listening to the granting address. It is true that in the tradition, thinking has been defined in relation to asking questions; that which thinking asks questions about here is the root of all that is, the *radix*, the first and ultimate ground *(Grund)*, and the latter has always been taken to be the essence, or better *das Wesende des Wesens*. At any rate, a thinking that tries to think in this manner is basically a form of questioning. In this sense, it was said in another essay that questioning is the *Frömmigkeit* of thinking. The word *Frömmigkeit* is related to the adjective *fromm*, and the latter is to be taken here in the original sense of *fügsam*. Questioning thus is the acquiescing suppleness which accommodates itself to what is to be thought.[93]

Be that as it may, it will be clear by now that before one can ask questions about language and about its essence, it is necessary first that language itself addresses itself to him and that he submit to its saying. If and when that happens, the essence of language becomes the address of language's own Being; thus the essence of language then becomes the language of Being. The title of the series of lectures can now be reformulated to read as follows: the mode of Being of language—the language of Being itself. But it is no longer a title; nor is it an answer; rather, it becomes our guideline on our way toward language.

We have learned already from our interpretation of the closing line of George's poem that "Where word breaks off no thing may be" refers to the relation between word and thing in such a way that the word itself *is* this relation which holds everything forth into Being. If the word did not have this meaning, the whole of things, the "world," would sink into the dark, including the "I" mentioned in the poem.[94]

We are attempting here to have an experience with language. To undergo an experience with something means to reach and attain it by going on the way. It should be clear that what is meant here by way cannot be identified with what the modern sciences call method. Method, taken in the sense which it has in modern science, is not a mere instrument which serves the sciences; rather, method is that which modern science serves.[95] Nietzsche was perhaps the first to realize that when in 1888 he wrote that what distinguishes the nineteenth century is not so much the victory of science but the victory of the scientific method over science. In modern science, the method not only calls forth and determines the themes to be investigated, it also keeps and maintains them within its own framework by subordinating them to itself. Today the entire power of knowledge lies in method, so that even the themes to be investigated belong within method. In thought this situation is completely different, because here there is neither method nor theme; here we find only the region which, as we have seen already, gives its free reign to what thinking has been given to think. Thinking abides in this region and merely walks the ways of this region. Heidegger notes here that he is aware that from the perspective of the sciences it is not just difficult, but even impossible, to understand this situation.

We try to speak about language and realize that what we are speaking about, namely, language, is itself always already ahead of us. Our speaking tries to follow language, but we continually remain lagging behind what we try to "capture." Thus when we speak about language, we remain entangled in a form of speaking which is persistently inadequate. This tangle dissolves the moment we pay attention to the peculiar properties of the *way* of thought and look around us in the region where thinking abides. And this region is everywhere open to the neighborhood of poetizing.[96]

We try to prepare ourselves for an experience with language. We have seen that to think first of all means to listen, not to ask questions but to let ourselves be told something. Thus if we are to reflect on the essence of language, language must first have addressed itself to us. In its own way, language must address itself to us; it must speak to us its own "essence." Language abides among us as this address. We hear it constantly; but we do not give it thought. Yet if we did not listen to it everywhere, we could not even speak one word. Language abides among us as the promising address, and its "essence" makes itself known to us as saying *(Spruch)*, as the language of its own Being. But we cannot yet quite hear this primal message *(Kunde)*, let alone "read" it. This primal message runs: the essence of language—the language of Being.[97]

If we try to get at least some idea of this message by turning to poets who have tried to poetize it, we find that poets such as Hölderlin and George have come to the conclusion that their own experience with the word also passes constantly into darkness and somehow remains veiled. We come to the same insight if we turn to thought. The relation between thing and word was among the earliest themes which Western thought attempted to bring into language, and it has tried to do so in the form of the relation between Being and saying *(Sagen)*. As we have seen, this relation overpowered thinking in such a way that it announced itself in one single word: *logos*. This word speaks simultaneously as the name for

Being and for saying. Thus neither in the poetizing of the poets nor in the thinking of the thinkers did language itself come to word as such. Neither the poetic experience nor the thinking experience with its saying brings into language language itself in its own Being.[98]

These reflections try to bring us to the point where, in the neighborhood of the poetic experience, we can have a meaningful experience with language. The final reason is that both poetizing and thinking move in the element (neighborhood) of language's saying; he who reflects on poetry finds himself always in that element in which also thinking moves, and that is the saying of language.[99] Also, both poetizing and thinking, moving within the element of the saying of language, owe their own saying to manifold experiences with language which usually remain unnoticed. As a matter of fact, what has been discussed here is very difficult to understand by a thinking which is dominated by calculation. Even when we start to think, listen to the poets, and thus stay in the neighborhood of poetry and thinking, we still do not yet really experience the neighborhood as such. We are on our way to it only if we turn back to where in reality we are already (hermeneutic circle). This turning back is very difficult to accomplish, and yet to turn back to where we are staying already is how we must walk along the way of thinking.[100]

Heidegger now returns to George's poem and points out that if there is no thing where the word is lacking, and if there is the thing where there is the word, then the word must itself be a thing. On the other hand, if the word speaking as a word were not to be a thing, then it would have to be a no-thing, a nothing. George suggests that word and thing are different; this notion entails that the word, which is supposed not to be a thing, not to be anything-that-is, keeps escaping us.[101] It also implies that within the domain of language, at the place where destiny provides the language that names, there is no word for the word. Our common conception rebels against this view: words are; we have names for them; they are like things; we put them in the dictionary. But all of that is so only because the dictionary can neither grasp nor keep the word by which terms become words, speak as words. Thus we must again ask the question of where the word and the saying *really* belong.[102]

The poetic experience with the word gives us nonetheless a clear hint: the word—no thing, not a being, nothing. When a word is available for things, we have an understanding of things; then and only then the thing *is*. The "is" too is not a thing; it is like the word. But it, too, cannot be cast out into the void of nothingness. The poetic experience with the word thus points to something that is very thought-provoking; it is that with which thinking has been charged from the beginning.[103]

The essence of the word conceals within itself something that "gives"

Being. We cannot simply say that the word as such "is," but in German one can meaningfully say *Es gibt das Wort*, literally translated "It gives the word." Heidegger interprets this expression to mean that the word gives itself and in so doing also gives Being: by virtue of the gift of the word, there is. . . . The situation which at the same time is simple and ungraspable, and which is called forth by the sentence, "The word gives . . ," reveals itself here as that which is properly worthy of thought. The poet has had some knowledge of this phenomenon, but his poetry has learned renunciation. Thinking tries to come to a better understanding of that. Yet something completely different is said in the poem in a completely different way, and yet the same is said as has been thought earlier concerning the relation between "is" and the word that is no thing.[104] Thus the neighborhood of poetizing and thinking is concealed within the farthest divergence of their saying.[105]

Heidegger then briefly recapitulates the two preceding lectures. The lectures as a whole make their way within the neighborhood of poetizing and thinking; in this manner we are on the way to the possibility of undergoing an experience with language. The first lecture listens to a poetic experience with the word and ponders its implications for thinking. The second lecture reflects on the way of this movement but tries to stay away from what is commonly called method and methodology. For thinking, the way rather belongs in what we could call the region, i.e., that which encounters us as the clearing that gives free, and where all that is cleared and all that conceals itself together attain the open freedom. To genuine thinking, the way is that which lets us reach out to that which reaches out for us by touching us. The way as understood here is somehow related to what Laotse called *Tao*.[106]

The third lecture must now try to bring us to the point where we indeed can have an experience with language. What is necessary now is that we stay in the neighborhood of poetizing and thinking. The way that is to lead us to this possibility is one that leads us only to where we are already; the way allows us to reach what truly concerns us in the domain in which we are already staying. We nonetheless still need a way, because we have not yet properly reached what concerns our Being.[107]

The way leads us to the region in which poetizing and thinking are neighbors. To be neighbors here means to dwell in nearness. Both are modes of saying *(Sagens)*. "To say" originally meant "to show, to make appear, to make free, to offer." What is offered here is the world which the saying shows by revealing and concealing it. The lighting and hiding offering of the world is the essence of language's saying. That is why we have chosen as our guide word: the essence of language—the language of Being.

In the phrase preceding the dash, language appears as the subject whose essence is to be determined; essence responds here to the *to ti estin*, the what a thing truly is. Thus the phrase says: You shall know and understand what language truly is as soon as you understand what the dash opens up for you. That says: the language *of* Being. The genitive here is a subjective one; thus the phrase says that Being possesses language. Furthermore, Being now means no longer "essence" but "to last, abide, endure, persist in its coming-to-presence." Being so conceived names what persists and abides, names what concerns us in all things, because it makes a way *(bewegen)* for all things. And it makes such a way because it, too, speaks. But it is not yet clear precisely how we have to think Being here and what is meant by speaking. That is the crux of our reflection on the essence of language. But our reflection itself is already on the way; and this way is within the neighborhood of poetizing and thinking. Our guide word gives us a hint about this way; it is by no means already an answer. To be neighbors means to dwell in nearness; poetizing and thinking are furthermore preeminent modes of saying. If these two modes of saying are to be neighbors in virtue of their nearness, then nearness and saying seem to be the same. If we can understand that, we may have reached the point where we may have an experience with language.[108] Note that Heidegger here explicitly adds: an experience with language, i.e., "*the language known to us.*"[109]

Be that as it may, we have seen that what concerns us as language receives its determination from the saying as that which makes ways for everything. The guide word beckons us away from the current conceptions about language in the direction of an experience with language as saying. We are convinced that we are so familiar with language that it is very difficult to take distance from these common conceptions. Furthermore, the common conceptions of language are rich "in truth." These common conceptions about language go back to Aristotle, who in *De Interpretatione* wrote that letters are signs of sounds, sounds are signs of thoughts or concepts, and the latter are signs of things. Thus, the sign relation constitutes the skeleton of the language structure. Later the term *sign* was taken in a manner which is different from the one originally intended by Aristotle; yet, however one interprets the sign here, it is and remains true that language is presented here in terms of sounds. This conception of language is important, yet it does not lead to what is the very essence of language.[110] Using some verses of Hölderlin, Heidegger focuses then on the idea that the saying of language structures the region as world, the world of heaven and earth, of mortals and gods. In the saying of language it comes-to-pass that world is made to appear. Language's saying attunes the dimensions of the world's structure and plays them in chorus.

All of that at first sounds very strange. Yet it points to simple phenomena which we can learn to see by heeding the way in which we are always on the way within the neighborhood of the various modes of saying, of which poetizing and thinking are preeminent. Neighborhood does not bring about nearness; rather, nearness brings about neighborhood. Thus, we must now ask: But what then is nearness?[111]

To answer this question would lead us toward a long path of thought, of which we can unfold here only a few steps. These steps do not lead forward, but rather they point backward to where we are already. Furthermore, they do not follow a certain order but rather constantly focus on the same thing.

What is meant by nearness is known to us in our everyday life. It is known also, and even with much greater precision, by modern science, including relativity theory and quantum mechanics. In all cases, space and time appear as that by means of which we measure distance, remoteness and nearness, and in all cases space and time appear as parameters. In this conception of nearness, what we mean here by nearness and neighborhood can never be *experienced*. We do not deny that some spatio-temporal relatedness belongs to every neighborhood and nearness; yet genuine nearness does not depend on spatio-temporal relations. Nearness as such is by its nature independent of space and time taken as parameters. People living next to one another need not relate to one another, be near to one another. People who are near to one another prefer to encounter one another face to face. Being face to face with one another originates in the original distance where heaven and earth, mortals and gods reach one another. Thus, if we are fully to understand what is meant here by nearness (*Nähe*), we must first rid ourselves of our calculative way of thinking. We can then focus on the making of the ways (*Bewegen*) which is at the heart of the world's four regions; it is there that we can experience the face-to-face (*das Gegen-einander-über*) of things with one another. This *Bewegen*, which makes things reach one another and holds them in the nearness of their distance, is nearness itself, and that paves the way for being face to face with one another. The nearness in regard to this making-ways is called nighness (*Nahnis*), a word which is formed in the same manner as like-ness, wilder-ness, etc. This aboriginal nearness cannot be approached further, and space and time as parameters cannot bring it closer to us or measure it.[112]

The essence of nearness as nighness is not lack of distance but the making of ways which pave the road for the face-to-face of the four regions of the world. Neither Aristotle's conception of time nor the "classical" conception of space can bring us closer to the essence of nearness, because both precisely exclude the possibility of a face-to-face encounter of their elements. That is the reason we could say that the simple relations implied in original nearness remain totally inaccessible to calculative thinking.[113]

In addition to our scientific conception of space and time, there is thus a more primordial one. Of these, Heidegger says that *Zeit zeitigt* and *Raum räumt* ("Time temporalizes" and "Space makes-space-for"). He admits that such a way of speaking is offensive from the perspective of our ordinary way of speaking. Yet we can learn to understand and appreciate them if we are able to come to a thinking experience of what is called *identity*.[114]

Time temporalizes, *zeitigt*. The German word *zeitigen* means "to make ripe, to make rise up, to call forth," but also "to mature" or "to effect" and "to produce." That which is so called-forth *(das Zeitige)* is that which rising has come up. But what is it that time temporalizes? It is what is together-at-the-same-time, that which is at-the-same-time *(das Gleich-Zeitige)*. And what is that? We have known it for a long time but have not yet thought it from the perspective of the temporalization of time. That which of time itself is at-the-same-time *(das Gleich-Zeitige der Zeit)* is the unity of past as having-been-ness, presence *(Anwesenheit)*, and that which one is waiting for *(Gegen-Wart)*, i.e., that which itself is waiting for our encounter and what we usually call the future. By temporalizing, time enraptures us *(entrückt uns)* into what is present-at-the-same-time and brings toward us the oneness of the has-been, the present, and the present-that-waits-for (future). In enrapturing us by bringing this oneness toward us *(ekstases)*, time begins to make ways in that which what-is-at-the-same-time grants to it, namely, the time-space *(Zeit-Raum)*. Yet time itself, taken in the wholeness of its essence, does not move; it rests in stillness.[115]

The same must now be said about space. It makes room for structured spaces and individual places; it makes them free and contains them; and it receives what-is-at-the-same-time as space-time *(Raum-Zeit)*. And space, too, taken in the wholeness of its essence, does not move; it, too, rests in stillness. Time's enrapturing and space's opening-up and receiving belong together in the same, in the play of stillness *(das Spiel der Stille)*. That which holds time and space together in their Being *(Wesen)* may be called the scope of time-space *(Zeit-Spiel-Raum)*, the "spatio-temporal" domain which gives free scope to things and events. This "spatio-temporal" domain makes ways for the face-to-face relations between the four regions of the world, heaven and earth, gods and mortals. That we may now call the world-play *(das Weltspiel)*.

The "process" which makes ways for the face-to-face relations of the four regions of the world lets nearness take place; it even *is* nearness, taken as nighness *(Nahnis)*. Perhaps one could call this "process" the appropriating event which lets stillness be.[116]

All of that can indeed help us have an experience with language. For we have seen that "to say" means "to show, to make appear"; it means to offer us the world in a revealing and concealing manner. Furthermore, we have also just seen that nearness manifests itself as that which makes ways in the "spatio-temporal" domain, so that the world's regions can face one another as the fourfold. We can now perhaps understand that and how the saying, as the essence of language, swings back into the essence of nearness. Careful reflection shows how nearness and the saying, taken as the Being of language, are really the same. But then language is obviously no longer a mere human "faculty" or ability. Its Being belongs to what is most proper to that which makes ways in the scope of the time-space, and which lets the four world regions face one another.

Thus language, taken as the saying of the world's fourfold, is no longer merely a "thing" to which speaking humans can have a relation such that this relationship would exist *between* man and language. Language, taken as the saying which makes ways in the world, is rather the relation of all relations. It relates, sustains, offers, and enriches the face-to-face encounter of the four regions of the world; it holds and keeps them, while it itself holds itself back in reserve. Reserving itself in this manner, language (as the saying of the world's fourfold) concerns us mortals who belong within the fourfold of the world and who can truly speak only as we respond to language.[117]

If that which makes ways in the world and, thus, holds the world's four regions in the single nearness of their face-to-face encounter, rests in the saying of language, then only this saying confers what we name with the tiny word *is*. The saying grants the "is" and releases it into the open that has been cleared. Once it has been so released, we mortals can repeat it after the aboriginal saying of language itself.[118]

CHAPTER 8

On Art and Art Works

In 1935, the year in which Heidegger delivered the lecture course *An Introduction to Metaphysics*, he presented a lecture in Freiburg on the work of art. Later he developed this lecture into three lectures; it finally appeared in the latter form in *Holzwege* in 1950.[1] As far as I know, that was the first time that Heidegger focused systematically on art works as such; the reflections on the history of aesthetics found in the *Nietzsche* volumes were part of a lecture course delivered later, in 1936–1937.[2] In 1935 Heidegger also gave a lecture in Rome, "Hölderlin and the Essence of Poetry," which later (with other essays on poems of Hölderlin) was to appear in *Hölderlin und das Wesen der Dichtung*.[3] The essence of poetry is also discussed in several other later works of Heidegger, notably in *On the Way to Language*.[4] In these latter essays and lectures, the stress is not directly on the Being of the work of art but rather on the essence of poetizing. I shall return to this issue in the next chapter.

In its present form, the essay "The Origin of the Work of Art" contains a brief introduction, in which Heidegger explains in what sense art is the origin of both the artist and the work of art; three major sections ("Thing and Work," "The Work and Truth," "Truth and Art"); a brief epilogue, in which Heidegger relates his own thoughts to modern aesthetics; and finally the significant *Addendum* of 1956, in which important clarifications are added and an attempt is made to prevent misconceptions from occurring.

In my commentary, I shall begin with the ideas developed in the epilogue; then I shall turn to the content of the three lectures, starting with the introduction. The observations made in the *Addendum* will be incorporated in the sections of the lectures to which they pertain.[5]

II. THE EPILOGUE (BY WAY OF INTRODUCTION)

In the epilogue,[6] about which Heidegger says only that in part it was written later than 1936, he first states that the reflections on the origin of the art work are concerned with the riddle that art itself is. It does not solve the riddle; it only makes an effort to begin to see the riddle.[7]

Specialized thinking about art and the artist is of relatively late origin, and so is the name for this kind of thinking, namely, *aesthetics.* Aesthetics treats the art work as an object, as the object of *aisthēsis,* of sensuous apprehension in the wide sense. Most people today call this apprehension experience. Aesthetics claims that the manner in which man experiences art gives us information about the essence of art. Experience is understood here as the source and the standard not only for the appreciation of art but also for the making of art. Heidegger suggests that it perhaps may be the case that experience as understood here is the element in which art really dies. The dying of art occurred so slowly that it has taken a few centuries. To be sure, people often speak today about important art works, and most are convinced that art is of eternal value. Yet these claims are very vague and suggest that today people are afraid of thinking. These half-baked clichés about immortal works and eternal value belong to an age in which great art, together with its essence, has departed from among us.[8]

Heidegger then quotes a few passages from Hegel's *Lectures on Aesthetics,* in which it is stated that art no longer counts for us as the highest manner in which truth obtains actuality for itself, that the form of art has ceased to be the highest need of the Spirit even though art may very well continue to perfect itself, and that with respect to its highest vocation, art is something past.[9] Heidegger explains that Hegel does not claim here that there will be no great works of art or no great movements in art; rather, he claims that from now on art no longer is a necessary and essential way in which the truth which is decisive for our historical Being comes-to-pass. It is this claim that the present series of lectures wishes to discuss.

But, Heidegger continues, this issue can be treated only after we have first considered the essence of art. We shall attempt a few steps in that direction by asking the question concerning the origin of the work of art. In so doing, it is essential that we stress the work-character of the work. What is meant here by origin will be unfolded by means of a reflection on the essence of truth.[10]

The truth referred to here does not coincide with what is generally recognized under this name. Usually one relates the true to knowledge and science, in order to distinguish it from the beautiful and the good, which are the names for the correlates of our non-theoretical activities.

Truth is the non-concealment of all that is, taken as such. Above all truth is the truth of Being. Beauty is not found alongside and apart from this truth. When truth is at work in the work, it appears; this appearance, taken as the Being of truth in the work, is beauty. The beautiful thus belongs to the coming-to-pass of the truth. Beauty is not merely relative to pleasure; it certainly is not actual purely as its object. It is perhaps not incorrect to say that the beautiful lies in form, but then one should realize that *forma* once took its light from Being as the "is-ness" of what is. In other words, one should realize then that Being first came to be as *eidos;* then *idea* fitted itself into *morphē;* then the unitary whole of *morphē* and *hylē,* i.e., the *ergon,* began to be as *energeia. Energeia* then became the *actualitas* of the *ens actu.* Then *actualitas* became *realitas,* reality; and reality became objectivity. Finally, objectivity became experience. In the manner in which in the Western world beings are related to what is real, a peculiar connection is concealed between beauty and truth: the history of Western art corresponds to a change in the conception of the essence of truth. But that means that art cannot really be understood in terms of either beauty or experience.[11]

Two observations are in order here. First, Heidegger objects mainly to an empiricist approach to aesthetic phenomena; and what he says about experience is addressed to the empiricist conception of experience, some traces of which, however, are still found in Kant. Heidegger himself uses the term *experience* in connection with works of art, but then he uses the term always in the sense of Hegel.

Secondly, Otto Pöggeler has claimed that the introductory remarks about the riddle that art is imply that Heidegger never developed a genuine philosophy of art; he also states that the *Holzwege* essay stems from Heidegger's "romantic" period (1933–1938), which he later tried to overcome. I do not share these views; I join Friedrich-Wilhelm von Herrmann, who holds that Heidegger, although he never developed a *philosophical aesthetics,* certainly presented us with a *philosophy of art,* thought from the perspective of the question concerning the meaning of Being. Yet I do agree with Jacques Taminiaux that the art lectures are not without inner tension, because of the fact that Heidegger oriented himself in these lectures to a retrieve of Hegel's aesthetics.[12] Let us now turn to the lecture series itself.

III. "THE ORIGIN OF THE WORK OF ART"

The lecture series itself begins with a section in which Heidegger explains that both the art work and the artist have their origin in art. Origin here means the source from which something springs; it is that which makes it possible for a thing to rise up as what it is and how it is; it is that from which and by which something is what it is and as it is. That which something is, as it is, we call its essence. Thus, the origin of something is the source of its essence. The question concerning the origin of the work of art therefore really asks about the source of its essence.

But whence is it that the work of art arises? One is inclined to say that it arises from the artist. Yet the artist himself is an artist only by virtue of the work of art that he produces; artists are those who bring forth works of art. Thus the work is as much the origin of the artist as such as the artist is the origin of the work. Both appear to spring from a source that is more primary than both; that is art itself. But when then is art taken as something that is distinct from the work in which it is found and from the human being who produces it? Can one speak about art "as such" at all? It appears that the only way to find an answer to this question is to examine that being in which art undoubtedly holds sway, and that is the work of art.[13]

The attentive reader will observe here that we are obviously moving in a circle, for it is said that we come to know what the work of art is only from the essence of art, and that what art is should be inferred from the work. The reader may even wish to demand that such a circle be avoided, because it violates the laws of logic. Yet it is not difficult to show that this circle cannot be avoided. In order to be able to distinguish works of art from other things, one must know what art is, whereas what art is can be gathered only from a comparison of art works. Thus we must try to carry out this circle. "This is neither a makeshift nor a defect. To enter upon this path is the strength of thought."[14]

In order to discover the essence of art which prevails in the work, we must thus go to the actual work and ask it what it is and how it is. A first thing we notice in all works of art is their thingly character. That does not mean that art works are just things like all other things; yet it is true that works of art are things. At first sight it seems superfluous to inquire into this self-evident thingly element in the art work, since the art work obviously is something over and above this thingly element. According to philosophical aesthetics, the art work says something more than the mere thing itself *(allo agoreuei);* it manifests something other than itself; it is an allegory. In the work, something other is brought together with the thing that the artist makes. "To bring together" in Greek is *sumballein;* thus the work is a symbol. That explains why for quite some time art works were discussed with the help of the concepts "allegory" and "symbol." Yet it is even then still the case that the one element in the work which manifests another element and joins with it is the thingly feature of the art work.

The thingly element of the art work seems to be some substructure upon which another, authentic, element is built.

Heidegger disagrees with this aesthetic theory. Yet it is still the case that if we are to bring to light the immediate and full Being of the art work, we must first focus on the thingly element of the work, and thus we must ask first precisely what a thing is.[15]

1. "Thing and Work" Our aim here is to come to know the thingness of the thing, the mode of Being characteristic of things. In order to do so, we must first familiarize ourselves with the domain to which all those beings belong which we call things. Heidegger makes a list: stones, lumps of earth, jugs, wells, clouds, thistles, hawks. According to Kant, the whole of the world, even God Himself, is a thing of this sort. Thus, in the language of philosophy both the beings in themselves and the beings that appear, i.e., all beings that in any way are, may be called things.[16]

But if the word *thing* can be used for all these beings, even including things made by man, as well as the so-called "ultimate things," i.e., death and judgment, then the word *thing* appears to designate whatever is not simply nothing. But taken in that sense, it is of no use to us when we try to understand the difference between thing and work. Furthermore, it is not proper to call God a thing; it is not even correct to call humans things. Heidegger even hesitates to call a deer, the beetle in the grass, or the blade of grass a thing. It seems more appropriate to call lifeless beings and objects of use things. "Natural things and utensils are the things commonly so called."[17] At any rate, there is a very wide domain within which everything can be called a thing *(res, ens)*, including even the highest and the last things, and a more restricted domain of "mere" things.[18]

If we limit ourselves to the latter, we can ask meaningfully in what the thingly character of these things then consists. This question has been raised since antiquity, because from the very beginning it was assumed that among all beings, things occupy the privileged position, so that when people began to wonder about the Being of beings, they really began to inquire into the thingness of things. In its long history, philosophy has given different answers to the question of what constitutes the thingness of things; these can be reduced to three: for some, a thing is the composition of substance and accidents; for others, it is the unity of a manifold of sensible properties; for still others, it is the fusion of matter and form.[19]

Heidegger now describes how in Greek philosophy a distinction was made between the *hupokeimenon* and the *sumbebēkota*, a distinction which in Latin was translated into *substantia* and *accidens*. Underneath this seemingly literal translation is concealed a *translation* of Greek experience into a completely different way of thinking. "The rootlessness of

Western thought begins with this translation."[20] Now, according to the common opinion today, this definition of the thingness of the thing as the substance with its accidents corresponds to our "natural" outlook on things, and our concern with things and our speaking about them have adapted themselves to this common view of the thing's thingness. Heidegger in passing points to the problem concerning the relationship between the structure of the simple propositional statement (the combination of subject and predicate) and the structure of the thing (taken as the union of substance and accidents). In his view, to this day it is still debated whether the thing-structure functions as the standard here or whether the proposition-structure is to be given preference. He himself is convinced that neither comes first; ". . . both sentence-structure and thing-structure derive, in their typical form and their possible mutual relationship, from a common and more original source."[21] We may thus conclude that the first interpretation of the thingness of the thing is not as "natural" as it originally appeared to be. This interpretation has become familiar in and through a very long tradition, which has forgotten the unfamiliar source from which it arose.[22] But this conception of the thingness of the thing not only is not well-founded, it also holds for any being whatsoever, not just for things in the narrow sense of the word. Finally, the conception does not really specify the true thingness of things.[23]

A second conception of the thing suggests that the essence of the thing is to be found in the unity of the manifold of sensible properties. This conception was widely accepted in modern philosophy. In this conception the thing is thus the *aisthēton*, the sum total of all that the sense of sight, hearing, and touch convey. A thing is nothing but the unity of the manifold of what is given to the senses; this unity is conceived of by one as sum, by others as totality, and by still others as form.[24]

This interpretation of the thing is obviously correct but nevertheless not necessarily the true one. This thing-conception, too, leaves us at a loss, because we never really first perceive a group of sensations; one perceives not isolated sensations, patches of colors, and noises but the storm whistling in the chimney; you hear the Mercedes in distinction from the Volkswagen. Thus much closer to us than all sensations are the things themselves. The second interpretation is therefore not so much an assault upon the thing as was the first interpretation; rather, it is an inadequate attempt to bring the thingness of the thing to the fore. In both interpretations the thing itself vanishes.[25]

The third interpretation is as old as the other two. Here it is stated that what gives things their constancy and what is the source of their particular mode of sensuous pressure is the matter which always is found together with some form. The thing is nothing but formed matter; and this conception also holds good for both natural and manmade things. This conception accounts for the thingly element we find in every work of art; this thingly element is obviously the matter of which the work consists. This matter is the substrate for the action of the artist, who gives it its proper form.

Heidegger has doubts about this conception, also. One could object to his position by saying that the distinction between matter and form is that conceptual scheme which in the greatest variety of ways is used for all theory about art works and all aesthetics. Yet in Heidegger's view, this fact does not prove that the distinction itself is adequately founded; it does not show either that this distinction originally belongs to the domain of art and art works. As a matter of fact, the range of application of this pair of concepts extends far beyond the field of aesthetics. Finally, Heidegger argues, the distinction was originally developed not to give an account of the thing character of works of art or, even less, of the essence of the work of art; it was not even developed to account for the thingness of things. It was developed rather to describe the typical mode of Being of equipment, where the form determines the kind of matter, whereas at the same time it itself is determined by the purpose to be served by the relevant piece of equipment. In Heidegger's opinion, there can be no doubt that matter and form have their proper place in an effort to determine the essence of equipment. Also, there is indeed a similarity between a piece of equipment and a work of art, namely, insofar as both are made by man. Furthermore, it is also the case that once the matter-form structure was discovered with reference to equipment, it appeared to be applicable to the intelligible constitution of every being. This latter application received an additional impulse from the biblical faith which teaches that all things are created by God and in which creation is understood as making or producing. Eventually the distinction between matter and form to account for the thingness of the thing became generally accepted, either in its original or in its Kantian interpretation. Yet this conception, too, does not really unfold the true thingness of the thing; nor does it help us in our effort to understand the essence of the work of art.[26]

In view of the fact that pieces of equipment are more similar to works of art than things are, it is perhaps possible to discover what a work is by distinguishing it from a mere artifact. To that end, Heidegger compares a pair of peasant shoes with a painting by van Gogh that depicts a pair of farm shoes. This comparison leads Heidegger to the view, defended also in *Being and Time*, that the essence of equipment as such consists in serviceability and in suitability. Yet it is particularly the reliability of the "real" shoes which makes them what they are for the farmer and enables him to discover the world and play a part in it. The farmer discerns this reliability without any advertence; for him to experience the reliability of the shoes is to comprehend what they are in truth. We, on the other hand, can comprehend what the farmer's shoes really are by means of van Gogh's painting. By means of this painting we, too, begin to realize that this equipment belongs to the earth and yet is also preserved in the world of the farmer.[27] As a matter of fact, the equipmentality of equipment first comes to appearance through the work and only in the work.

A brief observation is in order here. Schapiro has claimed that the shoes to which Heidegger refers here are van Gogh's own shoes, not the shoes of some farmer's wife. Thus Heidegger has just projected his "own social outlook with its heavy pathos of the primordial and earthy" into some picture of van Gogh. Although I do not deny that Heidegger's discussion of a painting by van Gogh is not without difficulties, I nonetheless feel that Schapiro's criticism is substantially irrelevant, in that it itself rests on the aesthetics which Heidegger precisely wishes to overcome.[28]

Be that at it may, Heidegger next asks what it is that is at work in the work. Van Gogh's painting discloses what the pair of shoes is in truth; this being now emerges into the unconcealment of its Being. In Greek, non-concealment is *a-lētheia*. Thus if a disclosure of a particular being occurs in the work, disclosing it as what and how it is, then there is *a happening of truth at work.*

In the work of art, the truth of a being has set itself to work. Some particular being comes in the work to stand in the light of its Being; the Being of this being comes into the steadiness of its own shining. The essence of art therefore would be: the truth of beings setting itself into the work.[29] Many people will object to these claims. First of all, one will say that truth belongs to logic, not to aesthetics; aesthetics is concerned with the beautiful. Secondly, one might think that in this view an attempt is made to revive the ancient conception that art is an imitation of nature. Thirdly, one might point out that it is not at all clear what is meant here by truth. What kind of truth is happening here? Can truth come-to-pass at all? Is truth indeed historical? Is the truth not inherently timeless?[30] Finally, is the expression "Art is setting into the work of truth" not needlessly ambiguous? In 1956, in the *Addendum*, Heidegger stated that in the essay itself it is expressly admitted that there is indeed an ambiguity. This "essential" ambiguity is connected with the fact that truth is here at once both subject and object, whereas both descriptions really remain unsuitable. If truth is the "subject," then the expression means truth's establishing itself in the work. Art is then conceived in terms of disclosing appropriation; yet Being is a call to man, and it never "is" without man. If one were to take art as the "object," then art would not be more than the result of human producing and preserving. Only when the relation between man and Being is properly understood will it be feasible to reformulate this and similar claims in a more appropriate language.[31]

Furthermore, the reader will still wonder about the following: Let us assume that the essence of the art work is indeed to be understood in terms of the coming-to-pass of the truth; why is the long detour, chosen in this first lecture, then not eliminated? If it is really one's intention to claim that the truth of Being happens in the work of art, then it makes no sense first to talk about the thingness of things and the equipmentality of equipment. Yet in Heidegger's view, the detour was necessary for a couple of reasons: 1) the commonly accepted conceptions of the work of art are still taken from these modes of defining thingness and equipmentality, and 2) these modes of defining obstruct the way toward the essence of the art work (just as they also obstruct the way to the thingness of things).[32]

Be that as it may, after a brief recapitulation of the argument, Heidegger concludes the first lecture by stating that ". . . the art work opens up in its own way the Being of beings. This opening up. . . , i.e., the truth of beings, happens in the work. In the art work, the truth of what is has established itself. Art is truth establishing itself in the work."[33]

2. *"The Work and Truth"* But what then is truth itself, if it sometimes comes-to-pass as art? And what is this establishing itself in the work precisely? To answer these questions, a number of preliminary remarks are necessary. First of all, we are limiting ourselves here to what Hegel has called "great" art. In these works the artist himself remains inconsequential as compared with the work itself. Furthermore, one should realize that great art works are now usually found in museums, where they are cut off from the world to which they belong. And even where they are not placed in museums or performed on "special occasions," they are usually isolated from their world. Even in its own square, the cathedral of Bamberg is without its true world. This withdrawal of world and this decay of world can never be undone. The works are no longer the works they once were. We still encounter the works themselves, and yet we encounter them as the ones that have been. As bygone works, they stand now over against us in the realm of tradition and the domain of conservation; they are there as "objects." Their standing before us is still a consequence of their former self-subsistence; yet they are no longer the same. Their genuine self-subsistence has fled from them. Thus, the whole art industry extends only to the object-being of the works, not to their genuine work-being.[34]

Since it is essential for the work to stand in certain relations, the work belongs as work in each case uniquely within the realm of those relations which it itself opens up. The work-being of the work is present only in

such an opening-up. We observed earlier that in the work a happening of
the truth is at work. The painting by van Gogh helped us to understand
this happening. In regard to this happening, it was asked what truth then
is and how it can happen. And we now ask these questions again with a
view to the work. In order to see more clearly what these questions
involve, let us look once more at the happening of truth in the work, but
now with the help of an example that cannot possibly be characterized as
representational art. Let us thus take a Greek temple, which portrays
nothing and simply stands there by itself in a valley; let us take the temple
of Poseidon in Paestum. The building contains the statue of the god, and
in this concealment it lets the god stand out into the holy enclosure
through the open portico so that the god *is present* in the temple by means
of the temple. And the presence of the god is in itself the expansion as
well as the delimitation of the enclosure of the holy. Yet the temple does
not fade away into the indefinite; the temple-work rather gathers around
itself "the unity of all the paths and relations in which birth and death,
disaster and blessing, victory and defeat, endurance and decline" acquire
the shape of destiny for human beings. The all-governing expanse of this
open, relational context is the *world* of a historical people.

Standing there, the building rests on the ground. As such it is in sharp
contrast with everything else that comes to appear as what it is by *phusis*,
the emerging and rising in itself and in all things. The temple also clears
and illuminates that on and in which man bases his dwelling, the earth.
The word *earth* must not be taken here in the sense it has in physics or
astronomy. Earth is that whence *phusis* brings back and shelters everything that arises, without violence. In all things that emerge, the earth is
present as that which shelters. Thus, the temple-work which stands there
opens up a world and at the same time sets the world back again on the
earth, which itself in this way emerges as what it is, namely, native
ground.[35]

In its standing there, the temple gives to things their look *(eidos)* and to
men their outlook on themselves, as long as the temple is a work, and as
long as the god has not fled from it. And it is the same with the statue of
the god: it is not a portrait; rather, it, too, is a work that lets the god
himself be present, and thus it *is* the god. Similar remarks can be made for
linguistic works of art.

But in what, then, does the work-Being of the work really consist? It
may suffice here to mention only two essential features of the work. The
first is that every work of art sets up a world. "Towering up within itself,
the work opens up a *world* and keeps it abidingly in force."[36]

Thus, to be a work of art means to set up a world. World is not the
mere collection of all the things that just happen to be there. But neither is

world a merely imagined framework which our imagination just adds to the sum of such given things. The world "does what as world it is supposed to do" *(die Welt weltet);* it holds sway *(welten = walten),* and as such it is more fully in being than the realm of tangible things in which we believe ourselves to be at home.[37]

World is thus never an object that stands before us and can be seen or touched. World is the ever non-objective to which we relate as long as we live as *Dasein,* and as long as we relate to Being. A stone has no world. Plants and animals likewise have no world; they just belong to an environment. But humans have a world, because they dwell in the openness of beings. It is the world that "determines" in what way things will be things; even the doom of the God who remains absent is a way in which the world holds sway *(weltet).* The work opens up a world, and in so doing it makes space for and liberates the open and establishes it in its structure; it installs and erects it. The work holds open the open of the world. We must now turn to the second feature of the work-being of the work.[38]

This feature consists in the fact that the work sets forth the earth. When a work is being created, is being brought forth out of a certain material (stone, wood, metal, color, tone, language), we say that it is being made of it, set forth from out of it. Now, just as the work requires the setting up of the world, so the setting forth is also needed. But what does the work set forth? We shall find out by comparing a piece of equipment in this regard with a work of art. In the equipment, the material almost completely disappears into usefulness. The material is all the better and more suitable the less it resists disappearing in the equipmental being of the equipment. But in the case of a work of art, in which a world is set up, the material does not disappear; rather, the work makes it come forth and come into the open of the work's world. In the work, rock comes to bear, metal to glitter, colors to glow, tones to sing, words to speak. All of that comes forth as the work sets itself back into the massiveness and heaviness of stone, into the hardness and luster of metal, into the lightening and darkening of color, into the sound of tone, into the naming power of the word. That into which the work sets itself back and which it makes come forth in this setting back of itself we call the earth.

Earth is that which comes forth and shelters. Upon the earth and in it, historical man grounds his dwelling in the world. The work moves the earth itself into the open of a world and keeps it there. The work lets the earth be earth.[39]

But why must this setting forth of the earth happen in such a way that the work sets itself back into it? The reason is that the earth itself shatters every attempt to penetrate into it; the earth is essentially self-secluding.

Thus to set forth the earth really means to bring it into the open as that which is self-secluding.[40]

Therefore, the setting up of a world and the setting forth of the earth are two essential elements in the work-being of the work. They belong together in the unity of the work-being; and yet it is not yet completely clear precisely how they can belong together. Thus we must still ask: What relation do the setting up of a world and the setting forth of the earth exhibit in the work itself?[41]

The world is the self-disclosing openness of the broad paths of the simple and essential decisions in the destiny of a people's history. On the other hand, the earth is the spontaneous forthcoming of that which is continually self-secluding, and to that extent also is sheltering and concealing. Both are essentially different from one another; yet they are never separated. The world grounds itself on the earth, and the earth works itself up through the world. They are not antagonistic opposites. In resting upon the earth, the world strives to surmount it; on the other hand, the earth, as sheltering and concealing, tends always to draw the world into itself and keep it there. The opposition of world and earth is a striving in which the "opponents" raise each other into the self-assertion of their respective essences. In their struggle with each other, each "opponent" carries the other beyond itself.

> The earth cannot dispense with the open of the world if it itself is to appear as earth in the liberated surge of its self-seclusion. The world, again, cannot soar out of the earth's sight if, as the governing breadth and path of all essential destiny, it is to ground itself on a resolute foundation.[42]

In setting up a world and setting forth the earth, the work of art incites this striving and lets it be as such; it even accomplishes this striving. The work-being of the work thus consists in the "fighting" of the "battle" between world and earth.[43] We now begin to see in what sense in the work the truth is at work. To explain further, let us try to answer the following questions: What is truth? In what way does truth happen in the work-being of the work? How does truth happen in the "fighting" of the "battle" between world and earth?

In his effort to answer these questions, Heidegger makes use of ideas developed in both *Being and Time* and *On the Essence of Truth*. He basically maintains the position reached in *On the Essence of Truth* but adapts the insights gained there to the problems raised by the work of art. Since I have dealt with most of these issues in the introductory chapter, I shall limit myself here to what is essential to comprehend Heidegger's position.

Heidegger begins his reflections on the questions mentioned by observing that we still know little about the essence of truth. This lack of knowledge is clear from the superficial manner in which in our everyday life we use the word. By truth we usually mean a particular truth, i.e., something that is true. A cognition articulated in a proposition can be such a truth; true gold and true friendship can be others. True gold means real gold. By the "real" we mean here that which in truth is. The true is what corresponds to the real, and the real is what is in truth.

But what is the essence of truth? Before we can answer this question, one should note that by essence we sometimes mean a basic feature held in common by a number of individuals. The essence then is discovered by the generic and universal concept, which represents the one feature that holds indifferently for many things. Here we do not take essence in that sense (= inessential essence). We are here concerned with the essential essence of truth; by essential essence we mean here that which is determined from a being's true Being.[44]

By truth we accordingly mean here the essence of what is true. In recollecting the Greek word *alētheia,* we think truth as the non-concealment of beings. In so doing, we are not demanding a revival of Greek philosophy. For from the very beginning, Greek philosophy itself did not remain in conformity with the essence of truth that lights up in the word *alētheia.* The essence of truth as *alētheia* was never thought out in the philosophy of the Greeks; nor has it been ever since.[45]

But why can we not be satisfied with the "normal" definition of truth? Truth means, as everybody knows, the agreement or conformity of knowledge with fact. Obviously, the fact must show itself to be a fact if knowledge and the proposition that expresses this knowledge are to be able to conform to the fact; otherwise the fact cannot become binding for knowledge and proposition. But how can a fact show itself if it cannot itself stand forth out of concealment? A thought or a proposition is true when it conforms to the unconcealed, i.e., to what is true. Propositional truth is thus correctness; no less, no more. The critical concepts of truth which since Descartes start out from truth as certainty are merely variations of the definition of truth as correctness. One thing is clear, however: the essence of truth as the correctness of propositions stands and falls with truth as the non-concealment of beings.[46]

Thus in thinking truth as non-concealment, we are not taking refuge in a literal translation of a Greek word; rather, we try to remind ourselves of what, unthought, underlies our familiar conception of the essence of truth as correctness. Without denying the correctness of the common conception of truth, we try to think the *essence* of truth, realizing that it is not we who presuppose the non-concealment of beings, but that the non-concealment of beings (i.e., Being) puts us in such a condition that in all our propositions we always remain within non-concealment. Furthermore, when I say that my statement is in conformity with X, then X must itself already be in some way unconcealed, and what is more, even the entire domain in which this "conforming to something" occurs must as a whole already come-to-pass in non-concealment. With all our correct propositions, we could not even presuppose that there is already something manifest to which we can conform ourselves, unless the non-concealment of beings had already exposed us to and placed us in that clearing in which every being stands and from which it withdraws.[47]

Before we can say how truth comes-to-pass as non-concealment, we must first try to get a better grasp of non-concealment itself. To this end, let us turn once more to beings. There are many things, and they are of very different kinds. Yet they all are and stand in Being. We know few of these things, and we have a perfect knowledge of none of them. What is, is never of our making, or even just the product of our mind. We can contemplate the whole of beings as a unity, as one; then we speak of all-that-is. In addition to all-that-is, there is still something else that comes-to-pass. In the midst of beings as a whole, an open place comes-to-pass; a clearing occurs which at the same time is a lighting. All-that-is can be only if it stands within what is lighted in this clearing. It is this clearing and this open domain which grant us humans a passage to the beings that we ourselves are not, as well as to the beings which we ourselves are. Thus, thanks to this clearing, beings are unconcealed.[48]

Yet beings can also be concealed, even though that, too, can take place only within the domain of the clearing. And concealment can even happen here in two different ways. Sometimes beings just hide themselves and simply refuse to show themselves. On the other hand, sometimes one being hides another; in that case concealment is not just a simple refusal but rather a dissembling. Now the clearing itself, too, is somehow concealed. And concealment happens here also in two different ways. The open place in the midst of beings, in which all things stand, is never a rigid stage on which the play of beings runs its course; it, too, happens only as this double concealment of simple refusal and dissembling. This double concealment belongs to the essence of truth as non-concealment; in its very essence, truth is also untruth.[49] First, denial, in the manner of simple concealment, belongs to non-concealment as clearing. For the coming-to-pass of the truth of Being is inherently finite; as a consequence, while it shows itself in letting beings be what they are, it itself hides itself (*Versagen*, "refusal"). At the same time, Being also can let beings be as what they are not and show them only in their seeming-to-be (*Verstellen*, "dissemble, dissimulate"). The process of dissimulation, fur-

thermore, also includes the concealing of the concealment itself. Thus
what Heidegger here calls *Verstellen* (dissimulation) includes what in *On
the Essence of Truth* was called errancy and mystery.[50]

In other words, dissimulation (= errancy and mystery) together with
the simple refusal constitutes the full essence of the non-truth inherent in
truth. Furthermore, truth and non-truth are constantly in contention as
original discord.

> Concealing denial is intended to denote that opposition in the essence of truth
> which subsists between clearing . . . and concealing. It is the opposition of the
> primal conflict. The essence of truth is, in itself, the primal conflict in which
> that open center is won within which what is, stands, and from which it sets
> itself back into itself.[51]

We must now return to world and earth. Being as the open happens in
the midst of beings. To this open belong both world and earth. Yet the
world itself is not the open which corresponds to the clearing, and the
earth is not simply the closed that belongs to concealment. Rather, the
world is in each case the clearing of the paths of the essential guidelines
and directions with which all decisions of a people comply to the degree
that they are intelligible. On the other hand, every decision founds itself
on something that is not-mastered, concealed, and even confusing. The
earth is not simply the closed but rather that which rises up as self-
closing. World and earth are always, intrinsically, and essentially in conflict. Only as such do they enter into the conflict of clearing and
concealing. Earth works its way up to world, and world grounds itself on
the earth only insofar as truth happens as the primal conflict between
clearing and concealing.

Truth can come-to-pass in more than one way. One of these ways is the
work-being of the work. Setting up a world and setting forth the earth,
the work is the "fighting of the battle" in which the non-concealment of
beings as a whole, i.e., truth, is won.[52] Thus, when we say that truth
comes-to-pass in a painting, we mean to say not that something is "correctly" portrayed but rather that in it world and earth in their counterplay
attain non-concealment.[53] In art works, truth is at work. Art works make
non-concealment as such come-to-pass in regard to what is as a whole;
they "let" self-concealing Being be as illuminating. Its light joins its shining to the work. This shining, joined to and into the work, is the beautiful. Thus beauty is one way in which truth comes-to-pass as non-
concealment.[54]

Heidegger concludes this second part of the essay by saying that we
may now have learned something about the essence of truth and about the

manner in which truth is at work in the art work. But in so doing, we have said nothing about the thingly dimensions of the work. By one-sidedly stressing the importance of the work, we overlooked one thing, i.e., that a work is something that is worked out. For one of the most obvious aspects of the work which sets it apart from all other beings is that it has been made, effected, brought forth in a medium that is intimately related to the thingly dimension of the work. Thus we must ask: What does it mean for a work that it has been brought forth, and what is the inmost essence of the work itself? And how do both relate to the happening of the truth? In order to answer these questions, we have to raise the question of truth once more. How can there lie in the essence of truth the inclination or impulse toward a work of art? Of what essence is truth that it can, and sometimes even must, establish itself in a work of art in order to be *as truth*? What is truth that it can or even must come-to-pass as art?[55]

3. *"Truth and Art"* Heidegger begins the third lecture with a brief summary of what has been argued for in the first two lectures.

Art is the origin of the art work and the artist. Origin is the source of the essence in which the Being of a being comes-to-presence. We seek the essence of art in the actual art work. The work itself has been defined by what is at work in the work; that is the coming-to-pass of the truth. This happening was described as the "fighting of the conflict" between world and earth. Response occurs in the concentrated agitation of this conflict; the independence and self-composure of the work are grounded here. Thus far we have taken the actuality of the work for granted. Yet it itself is as something that is effected. Now, the being-effected of the work can be grasped only in terms of the processes which bring it forth and preserve it. Thus it seems that in order to get to the origin of the work, we shall have to turn to the artist and the conserver, because our attempt to define the work-being of the work purely in terms of the work itself proved not to be feasible.[56]

In turning to the productive process, we tend to think of production as a bringing-forth. We realize that there are several ways in which one can bring something forth. The making of equipment and the making of art works are two privileged ways. We then make an attempt to distinguish these two basic modes of bringing-forth. In so doing, we can point to the fact that the Greeks seem to use the same word for "craft" and "art," namely, *technē*. Heidegger points out that this route is not leading very far. One of the reasons is that *technē* originally meant neither "craft" nor "art" but a certain way of knowing. For the Greeks, knowing is to be thought in terms of *alētheia*. *Technē* supports and guides all comportments toward beings. *Technē,* as a form of knowledge experienced in the Greek manner, is thus a bringing-forth of beings which brings beings out of concealment and into non-concealment. *Technē* never signifies the act of making.[57]

But if craft is not to guide our thinking about the productive process, what then is to guide us? There is no other way than to turn again to the work.[58] In light of what we have said about the work-being of the work, we can now say that to bring something forth is to cause something to emerge as a thing that has been so brought forth, and that "the work's becoming a work is a way in which truth comes-to-pass and happens." We now understand the questions mentioned earlier: but what then is truth that it has to happen in a thing that is brought forth?[59]

One should note here that we have shown already that truth is also non-truth insofar as the entire domain of the un-uncovered or not-yet-uncovered also belongs to truth. In non-concealment occurs the double refusal or restraint we mentioned earlier. Truth is the primal conflict in which the open is won in each case in some particular way, only such that in this open every thing can both show and hide itself, stand and with-draw. Whenever and however this conflict may come-to-pass in each case, clearing and concealing will move apart. In this way, the open as the place of conflict is won. The openness (truth) of this open (Being) can be this openness only as long as there is some being in this open in which the openness can take its stand. In taking possession of the open, the open-ness holds open the open and maintains it as such. The terms *to set* used earlier and *to take possession of* employed here must both be understood in terms of the Greek *thesis,* a setting up in non-concealment, and not in terms of the modern conception of thesis, in the sense of the positing of consciousness.[60]

Furthermore, Heidegger observes, one should note also that the claim concerning the self-establishing of the openness in the open implies a set of problems which cannot be explicated here. The non-concealment of Being belongs somehow to Being itself; thus Being itself must somehow let the place of openness, the clearing of the "there," come-to-pass. As is clear from the context, but particularly from the *Addendum,*[61] Heidegger refers here to the manner in which one is to conceive of the coming-to-pass of the ontological difference and the part which both Being and man have to play in it.[62]

Truth thus happens only by "establishing itself" *(sich einrichten)* in the conflict and the sphere opened up by truth itself. Two things should be observed here: 1) the expression "to establish itself" should not be under-stood in the sense given to it in the lecture on techology; thus here the term does not mean "to organize" or "to complete"; rather, it recalls the impulse or inclination on the part of truth according to which, in the midst of beings, it should be in the manner of work, or should itself occur as being. 2) One should not assume that truth exists in itself beforehand, somewhere among the stars, in order then later to descend among beings. In other words, the clearing of openness and the establishing in the open belong together. Both pertain to the essence of the happening of the truth. And this coming-to-pass of the truth is historical in many ways.[63]

Truth establishes itself in the beings that it has opened up when it "sets" itself into the work; other ways in which truth occurs are the act that founds a political state, the nearness of that which is not just a being but that being that is most in Being *(das Seindste des Seienden)*, the act of sacrifice, the thinker's questioning, etc. By contrast, science is not an original happening of the truth but merely the further cultivation of a domain of truth already opened up; science focuses on apprehending and confirming what shows itself to be possibly or necessarily correct within that domain. As soon as science goes beyond correctness and goes on to the truth and essentially discloses what is as such, it becomes philosophy.[64]

Be that as it may, from the preceding it is clear that because it belongs to the essence of truth to "establish" itself within that which is, in order so first to become truth, the impulse toward the art work lies in the essence of truth as one of its distinctive possibilities, by which it can itself come-to-pass as being *(seiend)* in the midst of beings. What is typical in this case is the fact that the establishing of truth in the work brings forth a being such as never was before and will never come to be again. Furthermore, the work is placed in the open in such a way that the work to be brought forth first clears the openness of the open into which it comes forth; as we have seen, it does so by setting up a world. What we call the "production" of a work of art is such a bringing-forth, which at the same time also brings forth the openness of beings, i.e., truth.[65]

We can now indicate more clearly in what the being-produced of the work precisely consists. First of all, truth establishes itself in the work. And truth as the conflict between clearing and concealing is present here in the opposition of world and earth. Truth wishes to be established in the work as the conflict of world and earth. This conflict is not to be resolved in the work; nor is it to be merely housed there; the conflict rather originates from it. The work must therefore contain within itself the essential characteristics of the conflict. In this conflict the unity of world and earth is fought to the end *(erstritten)*.[66] When through the work a world opens itself, it submits to the decision of a people the question of victory or defeat, blessing or curse, mastery or slavery. Thus the world itself does not decide anything; it merely shows what is not yet decided and still is without measure. In so doing it discloses the hidden necessity of measure and decision.

But at the same time, the earth comes to rise up. It shows itself as that which bears everything, as that which is sheltered in its own law and constantly closes itself. The world requires this decisiveness and measure while it lets beings choose their own paths. Earth, on the other hand, both bearing and towering up, tends to keep itself closed and to make everything surrender to its law. The strife between world and earth is not a fissure *(Riss)*, in the sense of a mere cleft that is just ripped open; rather, it is that kind of intimacy which shows that the two opponents belong together. The fissure brings the ones facing each other into the source of their unity, which itself flows from their common ground.

Truth thus establishes itself as the strife within a being, i.e., within the work that is to be brought forth, in such a way that the conflict mentioned opens up in that being. And truth establishes itself in that being in such a manner that this being itself occupies the open space of truth. But this occupying can come-to-pass only if what is so to be brought forth, i.e., the fissure, entrusts itself to the earth, which as self-secluding towers up into the open. Thus the rift must set itself back in the heavy weight of the stone, the hardness of the wood, or the glow of the colors. And as the earth receives the fissure back into itself, the fissure is first set forth into the open and placed within that which as sheltering and self-secluding towers up into the open.[67] The conflict that is so brought into the fissure and thus is set back into the earth is now determined and made stable; as such it is *Gestalt*. This *Gestalt* is the structure in whose shape the fissure becomes formed and molded. The so-ordered and structured fissure becomes the pattern in which the truth shines forth. What is here called *Gestalt* is always to be thought of in terms of that particular placing or setting and framing *(Ge-stell)* as which the work comes-to-presence, i.e., insofar as it sets itself up and sets itself forth.[68]

In the *Addendum*, Heidegger explains that the term *Gestell* used here should not be taken in the sense given to it in the lecture on technicity; thus here it does not mean the com-positing which is closely related to the pro-posing positing of modern science and philosophy. Rather, it means the totality of all the manners of setting as which the work occurs. There Heidegger also adds that the Greek sense of *morphē* (*Gestalt*, "figure, shape") is made clear by *Ge-stell*, also.[69]

Another thing is still to be noted here. In the production of the work, the conflict taken as fissure must be set back into the earth; the earth itself must be set forth and thus employed as the self-enclosing element. Yet that does not mean that the earth is used here or misused as matter or material; rather, the employment of the earth sets the earth free to be nothing but itself. Since this "use" of the earth *looks like* the employment of material in handicraft, it also *looks as if* the creation of the work is an activity of handicraft. That it obviously never is. Yet it always is an "employing" of the earth in the "fixing" of truth in the *Gestalt*.[70]

We must now turn to the second characteristic of being-produced. The making of equipment and the production of the work have indeed some elements in common. Yet they are essentially different. The making of equipment is never the effecting of the happening of the truth. Furthermore, the production is finished when a material has been so formed that it is now ready for use. On the other hand, the art work is distinguished by being produced in such a way that its being-produced is an integral part of the work; in the work, being-produced is expressly produced into the produced work, so that it stands out from the being so brought forth.[71] We are not referring here to the conception according to which the work should give us the impression of being made by a great artist. What we are stressing here is not the *N.N. fecit* but rather the mere *factum est*. In other words, the work must hold forth into the open the fact that the non-concealment of what is has come-to-pass here, and that as this happening it came-to-pass here for the first time. To be sure, "that it is made" is also a property of every piece of equipment. Yet in the equipment this property does not become prominent; it disappears in usefulness and serviceability. In the work, on the other hand, this very fact, that it *is as a work*, is just what must stand out. The more the work opens itself, the more luminous becomes the uniqueness of the fact that it is rather than is not.[72]

These reflections on the work's being-produced have brought us somewhat closer to the workly character and thus the "reality" of the work. We are now in a position to take the next step in our consideration, that step toward which everything said thus far was tending.[73] We can explain this step provisionally as follows.

The more solitarily the work, fixed in its *Gestalt*, stands on its own, and the more definitively it seems to cut all ties to humans, the more simply does the thrust come into the open that such a work *is*. Now, the more purely the work is itself transported into the openness of beings, an openness which in some sense it opens itself, the more simply does it transport us out of the realm of the everyday and ordinary, so that we may refrain from what we do usually, stay within the truth that is happening in the work, and let what is brought forth be the work that it is. This letting the work be a work we now call *the preserving* of the work. It is only for such preserving that the work yields itself in its being-made as present in the manner of a work.[74]

Just as a work cannot be without being made by artists who produce it (even though we do not have to raise the issue of the artist and his "experiences"), in the same way what is produced cannot itself come into being without those who preserve it (even though here too we need not ask about the "experiences" of the observers). Thus, although a work of art is always somehow tied to those who are willing and able to preserve it, it may very well be that works often do not find actual preservers who respond to the truth coming-to-pass in the work. Works can wait for preservers. Even the oblivion into which works sometimes sink is not nothing; it too is still a preservation that feeds on the work.[75]

To preserve a work means to let it stand within the openness of the beings that come-to-pass in the work. This letting-stand implies both a knowing and a certain willing. Both are to be thought here as belonging together: a knowing that remains a willing and a willing that remains a knowing; both constitute the entrance into and the compliance with the non-concealment of Being on the part of man who ek-sists, i.e., stands out within the essential opening-up of the clearing of Being. The resoluteness mentioned in *Being and Time* is thus not a deliberate action of a human subject but the opening up of *Dasein* out of its captivity in beings toward the openness of Being. At any rate, neither in the production nor in the preservation does the willing refer to the performance of a specific activity on the part of a subject that strives toward himself as the goal which he has set for himself.[76]

"Willing" here thus means the sober resolution of the ek-sisting self-transcendence which exposes itself "freely" to the openness of beings as it is set into the work here. Preserving the work as knowing, on the other hand, is the sober standing within the extraordinary awesomeness of the truth that is actually coming-to-pass in the work. This knowing-and-willing makes its home in the work; it does not deprive the work of its independence; it "does not drag it into the sphere of mere experience, and [it] does not degrade it to the role of a stimulator of experiences. Preserving the work does not reduce people to their private experiences, but brings them into affiliation with the truth, happening in the work."[77] In this manner it gives a foundation to our being-for-and-with-one-another, to our historically standing-out toward non-concealment. But most of all, knowledge in the manner of preserving has nothing at all to do with the "merely aestheticizing connoisseurship of the work's formal aspects" and qualities. This knowing is rather a being resolved and a standing within the conflict that the work has joined into the fissure.

The proper way to preserve the work is determined only and exclusively by the work itself, and it can occur on different levels of knowledge and with different degrees of scope, constancy, and lucidity. When works are put in a museum, that does not yet prove that they are being preserved *as works.* To restore a work or to handle it with the greatest of care, all of that still remains within the domain of art *business* and as such has nothing to do with preserving a work as such. A work comes-to-presence as a work only where it is preserved in the truth that comes-to-pass by the work.[78]

We must now return to a question raised earlier: what to say about the work's thingly character which is to guarantee its immediate and actual work-Being? It appears now that we no longer need to ask this question *in this fashion;* because in asking the question in this manner, we treat the work as an object and do not let it be as a work. What from the viewpoint of our everyday concern with things looks like the thingly element of the work taken as an object is, seen from the perspective of the art work, really its earthly character. The earth towers up within the work, because the work exists as something in which the truth is at work and because the truth in each case comes-to-pass only by installing itself within a particular being. However, in the earth, which is essentially self-closing, the openness of the open finds the greatest resistance and therewith also the abode of its constant stand, wherein the *Gestalt* is to be "fixed" in place.[79]

One could now argue that if that is so, then it was altogether superfluous in the first lecture to enter into a discussion of the thingly character of the work. In Heidegger's opinion, this conception is unfounded. To be sure, one cannot define the work-character of the work by means of the thing-character of the work; but the question concerning the thingly character of the thing can be brought on the right path only by way of the proper knowledge of the work-character of the work. And that is of the greatest importance, in light of the fact that the ancient ways of determining the thing-character of the thing led to a conception of beings as a whole which is totally inadequate to understand the essence of equipment as well as the essence of the work, and which, in addition, makes us blind to the original essence of truth.[80]

We have seen that one cannot define the thing-character of the thing by conceiving of it as the bearer of properties, or the unity of the manifold of sense data, or the matter and form structure which itself is derived from the structure of equipment. To truly understand the thingly character of the thing, one must focus on the thing's belonging to the earth. Now, the earth, which in its bearing and self-closure is not pressed in any direction, reveals itself truly only in its towering-up in the direction of a world; i.e., it reveals itself only in the opposition of the two. And their conflict is "fixed" in the *Gestalt* of the work and shows itself by it. Just as one cannot understand the equipmental character of equipment directly but must approach it through the work, in the same way the thing-character of the thing must be understood from the work-being of the work. This state of affairs also shows that in the work's work-Being, the coming-to-pass of truth is at work.[81]

One could object here that if the work indeed is to bring the thingness of things into the open, must the work itself then not have been brought into a relation with the things of the earth and, thus, with nature, and would Albrecht Dürer then not be correct where he says that in truth art lies already in nature? From a certain point of view, one could indeed say that art lies already hidden in nature; yet it is equally true that art, so hidden in nature, becomes manifest only through the work, because originally art lies in the work and nowhere else.[82]

CONCLUDING REFLECTIONS: ON THE ESSENCE OF ART

What was said about the reality of the work was meant to prepare us for a reflection on art itself, and the essence of art. If art indeed is, as we have suggested, the origin of the work, then art lets the artist as well as the preserver, each in his own way, originate in his essence. But what is art itself, and why do we call it an origin?[83]

Provisionally, we have defined art as the setting-itself-into-the-work of the truth. This definition was intended to be ambiguous. For, on the one hand, it says that art is the ascertainment *(Feststellen)* of the truth which establishes itself in the work's *Gestalt*. In the working of the artist, this event comes-to-pass as the bringing forth of the non-concealment of what is. But "to set itself into the work" also means to make the work-Being of the work happen as such, and that comes-to-pass as preservation. Thus art really is the producing preserving of the truth in the work; it is the coming-to-pass of truth.[84] That does not mean that truth was first somewhere else and now arrives here and manifests itself here. The clearing of what is, the opening of the open, comes-to-pass only as long as the openness, which arrives with *Dasein*'s thrownness, is projected as such. In the *Addendum*,[85] Heidegger notes that this ambiguity, which was intended as such, is not fully satisfactory as long as the relationship between Being and man in the coming-to-pass of truth has not been clarified more "delicately."[86]

Be that as it may, the truth, taken as the clearing and concealing of what is, comes-to-pass while it is being poetized *(indem sie gedichtet wird)*.[87] Now, all art, as the letting happen of the advent of the truth of what is, is, as such, in essence poetizing. The essence of art, on which both the art work and the artist depend, is the establishing-itself-in-the-work of the truth. It is due to the poetic essence of art that, in the midst of beings, art itself breaks open an open place, in whose openness everything then is in a manner different from the usual one. The working of the work should therefore not be compared with the working of a cause on the ontic level;

rather, it consists in a change, a coming-to-pass from out of the work itself, of the non-concealment of what is and, thus, of Being.

Yet poetizing is not an aimless imagining of arbitrary possibilities; nor is it the flight of mere fancies into the realm of the unreal. What poetizing, as illuminating projection, unfolds of non-concealment and projects ahead into the design of the work's *Gestalt* is the open which poetizing lets come-to-pass in such a way that only now, in the midst of beings, does the open bring these beings to shine. From that it is quite clear that it is impossible with Kant to conceive of the essence of poetizing in terms of the power of man's imagination. In the *Addendum* Heidegger notes once more that here too the relationship between Being and man is to be determined more carefully, such that the priority in the coming-to-pass of the truth of Being rests with Being itself and not with *Dasein*.[88]

It should be noted also that the essence of poetizing has been described here only in very broad strokes. It is to be determined further and constitutes an issue that is most worthy of questioning. Heidegger adds that it was not his intention to suggest that all arts are to be reduced to poetry or poesy. Yet it is certainly true that the work of language *(das Sprachwerk)*, i.e., poetizing in the more narrow sense, has a privileged position in the realm of the arts.[89] To see that, one must have the proper concept of language. Heidegger briefly typifies what he has in mind here and how he conceives of the essence of language. Since we have discussed the relevant issues elsewhere (namely, in the chapter on language and the chapter on thinking and poetizing), we need not dwell here on Heidegger's first attempt to articulate the essence of language and its relation to poetizing and, thus, also to all arts.[90] Yet it is relevant to briefly paraphrase how Heidegger characterizes the essence of poetizing.

The essence of art is poetizing. The essence of poetizing, in turn, is the originating institution *(stiften)* of the truth. *Stiften* is to be taken here in a triple sense for "bestowing" *(schenken)*, "grounding" *(gründen)*, and "beginning" *(anfangen)*. The setting itself-into-the-work of the truth that comes-to-pass in the work, thrusts up the extraordinary and destroys the ordinary; the truth that discloses itself here can never be derived from something else; what art founds can never be accounted for in terms of what is present already; thus, the founding of the truth has the character of an overflow, an endowing, a bestowal, a gift.[91]

Furthermore, the poetic projection of the truth that sets itself into the work is never carried out in the direction of an empty void. Rather, in the work, truth is thrown toward a people that in history comes to preserve it. But what is so projected is never just an arbitrary demand, so that the truly poietic projection is the disclosure of that into which *Dasein* as historical is already thrown. That is the earth. And for a historical people,

this earth is *its* earth, i.e., the self-closing ground on which it rests together with everything else that it itself already is, although still hidden
from itself.[92] But it also is its world, which prevails in virtue of *Dasein's*
relation to the non-concealment of Being. That is the reason that everything with which man is endowed in the projection must be drawn up
from the closed ground and expressly must be set upon this ground. In
this way, the ground is grounded as the one that bears.[93] Thus, since it is
in essence such a drawing-up, all production of art works has some
similarity with the drawing of water from a well. That does not mean, as
modern subjectivism in art claims, that all art is the work of genius.
Rather, the founding of the truth is a founding not only in the sense of a
free bestowal or gift; it is at the same time a founding in the sense of a
ground-laying grounding. The poietic projection comes from non-Being
in the respect that it does not take its gift from the ordinary. Yet it never
comes from non-Being insofar as that which is projected by it is nothing
but the withheld destiny of historical *Dasein.*[94]

Finally, bestowing and grounding both have in themselves the unmediated character of a beginning. Yet the unmediated character of this
beginning implies that this beginning prepares itself inconspicuously for
the longest time. Every genuine beginning already contains the end
within itself. A beginning, furthermore, also contains the undisclosed
abundance of the extraordinary, and thus the strife with the ordinary. Art
as poetizing is therefore also founding in the third sense of instigating the
strife of truth, i.e., in the sense of beginning. Every time the beings as a
whole as such require a grounding in the openness, art attains to its
historical essence as foundation. In the West this foundation came-to-pass
for the first time in Greece.[95]

What later was to be called Being was then and there set into the work
in a manner which would set the standard for all that was to follow. The
realm of the beings as a whole was later transformed into beings in the
sense of the things created by God. This transformation occurred in the
Middle Ages. In the modern age, beings became mere objects that can be
calculated and controlled. In each case, a new and essential world came-
to-pass. In each case, there happened the non-concealment of what is. In
each case, non-concealment established itself in work, and that was accomplished by art.[96]

> Whenever art comes-to-pass—that is, whenever there is a true beginning—a
> thrust enters history and history either begins or starts over again. History
> means here not a sequence of events in time, however important they may be.
> Rather history is the transporting of a people into its appointed task and also
> this people's entrance into its endowment.[97]

Heidegger concludes his reflections by stressing once more that in the statement "Art is the setting-itself-into-the-work of the truth," an essential ambiguity is hidden, in that truth here is at once the subject and the object of this setting. Furthermore, the terms *subject* and *object* themselves are not even suitable in this case, in that they prevent us from thinking the ambiguous nature itself. That cannot be accomplished in these lectures. Suffice it to note that art is essentially historical; as such it is the producing preserving of the truth in the work. Art comes-to-pass as poetizing, and poetizing is founding, which itself, in turn, is to be understood in the sense of bestowing, grounding, and beginning. Taken as founding in this triple sense, art is inherently historical. It is historical in the sense that it itself has a history. Above all, however, it is historical in the sense that it grounds history. "The origin of the work of art—that is, the origin of both the producers and the preservers, which is to say the origin of a people's historical ek-sistence, is art. And that is so because art is in essence origin: a distinctive way in which the truth comes into being, becomes historical."[98] Such reflections cannot force art and its coming-to-pass. Yet such an inquiry is the "preliminary" *(vorläufig)* and therefore indispensable preparation for the coming-to-pass of art.[99]

One may perhaps wonder where these reflections leave us with respect to the meaning and function of contemporary art. It is obvious that the "function" of the arts in our technological world must be quite different from the one they once had in Greece and in the Middle Ages. At first sight, it thus seems strange that Heidegger, following Hegel, limits himself to a reflection on great art, of which he himself, as did Hegel, explicitly admits that its time has passed. In a lecture given in Athens in 1967, Heidegger showed how a careful *retrieve* of Hegel's ideas about "great art" can teach us something important about the "function" of art today with respect to the coming-to-pass of the truth of Being. It is clear there also that the way in which contemporary man has an "experience" with the great works of art of the past which he preserves, has the same "function." At any rate, it is clear there that contemporary art can also be original; it too can be founding in a triple sense; it too can be historical in the dual sense just mentioned.[100] Yet it is true also that only thoughtful reflection can prepare the coming-to-pass of art.

CHAPTER 9

Thinking and Poetizing

I. INTRODUCTION

In the preceding chapter we have seen that for Heidegger poetizing is the essence of art as such. In "The Origin of the Work of Art," Heidegger develops the thesis that art is the establishing in the work of the truth. Since truth is the clearing and concealing of the beings as such and taken as a whole, truth comes-to-pass while it is being poetized. All art is essentially poetizing. Poetizing here means not the art of poetry but that in which all forms of art find their essence. It is due to the arts' poetic essence that in the midst of all that is, art is able to break open an open space, in whose openness everything is suddenly other than usual.

The essence of poetizing cannot be fully understood from the nature of the power of imagination (Kant). Poetizing is not an aimless and empty imagining of whimsicalities, nor is it the flight of mere notions and fancies into the realm of what is unreal and mere fiction. Poetizing is the illuminating projection which lets the open happen, so that now, in the midst of beings, the open can bring the beings to shine or to ring out.

To avoid misunderstanding, Heidegger clearly states that it is not his intention to claim that poetry is the essence of all art forms. The other art forms cannot be derived from poetry, nor can poetry be derived from any other art form. Yet Heidegger admits here that he shares Kant's view that among the arts poetry has a privileged position because of its close affinity with language. This view suggests that there must be a close relationship between art and language, also. This relationship becomes understandable the moment one realizes that there is an essential relationship between language and the non-concealment of beings.

The implications of these claims for Heidegger's conception of language and art need not occupy us here further, in view of the fact that they already have been raised in the preceding chapters. Yet it seems appropriate to dwell briefly on what Heidegger has to say about the relationship between thinking and poetizing and, thus, also about the relationship between the thinker and the artist, and about the thinker and the poet in particular.

In this chapter I thus wish to focus on the question of how in Heidegger's view the relationship between thinking and poetizing is to be understood. The question is important, and it has been raised in most of Heidegger's later publications. The issue has been studied by a number of commentators from different perspectives, but there are still questions for which the answers are lacking. There is common agreement on what thinking and poetizing have in common, but there is little agreement on the manner in which one is to think of their difference. Heidegger himself does not always characterize this difference in the same way, and his often-quoted statement that the poet names the holy and the thinker thinks Being lends itself to more than one interpretation.[1]

First I shall follow Heidegger in some of his works, written between 1935 and 1960, in order to see how he himself raises the issue and tries to think the belonging together of thinking and poetizing, as well as their unbridgeable difference. Obviously, no complete treatment of all the relevant passages will be attempted here. Also, I have decided to limit my discussion to those passages which in my view are important to understand how Heidegger determines the *difference* between thinking and poetizing.

Then I shall try to find a reasonable answer for the following questions: 1) Why is this issue, virtually never discussed by other philosophers, so important for Heidegger? 2) What are the reasons which led Heidegger to discuss the issue and give it such a prominent place in his later writings? 3) What is meant by "thinking" and "poetizing?" 4) What is to be understood by the expressions "original thinking," "original poetizing," "primordial poetizing," and "originating *(anfangendes)* thinking?" 5) What do thinking and poetizing have in common? 6) What constitutes their precise difference? 7) Why does Heidegger so hesitantly approach the issue, and why does he continue to discuss it time and again over a period of more than twenty-five years?

In my attempt to answer these questions, I shall be making use of ideas proposed by the leading commentators who have concerned themselves with the issue. Thus, what prompted me to write this chapter was not a dissatisfaction with the quality of the existing commentaries but rather the fact that even the best commentators, who have made a careful study of the problem, have finally come to a "disappointing" and somewhat "frustrating" conclusion. Richardson, for instance, who in his superb book on Heidegger has unfolded what Heidegger understands by thought, and who on many pages has turned to the relationship between thinking and poetizing, at the end of his book comes to the conclusion that Heidegger concerning this issue "gives us several hints, none of them wholly satisfying."[2] Kelkel, on the other hand, suggests that for Heidegger the relationship between thinking and poetizing is inherently problematic, because it is intimately concerned with the mystery of Being itself.[3] I do not disagree with these authors. Yet I wonder whether in what these and other commentators have said about the issue there is perhaps still something that has remained unsaid, although, to some degree at least, it is still sayable. It is this wonder which led me to the reflections to follow.

II. THE ARGUMENT IN THE TEXTS

The thesis that there is a close relationship between Being and language is thematized explicitly for the first time in *An Introduction to Metaphysics.*[4] It is in this context that Heidegger for the first time mentions an equally close relationship between thinking and poetizing, as well as an intimate relationship between thinkers and poets as far as their attention to the coming-to-pass of the truth of Being is concerned.[5] Yet in this lecture course, Heidegger does not yet give us a clear idea of how thinking and poetizing are to be distinguished from one another.

Between 1935 and 1946, Heidegger regularly returned to these issues, particularly in his elucidations of Friedrich Hölderlin's poems. He continued to stress both the close relationship between thinking and poetizing and their essential difference. Yet here, too, the question of how the difference is to be understood remained unanswered. Heidegger does mention there that the poet names the holy, whereas the thinker thinks Being; yet from the context, it is not clear precisely how that characterizes the essential difference between thinking and poetizing.[6]

In 1946 Heidegger wrote "The Saying of Anaximander," in which he explains that Being granted its light to the Pre-Socratics through some kind of special experience, on the basis of which they were able to bring Being into word. They conceived of Being in terms of *phusis, alētheia,* and *logos,* and in their response to Being's address they attentively listened to its saying.[7]

In a reflection on the question of how one is to "translate" the fragment under examination, Heidegger writes:

> Only in thoughtful dialogue with what it says can this fragment of thinking be translated [from the past into the present and from Greek into German]. How-

ever, *thinking is poetizing,* and indeed more than just one kind of poetizing, more than poetry and song. *Thinking of Being is the original way of poetizing.* Language comes into word, i.e., into its essence, in thinking. Thinking says what the truth of Being dictates; it is the original *dictare. Thinking is primordial poetizing,* prior to all poesy, but also prior to the poetics of art, since art shapes its work within the realm of language. All poetizing in this broader sense, and also in the narrower sense of the poetic, is in its ground thinking. *The poetizing essence of thinking* preserves the sway of the truth of Being.[8]

Heidegger speaks here about a thinking *of* and *by* Being that is equally a primordial poetizing and, thus, is more primordial than, and also at the root of, all "philosophizing" and of every engagement in the arts, including poesy. Thus he could later in a letter to Emil Steiger write that a poet is all the more poetizing to the degree that he is more thinking.[9] Secondly, one should observe here that Heidegger meanwhile has thoroughly rethought the relationship between Being and language; from now on, to think about Being is to concern oneself with the "essence" of language. The relationship to language, earlier maintained for the poet only, is now transferred to all thinking; yet what is called "poetizing" has herewith not lost its original importance. It is also clear that this relationship makes possible a meaningful dialogue between thinkers and poets, but the essay does not contain information on precisely how this dialogue is to be understood.

Finally, in the thinking *of* and *by* Being, which is also called primordial poetizing and as such is at the root of what we usually call man's thinking and poetizing, Being plays the privileged part.

A few years earlier, Heidegger had observed that the word *dichten,* which is derived from the old high German *tithôn,* is connected with the Latin *dictare* and *dicere.*[10] *Dictare* means "to say something repeatedly, to tell a person what to say, to dictate, to compose." These words have the same stem as the Greek *deiknumi,* which means "to show, make manifest, reveal something as what it is." Poetizing, therefore, means that saying which has the form of a making-manifest that shows. It receives the hints, given by the gods, and signals them through to the people. Poetizing is instituting, the founding which brings about what lasts. The poet is the one who institutes Being in the historical being of a people.[11]

In 1949, Heidegger added an introduction to *What Is Metaphysics?* and used the occasion to make a few very important changes in the postscript of 1943. In one of these passages, Heidegger writes that both thinking and poetizing originate from "originating thinking."[12] From the context it is clear that in 1949 Heidegger used the term *das anfängliche Denken* to refer to what in the "Anaximander" essay was called "original poetizing."

In my opinion, the most important passages on the relationship between thinking and poetizing are to be found in *On the Way to Language*, in which Heidegger published six essays written between 1950 and 1959. For our present purposes, I shall focus briefly on two passages which are immediately relevant to our concern in this chapter.

In the essay "Language in the Poem," written in 1953, Heidegger speaks about a thinking dialogue with the poets' works. There he states the following:

> Only a poetic dialogue with the poet's poem is a true dialogue: the poetizing conversation betweeen poets. But it is also possible, and at times even necessary, that there be a dialogue between *thinking* and *poetizing*, namely, for the reason that a distinctive, though in each case different, relation to language is proper to both. The dialogue of thinking with poetizing aims to call forth the coming-to-presence *(Wesen)* of language so that mortals may learn again to live within language.[13]

The relationship between thinking and poetizing is explicitly reflected upon in "The Essence of Language," which was written in 1957. It is difficult to understand how one can speak about the neighborhood of thinking and poetizing, in view of the fact that they obviously are two wholly different kinds of saying.[14]

Poetry and thinking seem to be as divergent as they can possibly be. Their being neighbors appears to be concealed within the extreme difference of their saying, and their divergence appears to be their real encounter. The neighborhood of poetry and thinking is obviously much more than a clumsy and cloudy mixture of two kinds of saying in which each awkwardly borrows from the other, even though sometimes it seems to be that way.

> But in truth, poetry and thinking are in virtue of their essence held apart by a delicate but luminous difference, each held in its own darkness: two parallels, in Greek *para allēlōn*, next to one another and against one another, transcending and surpassing one another, each in its own fashion. Poetry and thinking are not separated if separation is to mean cut off into a relational void. The parallels intersect in the infinite. There they intersect in a cut (or section) that they themselves do not make. By this cut, they are first cut, engraved into the design of their neighboring essence. This design is the fissure, which tears poetry and thinking open so that they can be near to one another. Thus the neighborhood of poetry and thinking is not the result of a process by which poetry and thinking—no one knows from where—first draw near to each other and in this way establish a nearness or neighborhood. The nearness that draws them near is itself the happening of the appropriation *(Ereignis)* by which poetry and thinking are directed into their proper essence.[15]

But if the nearness of poetry and thinking is a nearness of saying, then we must in our thinking assume that the appropriating event abides or holds sway as that aboriginal saying in which language itself grants us its own essence.[16]

III. ISSUES TO BE DISCUSSED

A first problem to be discussed in light of the texts presented in the preceding section is the question of whether or not the issue about the relationship between thinking and poetizing is an important one for Heidegger, and if so, why.

The answer to the first part of this question is obviously an unqualified yes. The issue is of vital importance, in that it immediately pertains to the matter worthy of being thought by a thinking that must focus on the coming-to-pass of the truth of Being. Thus Heidegger does not discuss poetry to make an otherwise dry and boring discussion more interesting; rather, he thinks about certain poetic works because in them the poet authentically responded to the soundless voice of Being's address. And he raises the issue about the precise relationship between thinking and poetizing because it is essential to a proper understanding of the response that man is to give to the aboriginal saying of Being as *logos*.[17]

In dealing with the issue, Heidegger is fully aware of the fact that most philosophers reject the idea of a poetizing thinking, because it seems to be, and often is, "adventurous." Heidegger is aware of the danger. He even admits that authentic thought can be threatened by the good and salutary danger of the proximity of the singing poet. The poetizing character of thinking has been veiled for a long time, and wherever it begins to manifest itself, it is constantly exposed to the danger of remaining caught in the utopia of a half-poetic understanding.[18] Heidegger is also aware of the fact that many poets object to the so-called thinking interpretation of poems given by philosophers.[19] He furthermore does not suggest that he is the first one to raise the issue. Several authors in the past have pointed to the fact that both philosophy and poetry belong to the same cultural region, one which is often opposed by that which is brought to light by the sciences.[20] Others have said often that both concern themselves with language in a manner which methodically is still not yet carefully determined (Nietzsche). Yet in Heidegger's view, these authors tried to relate thinking and poetizing as it were from the outside, and most of them treated the issue in a rather superficial manner. Heidegger himself asks the question about their relationship in order to point to a dilemma from which we feel unable to escape. This dilemma originates from their apparent belonging together.[21] Poetizing and thinking are two different modes of saying which concern themselves with the same in different ways, the saying of Being.[22]

Finally, Heidegger is equally aware of the factors which have prevented most philosophers from genuinely reflecting on the issue: the assumed opposition between the rigor of philosophical thought as opposed to the so-called free employment of man's creative imagination, the importance given to logical and calculating thinking in philosophy, the primary position of the proposition in philosophical discourse, the idolatry of *ratio*, the privileged position of the concept in systematic philosophy, the alleged opposition between philosophy, on the one hand, and poetic and mythic thinking, on the other, etc.[23]

The answer to the second part of our question is already somehow indicated in the preceding reflections. Yet it is of some importance here to unfold in a more systematic fashion the reasons Heidegger had for his position. It seems to me that we can give at least five different, but closely related, sets of reasons which explain why Heidegger thought he had to return so persistently to the issue.

First of all, there is the all-encompassing concern to come to a genuine understanding of what it means to think philosophically. This concern led Heidegger to a radical critique of Western philosophy since the time of Plato, and of classical metaphysics in particular. The "logical" outcome of the entire metaphysical movement in the West since Plato and Aristotle has come to the point where modern science and technology have completely taken the place of thought.[24] Heidegger gradually began to realize that overcoming metaphysics inherently implies giving up the scientificity of philosophy, if taken in the form in which it was understood between Plato and Nietzsche.[25] Philosophy is not a science, and, thus, its "organon" cannot possibly be classical logic. But if thought has really nothing in common with science and our scientific way of thinking, are there then perhaps other forms of thinking to which it may be related and with which it is to be compared? As other possible modes of thought relevant here, Heidegger regularly mentions poetizing and *muthos*. In his view *muthos* and *Dichtung* are intimately intertwined, and both have an essential affinity to thinking.[26]

Furthermore, the more Heidegger concerned himself with thought, the more he began to realize how much even the greatest thinkers depend on the manner in which Being itself in each epoch of history addresses itself to man.[27] This realization led to penetrating reflections on the essence of language, and that, in turn, confronted him again with the fact that both the thinker and the poet are concerned primarily with language, i.e., with the language of Being as well as man's authentic response to its address.

Then there is what I would like to call the socio-political dimension of Heidegger's philosophy, which again pointed in the same direction. Already in *Being and Time* Heidegger had strongly stressed that historical

Dasein, as Being-in-the-world, ek-sists essentially in Being-with-others, so that its historizing really is a co-historizing which is determinative for the destiny of the community and people to which each man belongs.[28] These ideas were then taken up in Heidegger's rectorial address, where an attempt was made to explain the function of the university in the life of the community and the function of philosophy in that overall framework.[29] In *An Introduction to Metaphysics,* he describes the Greek *polis* as the place wherein and as which historical *Dasein* is; it is the place in which, out of which, and for which history happens. To this place belong the gods, the temple, the priests, the festivals, the games, the poets, the thinkers, the ruler, the council, the assembly of the people, the army, and the fleet.[30] It is in this community that the unconcealment of Being occurs, and it is achieved there by various forms of work: ". . . the work of the word in poetry, the word of stone in the temple and statue, the work of the word in thought. . . ."[31] Here, too, we find the poet and the thinker again characterized in the same way, namely, as the ones who are concerned with the work of the word.

Then there is Heidegger's growing concern with the Pre-Socratics and the Greek poets. This concern led to the realization that it is incorrect to assume that originating thinking *(das anfangende Denken)* at that time was "scientific" in the sense in which it later would become so in Plato and Aristotle. Furthermore, in the case of Parmenides it is almost impossible to distinguish between thinking and poetizing. It is particularly here that Heidegger began to realize that underlying the poetizing of poets and the thinking of thinkers, there must be a more primordial form of thinking involving both Being and man which is sometimes called primordial poetizing and sometimes originating thinking. As far as the part of man in this thinking is concerned, it involves not yet anything more than his attentive and docile listening to the aboriginal saying of Being itself. This first response can then be taken up and articulated by man, either by making the already existing language say things and show a world which it before had not yet said and shown (authentic poetizing) or by returning to the language already spoken in order then, by means of a re-collecting re-trieve, to make the unsaid come to light in the said (authentic thinking). Such a re-trieve is particularly important if it focuses on what was said by "great" poets and "deep" thinkers.[32]

Finally, we may perhaps mention here Heidegger's concern with theology. If it is true that metaphysics is to be overcome, and if it is also true that metaphysics has become an integral part of dogmatic theology, then classical dogmatic theology is to be overcome to that extent as well. Today we find ourselves in a world which is "possessed" by science and technology, and that which most people call "philosophy" is really no more than a "scientific" dealing with science and technology. In such a world and in such a philosophy, there is no room for the holy and, thus, no room for God. We no longer know what the holy means. Perhaps that may change again, if through poetry we let ourselves be led back to the homeland of our historical dwelling, which is the nearness of Being.

> In such nearness, if at all, a decision may be made as to whether and how God and the gods withhold their presence . . . whether and how the day of the holy dawns, whether and how in the upsurge of the holy an epiphany of God and the gods can begin anew. But the holy, which alone is the essential sphere of divinity, which in turn affords a dimension for the gods and for God, comes to radiate only when Being itself beforehand and after extensive preparation has been illuminated and is experienced in its truth.[33]

Throughout his reflections on the work of Hölderlin as well as in the epilogue to *What is Metaphysics?* Heidegger constantly describes the work of the poet as one who is concerned with the naming of the holy.[34]

The question concerning the relationship between thinking and poetizing is thus an important one for Heidegger, and there are many reasons why that is so. One wonders why Heidegger so hesitantly approached the issue. It is mentioned first in the thirties, and it is then touched upon on many occasions over a period of more than twenty-five years. Could it be that Richardson is correct when he (commenting on Heidegger's own words) says that the main reason for this state of affairs is to be found in the fact that the poetizing character of thinking and, thus, its common root with poetry and poesy in original poetizing or originating thinking had to remain somewhat hidden until one learned to comprehend the genuine nature of language, i.e., of Being as the process of *logos?* For if that indeed is correct, then it is understandable that a clearer exposition of Heidegger's view could not be expected before *What Evokes Thought?* and *On the Way to Language.*[35]

We must now turn to the most important and most difficult question raised in the beginning of this chapter: For Heidegger, precisely what is the relationship (i.e., identity and difference) between thinking and poetizing? William J. Richardson, who in his book *Heidegger: Through Phenomenology to Thought* was concerned primarily with clarifying Heidegger's position on thinking, has made a careful study of the issue. As we have mentioned already, toward the end of this important book the author concludes that Heidegger has given us several hints in regard to this question but that none of them is wholly satisfactory.[36]

First, one could say that Being comes into words through both poet and thinker by reason of their authentic responses to Being's address, which has the structure of re-collection. In this response, Being comes (future) as having-been in what is (past), and it is now made present in words (present). It is the nature of the past which distinguishes poetry from thought. For the poet, the past would be that through which he experiences Being (i.e., the world or the holy) and to which the poet, in response to Being's address, gives a name. This *original naming* holds the primacy for the poet.[37] For the thinker, on the other hand, the past is Being as already brought into words in one way or another; the thinker must retain Being, articulated in these words, by a constantly renewed retrieve. Thus, *retrieve* holds the primacy for the thinker. In this interpretation the thinker plays a role in the event of language which is analogous to that of the conserver in a work of art.[38]

Then, one could also say that in his poetizing the poet moves from language's aboriginal utterance *(logos)* to articulation *(Verlautbarung)*,[39] whereas in his thinking the thinker moves back from articulation to primordial utterance.[40] The thinker thus lets Being shine forth by retrieving the authentic meaning of words. Yet in Richardson's own view, this explanation cannot account for the fact that poetry, too, is fundamentally a thinking;[41] it does not explain either how thought differs from poetry, when the thinker for his part also brings Being into words.

Finally, one can derive a third interpretation from Heidegger's claim that the thinker utters Being and the poet names the holy.[42] In the "Letter on Humanism" Heidegger wrote that Being, as the sending which sends truth, announces itself in poetry, without being manifest already as the history of Being.[43] One could thus understand the holy as Being considered as revealment, whose concomitant concealment is not experienced as such. In thinking, on the other hand, Being would be experienced as the process of *a-lētheia*, i.e., revealment and concealment, and brought to expression as such.

Richardson finally concludes: "Could we find a more original simplicity if we reduced all three explanations to this: in poetry Being is uttered, but not as Being; in thought Being is uttered as such. Fine, but is the formula not still a bit too formal?"[44]

In principle, I agree with the author that these indeed are possible, valid interpretations. Yet it seems to me also that these interpretations can be further articulated by adding to the first one an explicit reference to the future, and in the second distinguishing between the "aboriginal" thinking and poetizing saying, on the one hand, and the thinking and poetizing responses by thinkers and poets, on the other. In this way we shall perhaps be able to give a more articulated explanation of the third, as the reflections to follow, I think, will show.

In my view, to explain the difference between thinking and poetizing, it is important at first not to focus exclusively on those we commonly call

philosophers and poets. The response to the thinking and poetizing saying of and by Being is a listening response to which every human being
who is authentic is invited. This response can be articulated in two ways.
Firstly, one can realize that Being has already taken a concrete "form"
(world), which the aboriginal as well as the responding saying attempts to
overcome. In this case the saying of Being and the articulated response by
man are called poetizing, *dichtend.* The basic characteristic of poetizing
consists in bringing Being into words in a truly originating manner; that
constitutes the "creative" element in poetizing, which envisions and institutes a "new" world, i.e., a world with new options and possibilities. In
this case, the human response thus tries to bring into words as carefully as
possible the "dictation" of Being itself. In the final analysis, the twofold
poetizing saying institutes *(stiftet)*, brings about *(erwirkt)*, and founds
what remains, i.e., Being.[45] It also "determines" what a human being is,
what a people is, because it "determines" in what world they will live.[46]

However, in the second type of response, one can also realize that
every articulation of the meaning of Being in any given world is inherently affected by negativity during each epoch of its history, so that
everything said and thought, including the aboriginal saying of Being,
and most certainly man's response, contains something unsaid and something still unthought. This phenomenon is to be brought to light by
thinking. Thus the basic characteristic of the thinking act consists in
returning to what is already said and thought (which, as far as every
original response is concerned, presupposes poetizing), in order to think
again the unsaid and unthought in what has been so said and thought. The
poetic saying is oriented primarily toward what is to come, something
novel, something which as such has never been. The thinking saying is
oriented primarily toward what has already been said and toward what is
to come only through the dialogue with the "poets."

This interpretation would also account for the fact that Heidegger is so
adamant in proving that the great thinkers of the West's beginning were
just as much poets as they were thinkers, because they were the first to
bring the address of Being into words, and to bring it to the attention of
their people as something that is constantly to be thought, to be taken as
something in which particularly the still unsaid is that which is to be
thought time and again.[47]

But even though it is good not directly to begin with those we usually
call philosophers and poets, it is and remains true that there are humans
who think and poetize in a privileged manner; those we call "our"
thinkers and poets. Yet it is true also that great poets think and great
thinkers often poetize.

IV. CONCLUSION

In Heidegger's later philosophy, a thinking concern with language begins to come to the fore. Being is then thought as *logos* and language. This way of thinking about Being has important implications for the manner in which one conceives of the relationship between thinking and poetizing. I do not think that Heidegger's position in this matter has changed considerably since the thirties, even though his way of speaking about it has changed notably. This change is particularly obvious from the fact that the original address of Being is sometimes articulated as an original poetizing, an originating thinking, and more often in the later works as the aboriginal saying.

Being addresses itself to humans; the lightning flash of its address can in principle be seen by everybody who has come to authenticity and, thus, has not yet fallen, or no longer is the victim of the dominating scientific, technological, and thus nihilistic view of the world. Yet among those who see the lightning and hear the soundless voice of Being, some humans occupy a privileged position. Heidegger calls them the thinkers and the poets.

All humans live in communities. In some form or another they belong to a people; and each people has its own language, its mother tongue, and perhaps even its own set of dialects.[48] Poets and thinkers have a special concern for language, for the language *of* and *by* Being *(logos)* as well as for the language which as members of a people they themselves speak. Thinkers and poets bear great responsibility for the life of the community to which they belong; but they share this responsibility with other members of the community, and it need not occupy us here.

The thinker and the poet are concerned with the same, but not in the same way. They are concerned, each in his own way, with providing an authentic response to the soundless voice of Being. They differ in the manner in which they so respond. The poet is, standing in the present, oriented primarily toward what is to come in light of what is as having-been; the thinker, on the other hand, is concerned with the unsaid in what has already been said about what has been, is, and will be. Both the thinker and the poet presuppose in their poetizing and thinking responses that before they can begin to respond in poetry or thinking, they must first properly have seen the lightning flash and heard the soundless voice of Being. Thus their authentic responses still have, each in its own way, the character of the originating thinking in which through its aboriginal saying Being dictates the primordial poem to those men who are willing and able to listen. Fully realizing the tension *(polemos)* that lies at the root of the identity and difference of any concrete world and Being itself, they formulate their authentic responses in such a way that every "needless" limitation found in this world and its language will be overcome, either by showing new possibilities and options "prophetically" or by retrieving them from what already has been said by other poets and thinkers. And yet in a deep sense, their poetizing and thinking really remain the poetizing and thinking of and by Being, even though they take place in the *Da* of Being, in those humans who have seen and heard and have lent their ears in docility to the silent word of Being's saying.

Thus poets and thinkers have in common that both, to some degree at least, try to overcome the negativity which is inherently intrinsic to every concrete sending of Being. Yet the poet who names the holy is concerned with the positive dimension of Being more than with the negative, whereas the thinker who tries to think the unthought and unsaid in what already has been thought and said is more directly concerned with the negative dimension of the various forms of Being's sending which have already come-to-pass.

> Poetizing is instituting *(Stiften)* by the word and in the word. But what is instituted in this way? That which will remain . . . the poet names the gods and all things with respect to what they are. This naming does not consist in labeling something already previously known with a name; rather, by speaking the essential word, the poet's naming first nominates a being to what it is. Thus it becomes known *as* being. Poetry is the founding of Being in the word.[49]

"The poet gathers the world in a saying whose word remains . . . a shining in which the world appears in such a way as if it were seen for the first time."[50] The poet brings things into words; that means "to raise into word something formerly unspoken and never said before and to let what until now remained hidden appear through the saying."[51] Thinking, on the other hand, "deals with the arrival of what has been and is recollection."[52] Thinking fully realizes that never and in no language is it the case that what is spoken is also that which is being said.[53]

CHAPTER 10

Science and Metaphysics
in the Modern Era

I. INTRODUCTION. MODERN SCIENCE AND MODERN METAPHYSICS

Heidegger had a rather sophisticated knowledge of the sciences, particularly physics, biology, and history. He studied mathematics, physics, and history at the University of Freiburg and remained interested in these sciences throughout his life. Carl von Weizsäcker reports that Heidegger's knowledge of the natural sciences was exceptional and that he was able to maintain high-level conversations on scientific issues with leading scientists of his time (Werner Heisenberg, Victor von Weizsäcker, et al.).[1]

As a philosopher, Heidegger concerned himself regularly with the meaning of modern science. Important ideas about the sciences, particularly about the natural and the historical sciences, are found in *Being and Time, What is Metaphysics?, What is a Thing?, Holzwege, Vorträge und Aufsätze, Gelassenheit, Was heisst Denken?,* and the *Nietzsche* volumes.[2] In his lectures and essays on the sciences, Heidegger was not interested in logical and methodological issues, however important they may be. His main interest rather focused on an effort to understand the meaning of modern science and to comprehend its relationship to modern metaphysics.

In the secondary literature, Heidegger's position in regard to modern science has been discussed quite regularly.[3] Since I myself have already written on several aspects of Heidegger's "ontology of science," I have decided to limit myself here to a brief reflection on Heidegger's conception of the precise relationship between science and metaphysics in the modern era.

In a lecture presented in 1938, Heidegger states that the origin of modern science must be understood from the perspective of the origin of modern metaphysics.[4] In his view, each concrete form of metaphysics founds the era or epoch in which it comes about, by giving that epoch the ground for its course in history, which in each case is defined by a determinate interpretation of beings and a determinate conception of truth. This "ground," this "truth," and the "domain" over which they range are for each epoch that which is most questionable, because they constitute what for that era Being has come to mean. Thus, the essence of an epoch must be understood from the coming-to-pass of the non-concealment of Being as it dominates that epoch.[5]

Among the phenomena which are essential to our own era, *science* and *technology* certainly occupy an important place. There are obviously other phenomena which are equally essential to our modern era. For one thing, in the modern era *art* has become the subject matter of aesthetics; as we have seen elsewhere, that means that works of art have become objects of a special experience, and that art is conceived here as the expression of a man's life.[6] Furthermore, man's doing in general is now universally interpreted as *culture*, i.e., as the realization of the highest values through the cultivation of the highest goods of mankind.[7] Finally, we also have as a typical characteristic of our modern epoch the de-divinization of nature and of the entire world.[8]

In Heidegger's opinion, the important question to ask in regard to these facts concerns the kind of Being and the interpretation of truth which lie at the root of these phenomena. In this lecture he limits himself to some questions: 1) What is the essence of modern science? 2) What conception of Being and truth is at the root of this view? 3) What is the relationship between modern science and modern metaphysics, and what does this relation tell us about the essence of the modern era? In my attempt to explain how Heidegger answers these questions, I shall use several essays and lectures on science written between 1938 and 1953, but particularly some sections of *What is a Thing?*

II. MODERN SCIENCE IN CONTRAST TO ANCIENT AND MEDIEVAL SCIENCE

According to Heidegger, the expression "modern science" refers to some-thing that is essentially different from the medieval *doctrina* as well as from the Greek *epistēmē*. This basic difference is founded upon a differ-ent interpretation of Being, and correspondingly upon a different kind of "seeing" and questioning. That is why it is impossible to conceive of ancient and modern science as two forms of knowledge which differ merely in degree, and to claim that modern science has made great prog-ress in comparison with ancient science.[9]

But even for those who do admit an essential difference between an-cient and modern science, it has not been easy to determine this difference in detail. One often characterizes modern science, in contradistinction to ancient and medieval science, by saying that modern science starts from facts, while ancient and medieval science started from general speculative concepts and propositions. There is some truth to this claim; yet it is also undeniable that ancient and medieval science observed facts and that modern science works with universal concepts and propositions. Thus, both ancient and modern science are concerned with facts and with universal concepts and statements. The contrast between the ancient and modern attitude in science can be explained only by paying attention to the manner in which in both cases the facts are conceived and to the question of how in each case universal concepts and statements are established.[10]

It is important to note here that all great scientists of the sixteenth and seventeenth centuries were also philosophers. They clearly understood that there cannot be any "bare" facts; a fact is only what it is in light of the fundamental conceptions with which man approaches nature and natural events. One of the basic weaknesses of modern positivism is that one does not sufficiently stress the strong relationship between theory and fact. This relationship (and thus also the relationship between science and philosophy) is again maintained today by many leading scientists, such as Niels Bohr, Werner Heisenberg, Albert Einstein, etc.[11]

Secondly, the difference between the ancient and modern conceptions of science is often characterized by saying that the latter, contrary to the former, uses experiments and proves its insights empirically. But both experiment and test, to get information concerning the things and events, were already used in ancient Greece and in the Middle Ages. One should not forget that this kind of "experience" is implicit in all technological contacts with things in the arts and in the use of tools. Here, too, it is thus not the experiment or test as such but the manner in which experiments and tests are set up and the intention with which they are undertaken that are different in both cases. In modern science, the manner of experimentation is connected with the kind of conceptual determination of the facts and with the hypotheses used in the effort to find an answer for the questions that can be asked in regard to them.[12]

Thirdly, it is often said that it is characteristic of modern science that it uses calculations and measurements. But they were also used in ancient Greece and in the Middle Ages. It is again the manner in which both are being employed that is characteristic for modern science.[13]

III. THE ESSENCE OF THE MATHEMATICAL

These three ways of characterizing modern science vis-à-vis ancient and medieval science thus remain inadequate as long as we do not find the

basic characteristic of modern science, i.e., that which rules and determines the basic movement of modern science as such. This characteristic
consists in the typical metaphysical projection of the thingness of the
things in modern science. One could indeed say that this characteristic is
intimately connected with the mathematical character of modern science,
but then again it is essential that this characterization be properly understood. This characterization of modern science is also in harmony with an
often-quoted statement of Kant: "However, I maintain that in any particular doctrine of nature only as much genuine science can be found as
there is mathematics to be found in it."[14]

Yet one should keep in mind that the answer to the question of what is
meant here by "mathematics" cannot be taken from the science of
"mathematics" alone because this science is only a particular form of the
mathematical.[15] The word *mathematical* stems from the Greek word *ta
mathēmata*, originally "that which can be taught and learned"; thus
mathēsis originally meant the teaching and learning as well as that which
is taught and learned. Furthermore, teaching and learning should be taken
here in a very broad sense, i.e., in a sense not yet connected with any
official institution of learning. To fully understand what the Greeks
meant by *ta mathēmata*, one must compare it with that from which they
tried to distinguish it: *ta phusika*, the things insofar as they originate and
come forth from themselves; *ta poioumena*, the things insofar as they are
produced by man; *ta chrēmata*, the things insofar as they can be used and
stand at man's disposal, regardless of whether they are natural or manmade things; *ta pragmata*, the things insofar as man has to do with them,
works on them, uses them, transforms them, looks at them, examines
them, etc. The term *ta mathēmata* refers to things insofar as they can be
learned, i.e., insofar as they can be understood in terms of something one
knows already.[16]

In this light, it is thus understandable why Heidegger can claim that the
very essence of modern science is to be found in research *(Forschung)*. To
see that, one must realize first that research consists in a number of
closely related procedures. In these procedures one limits himself to a
clearly delineated realm of beings. Thus the expression "procedures" does
not just mean "method." For, as we have seen already,[17] the methodical
way of proceeding presupposes that there is already an open realm in
which a science can move. The opening-up of such a realm is precisely the
fundamental operation of research. The delineation of a definite realm of
Being is brought about by a projection *(Entwurf)*, by means of which a
certain aspect of things is taken as the exclusive theme of investigation. It
is by such a projection that the realm of beings characteristic of a particular science is clearly defined, that the access to that domain acquires its

methodic direction, and that the structure of the conceptual explanation received its first orientation.[18]

In Heidegger's opinion, one sees all of that most clearly in the rise of modern mechanics. What is decisive for its development consists in the application of a *special* kind of mathematics for the determination of the character of natural processes and events. It consists in the manner in which "nature" itself becomes projected with the help of *modern* mathematics; and modern mathematics can proceed "mathematically" because it itself is already "mathematical" in the original meaning of this term. As we have just seen, originally *ta mathēmata* referred to that which man, in his theoretical consideration of beings and in his practical concern with them, has learned, to what we know already in advance, know a priori. Since numbers and elementary quantitative relationships certainly occupied a privileged position among all the things the Greeks already knew beforehand, it is understandable that gradually the expression *ta mathēmata* received the meaning we now attach to this term. Yet when Greek physics developed into mathematical physics, the term *mathematical* still expressed first and foremost that in and for modern physics, something beforehand was made into what-is-known-already. And, in regard to that particular type of knowledge one was looking for, that meant concretely the specific projection of that which henceforth would be called "nature" and "natural."[19] Let us try to explain with the help of a brief digression, which will focus on Newton's *Principia*.

IV. THE MATHEMATICAL CHARACTER OF MODERN NATURAL SCIENCE

Modern mathematical physics obviously did not appear all at once. Its beginning occurred in the late Scholasticism of the fifteenth century.[20] The sixteenth century brought sudden advances, but also setbacks. Only during the seventeenth century were the decisive clarificatons and foundations of mathematical physics accomplished. The entire development found its first systematic expression in Newton's major work, *Philosophiae Naturalis Principia Mathematica* (1686–1687). This work is not only the culmination of all preceding efforts in mathematical physics; it is also the foundation for the subsequent development of the natural sciences.[21]

This monumental work is preceded by a short introduction entitled "Definitiones." It contains Newton's definitions of quantity of matter (= mass), quantity of motion (= momentum), and various forces. Then follows an important scholium, which contains statements about absolute and relative space and time, and absolute and relative motions. Next follows a section entitled "Axiomata, sive Leges Motus." After this section the proper content of the work follows, and it is divided into three "books," two of which are concerned with the motions of bodies and the third with the system of the world. We shall limit ourselves here to some brief remarks on Newton's first law, known as the principle of inertia.[22]

The first law states that "every body continues in its state of rest, or uniform motion in a straight line, unless it is compelled to change that state by forces impressed upon it."[23] In the preface to the second edition, Cotes observed in 1713 that this law was immediately accepted by all natural scientists.[24] Today most students of physics do not puzzle over this law, either, and consider it to be self-evident. Yet one hundred years before Newton put the law in this form, it was still completely unknown. Furthermore, it was "discovered" not by Newton but perhaps by Galileo. Also, Galileo never formulated the law in general terms; that was done by Baliani. Descartes tried to ground it metaphysically, whereas Leibniz employed it as a metaphysical principle. What interests us here is the question of precisely how the "mathematical" becomes decisive in the application of this law.[25]

V. THE ESSENCE OF THE MATHEMATICAL PROJECTION

The law speaks about a body which is not forced by impressed forces (*a viribus impressis non cogitur*). Where does one find such a body? There is also no experiment known which could bring such a body to direct perception. Modern science thus requires as a basic assumption a representation of things which contradicts ordinary experience. In other words, modern science claims to be based solely on facts given in experience; and yet its first and basic law speaks of things which do not exist. That shows us something important as far as "the mathematical" is concerned. For

> the mathematical is based on such a claim, i.e., the application of a determination of the thing, which is not experientially created out of the thing and yet lies at the base of every determination of the things, making them possible and making room for them. Such a fundamental conception of things is neither arbitrary nor self-evident.[26]

We cannot follow here the long controversy which brought it into power, nor can we determine in detail why it required a change in the entire approach to natural things and the development of a new mode of thought. Yet we shall try to typify this "battle" and this change with the help of an example.

According to Aristotle, heavy bodies are supposed to fall downward and light bodies must move upward. That is what according to their nature they have to do. Furthermore, of the heavy bodies, those fall faster which are mixed with less light bodies; the more weight a body has, the faster it will fall. Now, it was a decisive insight on the part of Galileo to realize that all bodies must fall with the same velocity. Galileo (perhaps allegedly) performed a public experiment from the leaning tower of Pisa, involving bodies of different weights. Although the bodies did not arrive on the ground at exactly the same time, Galileo nonetheless maintained his position. His opponents, on the other hand, interpreted the outcome of the experiment obviously in favor of Aristotle's theory. Because of this experiment, so the story goes, the opposition against Galileo increased to such an extent that he had to give up his position at the university and leave Pisa.[27] What is important in this story is the following:

Both parties saw the same facts, but they interpreted them differently. *They made the same events visible to themselves in different ways.* Both thought something *along with* the same phenomena, something a priori, something that in their opinion was connected with the *essence* of bodies and the *nature* of their motions.[28] What Galileo thought along in advance of the experiment concerning motion was the a priori conviction that the motion of every body is uniform, if every obstacle has been removed, and that every body's motion changes uniformly when an equal force affects it, regardless of its weight. In 1638 Galileo wrote in his *Discorsi:* "I think of a body thrown on a horizontal plane and every obstacle excluded. This results in what has been given a detailed account in another place, that the motion of the body over this plane would be uniform and perpetual, if this plane were extended infinitely."[29]

Thus in the first formulation of Newton's first law, Galileo says *mente concipio,* "I think in my mind," of something movable that is entirely left to itself. I think in my mind, I give myself a determination of things in advance, a priori. There is a prior grasping of what should be uniformly determinative of all bodies as well as of their motions. All bodies are alike as far as motion is concerned; there are no privileged motions; all places are alike, also, and so are all moments of time. Every force becomes determinable only by the change of motion which it causes. Change in motion is really a change in place. All determinations of all bodies have one basic characteristic as their origin: natural processes are nothing but the space-time determinations of the motions of point masses. This basic characteristic of nature also circumscribes its entire realm as being everywhere uniform.[30]

In Heidegger's opinion, we are now in a position to describe the essence of the mathematical more clearly. Until now we said only that it is a taking cognizance of something in which man's knowledge gives to itself and from itself in advance what it itself takes a thing to be, thus giving itself what it already had before. We can now specify this result further in the following manner.

The mathematical, as *mente concipere*, as thinking in one's mind, is a *projection* of the thingness of the things under consideration, which opens up a domain in which only things of a certain kind can show themselves. In the projection there is *posited* in advance what things are to be taken to be, and how they are to be evaluated. Such taking-for and evaluating are called in Greek *axioein*. The anticipating determinations and assertions which are implicit in the projection are called *axiōmata;* and Newton thus correctly called them so. Insofar as every science is expressed in propositions, the cognition which is posited in the mathematical projection is of such a nature as to set things on their foundation in advance. Thus axioms are fundamental propositions a priori. The mathematical projection is the anticipated conception of the essence of the bodies to be examined in natural science. The projection sketches in advance the ground plan of the structure of every natural thing, as well as of its relation to every other thing.[31]

The ground plan at the same time provides the measure and scope of the realm which, in the future, will eventually encompass all things of that kind. Nature thus no longer is an inner capacity of a body, *archē kai aitia tou kineisthai kai ēremein*,[32] which determines its form of motion and place, it is rather the realm of the uniform space-time context of motion, which is described in the axiomatic projection. Thus nature now becomes the closed totality of the motions of spatio-temporally related point masses. And, as we have mentioned already, into this outline of what, because of the a priori projection, from now on is supposed to be "nature," is furthermore subsumed the idea that motion is just change of place, that there are no privileged motions and that there is no privileged direction of motion, that space has the property of isotropy, that time has the character of isochrony, and finally that force must be determined by the motion which it is able to produce.[33] In other words, the axiomatic projection determines the conditions which must be fulfilled in order that a thing be a natural body.[34]

The realm of nature which is so axiomatically determined in outline by this projection also requires for the bodies within it a mode of access that is appropriate to the axiomatically predetermined objects. Thus the mode of questioning and the cognitive determination of nature are now no longer ruled by common opinion and traditional concepts. Bodies no longer have qualities beyond those projected in the mathematical projection itself; they simply have no other qualities, powers, or capacities. Natural bodies are nothing but what they show themselves to be within this so-projected realm. Their entire mode of being, their thingness as such, is determined by space and time determinations, masses, and forces. How they will show themselves is predetermined by the mathematical projection. Thus, the projection also codetermines the "perception" of what shows itself, our studying what shows itself, and our experiencing it. The projection posits in advance the conditions to which natural beings must respond in one way or another. The *experientia* thus becomes *experimentum*. Modern science is therefore experimental *because* it is mathematical. In other words, experimentation is necessary because of the a priori character of the projection.[35]

We mentioned before[36] that in this regard, too, there is an essential difference between modern science and medieval *doctrina* and Greek *epistēmē*. We now see better why that is so. For neither the Greek nor the medieval philosophers ever did come to genuine experimentation, nor could they do so, in view of the fact that neither *doctrina* nor *epistēmē* was science in the sense of research. To be sure, these people did know what *empeiria* or *experientia* meant: the observation of things, their properties, and changes under varying circumstances and conditions which, provided it be systematically performed, leads to knowledge of the way in which things as a rule are and behave. It is true also that in their observations they sometimes made use of measurements and numbers, and in certain instances they even employed devices and instruments. But all of that was not an experiment in the modern sense of the term, because the decisive element, as far as our modern research experiments are concerned, was still missing. To perform an experiment means to prescribe a condition according to which a certain kinetic whole *(Bewegungszusammenhang)* can be mastered in the necessity of its course, and can be mastered beforehand by our calculations. In other words, an experiment in the modern sense of the term is suggested and governed by laws, which in turn point to "facts" which will verify or falsify those laws. Laws, which have the character of hypotheses, are not arbitrary hypotheses, but they are developed from basic conceptions of nature which the scientists have formed in and through their original projection, by means of which they beforehand clearly demarcated a priori the region of things which would constitute the realm of their investigations. Thus the more they are able to exactly project the basic conception of nature, the more they will be able to perform their experiments in an exact way.[37]

Because the projection established a uniformity of all bodies according to the relations between the four basic "variables," it also required a universal and uniform measure, i.e., a numerical measurement. In this way, the mathematical projection of Newton led to the development and application of a certain kind of mathematics, in the narrow sense of the term. Modern science did not arise because people learned to make mathematics an essential part of the study of nature. Rather, the fact that a particular kind of mathematics could ever become an essential part of the study of nature is a consequence of the mathematical projection of nature. Analytic geometry (Descartes), infinitesimal calculus (Newton), and differential calculus (Leibniz) became possible and necessary on the ground of the basically "mathematical" character of modern thinking.[38]

VI. SPECIALIZATION AND MANAGEMENT

Once the mathematical character of modern physics is properly understood, it is relatively easy to understand its other basic characteristics, such as its concern with regularity and law, its experimental nature, its need for further organization and specialization. As for the latter, Heidegger claims here again that each science which is founded on the projection of a well-delineated realm of objects is necessarily always this particular and individual science, to be distinguished from possible other sciences. In the further unfolding of the original projection by means of its methodic procedures, each individual science again demarcates determinate subfields for special investigation. Thus specialization is necessarily connected with science taken as research. Furthermore, specialization does not proceed arbitrarily; it is oriented and guided by another important characteristic of modern science, namely, the fact that each science implies systematic management *(Betrieb).*[39]

The term *management* is not used here in a pejorative sense. Yet in view of the fact that science is essentially management, there is always a real danger that it becomes *mere* management and even mere "business." The management of science becomes mere management and business when, in its methodical procedures, it does not keep itself open and free by continuously and originally performing its basic projection time and again, but leaves this projection as it were behind itself as a mere given which does not require any further ascertainment, in order to focus exclusively on results and their further development and application.[40]

And because modern science as research intrinsically has the character of systematic management, institutionalization is also necessary in modern science. Institutes, departments, societies, academies, journals, all have become necessary. Yet this state of affairs contains the danger that one secures the priority of the method over that being (namely, nature or history) which is objectified in modern research.[41]

Furthermore, research today is also necessarily oriented toward technology, provided technology is taken here as what it is according to its very essence. Technicity keeps research efficient in its work and guarantees its genuiness. It also makes the necessary specialization possible, justifies it, and makes it understandable.[42]

In this very complex manner, scientific knowledge taken as research calls the beings to account for the question of how and in how far they can be made available to man's pro-posing and positing presentation *(Vor-Stellung)*. Research disposes of beings either when it is able to pre-calculate them in their future course or when it is able to post-calculate the past. In this pre- and post-calculation, nature and history become posited; they become the mere object of man's clarifying, positing presentation, which reckons on nature and reckons with history. Only that which in this way becomes object, *is*. Science becomes research only when the Being of beings comes about in a pro-posing, positing presentation which aims at bringing each being before itself in such a way that calculating man can be sure of it. Science becomes research when and only when the truth of beings has been changed into the certainty of man's own pro-posing, positing presentation.[43]

VII. THE METAPHYSICAL MEANING OF MODERN SCIENCE

We must now ask what the metaphysical ground is of modern science and what that which constitutes the metaphysical ground of science as research teaches us about the essence of our modern epoch. One could say that the essence of the modern epoch consists in that modern man has freed himself from all medieval conditions and, thus, has freed himself unto himself. This characterization of the modern epoch is true; yet, as we shall see shortly, it is misleading. It is also true that man's vindication of his own freedom has led to subjectivism and individualism; but it is equally true that in no other epoch has one ever seen an objectivism and collectivism that can be compared with that of modern times. Even the statement that the interaction of subjectivism and objectivism determines the essence of the modern era does not yet go to the heart of the matter.[44]

In Heidegger's view, the decisive factor in the constitution of the modern epoch is not so much the fact that man frees himself unto himself but the fact that the essence of man himself has changed. Man changed from being a *zōion logon echon* and God's child into being a subject. The word *subject* is derived from the Latin *subjectum*, which as a technical term is the translation of the Greek *hupokeimenon*, "that which lies before or underneath" and thus as ground gathers everything toward itself. Taken in this sense, the term does not yet necessarily refer to man. Yet in the modern era, to say that man is the first and true subject was tantamount to saying that man is that being upon which all other beings are founded, as far as their mode of Being and their truth are concerned. In this way, man becomes the center of reference of being as such and the measure of all things. But that, in truth, was possible only because the conception of the beings as a whole had changed. The beings as such taken as a whole no longer constitute the totality of all that emerges and abides, or the totality of all beings created by God, but rather the totality of all beings proposed to man as subject. Opposed to man-as-subject and pro-posed and posited by him, the entire world of things has meaning only in regard to him. In the modern era, the beings as such taken as a whole *(das Seiende im Ganzen)* are to be taken in such a way that they are beings only insofar as they are posited by man's pro-posing presentation and fabrication. Thus things are to the degree that they can be pro-posed and posited by man. Therefore, what truly characterizes our modern epoch consists in the fact that being *is* merely as objectified, *is* merely as posited pro-posedness.[45]

From this decision about the meaning of beings, very important consequences follow. First, if the world appears merely as something that has meaning only in regard to man, then the basic task of man becomes one of conquering the world. And man conquers the world by means of objectifying projections, calculations, designs, and techniques. Furthermore, anthropology as a philosophical discipline of utmost importance is born. The more the world of things is conceived as that which is to be conquered, and, thus, the more objective all beings begin to appear, the more subjective the subject becomes and begins to claim priority, and the more a doctrine of the world changes into a doctrine of man. It is then also understandable why philosophical anthropology proposes some form of humanism, which, in the final analysis, is no more than an account of the moral and aesthetic dimensions of man. It is then understandable, also, why man begins to develop a "picture of the world," a world view, and why eventually a philosophy of life had to develop. For as soon as the world of things becomes the mere object of man's pro-posing positing, and in this sense a mere "picture," man begins to seek ways of looking at it. Furthermore, if beings attain their status as beings merely to the extent that they are absorbed in some way or other in man's life, then one begins to account for these beings merely in terms of man's "living experiences."[46] From all of that, it finally becomes understandable why people in the nineteenth century felt the need to begin to search for values. For the moment beings become mere objects of man's own pro-posing and positing presentation, man has to compensate for the loss of their meaning by ascribing "values" to them, in such a way that these values can become the goal of all man's interactions with things. These interactions with beings then are no longer "natural" but become understood as "culture"; values become "cultural values," and, thus, the goal of all human activity is placed in the service of man himself. Finally, these values themselves become again reduced to the level of mere objects, pro-posed and posited by man himself as the goals which he needs to sustain his own activities in his effort to establish his place in the world.[47]

In Heidegger's opinion, the origin of the entire modern epoch is to be sought in the philosophy of Descartes, who for the first time tried to determine the metaphysical meaning of the mathematical. To fully understand Descartes's position in regard to both the mathematical and metaphysical, one should realize that before the modern conception of the mathematical emerged, the authoritative source of truth was taken to be that of the Christian faith. If one wished to discover the truth about what is, one had to turn to the Scriptures and the tradition of the Church. Before the modern era, there really was no worldly knowledge; the so-called natural knowledge, which was not based on revelation, did not have its own form of intelligibility, or its own independent ground. On the other hand, in the essence of the mathematical as it was understood in the modern era, we find the specific will to a new formation and self-grounding of man's knowledge as such. The detachment from revelation and the rejection of tradition are only the negative consequences of the mathematical projection. There is not only a liberation in this mathematical projection but also a completely new experience of freedom, i.e., a freedom which binds itself only to obligations which are self-imposed.

In view of the fact that natural science, modern mathematics, and modern metaphysics all emerged from the same root, and because of the fact that metaphysics, of these three, reaches farthest and deepest, it is metaphysics which will have to explain its own "mathematical" foundation and ground.[48]

VIII. DESCARTES AND THE ORIGIN OF THE MODERN ERA

Most scholars hold that modern metaphysics begins with Descartes. Heidegger first gives a brief description of the usual interpretation of Descartes's work. According to this view, during the Middle Ages philosophy was completely dominated by theology and gradually degenerated into a mere analysis of concepts and explanations of traditional opinions and theses. It petrified into a strictly academic knowledge which had no relevance for life, and was unable to enlighten the world as a whole. Descartes liberated philosophy from this disgraceful position. He introduced a new approach to philosophy; he began by doubting everything, but eventually he was led to something that cannot possibly be doubted: the doubting skeptic must be, and must be present, in order to be able to doubt at all. If I doubt, I must admit that I am. The "I" in the "I am" is thus indubitable; the human subjectivity came to be the center of thought. In view of the fact that reflection upon man's knowledge is to be developed at the very beginning of philosophy, a theory of knowledge must precede any theory of the world. Epistemology is to provide us with the foundation of philosophy, and this insight constitutes the main difference between modern and medieval philosophy.[49]

According to Heidegger, this interpretation of Descartes's work and significance is nothing but a bad novel. For the main work of Descartes is not an epistemology but his *Meditations on First Philosophy*, which is concerned, like Aristotle's *prōtē philosophia*, with the question concerning the Being of what is, concerning the thingness of the things. In trying to deal with this question, Descartes assumes that the proposition constitutes the guide for the question about the Being of beings.[50]

In developing his "new" philosophy, Descartes was certainly influenced by Scholasticism and particularly by Suarez's interpretation of Aristotle and Scholastic philosophy. Thus his main work reflects his argument with this tradition as well as his will to take up anew the question concerning the Being of beings, the thingness of things, the question of "substance." Yet Descartes lived during a time in which, for a century, mathematics had already been emerging more and more as the true foundation of thought. In other words, it was a time "which, in accordance with the free projection of the world, embarked on a new assault upon reality." But that means that Descartes was not a skeptic, nor did he try to promote an ego-perspective and modern subjectivism. Just the opposite is the case. Descartes wanted to make a contribution to the new mode of thought, which was trying to bring to clarity and unfold in its innermost essence "the at first dark, unclear, and often misinterpreted fundamental position" which thus far had progressed only by fits and starts. The mathematical, which "wills to ground itself in the sense of its own inner requirements," expressly intended to manifest itself "as the standard of *all* thought."[51] Descartes fully participated in this work of reflection on the fundamental meaning of the mathematical. Now, in view of the fact that this reflection was really concerned with the totality of all that is and man's knowledge of it, this reflection had to take the form of a reflection on metaphysics. "This simultaneous advance in the direction of a foundation of mathematics and a reflection on metaphysics above all characterizes his fundamental philosophical position."[52] In Heidegger's view, one can see that very clearly in Descartes's *Regulae ad directionem ingenii*, which constitutes an early work that remained unfinished and appeared in print only posthumously in 1701.[53]

In this work, Descartes tried to formulate and prove basic and guiding theses which were to lay the foundation of the mathematical, in order that the mathematical approach, as a whole, could become the measure of every inquiry of the human mind. In other words, Descartes tried to formulate the idea of a universal science, to which every inquiry must be directed and ordered as the one and only authoritative science.[54]

Heidegger discusses only three of the twenty-one rules, just to convey to the reader a notion of the aim and the "spirit" of the work. The third rule states that "concerning the objects before us, we should pursue the questions, not what others have thought, nor what we ourselves conjecture, but what we can clearly and insightfully intuit, or deduce with steps of certainty; for in no other way is knowledge arrived at." The fourth rule speaks about method, i.e., about the manner in which one in general is to proceed, and states that this "procedure" decides in advance what truth one will seek out in things. "Method is necessary for the discovery of the truth of nature." Thus method is not just one element of science among others but rather the primary component which determines what can become object and how it will become an object. Finally, the fifth rule reads:

> "Method consists entirely in the order and arrangement of that upon which the sharp vision of the mind must be directed in order to discover some truth. But, we shall follow such a method only if we lead complex and obscure propositions back step by step to simpler ones and then try to ascend by the same steps from the insight of the very simplest propositions to the knowledge of all the others."[55]

In Heidegger's opinion, it is essential that one understands how these reflections on the mathematical affect Descartes's argument with traditional metaphysics and how, starting from there, the future destiny and form of modern philosophy are determined. We have seen already that to the essence of the mathematical as a projection belongs the axiomatical, the formulation of basic principles upon which everything else is to be based in the proper order. Thus, if Descartes's *mathesis universalis* is to give a foundation to the whole of knowledge, it requires the formulation of special axioms which must be absolutely first, intuitively evident in and of themselves, and, thus, absolutely certain. Furthermore, these axioms must establish a priori, concerning the whole of what is, what is in being and what Being means, from where and how the thingness of things is to be determined. Descartes accepts from the tradition that that is to happen along the guidelines of the proposition. The tradition had taken the proposition, like the things, to be present-at-hand, and thus to be the present container of Being. Yet for a basically mathematical position, there can be no pre-given things whatsoever. Thus the proposition cannot be just any arbitrary one; it must be a basic proposition which must itself be based on its own foundation; it must be the basic principle absolutely.

One must thus try to find a principle of all positing, a proposition in which that about which it says something (the *subjectum*) is not at all taken from somehwere else.

> That underlying subject must as such first emerge for itself in this original proposition and be established. Only in this way is the *subjectum* a *fundamentum absolutum*, purely posited from the proposition as such, a basis and, as such, a *fundamentum absolutum* at the same time also *inconcussum* and thus indubitable and absolutely certain. Because the mathematical now sets itself up as the principle of all knowledge, all knowledge up to now must necessarily be put into question, regardless of whether it is tenable or not.[56]

For Descartes, the main issue thus is not to find a basic law which is valid for the realm of nature but rather to discover the highest principle for the Being of what is as such. This absolutely mathematical principle cannot have anything above it or in front of it, nor can it permit anything that might be given to it beforehand. The only thing that is given here is the proposition itself as such, the positing, the thinking that asserts. Thus the positing has only itself as that which can be posited. Only when thinking thinks itself is it mathematical in an absolute sense and does it take cognizance of that which it already has. If this thinking positing directs itself to itself, it may rightly claim that, whatever is asserted, the asserting or thinking is always an "*I* think." Thinking is always "*I* think," and therein lies "*I* am." In the "I posit," the "I" as the positor is co- and pre-posited as that which is already.[57]

In the essence of the thinking positing lies the proposition: *I posit.* It is the only proposition which gives to itself what lies within it. In it we find two claims. First: *I* posit; in each positing what is posited first is the *I* which posits, the *subjectum* of the positing as such. Thus it came-to-pass that the "I" became the subject in a privileged sense. Herein the character of the *ego* remained unnoticed; instead, the subjectivity of the subject is determined here by the I-ness of the "I think." It is important to note that this "I," which from now on is taken to be *the subjectum,* is, in its meaning, nothing subjective at all, if the latter term is taken in its common sense. It becomes subjectivistic only when its essence is no longer understood.

The second claim is connected with the first. Before Descartes's time, every thing present-at-hand, taken for itself, was called a *subjectum.* But now the "I" has become the privileged subject, that with respect to which all other things first become determined as such. These things receive their thingness only through the founding relation to the highest principle and its subject; consequently, they must be taken to be that which lies over against the subject as its *objectum*. Thus the things become objects, and the term *object*, too, receives here a completely new meaning.[58]

The "I," taken as "I think," becomes the ground upon which from now on all certainty and truth are based. Furthermore, thinking becomes at the same time the guideline for the determination of Being, i.e., the categories. And in view of the fact that thinking is the fundamental act of reason, reason now becomes explicitly posited, in harmony with its own demand, as the first ground of knowledge and the guideline of the determination of the Being of what is.[59] As we have seen already, that is true not only for the Being of things but equally and even more so for the Being of man himself.

CHAPTER 11

On the Essence of Technicity

Article I: Dessauer, Jünger, and Heidegger on Technology

The question concerning the essence of technicity *(Technik)* occupies an important place in Heidegger's later thought. In his view, technology is the "logical" outcome of traditional metaphysics, which concerns itself with beings and not with Being itself. As far as I know, the issue is raised for the first time in the *Nietzsche* lectures, namely in "Die ewige Wiederkehr des Gleichen und der Wille zur Macht" of 1939[1] and in "Seinsverlassenheit und Irrnis."[2] Heidegger returned to the essence of technology in the essay "What Are Poets For?" (1946)[3] and in a series of four lectures delivered in Bremen in 1949 under the general title *Insight into What Is*, in which both "The Question Concerning Technology" and "The Reversal" were presented for the first time.[4] Finally, he speaks about technology in *Gelassenheit* (1955) and in *Identity and Difference* (1957).

Heidegger was obviously not the first to raise the question concerning technology and technicity. Of the many authors who have concerned themselves with technology and its many implications, we must focus for a moment on Friedrich Dessauer and Friedrich Georg Jünger, with whose ideas Heidegger was familiar.[5] It should be noted that with the exception of Norbert Wiener,[6] most other contemporary authors who have made a careful study of technology wrote on technology after Heidegger had already formulated his definitive position in regard to the most important issues to be raised from the perspective of the coming-to-pass of the truth of Being. That is true notably for such authors as Jacques Ellul, Georg Klaus, Karl Steinbuch, and Jürgen Habermas.[7]

Friedrich Dessauer has been one of the best-known philosophers of technology in Germany.[8] He concerned himself intensively with technology between 1924 and 1960. K. Tuchel, who has made a careful study of Dessauer's basic ideas, summarizes the latter's position in the following statement:

> All the technological realizations are preceded by, and the realm of pre-established solutions is founded upon, the plan of God, which is the real ground and presupposition of all technology. Its essence can be transparent only to one who reconciles both the naturally given and the final fashioning of it to the Biblical act of creation, and who understands technological inventions in the sense of a *creatio continua*.[9]

Dessauer's philosophy, which is partly theological and partly philosophical, is inspired by the basic ideas of neo-Platonism. In his opinion, technology cannot be understood in an instrumental manner, i.e., as something that flows from the natural sciences and is "steered" by economics. In his view, the source of everything that is technological is to be found in a typical human activity called invention. The independence and autonomy of technology with respect to both economics and the natural sciences are guaranteed by the fact that technology has its origin in an irreducible "experience" which is typically its own. When God created the world, a great number of his ideas concerning the world were materialized directly; many other ideas were still to be materialized through the continuing creation of man's technology, which in and through invention discovers these latter ideas and realizes them. In 1958, in his *Streit um die Technik*,[10] Dessauer devoted part of a chapter to Heidegger's conception of technicity. It is quite clear from this critical exposition that Dessauer did not fully understand Heidegger's "philosophy of technicity" and was able to interpret it only from his own perspective. Dessauer feels that there are several important insights which Heidegger's reflections have brought to light; yet there are others which for Dessauer are totally inadequate and unacceptable.[11] Dessauer's own ideas and his criticism of Heidegger need not occupy us here further. Egbert Schuurman has given us a clear exposition of them, as well as of Heidegger's possible response to Dessauer's critique.[12] Suffice it to mention here two things only: 1) Heidegger must have known Dessauer's position; although he does not discuss Dessauer's ideas explicitly, there are some indications that he was familiar with his views. 2) Heidegger was unable to make use of Dessauer's ideas, in view of the fact that Dessauer's philosophy of technology is at root an anthropological determination of technicity, which Dessauer attempts to justify by constructing a metaphysical or religious explanation behind it which is supposed to undergird it. Yet in Heidegger's view, any merely anthropological conception of technicity is unacceptable, and it cannot be saved by metaphysical or religious conceptions that are added to it.[13]

The relationship between Heidegger and Friedrich Georg Jünger is more complex. Jünger (not to be identified with Ernst Jünger, whose work will be discussed in chapter 12), is not a philosopher but a poet and novelist, and as such he never developed a systematic philosophy of technology. He was very much concerned with the suprapersonal power in modern technology, and also with a possible deliverance from its "demonic" development.[14] Jünger tried to understand technology as a cultural force in both its origin and its unity; he usually expressed quite convincingly what people experience and feel in the face of technology. His view has some similarity with that developed by Oswald Spengler, for whom man is a predator, technology a tactic and a means to power. But this will to power is also his destiny: it leads to destruction. Man uses himself up in his will to power.[15] Yet where Spengler's position stresses a "heroic" element, despite the disastrous outcome, Jünger stresses anxiety and concern; where Spengler does not believe that there is still hope (the decline of the West is inevitable), for Jünger there still may be hope.

In Jünger's view, modern man turns to technology in order to orient himself toward the future. It is a utopia. Where classical utopias are built on the greatness and the power of the state, technology has now taken over this role of the state. "A utopia requires a scheme that is susceptible to rational development; technology is the most useful scheme of that kind which is presently available."[16] Initially people were very optimistic about the progress which technology was to bring about. Gradually, authors became more skeptical. Jünger himself is a downright pessimist; technology inevitably leads to destruction. Through technology we achieve just the opposite of what we wish to achieve. It leads to more work, less freedom, and ultimately death and total destruction.[17]

Technology "is a deadly power evoked by Cartesian thought and inspired by the will to power. Technological power is a suprapersonal power bearing the character of necessity."[18] We can avoid the disaster implicit in technology by another form of thinking, which learns again to keep and tend nature, and to care for the earth. In his later writings,[19] Jünger is deeply influenced by Heidegger and suggests that he has now found a genuine basis for the hope of deliverance from the catastrophic development of technology.[20]

As Jünger sees it, this deliverance must eventually come from a form of thought which is not just calculating, and from language as it is presupposed in every form of calculation and objectification. That does not mean that the extreme danger would still not be there. First of all, one cannot just lay technology aside as an instrument which one no longer needs. To lay technology aside is "beyond the capabilities of man and is at the present time something impossible."[21] It is much more likely that man himself will become part of technology, an instrument, or even its raw material. Already at this time, humans are often reduced to being parts of larger machines.[22] If one takes the technical plan as a whole, then there is often little difference between men and machines. In this plan all components and elements are normed and numbered, and man too is often no more than a number. In many cases he is just a replaceable part in a complex business project.

There still is hope. Deliverance can still come by the cultivation of a meditating and non-calculating way of thinking, as well as from a return to language in the original sense. "We ourselves are 'language'; and where we are not 'language' we are no longer able to encounter one another."[23]

Yet even though it is true that in his later work Jünger was indeed deeply influenced by Heidegger, it cannot be denied that in his earlier publications Heidegger himself must have been somehow influenced by Jünger; he never refers explicitly to Jünger's publications,[24] but he derived certain ideas and expressions from them. The latter are usually placed in quotation marks.[25]

In the present essay I shall present a brief paraphrase of the main ideas contained in the essay "The Question Concerning Technicity," where I shall also discuss some ideas proposed in "What Are Poets For?", *Gelassenheit*, and *Identity and Difference*. I finally shall conclude this chapter with a brief paraphrase of the most important insights contained in the lecture "The Turning."

Art. II: Heidegger's Lecture on Technicity (1949)

I. INTRODUCTION

In 1949, Heidegger delivered a series of four lectures in Bremen, entitled *Insight into What Is*. He literally repeated this series later at Buhlerhohe in the spring of 1950. The titles of the four lectures were "The Thing," "The Com-positing," "The Danger," and "The Turning."[26] The second lecture was later enlarged and in this new form presented in Munich in a series of lectures presented by different leading scholars, entitled *The Arts in the Technical Age*, and organized by the Bavarian Academy of Fine Arts. Heidegger's lecture was presented there on 18 November 1953. It was later published in this enlarged form in *Vorträge und Aufsätze*,[27] as well as in the third volume of the yearbook of the Bavarian Academy, which was edited by Clemens Graf Podewils[28] under the title *Die Künste im technischen Zeitalter*. It then also received a new title: "The Question of Technicity."

The lecture "The Turning" ("Die Kehre") was first delivered in Bremen in December 1949 in the series *Insight into What Is* mentioned above. It was first published in its original, unchanged form in 1962, together with the second lecture of the same series, taken in the revised form.[29]

In the German language, there are two different words for the English word *technology*, namely, *Technik* and *Technologie*. Heidegger is in these lectures primarily concerned with *Technik*, not with *Technologie*. In order to be able to distinguish these two in English, I am following William J. Richardson in translating *Technik* as "technicity" and reserving "technology" for *Technologie*. Furthermore, I shall translate *Gestell* as "compositing" and *Bestand* as "the constant standing-reserve."[30]

II. TECHNICITY VS. THE ESSENCE OF TECHNICITY

In the essay on technicity, Heidegger first indicates with a few brief statements what it is that he wishes to discuss, how he plans to do that, and why the issue is to be raised. The lecture will take the way *(methodos)* of thinking, and this way inherently will lead us through language. Its aim is to prepare us for a free relationship with technicity; that is necessary because today we are all unfree and chained to technology, in view of the fact that we no longer know our real relationship to technicity. And we shall remain unfree and chained to technicity, whether we affirm or deny this fact, as long as we do not learn to think the essence of technicity. Technicity is not the same as the essence of technicity; thus, our relationship to technicity will be free if and only if it opens our human ek-sistence to the essence of technicity. Today many people conceive of technicity as something that is neither positive nor negative in itself; technicity can be used positively or negatively, and man will have to make a decision about this use. The conception that technicity is something neutral makes us blind to the true essence of technicity.[31]

It is important to note here that, contrary to other authors who have concerned themselves with technicity and technology, Heidegger does not begin with detailed analyses of the numerous phenomena which modern technology has made available to us. Rather, he turns immediately to the essence of technicity and claims that if we were to concern ourselves with everything that bears the stamp of modern technology, the way toward the essence of technicity would be closed from the start.[32]

III. TECHNICITY AS A MODE OF REVEALMENT (*A-LĒTHEIA*, TRUTH)

According to a very old tradition, we understand by the essence of a thing that which the thing is, the *what* of the thing. Now, everyone today knows that the question concerning the essence of technicity can be answered by two simple statements: 1) technicity is a means to an end, and 2) it is a human activity. The instrumental and the anthropological definitions of technicity belong together.

In Heidegger's view, these definitions are correct both for the earlier handwork technology and for modern machine technology. The instrumental definition is even "uncannily" correct; for the more technicity reveals itself as something inhuman, the more one tries to define and pursue it as a means or an instrument that is to be controlled. As a matter of fact, it is precisely because this definition is a correct one that many people today think that we shall bring about the right relationship to technicity and, thus, master and control it if we just learn to manipulate technicity itself in the proper manner. Yet, in view of the fact that the merely correct is not yet the true,[33] the instrumental definition does not yet uncover technicity in its very essence. The true comes-to-pass only at the point where a thing is uncovered in its essence, and only the true brings us into a genuinely free relationship with that which concerns us from its essence.[34] Heidegger tries to prepare us for this truth by inquiring into two different but related directions; the first leads through causality, whereas the second passes through the word *technē*.

To arrive at the true conception of technicity, we shall try to seek the true by way of what is correct. We must thus ask what the instrumental itself truly is. For centuries the instrumental has been said to belong to the domain of means and ends, and the latter have been considered there as causes. Thus a brief reflection on causality seems in order here.

For many centuries, Aristotle's doctrine of the four causes was widely accepted without much criticism. It may be that the time has come now to ask why there are just these four causes, namely, the material, the formal, the efficient, and the final cause. We must then also ask what the unity of these four causes is and just what their origin is. The question of what technicity is will remain dark and groundless as long as we fail to address these questions about causality and instrumentality.

To prepare an answer for these questions, Heidegger turns to Greek philosophy. What we now call "cause" was called by the Greeks *aition;* it carried the connotation of indebtedness to someone or something. This indebtedness, however, included for the Greeks more than the four causes mentioned. One sees that immediately when one reflects on man where he functions as "efficient cause." Man is much more than just an efficient cause, i.e., the one who makes and fashions; he must also think and reflect, and in so doing he is in a position to relate to another way of being indebted to. This thinking and pondering was called in Greek *legein*, and it is in turn connected with *apophainesthai.* According to

Heidegger, it signifies thus a leading-forth, a bringing-to-presence. The four forms of causality taken in the sense of indebtedness show their unity in that they "bring something forth into presence."[35]

Yet for a long time we have been accustomed to present cause as that which brings something about, makes it. From that perspective, the efficient cause sets the standard for all causality. Yet Aristotle, who originated the doctrine of the four causes, never claimed that causality has something to do with bringing something about. What Aristotle meant can be seen clearly in the example of a silver chalice. Some kind of *matter,* namely, silver, is co-responsible for the sacred vessel. But the vessel is equally and as such indebted to the particular *form* or *shape* which gives it its characteristic aspect, as well as to its *telos*. It is the *telos* which in advance confines the chalice within the realm of the sacred; it is thus also the *telos* which gives it its meaning and ultimately determines what it will be. The *telos* is responsible for the manner in which matter and shape are together responsible for the sacred vessel. Finally, there is the silversmith. Aristotle conceived of him not as the *causa efficiens* but rather as the one who considers carefully and gathers together *(legein)* the three other ways of being responsible discussed already, so that they can come forward in appearance together *(apophainesthai)*. Thus, the three mentioned ways of being responsible for the chalice "owe thanks" to the pondering of the silversmith for the fact *that* they are and *how* they came into appearance as such. The silversmith takes part in the indebtedness of the sacred vessel as "the whence of the sacred vessel's bringing-forth and resting in itself."[36] In other words, the others ways of being indebted are indebted to the silversmith for the "that" and the "how" of their being brought into play and for the arriving into appearance of the sacred vessel.[37]

But in what sense do these four different forms of being indebted constitute a unity? This question must be raised especially today, now that we have completely forgotten what *aition* originally meant. Today we understand being responsible for and being indebted to in a moral sense, or we continue to construe them in terms of some making or effecting. Yet for the Greek way of thinking, the four ways of being responsible bring something into appearance, let it come forth into presence *(Anwesen)*. They set something free and start it on its way to arrival. As such, this starting something on its way is at the same time an occasioning, an inducing to come forward *(Veranlassen)*, as well as a leading-forth *(Her-vor-bringen)*. The four ways of occasioning let what is not yet present as such arrive into presence, come-to-presence. In the *Symposium,*[38] Plato calls this leading-forth out of the non-present into the present *poiēsis*.[39]

It is of the greatest importance to understand *poiēsis* here in its full sense; it includes the bringing-into-presence of all manufacturing, but also all artistic and poetic leading-forth; it even includes the leading- or bursting-forth of *phusis*. *Phusis* is *poiēsis* in the highest sense,[40] for what comes-to-presence by means of *phusis* has its bursting-forth in itself, and not in the artist or the artisan. But we still must ask precisely how the leading-forth itself, in which the fourfold way of occasioning plays, comes-to-pass. Occasioning is related to the coming-to-presence of that which at any given time comes to appearance in that leading-forth which leads something from concealment into non-concealment and, thus, reveals it. The Greeks used the word *alētheia* for "revealing." *Alētheia* was translated first as *veritas* and is now commonly translated in English as "truth." We usually understand by truth the correspondence of the pro-positing presentation with the thing so pro-posed and presented.[41]

It should be noted here again that for Heidegger truth is an original happening; it is the revelation of Being. In his view we still find traces of this conception, common among the Pre-Socratics, in the works of Aristotle. In the modern era, when truth was reduced to correctness, this conception became completely forgotten. When truth became reduced to correctness, man himself became the center and focal point of all beings. And when man began to circle about himself in search of certainty and security, thinking gradually became a pro-posing, positing presentation, and the Being of beings changed into sheer objectivity. All of that prepared the way for the modern nihilist era of technicity, concerning which man, thus, has completely lost the truth. Instead of concerning himself with Being and seeing everything in the light of that perspective, man, in his science and technological concern, gives his attention exclusively to beings. "Heidegger pleads for reflective consideration for Being or devotion to Being to show that the *origin* of technology is a *truth-event*."[42]

Yet one will still wonder what the mode of Being characteristic of technicity has to do with revealing, truth, *alētheia*. In Heidegger's opinion, the answer to this question has to be: everything, provided, obviously, the preceding reflections hold good. Furthermore, he argues that one can arrive at the same insight by focusing on the original meaning of the Greek word *technikon*, from which our word *technicity* is derived.[43]

Technikon means that which belongs to *technē*. *Technē* names the activities and skills of the craftsman and the artist, as well as the liberal and fine arts themselves. *Technē* belongs to *poiēsis*, to leading-forth; it itself is something poietic. Before Plato, *technē* still coincided with *epistēmē*, both of which signified "to ken, to know, to have insight." Even for Aristotle, for whom *technē* had already become a bringing-forth, *technē* is nevertheless primarily still a way of revealment, a form of *alētheuein*. "The faculties by which the soul expresses truth, by way of affirmation or denial, are five in number: *technē, epistēmē,* practical wisdom, theoretical wisdom, and *nous.*"[44] Thus *technē,* too, is a form of revealment; it reveals whatever does not bring itself forth. What is essential in *technē* is not the making or the manipulating, or even the using of means, but rather the revealing which was mentioned earlier. But that means that we are led once more to the view that technicity comes-to-presence in that realm in which revealing (non-concealment, *alētheia,* truth) comes-to-pass.[45]

One will now object that even if all of that were correct, it still would not hold for modern technicity, which makes use of complex machines, and it is precisely the latter situation that is disturbing today; it is modern machine technology that makes us ask the question concerning technicity in the first place. Today technicity is intimately related to the sciences, and, thus, it is fundamentally different from anything that mankind had at its disposal in earlier times. Heidegger does not deny the close relationship between modern science and modern technicity; yet in his view this relationship and interdependence is mutual. One should not forget that modern science is impossible without very complicated machines of all kinds. In Heidegger's opinion, it is not at all evident in what this reciprocal relation and interdependence precisely rests; yet he decides not to examine this issue here further. In his view, it suffices to stress the following points: Ancient and modern technicity are both forms of revealment; they differ in the manner in which they reveal, and this difference is connected with the fact that modern technicity is closely related to modern science. But in what does this difference precisely consist? For Heidegger, the basic difference between ancient and modern forms of technicity is to be found in the fact that the former leads-forth in the sense of *poiēsis,* whereas the latter has the form of a challenge, which puts to nature the unreasonable demand that it supply energy which can be extracted and then stored and finally used. Thus modern technology challenges, demands, and posits *(stellen).* Energy which was concealed in nature is unlocked, transformed, stored, distributed, used. And all of these human activities are ways of revealing, even though in this case the revealing never comes to its end. Modern technicity demands that everything which it reveals stands there not merely as an object but rather as something that is constantly ready for. . . . Thus what is ordered about by modern technicity has its own typical mode of standing. Heidegger calls it *den Bestand,* "the constant standing-reserve."[46]

The origin and the implications of this demand of modern technicity were discussed a few years earlier in the essay "What Are Poets For?", where Heidegger, among many other issues, focused on the implications of the fact that in the era of modern metaphysics, man is so preoccupied with beings that he now is completely unable to relate to Being. In that context he makes the claim that for metaphysics thinking has become a pro-posing and positing presentation. Man posits before himself the world as the totality of all that is objective, and he posits himself before the world as the subject. Man sets the world up in the direction of himself and tries to get total control over nature. Where nature taken by itself is inadequate or not satisfactory, man's pro-posing and positing presentation reorganizes and reshapes it.[47] In this way man really purposely asserts himself. His self-willing everywhere just reckons with things and humans as if they were mere objects. What is so reckoned becomes then mere merchandise, and man himself becomes merely a businessman and a merchant.[48] Man constantly produces new things where they are lacking; he removes things when they are in his way. "Man interposes something between himself and the things that distract him from his purpose. Man exposes things when he boosts them for sale and use."[49] Man places himself over against the world of objects, and he sets himself up as the one who wills and pushes through all this producing and objectifying.[50]

Heidegger sees in all of that the Being of beings, which in the era of modern metaphysics comes-to-presence as will to will. When the Being of beings appears as will to will, man's willing begins to appear in the form of self-assertion, and this self-assertion forces everything under its dominion and control. For such a willing, everything turns into material for a self-assertive production. The earth and the heaven become just raw material. Even human beings are considered to be material of which one can dispose in light of certain proposed goals. The unconditioned establishment of the unconditioned self-assertion ultimately emerges from the hidden nature of technicity, which only in modern times begins to unfold as the destiny of the truth of all beings taken as a whole. From the same essence of modern technicity, modern science and the conception of the total state have also emerged. And the same can be said for the means and modes that are developed for the formation of public opinion, and of man's conception of everything in his world.[51]

According to the technical conception of the world, everything is producible and the products of this production can always be delivered by means of the market. In this self-assertive production, the essence of man and the essence of the things dissolve into their calculable market value. Technological dominion spreads itself now over the entire earth ever more quickly, ruthlessly, and completely. Modern man does not realize that in all of that he has become exposed to the real danger that he himself will lose his selfhood to this process of unconditional production. By his own uncontrolled self-willing, with which he tries to respond to the appeal made by the essence of technicity, he becomes in an essential sense endangered and in need of protection. But the "salvation" and the protection which he needs cannot possibly come from technicity itself.

What is particularly frightening in all of that is not so much the atomic bomb; what long since has been threatening man with death, the "death" of his own essence, is the unconditioned character of his mere willing, of his purposeful self-assertion in everything: "What threatens man in his very essence is the willed view that man, by the peaceful release, transformation, storage, and channeling of the energies of physical nature, could render the human condition, man's Being, tolerable for everybody and happy in all respects."[52] What is above all threatening is thus the opinion that "this imposition of production can be ventured without any danger" and that one can always find an escape from the danger. What threatens man in his essence is the idea that technicity puts the world in order, while in fact this ordering eliminates all true order and hierarchy, in that it subjects everything to the uniformity of production. What threatens thus is the fact that technicity itself prevents the appearance of any experience of the true essence of technicity. For while technicity "is developing its own self to the full, it develops in the sciences a kind of knowing that in principle is debarred from ever entering into the realm of the essential nature of technicity."[53] Yet for Heidegger, modern man is not without all hope. For there still is the possibility for some humans at least to see the threat and the danger as such. As we shall see, both poets and thinkers have an important part to play here.[54]

But let us return to the *Bestand,* the constant standing-reserve, the fund, which Heidegger uses to characterize the manner in which everything comes-to-presence which belongs to the challenging revealment typical of technicity. What is the origin of the idea of nature as constant reserve and of the challenging attitude which rules man's behavior? As we have just seen, both are related to the subjectivism and voluntarism of modern metaphysics and therefore also to the development of modern science. Physics sets nature up as a coherent framework of forces that can be calculated in advance and then controlled. The challenging revealment held sway in physics long before machine technology developed.[55]

But even though the ideas of nature as constant reserve and of the challenging attitude which rules man's behavior are related to modern metaphysics, they do not really have their origin in man and his activities. Man indeed executes the challenging revealment; but no more than the silversmith causes the leading-forth of the chalice does modern man cause the challenging revealment. On the contrary, man is himself challenged to challenge the forces of nature. In a way, man himself belongs more originally to the standing-reserve than does nature; in the preceding, we have already indicated that by using expressions such as "human material" and "human resources." Yet, even though man is challenged more originally than the forces of nature, he nevertheless is never just part of the standing-reserve, insofar as he at least takes part in the revealment. Thus, any effort to determine more carefully what is really meant by the constant standing-reserve and the positing, ordering, and challenging that are related to it is beset with great difficulties, in view of the fact that, as we have just seen, man has no control over non-concealment itself, in and through which, at any given time, what is actual shows itself. The fact that what is actual shows itself in this way or in another is not brought about by man, not even by thinkers or poets. Even the thinkers and the poets merely respond to what addresses itself to them.

If that is so, then it is also clear that here, too, man for his part is unable to bring about the standing-reserve of nature. Only to the extent that man for his part already has been challenged to exploit the forces and energies of nature can this revealing which demands, challenges, and orders come-to-pass. And as we have just said, man himself is even more originally and radically challenged than are the forces and energies of nature. That is the real reason why he can never be completely transformed into a mere standing-reserve.[56]

But if the non-concealment, within which the challenging ordering unfolds, is never just the work of man, where and how does this revealing then come-to-pass? Heidegger formulates his answer to this question as follows: "When man, investigating, observing, pursues nature as an area of his own conceiving, he has already been claimed by a way of revealing that challenges him to approach nature as an object of research, until even the object disappears into the objectlessness of mere standing-reserve."[57] Heidegger use the term *Ge-stell* for the challenging claim which gathers man and makes him concentrate upon ordering what is actual to reveal itself as mere standing-reserve. The word is used in everyday German for stand or rack, frame, framework, support, holder, etc. Heidegger does not use it in this manner; for him the term is meant to suggest the way in which all that is comes-to-presence for man today. Relating it to words such as *Gebirg, Gemüt,* he takes *Ge-stell* to relate to that gathering that gathers together all the modes of challenging revealment which are built on the verb *stellen.* I thus translate it as "com-positing." Heidegger is fully aware of the "arbitrariness" with which he here seems to "misuse" a common word of the German language; yet he feels justified in using the word in a technical sense to refer to the essence of modern technicity.[58]

Heidegger furthermore states that the term *com-positing* expresses not only the provocative commanding which belongs to modern technology but also the leading-forth into presence which was characteristic of what the Greeks called *poiēsis*. Modern and classical forms of production do indeed differ fundamentally in character; yet they continue to be essentially related, insofar as both are ways of revealment of the truth *(des Entbergens, der alētheia)*. Heidegger moreover returns again to the relationship between modern technicity and modern science. Historiographically, it is correct to state that modern technicity first arose when it was capable of utilizing the mathematical sciences of nature. Yet historically this claim fails to reach the truth *(das Wahre)*. Modern physics prepared the way not for technicity but rather for the essence of modern technicity; on the other hand, one can say also that the modern sciences of nature are grounded in the coming-to-presence of the essence of technicity.[59] Even though it was never perceived to do so, it is nevertheless still true that the coming-to-presence of modern technicity governed the rise of modern science, so that we may finally say that "that which, according to the historiographical establishment, is the later, i.e., modern technicity, is, in view of the coming-to-presence that governs within it, the historically earlier."[60] Although modern technicity makes use of the natural sciences, it is still incorrect to call technicity applied science. Precisely because the essence of modern technicity lies in the com-positing, it must make use of the natural sciences.[61]

IV. THE DEFINITION OF TECHNICITY FROM THE PERSPECTIVE OF THE
SENDING OF BEING

Heidegger then briefly recapitulates the argument developed thus far. It is clear by now that he rejects any anthropological or instrumental conception of technicity. For man it is not possible to enter into an independent relation with technicity. The latter thus is not merely a human affair, because man is originally placed on the way to revealment, and in that process Being plays the leading part. Revealment does not come-to-pass through man alone; he is claimed for that purpose by Being, which is in need of him. It is the *Ge-Stell,* the com-positing, which as the sending of Being sends man into this way of revealment.[62]

Com-positing is nothing technical; it is the way in which today what is actual reveals itself as the standing-reserve. This revealing does not happen independently of man's doing, and yet it is not the work of man alone, either. Com-positing is the gathering together which belongs to that positing which challenges man and puts him in the position to reveal what is actual and to order it to be constantly available. Thus man stands within the domain of the com-positing as the one who is so challenged. It is the essence of modern technicity that starts man on the road of that form of revealing through which what is actual becomes nothing but standing-reserve. It is the *Ge-stell,* the com-positing, which sends him on this way. Heidegger calls the sending which gathers and starts man upon a definite way of revealing, *das Geschick*, which is a sending which destines. It is this destining which determines the essence of all history *(Geschichte)*,[63] which, in turn, constitutes the subject matter of historiography. Although this destining sending which reveals holds complete sway over man, it is nevertheless never a fate which compels him. "For man becomes truly free only insofar as he belongs to the realm of sending and so becomes one who listens, not one who simply obeys."[64]

A few years later (in 1957), Heidegger clarified the implications of this state of affairs in the following manner: In *Identity and Difference*, speaking about the present epoch, the atomic age, he wrote that it is the age in which Being comes-to-presence as the world of technicity. Then he asked: But is it correct to simply identify Being with the world of technicity? Obviously not, precisely because technicity hides and prevents us from catching sight of the true constellation of Being and man. In the world of technicity, everything is interpreted in advance in terms of man, in terms of that which man makes (an idea to which we shall return shortly). Technicity refers to a "plan" which man projects, and, finally, it compels him to decide whether he will become the servant of this plan or not.[65] But in such a conception of the totality of the technical world, we reduce everything to man and fail to hear the claim of Being. And yet it is true that today Being "appears" as the world of technicity.

Let us therefore stop conceiving of technicity as something merely technical, as something that man and man alone makes, hence in terms of man and his machines. Let us listen instead to the claim placed in our age not only on man but also on all beings, nature, history, with respect to their Being. Today everything is challenged, including our whole human existence. Beings make a claim on us with respect to their aptness to be planned and calculated; Being is challenged to let beings appear within the horizon of what can be calculated; man himself is challenged to secure all beings that are his concern as the substance for his calculating and planning. The name for the gathering of this challenge, which today places Being and man opposite to each other such that they challenge each other and therewith all that is, is the *Ge-Stell*, the com-positing.[66]

That in which and from which Being and man concern each other in our technical world claims both in the manner of the com-positing. This state of affairs is more real than all atomic energy taken together and more real than the entire world of machinery, more real even than the driving power of organization, communication, automation, etc. We are so taken up with what we encounter within this com-positing that every form of speaking about it sounds strange. Yet it is the case that the belonging together of Being and man which prevails and challenges both Being and

man today, i.e., the com-positing, also drives home to us both *that* and
how man is delivered over to the ownership of Being and Being is appropriated to the essence of man. Thus, within the domain of the com-
positing prevails a strange ownership and a strange process of
appropriation.

Appropriating event, Heidegger explains here once more, is a key term
that cannot be properly translated in any other language; in this regard it
is similar to *logos* in Greek and *tao* in Chinese. It is in each case a
singulare tantum and refers to something that, at each time, occurs
uniquely. What we now experience in the com-positing as the constellation of Being and man through the world of technicity is the prelude to
the genuine event of appropriation, one in which the mere dominance of
the com-positing will be overcome. Such a transformation of the com-
positing into a more "original" event of appropriation would bring the
appropriate recovery of the world of technicity, "such that technicity
would be brought from its dominance back to servitude."[67] This event is
not far away, Heidegger believes. It speaks already to us directly from the
very nearness of that neighborhood in which we already reside and dwell.
This event is at the same time that domain through which man and Being
reach each other in their true essence, that in which they will achieve their
essence and will finally lose all those qualities with which metaphysics has
endowed them. To think this event of appropriation, thought must receive the necessary means, not from the world of technicity but from the
structure of language.[68]

In his essay on technicity, to which we must now again return, Heidegger is particularly concerned with explaining *that* and *how* man must try
to find a "free relation" to the essence of technicity, one in which Being
and man will be properly drawn to one another. *(Beziehung—ziehen.)* It
is to be noted here that we already stand within the relation that we are
seeking. "Thus the question 'How can we take up a relation to it?' always
comes too late."[69]

The com-positing is a form of revealment which tends to intensify and
even perpetuate itself. For the more the world of things dissolves into the
standing-reserve and man is revealed as the one who holds sway over it,
the farther away man is from experiencing himself as the one who is
commanded and controlled. But the more man is removed from truly
experiencing himself as the one who is ordered and commanded, the
nearer he is to the edge of the abyss, i.e., the possibility that he himself,
too, may be dissolved into the standing-reserve. "Threatened in this way,
he exalts himself as lord and master of the earth and boasts that everything is created by man."[70] It begins to look as though man encounters
everywhere only himself. But such a response to the danger only removes

man further from experiencing himself as the one who is ordered and commanded by the com-positing.[71]

And yet man is free. But one should observe here that the essence of freedom originally is not connected with man's will or with the "causality" of human willing. Freedom originally governs the open, that which has been cleared, lighted up, and revealed. Thus, freedom stands in the closest relationship to the coming-to-pass of the truth. And yet that which frees in the final analysis always remains concealed; it always continues to conceal itself. This mystery is Being itself.[72]

Thus when we consider the essence of technicity, we experience the com-positing as a sending and, thus, as a revealing which somehow destines man. Yet this destining does not force him to engage blindly in technicity, or to rebel helplessly against it, as if it were the work of the devil (Ernst Jünger). On the contrary, when we open ourselves to the essence of technicity, we find ourselves already taken into a claim which frees.[73]

Obviously, since the *Geschick*, the sending that destines, at any given time starts man on a certain path of revealing, it is always possible that man will no longer see any other mode of revealing and thus become blind to the one through which man will be admitted to the essence of what is nonconcealed. Placed between two extreme possibilities, man is endangered by Being's sending itself. The sending which reveals, but at the same time also destines, is thus as such, in every one of its concrete modes, and therefore also necessarily, the danger.[74]

This danger is that man may misconstrue the genuine meaning of the sending. For "whatever a sending of revealment may be and whenever it may happen, there is a danger that it will be misinterpreted. The misinterpretation consists mainly in man's fixing upon what is revealed, a preoccupation with the immediate which blocks the mystery from out of which revealment is sent. . . ."[75] "Thus where everything that comes-to-presence exhibits itself in the light of a cause-effect relationship, there even God, for representational thinking, can lose all that is exalted and holy, the mysteriousness of His distance."[76]

When Being's mittence which destines reigns in the form of com-positing, it becomes the supreme danger, because in that case it can come-to-pass that man no longer encounters his own essence. He himself may come to the point where he, too, is to be taken as standing-reserve. Man will again try to convince himself that he truly is the lord of all that is, and that all he encounters is only insofar as it is his construction. But that gives rise to a final illusion, namely, that man everywhere and always encounters only himself. Man then fails to see himself as the one who is addressed and as the one who ek-sists, from out of his very essence, into the realm of an exhortation, an appeal, a claim. Furthermore, as we have seen already, the com-positing also banishes man into a kind of revealing which is really no more than a calculating ordering. And where this ordering dominates, it eliminates at once every other possibility of reveal-ment. But that implies that the truth as such becomes hidden and masked. Above all, com-positing conceals the revealing which, as *poiēsis*, lets what comes-to-presence come-forth into appearance.[77]

A few years later, in *Gelassenheit* (1955), Heidegger would further elaborate on this basic idea. In the "Memorial Address" for Conradin Kreutzer (1955),[78] Heidegger states that in modern philosophy a radical revolution was prepared which eventually would lead to a completely new relation of man to the world and also to a new conception of man's place in it. The world is from now on no more than an object of calcula-tive thinking, from whose influence nothing can escape. Nature is no more than a source of energy for modern technology and industry. Par-ticularly through the discovery of atomic energy, man has come to believe that in the near future the world's demands for energy will be ensured forever; since atomic power stations can furthermore be built everywhere on earth, the procurement of energy will no longer be tied to only certain rich countries. The main question for modern science and technology is now no longer where to find sufficient quantities of energy but rather how we can protect mankind against the enormous dangers which atomic energy use appears to imply.[79]

It is quite generally assumed that man will be able to control atomic energy and thus that a completely new era of technical development will begin which will open totally unexpected possibilities in many areas. One does not realize that man from now on will "be encircled ever more tightly by the forces of energy" and that "these forces, which everywhere and every minute claim, enchain, drag along, press, and impose upon man . . .—these forces, since man has not made them, have moved long since beyond his will and have outgrown his capacity for decision."[80]

Today many people are aware of the enormous danger created by atomic bombs. Yet few people stop to consider that today with all techni-cal means an attack is being made on the life and nature of man himself. What is most uncanny, however, is not so much the fact that our world is becoming entirely technical but rather the fact that we are not prepared for the total transformation, and that we are still unable to confront it reflectively and meditatively.[81]

A first thing one must realize here is that no one, no scientist, no engineer, no technician, no person concerned with industry and econ-omy, no political agent or body, and no poet or philosopher, can stop this development or even give it a direction. No person and no human organization is still capable of gaining control over what is developing here. In light of this development, man is helpless and defenseless unless he puts a meditative thinking resolutely against a merely calculative form of thinking.[82]

But what is meditative thinking capable of contributing to our actual situation? Obviously, it will not propose to condemn science and technology, and to get rid of them altogether. Instead, it must try to propose a manner of dealing with science and technology such that we can meaningfully use them without allowing them to dominate and enslave us. Thus saying both yes and no to technology does not make our relation to technology ambiguous. We can let science and technology enter our daily life, and at the same time let them alone, as things that are by no means absolute but always remain dependent upon something more eminent. Heidegger calls this comportment toward technology "releasement toward things."[83]

Once modern man were to acquire this new comportment, he would also be able to see things in a new light and not just in a technical manner. He would then discover that there is a meaning hidden in modern technicity which is not invented or made by man himself. This meaning does show itself in an indirect manner, and yet it hides itself also at the same time. "That which shows itself and at the same time withdraws is the essential trait of what we call the mystery." The comportment which enables modern man to remain open to the meaning hidden in technicity is called "the openness to the mystery." "Releasement toward things and openness to the mystery belong together. They grant us the possibility of dwelling in the world in a totally different way."[84] Yet releasement toward things and openness to the mystery do not occur of themselves. They come to flourish only through a meditative thinking that is both persistent and courageous.[85] But how then is one to come to this meditative thinking that will lead modern man to releasement toward things and to openness to the mystery, and how is one to break the power of modern technicity and its grip on modern man? And what or who is to play the leading part here? In order to find answers for these questions, we must return once more to the com-positing.[86]

V. THE COM-POSITING AS THE DANGER AND AS THE SAVING POWER

We have seen that com-positing not only conceals a former way of revealing (namely *poiēsis* as leading-forth), it also conceals revealing itself, and with it also that wherein non-concealment (= truth) comes-to-pass. Thus, com-positing really prevents the shining-forth and holding-sway of the truth of Being. What is dangerous here is not technicity itself; rather, it is the very essence of technicity, taken as a sending which reveals and destines, that is the true danger. And the danger to man does not come first and foremost from the potentially lethal apparatuses of technology, however awesome their powers may be; the main danger is that, because of the com-positing, it could be denied to man to enter into a more original form of revealing, and to experience the call of a more primordial truth.[87] Thus, where the com-positing holds sway, there indeed is the danger in the highest degree.

Yet Hölderlin tells us that where the danger holds sway and reigns, there the saving power also grows. For even in the period in which we experience Being in its most extreme poverty, the com-positing still somehow harbors the more original truth; thus, in the very withdrawal lies the saving power. Here "to save" does not mean what it usually means, namely, to seize hold of a thing that is threatened by ruin in order to secure it in its former continuance. Here it means to fetch something home into its genuine essence and to bring this essence into its true appearance. That is what the com-positing, which is also the greatest danger, nonetheless has the power to do. At the very moment when Being withdraws, the saving power takes root in this withdrawal. If this claim applies to the essence of technicity, then the com-positing must harbor in itself the growth of the saving power. To discover this saving power, we must more carefully look into the danger which is intrinsic in the com-positing.[88]

We have called the com-positing the essence of technicity. Usually we take the term *essence* to refer to that which a thing is, its whatness or quiddity. Heidegger explains that in the expression "the essence of technicity," the word *Wesen* ("essence") is to be taken in a different sense, namely, verbally for the manner in which something holds-sway, unfolds, and finally decays. Thus the word *Wesen* taken in a verbal sense refers to the manner in which a thing comes-to-presence. Now, the latter is furthermore to be taken such that it also signifies "to last, to endure" *(währen)*, even though *essence* does not refer here to the permanent and invariable what of things. For it can never be proven that the "enduring is based solely on what Plato thinks as *idea* and Aristotle thinks as *to ti ēn einai*, that which a particular thing has always been, or even what metaphysics in its most varied interpretations thinks as *essentia.*"[89] Yet neither is the essence of technicity a mythological abstraction perpetually suspended over all that is technological. Com-positing comes-to-presence; it lasts and endures as the sending of revealment. Heidegger here recalls that Goethe once used the verb *fortgewähren*, in which he combined the verb *fortwähren* ("to endure permanently") with the verb *gewähren* ("to grant") to create a new verb with the meaning "to grant permanently." If we now think more carefully than before what it is that actually endures, we may perhaps say that only what is granted will endure and that which endures primarily out of the earliest beginning is what truly grants.[90]

But all of that seems to run contrary to what was argued for earlier. If com-positing is a sending which destines and gathers together into revealing, which itself, in turn, is something that challenges, how can one then still speak here about granting? In Heidegger's view, we must realize that com-positing is a sending which destines man in such a way that it starts him upon a way of revealing. This sending thus gives man access to something which of himself he cannot invent or make. And as we have seen, this sending is both the extreme danger and the saving power. Thus "every sending which reveals, comes-to-pass from a granting and as such a granting."[91] This granting conveys to man that share in revealing that the coming-to-pass of the truth of Being needs. So needed and used, man is granted to belong to the happening of the truth. But if that is so, then the granting which sends man into revealment is also the saving power. For it lets man enter into the highest dignity of his own mode of Being; this dignity consists in keeping watch over non-concealment. It is in this sense that the coming-to-presence of technicity harbors in itself the rising of the saving power. Everything thus depends on our pondering this rising, our re-collecting it and watching over it.[92]

In so doing, we must realize that, as we have seen, the essence of technicity is ambiguous; an ambiguity manifests itself here that points to the mystery of all revealing and truth. On the one hand, com-positing challenges us forth into an ordering that blocks every view into the coming-to-pass of the truth. On the other hand, com-positing comes-to-pass in the granting that lets man endure so that he may be the one who is needed and used for the safekeeping of the coming-to-presence of truth.[93] In other words, the question concerning technicity is really the question about the revealing and concealing in which the coming-to-presence of the truth itself comes-to-pass.[94] Thus it helps us to look into the danger and to discover in it the growth of the saving power. Yet this looking itself does not yet save us; it merely summons us to have hope in the growing light of the saving power.[95]

The coming-to-presence of technicity threatens all revealing with the possibility that all revealing will be consumed and that everything will begin to present itself only in the non-concealment of the standing-reserve. It is clear that man's activity alone can never counter this danger directly. But man can think the fact that all saving power must be of a higher essence than that which is so endangered.

But is there perhaps a more primordially granted revealing that will bring the saving power into its first shining-forth, in the midst of the danger which in our atomic age more conceals than shows itself? Let us not forget, Heidegger observes, that there once was a time in which the name *techne* referred not only to technicity but also to the revealing which brings forth the truth into the splendor of radiant appearance. *Techne* then meant also the bringing-forth of the true into the beautiful (*poiesis*). As art, *techne* was then one single manifold revealing; it was then also *promos*, first, leading, brave, and capable, i.e., yielding to the holding-sway of the truth.[96]

At that time art was not yet artistic, and works of art were then not yet enjoyed "aesthetically." Art was then simply called *techne*, because it was taken to be a revealing which brings forth and makes present. Could it perhaps be that "revealing lays claim to the arts more primarily, so that they for their part may expressly foster the growth of the saving power?"[97] No one knows. Yet we can say that that is a genuine possibility, provided that art is not just taken aesthetically, and provided our reflection upon art does not shut its eyes to the constellation of the truth of Being.[98]

CONCLUSION

Heidegger concludes the lecture with a few brief remarks. Questioning in this manner, we bear witness to the crisis which consists in that, preoccupied with technicity and preoccupied with aesthetics, we no longer guard and preserve the coming-to-presence of art. Yet the more we thoughtfully question the essence of technicity, the more mysterious the essence of art becomes. The closer we come to the danger and the more brightly the ways into the saving power begin to shine, the more questioning we become. For questioning is the acquiescing suppleness of thinking.[99]

Article III: "The Turning" (1953)

Heidegger begins this lecture with a brief summary of what was said in the preceding lecture about the danger intrinsic in technicity. He stresses once more the point that the danger referred to here should not be identified with the dangers which press on modern man everywhere and every hour, so to speak, or with the danger caused by atomic bombs. The true danger is the concealment and misplacement of Being.[100]

The present sending of Being is that of the com-positing; it is one modality of the coming-to-presence of Being, and it eventually will pass over into another modality, which is now still hidden for us. For it is the destiny of Being that it has to send itself time and again. When a change in Being takes place, it sends itself into another modality of its coming-to-presence in such a way that the earlier modality is not eliminated, struck down, or destroyed.

But if com-positing as the essence of technicity is the modality in which Being has sent itself in our age, it follows that technicity can never be mastered by means of a human activity alone; for that would imply that man is the master of Being. Yet, on the other hand, Being needs man: the essence of technicity cannot be guided into a change without the cooperation of man's essence; for the coming-to-presence of Being needs man's Being in order to be preserved as Being, i.e., as the Being of beings. But that does not mean that man could ever overcome technicity by himself. The essence of technicity will be transcended only if man is able to enter into technicity's still-hidden truth. The overcoming of com-positing, as one sending of Being, comes-to-pass out of the arrival of another sending, which cannot be calculated scientifically in advance, or constructed metaphysically.

Man is indeed needed for the overcoming of the essence of technicity. But he is needed in a manner which is in harmony with his own mode of Being. Thus contemporary man must first find his way back into the depth and scope of his own essence. And his essence is intimately connected with his relation to the truth of Being, for whose coming-to-pass he is needed.[101]

The next thing to do here is to think the coming-to-presence of Being itself as something that is worthy of thought. But how is one to do that today? Certainly not by first asking what we should do, but rather by pondering how we are to think. For thinking is man's genuine doing, because it brings the coming-to-presence of Being to language. Language first grants the way which everyone must go who wants to think. Without language, every doing lacks the dimension within which it can move and work. Language is the originary dimension within which man's way to be is capable of responding to Being's claim and of belonging to Being in responding. What is called thinking here is precisely this originary responding. Thinkingly we learn to dwell in the realm in which the overcoming of Being's present sending (= com-positing) must come-to-pass.[102]

We have seen that the real danger consists in the essence of compositing. Being here turns away from its own coming-to-presence into the forgottenness of its coming-to-presence and against the truth of its own coming-to-presence. In the danger itself, a first turning (Kehre) thus holds sway. In this first turning, the possibility of a second turning is hidden. In this second turning, the forgottenness of the coming-to-presence of Being turns in such a way that the truth of the coming-to-presence of Being enters beings properly. Presumably, this second turning comes-to-pass only if the danger really comes to light as the danger which it is. The arrival of this turning may already be imminent; yet no one knows when and how it will come-to-pass, full of destiny. Man's mode of Being is such that intrinsically he is the waiting one, who waits for the coming-to-presence of Being and who must shepherd Being thinkingly.[103]

But when the danger is as danger, there come-to-pass first the turning of the forgottenness of Being, and then also the upholding *(Wahrnis)* of Being, and finally also the world. That world comes to be as world, and that thing comes to be as thing, that is the arrival of the issuance of Being, the arrival of Being's truth.[104]

Thus, the self-withholding of the truth of Being, which tries to hold it in forgottenness, hides a yet ungranted favor, namely, that a turning will come-to-pass, a turning of Being's forgottenness into Being's truth. Thus, where danger is as danger, there also is the freeing of Being. This turning, however, can happen only abruptly. It is not brought about by anything except Being itself; and it is certainly not brought about in a cause-effect relationship. The abrupt opening up is the flashing of a light-ning flash. It brings itself into its own light, which it has brought along. When the truth of Being flashes in the turning of the danger, the coming-to-presence of Being opens up and the truth of Being's issuance comes-to-pass. It can come-to-pass also in the epoch of technicity's com-positing.[105]

In this flashing, Being comes-to-presence; in this way it comes into its own lighting. Heidegger calls the appearance of the flash of the truth of Being the insight *(Einblick)*. The expression "insight into that which is" names the event of the turning of Being. It is the appropriating event itself, through which the truth of Being comports itself to Being which was without truth. It names the constellation within the coming-to-presence of Being. Thus, it is by no means just a look that we humans, from out of ourselves, cast into that which is. Insight is the appropriating event of the constellation of the turning of the com-positing. Thus, the "it is" must be claimed first with regard to Being and not with regard to beings. That which makes up the Being of beings is Being itself. The same is true also in the case of the com-positing.[106]

It cannot be denied that the disposing in the com-positing displaces things, the nearness of the world, and even its own displacing. Yet in every displacing of the com-positing, the clearing of the world emerges and continues to open up, while the truth of Being keeps flashing, as long as the com-positing emerges in its essence as danger. Thus even within the com-positing there still is an essential sending of Being.[107]

When this insight comes-to-pass, the mortals are the ones that are lit up by it. Only when man's coming-to-presence within the appropriating event of the insight relinquishes the human stance and projects itself in the direction of the insight and away from itself does man respond in his Being to the claim of the insight. Responding in this manner, man may anticipate the divine in the world. For if God is, He too is a "being," and as a "being" He stands within Being and its coming-to-presence; but the latter comes-to-pass only from the governing of the world.

Only when this insight comes-to-pass does the essence of technicity as com-positing open up; only then do we realize that the truth of Being as world remains withheld from us in the disposing of the com-positing; only then do we note that every mere willing on the part of man persists in disregarding. For in that case, every mere ordering of the world remains without truth, caught up in mere calculative thinking and in a merely technical pro-posing. And the same is true for all historiological thinking, which as such never gets to the appropriate relationship with the essential source of the sending in the coming-to-pass of the truth of Being. For what is at issue in that case is not the description of a historical situation but rather the constellation of Being which addresses itself to man.[108]

We who stand under the domination of technicity (radio, television, etc.) still do not hear and see the deepest mystery of Being within the domination of the com-positing.[109] Whether God lives or remains hidden is not decided by man's religiosity or, even less, by the theological aspirations of philosophy and science. The constellation of Being determines whether God comes-to-pass as God. So long as we do not experience that thinkingly, we can never belong to what will be. Does insight into what is indeed come-to-pass already? Do we already see the flashing of Being in the coming-to-presence of technicity?[110]

CHAPTER 12

On Ethics and Politics

No dimension or aspect of Heidegger's philosophy has evoked a more direct and straightforward criticism than his attitude in regard to practical philosophy, taken both as ethics and as social and political philosophy. Many people who have written about his practical philosophy have tried to link it directly to National Socialism, either because of Heidegger's involvement with National Socialism in 1933–1934 or because of the unwarranted claim that his philosophy inherently would lead to some form of totalitarianism and to National Socialism of the type promoted by Hitler in particular.[1]

Heidegger was asked more than once[2] to clarify his position in regard to ethics and political philosophy. According to the critics, in each case the answer given was patently inadequate and suggested an unacceptable position in regard to both ethics and political philosophy, a position to be identified with nihilism, totalitarianism, or Nazism.[3]

There are very few texts in which Heidegger explicitly makes a claim about ethical and political issues and, thus, very few texts on which one can base any claim about Heidegger's position in regard to practical philosophy. There are, on the other hand, a number of statements in which Heidegger himself states that his thinking moves in a domain which lies before the distinction between theory and practice.[4] But here, too, it is not immediately clear in what sense this claim is to be understood: is it Heidegger's position to defend the view that making this very distinction is characteristic of the metaphysical tradition he is trying to overcome? Or is it perhaps his opinion that the distinction indeed is to be made, but that it can be made legitimately only after the foundations of thinking have been laid in some kind of "ontological" reflections? Furthermore, what would be the precise implications of such a position? If one assumes that in Heidegger's philosophy there is still room for ethics and political philosophy, what would be the basic theses of the ethics and the political philosophy to which one would come if one were to make the implicit ideas explicit?

Many critics have rejected any form of practical philosophy based on Heidegger's thinking on the ground that such a practical philosophy would have to be hermeneutical in character, whereas for them a hermeneutical, practical philosophy is doomed to failure in principle, because it would consist in an idealization of the past and, thus, be bound to maintain the status quo. As an introduction to the critical reflections to follow, it seems important to examine these claims briefly.[5] To this end, we must ask first how the expression "hermeneutical, practical philosophy" is to be understood.

In his book *Metaphysik und Politik*,[6] Joachim Ritter writes that practical philosphy is inherently hermeneutical, in that it consists in reflections on what has become already *(geworden ist)*. In his opinion, one sees that already most clearly in Aristotle's practical philosophy. Criticizing Plato, Aristotle tried to show that in the domain of the practical (which among other things includes both ethics and political philosophy), the good toward which one aims and with which all practical knowledge is concerned is not given in advance as an object but rather is something that is to be materialized in a concrete situation from which it, as it were, comes toward the one who acts. To be able to "move" in a historical situation presupposes that one is a man of experience and that one has acquired certain definite and stable dispositions. Thus, for Aristotle life means practice, activity, doing. Each man must build up his world in action, and for this action he must find the proper measure. If he wishes to behave "ethically," he must observe what possibilities for right action are already present in the community in which he lives. Man's dwelling place is structured by custom, *ethos*, and its institutions. That is the main reason why ethics is and remains related to the political and why the ethical is to be understood universally from the formation and the design of the *polis*, c.q. the community. Thus practical philosophy is hermeneutical *because* it relates the ethical to the political and tries to explain action according to "reason," i.e., a form of reason which has already been *institutionalized*. But practical philosophy is today even hermeneutical in a very special sense, because it now finds itself in a time in which one's heritage has been questioned quite universally and in which one thus must try to re-establish through reflection the *ethos* which has come into a severe crisis situation and is no longer carried on as a self-evident tradition.[7]

For many critics, on the other hand, a hermeneutical, practical philosophy is unacceptable, because it leads to ethical nihilism. For how can one, in a context where history is explicitly accepted as a power as well as something that can and is to be "made," and where one, in addition, finds himself in a historical crisis, still re-establish rationality, reasonableness, and the obligatory character of institutions, norms, and laws by means of reflections alone? In other words, if in such a situation practical philosophy is conceived of as hermeneutical, that seems to imply that all action is guided only by different types of ideology.[8]

And yet, in my opinion, it seems virtually impossible to deny that practical philosophy is inherently hermeneutical; in addition to Ritter, that has been shown also by Hans-Georg Gadamer.[9] Thus it makes little sense to criticize Heidegger for having attempted *to lay the foundations* for a hermeneutical, practical philosophy. On the other hand, it should be readily granted that such a practical philosophy is affected by great difficulties and grave problems. Hermeneutic philosophy always stands in a tension which flows from the fact that "life" and knowledge belong together and yet also are opposed to one another. Furthermore, philosophical reflection is only one form of knowledge which can easily be distinguished from other forms of knowledge (the pre-ontological, the scientific, the religious, etc.). Yet philosophy, including practical philosophy, is not just a "theory" of the practice. Philosophy is inherently practical; it is meant to guide the *praxis,* and it is thus directly related to the practical, even though it itself refrains from decisions about the aims, the goals, and the means of the practice. In other words, practical philosophy, when it formulates guidelines for the practical, the ethical and the political domain, is not yet directly concerned with the concrete ethical and political domain itself. And yet it is not just political rhetoric; nor can it separate decision from knowledge. Practical philosphy must realize, furthermore, that it must avoid becoming politicized, while at the same time it must accept that it itself already implies ethico-political presuppositions and prejudices. That seems to be one of the reasons why hermeneutic phenomenology intimately relates existential analyses to existentiell decisions, even though it carefully tries to distinguish the existential from the existentiell. Yet let us never forget that these, and similar, difficulties affect all practical philosophy, and that in many forms of practical philosophy these problems have not even been seen and discussed yet.[10]

From these brief reflections, it will be clear that in this chapter, contrary to the preceding ones, we shall sometimes be concerned not so much with an interpretation of claims made by Heidegger himself as with a critical analysis of claims which other philosophers have made about his "practical" philosophy. The latter is the case particularly for our reflections on the status of political philosophy in Heidegger's later works. Instead of having to reflect on the meaning of certain difficult statements of Heidegger himself, we must then try to explain why in Heidegger's later work there are virtually no claims that pertain to what we commonly call "political philosophy."

One final remark is in order here. We have seen that in hermeneutic philosophy, as is the case in many other conceptions of philosophy, ethics is very closely related to political philosophy. In the brief reflections on Heidegger's practical philosophy to follow, it appears nevertheless desirable to make an explicit distinction between the two. The reason has little to do with the issues themselves but is of a merely practical nature, as we shall see.

Article I: Heidegger on Ethics

The publications on Heidegger's conception of ethics roughly fall into four different categories. First, there are essays which simply rest on some misunderstanding.[11] Secondly, there are the publications in which authors who belong to a different orientation in philosophy look at Heidegger's philosophy and criticize it, either becase it does not contain an explicit ethics or because it contains an implicit ethics which they believe leads to anti-humanism, nihilism, totalitarianism, National Socialism, etc.[12] Then there are those treatises in which the authors are positively inclined toward Heidegger's philosophy as a whole, admit the thesis that Heidegger never developed a philosophical ethics, and suggest that such an ethics nonetheless could be developed and that such an ethics would not be at all in conflict with Heidegger's own deepest intentions.[13] Finally, there are the treatises which make an effort to explain Heidegger's position and try to understand the basic motifs from which this position ultimately appears to flow.[14] In harmony with the basic aim of this book, in this chapter I shall join the last group of authors and limit myself to Heidegger's position in regard to ethics as it is found in his later philosophy. To be more specific, I plan to make a few comments on Heidegger's remarks on ought and values in *An Introduction to Metaphysics* (1935), the "Letter on Humanism" (1947), and some other essays and lectures of the same time. Obviously it would have been very important to dwell critically on the publications from the first three categories mentioned, but that would lead us far beyond the scope of the present study. I shall mention these publications only where they immediately pertain to the issues raised by Heidegger himself in the works just mentioned.

Although these reflections are concerned with Heidegger's later philosophy, in this case nontheless a few remarks about Heidegger's earlier
view on ethics appear to be in order.

It is well known that in *Being and Time* and other works of the same
period, Heidegger very often uses a language which one usually expects
to find in treatises on ethics. The concepts of guilt, conscience, call,
authenticity, resolve, resoluteness, etc. play a very important part in the
second division of the first part of *Being and Time.* Yet Heidegger makes
it clear that in this work he is concerned not with ethics but only with
fundamental ontology. Already in the fifth section of the book, in which
he tries to show that the analytic of *Dasein* is to lay bare the horizon for
an interpretation of the meaning of Being as such, Heidegger places ethics
on a par with a number of other human disciplines and then distinguishes
all of them from the fundamental ontology with which he himself in this
work is primarily concerned. "*Dasein's* way of behavior, its capacities,
powers, possibilities, and vicissitudes, have been studied with varying
extent in philosophical psychology, in anthropology, in ethics, and political science, in poetry, biography, and the writing of history, each in a
different fashion."[15]

Heidegger does not deny that the efforts mentioned here possess an
existentiell primordiality; yet he doubts whether they have been carried
out with a comparable primordial existentiality. In his view, only "when
the basic structures of *Dasein* have been adequately worked out with
explicit orientation towards the problem of Being itself, will what we
have hitherto gained in interpreting *Dasein* get its existential
justification."[16] From that it is clear that in *Being and Time* we shall find
not an ethics but merely a study which, among other things, is concerned
with the laying of the ontological foundations of a possible ethics and of
the other human disciplines mentioned. Thus, when in the second division of the book he comes to speak about the phenomena mentioned,
Heidegger constantly warns the reader that his concern is with fundamental ontology, not with ethics or moral theology.[17]

In a lecture course of 1928, *Metaphysische Anfangsgründe der Logik im
Ausgang von Leibniz* (1928),[18] Heidegger clarifies his position with respect to the relationship between fundamental ontology and ethics in
greater detail. In *Being and Time,* it was suggested that fundamental
ontology is concerned (among other things) with the ontological foundations of ethics. In 1928 Heidegger points out that fundamental ontology
tends toward a primordial, metaphysical transformation, which becomes
possible only when Being itself is understood in its complete problematic.
Thus in addition to fundamental ontology, there is another part of
metaphysics, to which Heidegger there refers with the term *metontology*

and which is to concern itself not just with the Being of man but with the Being of all beings taken as a whole. Then he adds: "And here also in the domain of a metontological and existentiell questioning is the domain of the metaphysics of ek-sistence; (here the question of an ethics may be properly raised)."[19]

From all of that one can conclude that although in his early period Heidegger did not have the intention of developing a philosophical ethics, he nonetheless did not exclude its possibility or necessity. Rather, he himself had decided first to focus on the question concerning the meaning of Being. To that end he started with the development of a fundamental ontology which concerned itself with the Being of *Dasein* and which was to lay the foundation for the ontological study of Being itself. Heidegger envisioned at that time a metontology which was to concern itself with the Being of all beings taken as a whole, as well as a metaphysics of ek-sistence or philosophical anthropology. Now, in his opinion it is impossible to develop a philosophical ethics except on the basis of such a metontology and metaphysics of ek-sistence.

Although Heidegger does not explicitly claim so, one may nevertheless add here that he was of the opinion that the classical ethical treatises, written since the time of Plato, contain metaphysical assumptions that are unjustified and unjustifiable and that, on that ground, they are to be overcome. I thus tend to agree with Boelen where he writes that:

> Heidegger's thinking on the various forms of traditional ethics could be summarized by the statement that they all have failed, although in different ways, to work out their "explicit orientation toward the problem of Being itself." In other words, they have failed to think man's fundamental ethos; they have left unthought Being as the *essential* "dwelling place" of human ek-sistence. . . . Traditional ethics has been the *logic* of *mores* rather than the *logos* of *ethos*.[20]

Let us now turn to Heidegger's later works, in order to see what attitude he adopts in regard to philosophical reflections on moral issues and on the philosophical discipline called "ethics" in particular. As we mentioned before especially *An Introduction to Metaphysics* and the "Letter on Humanism" contain remarks that are of great importance in this regard.

In the lecture course *An Introduction to Metaphysics* (1935), Heidegger tried to give a foundation to metaphysics by asking once more the question concerning the meaning of Being. After a brief analysis of the etymology of the word *Being* and of its grammar, Heidegger examines the meaning of Being in terms of certain modalities which we usually "oppose" to Being, namely, becoming, seeming, thinking, and "having-to" (obligation). The treatment of the relationship between Being and the ought is very short. That is in all likelihood because Heidegger "ran out of time" in the course.[21]

Be that as it may, Heidegger claims here that classical metaphysics considers thinking to be the foundation and the determining ground of Being, whereas Being itself is surmounted by the ought. One sees that most clearly in modern metaphysics, but basically the same insight is already found in Greek philosophy. For although the modern ethics of the "ought" *(Sollen)*, and most certainly the ethics of values, are of relatively recent origin, their basic assumptions can already be found in the philosophy of Plato. For Plato, the *idea* is the prototype of what is, and it presents a certain view *(eidos, Aussehen)*. For Plato the view of all views, the idea of all ideas, the supreme idea, is the *idea tou agathou,* the idea of the good. The good is for Plato the standard as such; it is that which first endows Being with the power to become a prototype of its own. Yet in view of the fact that Being receives this power from the idea of the good, the idea of the good itself must stand *epekeina tēs ousias,* i.e., beyond Being. In this manner, Being itself, taken as *idea,* comes to stand in opposition to something else on which it itself is dependent. It is important to realize that in this case the ought is not superimposed on Being from the outside, so to speak. As soon as Being is interpreted as *idea,* it "automatically" brings with it a relation to the prototypical, the ought. But in this way, something is set above Being, "something that Being never is yet, but always *ought* to be."[22]

Yet this distinction between Being and the ought did not come into its own before the modern era, when "thought as the *logos* of statement *(dialegesthai)* assumes the crucial role" and "thought becomes dominant in the form of self-sufficient reason."[23] This development reaches its completion in the philosophy of Kant. In the *Critique of Pure Reason,* Kant appears to take nature to be the totality of beings insofar as they can be determined by mathematical physics. Opposed to nature understood in this way is then what Kant calls the *categorical imperative,* which is equally determined by reason and as reason. When he compares it with and relates it to nature, he calls it explicitly the *ought (Sollen).*[24]

Heidegger next briefly indicates how Fichte made the opposition between Being and the ought the foundation of his philosophical system as a whole, but he then states that, speaking generally, in the nineteenth century the privileged position was given by philosophers neither to Being nor to the ought but rather to beings taken in the sense in which they are determined by the natural and human sciences, including history. It is clear that in this way the ontological status of the ought became questionable and its role as criterion and standard was endangered. Those who were concerned with ethics felt that the ought was to receive a new ground and that this ground was to be derived from the ought itself; the categorical obligation attached to every moral ought had to present its own justification. It was argued that such obligation could be derived only from something which in and by itself is able to raise a moral claim, something which has an intrinsic *value*, which is itself a *value*. From then on, values as such became the foundation of the moral ought and the entire ethical "system." One soon realized that values as such are opposed to the Being of the beings taken as facts, and that for that reason they themselves cannot be. One cannot say that values are; yet one can say that they have validity. Finally, values became ultimately the "crucial criteria" for all realms of beings, and one began to consider history as the process in which these values are realized.[25]

In Heidegger's opinion, what happened here was really the following: One had learned from Plato that Being may be conceived as idea and that the idea is to be conceived as a prototype and, thus, as a measure. One then took Plato's ideas, re-interpreted them in terms of values, and interpreted the Being of the beings from the perspective of values. Realizing that the statement that values have validity can easily be misunderstood in a subjectivist sense, it was then said that values have a Being of their own, and that undoubtedly meant for these authors that values, too, in some sense or other have the presence of something that is already there. Although these authors stressed the point that this presence cannot possibly be taken in the sense of the presence of tables and chairs, it is nonetheless obvious that with the claim about the Being of values, a maximum of confusion was created.[26]

Heidegger concludes these reflections on an ethics built upon the concept of values with a few remarks about Nietzsche's philosophy: "How stubbornly the idea of values ingrained itself in the nineteenth century can be seen from the fact that even Nietzsche, and precisely he, never departed from this perspective."[27] To substantiate this claim, Heidegger points out that the subtitle of Nietzsche's last work, *The Will to Power*, is *An Attempt to Re-evaluate All Values*, and that the third book of this work is called "An Attempt to Establish New Values." Yet, in Heidegger's view, this preoccupation with values was the basic weakness of Nietzsche's philosophy: "His entanglement in the thicket of the idea of values, his failure to understand its questionable origin, is the reason why Nietzsche did not attain to the true center of philosophy."[28] The implication of this statement obviously is that the same thing is true for any other philosophical ethics which gives the privileged position to the concept of values.

It is clear from these reflections that it would be rather difficult to derive from them the thesis that in 1935 Heidegger was of the opinion that philosophy should not concern itself with moral issues and that a philosophical "ethics" is impossible or irrelevant. Yet two theses can be established on the basis of these reflections which in my opinion are of great importance. First of all, Heidegger rejects any attempt to develop a philosophical ethics which gives the privileged position to the concept of values. This criticism has been taken up and developed further by several authors since 1935 and need not occupy us here further.[29] Secondly, Heidegger also criticizes every form of ethics in which metaphysical assumptions of any kind play an important part. His attitude in regard to ethics thus runs parallel here to his attitude in regard to sacred theology.[30] Let us now turn to the "Letter on Humanism" and see how these ideas are articulated further.

The second time Heidegger turned to ethics was in the "Letter on Humanism."[31] There he spoke against humanism, against logic, and again against values; instead, he defended the view that the Being of man consists in Being-in-the-world; he referred to Nietzsche's word on the "death of God" and thus seemed to speak "against all that humanity deems high and holy" and to defend some irresponsible and destructive form of "nihilism." Heidegger realized that that is the way it has to look to many people who hear talk about humanism, logic, values, world, and God, who accept these "things" as positive, hear something about opposition to these, and thus feel threatened in what is most dear to them. These people do what all of us often do: "We pitch everything that does not stay close to the familiar and beloved positive into the previously excavated pit of pure negation which negates everything, ends in nothing, and so consummates nihilism."[32]

In Heidegger's view, to think against values is not tantamount to defending the view that everything which one usually interprets as a value is really valueless and thus that culture, art, science, human dignity, world, and God are without value and meaning. Rather, one should realize that we rob everything of its true worth by characterizing it as a value. For by assessing something merely as a value, we make that which we so value a mere object of our own estimation. But the Being of a thing is not exhausted by its being an object for a subject. And that is true particularly where objectivity takes the form of value, because every valuing, even if it values in a positive manner, is and remains a subjectivizing; it does not let beings be. To call God the highest value is to degrade the true essence of God.[33]

Furthermore, to speak about man in terms of his being a Being-in-the-world is not tantamount to stating that man is merely a worldly creature understood in a Christian way, i.e., a creature turned away from God.

For, " 'world' does not in any way imply earthly as opposed to heavenly being, nor the 'worldly' as opposed to the 'spiritual.' " The term *world* does not refer here to beings or to a particular realm of beings; it simply means the openness of Being.[34] Thus the claim that man's essence consists in Being-in-the-world "contains no decision about whether man in a theologico-metaphysical sense is merely a this-wordly or an other-wordly creature."[35] Nor does it negate the true humanity of man. What is meant in these and similar claims is that one cannot meaningfully speak about God and man if one does not make a serious effort to overcome classical metaphysics by trying to think the truth of Being. But "to think the truth of Being at the same time means to think the humanity of the *homo humanus*."[36] In *What Evokes Thinking?* Heidegger expressed the same idea as follows: "Every philosophical, i.e., thinking, doctrine of the essence of man is *ipso facto* a doctrine of the Being of beings. And every doctrine of Being is *ipso facto* a doctrine of the essence of man."[37]

But if the humanity of man must be related essentially to the thinking of Being, does this ontology then not have to be supplemented by an ethics? In his attempt to answer this question, Heidegger first mentions that shortly after the publication of *Being and Time*, a young friend asked him when he would write an ethics. Heidegger admits that where the essence of man is thought solely from the question concerning the meaning and truth of Being without in any way elevating man to the center of beings, it is understandable that one wants directives and rules which state how man, experienced from the ek-sistence toward Being, ought to live. And that is true particularly in our own epoch, in which man's perplexity has grown immeasurably. "The greatest care must be fostered upon the ethical bond at a time when technological man, delivered over to mass society, can be kept reliably on call only by gathering and ordering all his plans and activities in a way that corresponds to technicity."[38]

And yet this urgent need does not release thought from its basic task of thinking what is most worthy of being thought, i.e., the truth of Being, because Being, as prior to all beings, is their guarantor and their truth.[39] In other words, even if one grants that no one can disregard his own predicament, and that it is everyone's task to secure the existing bonds, however tenuously they may hold human beings together today, even then thought cannot be released from its most important task, because the forgottenness of Being is at the root of the actual situation in which man finds himself today.[40]

Heidegger next turns to the question of what ontology and ethics themselves then are. Can one still assume without further ado that what these two names designate indeed is still near and proper to the task of thinking? Let us assume for a moment that all thinking in terms of disciplines has become superfluous and that a thinking which tries to think outside the domain of disciplines therewith becomes more "disciplined"; would then the entire discussion about ontology and ethics and their mutual relationship not become superfluous as well?[41]

The disciplines "logic," "physics," and "ethics" originated in the school of Plato at a time when thinking became philosophy, and philosophy, in turn, became *epistēmē*, science, and science itself became part of an educational framework and of academic pursuits. Prior to Plato and Aristotle, the Greeks did not make a distinction between these disciplines; yet their thinking then was not illogical, unnatural, or immoral. As a matter of fact, they thought about *phusis* "in a depth and breadth which no subsequent physics was ever again to attain."[42] Furthermore, the works of Sophocles preserved the *ethos* more primordially than Aristotle's lectures on ethics.[43]

Heidegger uses a fragment of Heraclitus to elaborate on this idea. Fragment 119 states: *ēthos anthrōpōi daimōn*. This phrase is usually translated as "A man's character is his *daimon*." In Heidegger's opinion, *daimōn* here means the god, whereas *ēthos* means the dwelling place or abode. Thus the fragment states that man as man dwells in the nearness of God. A story about Heraclitus which is reported by Aristotle[44] is in harmony with this interpretation. In it Aristotle reports that strangers who visited Heraclitus found him warming himself at a stove. They were surprised and stood there baffled. Then Heraclitus asked them to come in with the words: "For here too the gods are present" *(Einai gar kai entautha theous).*[45]

Be that as it may, if, in harmony with the basic meaning of the word *ēthos*, we take the word *ethics* to refer to the fact that it ponders the abode of man, then "that thinking which thinks the truth of Being as the primordial element of man, as the one who ek-sists, is in itself the original ethics."[46] One will obviously say that a thinking which ponders the truth of Being and which defines the essence of *Dasein* in terms of ek-sistence from the perspective of *Dasein*'s belonging to Being *(ēthos)* remains a purely theoretical presentation of Being and of man and, as such, still has little to do with practical philosophy, which is supposed to provide us with practical guidelines and directives. Heidegger responds by saying that thinking is neither theoretical nor practical, and that it occurs before this distinction can be made.

> Such thinking is, insofar as it is at all, the re-collection of Being and nothing
> else. Belonging to Being, because thrown by Being into the preservation of its

truth and claimed for such preservation, it thinks Being. Such thinking has no result. It has no effect. It satisfies its essence in that it is. And it is by saying its matter . . . it lets Being be.[47]

But that does not mean that this thinking is "morally" irrelevant. One should realize that in the final analysis, only insofar as man, standing-out into the truth of Being, belongs to Being can Being itself grant the assignment of those directives that must become law for man. "In Greek to assign is *nemein. Nomos* is not only law but more originally the assignment contained in the dispensation of Being. Only the assignment is capable of dispatching man into Being. Only such dispatching is capable of supporting and obligating. Otherwise law remains merely something fabricated by human reason."[48] Thus Heidegger concludes that even more essential than the institution of rules is that each man finds the way to his abode in the truth of Being, because this abode first yields the experience of something one can hold on to. "The truth of Being offers a hold for all conduct."[49] The relationship of the thinking of Being to theoretical and practical behavior should now be clear. For the thinking of Being exceeds all contemplation, because it cares for the light in which all seeing *(theōria)* can first live and move. Thus it is a deed, and a deed which even surpasses all *praxis.* "Thinking towers above action and production, not through the grandeur of its achievement and not as a consequence of its effect, but through the humbleness of its inconsequential accomplishment."[50] For people who think from the perspective of our everyday life, these claims are meaningless. We measure the greatness of a thought by its influence, and we measure deeds by the successful achievements in the order of the *praxis.* Yet, in Heidegger's view, then one forgets again that the thinking of Being is neither theoretical nor practical; it is not even the conjunction of these two forms of behaving.[51]

From these reflections, it is clear again that Heidegger does not claim that the thinker should not concern himself with moral issues and thus with reflections which are ethical in character. He does not even reject the possibility and necessity of a philosophical ethics. It is true that he maintains his negative attitude in regard to every form of ethics which is built upon the conception of values; as far as this approach to ethics is concerned, Heidegger once remarked that he would give preference to Kant's over that of Max Scheler.[52] It is true also that Heidegger was of the opinion that the meaning which an ethics will have in the future will depend on the manner in which a new approach to thinking will be developed concretely.[53] Yet all of that should certainly not be construed to mean that in Heidegger's view ethics is to be eliminated. It is clear also

that there is absolutely no ground to defend the view that the ethical
position which is implicit in Heidegger's own way of thinking would lead
to nihilism, or that in his later thinking Heidegger is no longer able to
give a foundation to responsibility and obligation.[54]

Article II: On Heidegger and Politics

In reflecting on Heidegger's conception of politics and the relation between thinking and the political practice, one finds oneself somehow in a
vicious circle. On the one hand, in order to be able to relate critically to
Heidegger's ideas, one must already have a conception about what ideally
the relationship between philosophy and politics should be. On the other
hand, in formulating these ideas, one must formulate and justify this
conception with the help of a metaphysical philosophy, which Heidegger
precisely tries to overcome. One could argue with Marxism that the
function of philosophy is inherently and exclusively "political"; in that
case there is something basically wrong with Heidegger's philosophy, at
least as long as philosophy and politics are understood in the manner in
which Marxism understands them. But what Heidegger understands by
thinking can by no means be placed on a par with what Marx understood
by philosophy in his theses on Ludwig Feuerbach. Furthermore, the term
political, which is so predominant in the Marxist literature, is virtually
absent in Heidegger's thinking. Does the term *the political* not suggest a
fragmentation in our conception about what is which is totally counter-
productive to what reflections on "the political" try to achieve? Should
we not be concerned primarily about the world in which we live, and is
this world not primarily the concrete form or structure which Being
adopts in the coming-to-pass of its truth? But if that is the case, is
Heidegger's philosophy then not "political" through and through, and
"political" in a sense which is much "deeper" than the one we find in
many philosophical treatises concerned with politics?

One could also say, with some logical positivist and critical rationalist
authors, that a philosophy which cannot demonstrate its relevance for
our technocratic planning is totally superfluous. Seen from this perspective, Heidegger's thinking seems to be superfluous in a superlative degree, simply because of the fact that it rejects calculative thinking as
meaningful for the manner in which we concern ourselves with our
world, which is the building structure of Being itself. Yet here again it is
obvious that at the root of Heidegger's thinking we find the conviction
that a scientific philosophy in the sense of logical positivism and critical
rationalism really constitutes the end of philosophy in the strict sense of

the term.[55] Heidegger does not hesitate to state that in his own opinion, thinking and logical positivism are two opposing extremes.[56]

Thus in speaking about Heidegger and politics, it makes little sense to characterize and criticize his position merely from the outside, so to speak. Furthermore, such a procedure can be turned around. Thus, it is more important to try to understand how in Heidegger's view the relationship between thinking and the "life of the people" is to be understood. Once we have come to a proper understanding with respect to this point, we can turn to a critical evaluation.

Yet the drift of the preceding remarks is not to defend the thesis that there could be a genuine form of thinking which would be totally "apolitical," in the sense of "irrelevant for the life which people have to live in their world." On the other hand, however, it is equally incorrect to defend the view that philosophy is to be surrendered to politics; a philosophical position which is philosophically respectable cannot just be a tool in the hands of some clever politicians. As far as Heidegger's work is concerned, it has often been said, on the one hand, that there is no concern with politics in his philosophy and, on the other, that his philosophy is really no more than an attempt to justify National Socialism as a political movement. It does not take much reflection to realize that neither of these claims can be correct or even remotely relevant to the state of affairs and the actual historical events. Not even in 1933 and 1934 did Heidegger ever try to philosophically justify National Socialism, as it was understood by the NSDAP. On the other hand, his concern with "political" issues is obvious both in *Being and Time* and in the later works, as we shall see shortly.

As far as Heidegger's attitude in regard to politics in general and to political philosophy in particular is concerned, it must be said first that there is quite a bit of literature on this subject.[57] That is understandable, especially because of Heidegger's involvement with politics in 1933 and 1934. As for his attitude with respect to National Socialism, it seems that by now we are relatively well informed about the facts as they actually took place. Yet it is still much less clear how one is to understand these facts, and there is certainly not yet common agreement on this matter. It seems to me that François Fédier and Beda Alleman have provided us with the most important information about the historical events;[58] I also think that the interview with Heidegger that appeared in *Der Spiegel* contains important remarks which to some degree clarify a number of points.[59] In my opinion, the best known studies on Heidegger's attitude in regard to political ideas are found in the works of Alexander Schwan, Jean-Michel Palmier, and Otto Pöggeler.[60]

If it had not been for Heidegger's involvement with National Socialism during the period in which he was rector of the University of Freiburg, a position which at that time "automatically" implied membership in the NSDAP, probably nobody would have expected that in a treatise on his philosophy a chapter on his political philosophy would be mandatory. Even though it is the case that the work of every philosopher is politically relevant in some sense, it is nonetheless also true that the work of many philosophers has been written about without the addition of explicit chapters on their political philosophies.

In Heidegger's works written before 1933, there are no explicit remarks about political ideas or even about the political situation. The same is true for almost all works written after February 1934. The few and mostly brief remarks about politics and political philosophy are so ambiguous that it is very difficult to interpret them, except perhaps in the light of the events which took place in 1933 and the beginning of 1934; but even in that case it is extremely difficult to prove that such an interpretation is objective.

As for the meaning and the implications of the events which took place between May 1933 and February 1934, it seems to me that the essays by Fédier, Alleman, Pöggeler, and Palmier can be read fruitfully.[61] On the other hand, the publications by Theodor Adorno, Mrs. T. Cassirer, J. P. Faye, P. Hühnerfeld, G. Lukács, Karl Löwith, R. Minder, M. de Gandillac, G. Schneeberger, A. Schwan, and E. Weil are (partly) incorrect, tendentious, and sometimes even defamatory, slanderous, and shabby.[62] During this ten-month period Heidegger wrote his rectorial address, "Die Selbstbehauptung der deutschen Universität,"[63] and a number of brief essays published in local newspapers, student newspapers, or pamphlets. When in his interview with *Der Spiegel* Heidegger was questioned about his contributions to local newspapers, he obviously did not deny the fact, but he added the following statement: "When I took over the rectorship it was clear to me that I would not see it through without some compromises. I would today no longer write the sentences which you cite. Even by 1934 I no longer said such things."[64]

These and similar statements taken from pamphlets, as well as some statements made in the rectorial address, are taken by many to express a deep-seated and long-lasting affiliation with the National Socialist movement, taken in its worst possible interpretation, and a clear sign of Heidegger's insincerity and irresponsibility. Yet anyone who has made a careful study of the available documents and publications knows that neither claim is true. Heidegger's affiliation with the Nazi movement lasted about ten months. There is no evidence in his works of his sympathy with this movement before 1933, and there is quite a bit of evidence for his explicit rejection of Nazism after February 1934. Thus it seems to me that anyone who defends the view that there is an intrinsic link between Nazism and Heidegger's later philosophy or between Nazism and the ideas proposed in *Being and Time* is simply mistaken. Personally, I am convinced that the evidence provided by Palmier and Fédier suffices to warrant this claim.[65] Obviously, the point is not to condone Heidegger's behavior in 1933 and 1934, because that behavior was indeed unacceptable on several counts. Yet it is impossible to defend the thesis that this behavior merely made manifest a political philosophy that had always been there and always would remain there.

The basic mistake which Heidegger made in 1933 was letting his colleagues talk him into believing that because of his fame and respect he would be able to run the University of Freiburg basically free from all outside political intervention, provided he would "play the game," i.e., become purely formally a member of the NSDAP, speak the "proper" language, and not antagonize the "authorities." Heidegger did succeed in preventing the posting of anti-Semitic posters, maintaining Jewish professors, preventing the burning of "unacceptable" books, appointing two well-known anti-Nazi deans, etc. Yet the price he had to pay was enormous, and after ten months he resigned. From February 1934 he was haunted by many Nazis, particularly by such Nazi philosophers as E. Krieck and P. Bäumler. Spies were sent to his lectures, his scholarly activities were made difficult (Descartes congress), and he was forbidden to publish. The details can also be found easily in Fédier, Alleman, Pöggeler, and Palmier.[66]

In Heidegger's later works, there are a few rather isolated statements which often have been quoted to substantiate the (mistaken) thesis that Heidegger's philosophy as a whole implies the political position made concrete in the Nazi movement. Two of these are found in *An Introduction to Metaphysics*. Commenting on a line from Sophocles' *Antigone*, Heidegger writes there:

> It speaks not of *poros* but of *polis*, not of the paths to all realms of beings but to the foundation and scene of man's *Dasein*, the point at which all these paths meet, the *polis*. *Polis* is usually translated by state or city-state. This does not capture its full meaning. *Polis* means rather, the place, the *Da* [there] wherein and as which historical *Da-sein* is. The *polis* is the historical place, the *Da in* which, *out of* which, and *for* which history happens. To this place and scene of history belong the gods, the temples, the priests, the festivals, the game, the poets, the thinkers, the ruler, the council of elders, the assembly of people, the army, and the fleet. All this does not first belong to the *polis*, does not become political by entering into a relation with a statesman and a general and the business of the state. Rather it is political, i.e., at the site of history, provided

there be for example poets who indeed are and are nothing but poets, priests who indeed are and are nothing but priests, rulers who indeed are and are nothing but rulers. And provided "be" means: as violent men use power to become pre-eminent in historical being as creators, as men of action. Pre-eminent in the historical place, they become at the same time *apolis,* without city and place, lonely, strange, and alien without issue amid the beings taken as a whole, at the same time without statute and limit, without structure and order, because they themselves *as* creators must first create all of this.[67]

Some interpreters take this passage to indicate Heidegger's long-standing preference for totalitarianism in general and for National Social-ism in particular. To substantiate this claim, they sometimes relate this passage to a statement taken from the interview with *Der Spiegel,* in which Heidegger explicitly said that it was a decisive question for him how a political system can accommodate itself to our technological age, and which political system it could be. "I have no answer to this question. I am not convinced that it is democracy."[68] Furthermore, these interpre-ters claim, the passage cited above strongly suggests that those who do not have the strength to create what is necessary for the state on their own must just follow the leaders; and among the leaders mentioned particu-larly, the statesman, the *Führer,* occupies a privileged position. Karsten Harries, who has developed this line of argument in detail, heavily relies (among other sources) on Schwan's interpretation of Heidegger's "polit-ical philosophy" and interprets from that perspective Heidegger's rec-torial address, as well as several statements found in Heidegger's later works.[69] Yet it seems to me that Gregory Schufreider[70] has competently shown that this way of thinking "is guided in advance by a desire to find [it] consistent with the Nazi involvement. . . ."[71] Furthermore, Schuf-reider also correctly observes that any attempt

> to align Heidegger's work with totalitarianism on the basis of a pair of brief and all too fragmentary passages, will not stand the test of their careful examination and in fact obscures the very conception they are designed to develop. The idea of the *polis* as the site of history, as that place at which the destiny of a people is formed, rules out its being instituted by an individual, the statesman, since its very conception entails that it be founded as a work in the intersection of the various paths which contribute to the establishment of a community, in their "conversation with one another."[72]

Another short passage often quoted by those who affiliate Heidegger's philosophy with the political conception incorporated in National Social-ism is found in another section of *An Introduction to Metaphysics,* where Heidegger toward the end, speaking about treatises on values, writes:

All these works call themselves philosophy. The works that are being peddled about nowadays as the philosophy of National Socialism but have nothing whatever to do with the inner truth and greatness of this movement (namely the encounter between global technology and modern man)—have all been written by men fishing in the troubled waters of "values" and "totalities."[73]

It is obviously easy to conclude that even in 1935, not to mention 1953, when the work was first published, Heidegger was still a convinced protagonist of National Socialism. In my opinion, Schufreider is again correct where he states that nothing is really gained by such simplistic reflections. Anyone who wishes to fully understand what this remark on "the inner truth and greatness of this movement" really means will have to place it within the broad context of Heidegger's concern with technicity, the work of Ernst Jünger, his concern with the meaning of Being in the atomic age, and (obviously) the political situation of the time and Heidegger's involvement in it.[74] As far as all of that is concerned, it seems to me that Palmier has made a great contribution by critically analyzing and unfolding these issues, events, and their implications in detail.[75]

I agree with Palmier that there was a short time in Heidegger's life in which he saw in Hitler the head of a nationalist party with a social character which indeed realized the ideal Jünger had projected and formulated in his book *Der Arbeiter.*[76] The mistake which Heidegger made in 1933 is one that was made by numerous Germans at that time, both inside and outside academia. Furthermore, that which Heidegger's publications of 1933 and 1934 try to promote is not the party's interpretation of National Socialism but rather the ideal portrayed by Jünger, which, at that time, Heidegger believed could be materialized by the National Socialist movement, which had just gained power. Heidegger never gave up this ideal, even though he protested against the errors made by National Socialism. In his later view, Nazism is no more than a simplistic and dangerous caricature of Jünger's ideal; Nazism is still caught in the grip of the metaphysics of the will to power. The party's interpretation of the meaning of National Socialism is no more than a symptom of the "spirit" of a metaphysics that is to be overcome. Seen from this point of view, Heidegger's later work is the only authentic attempt to overcome National Socialism, in the sense that it recognizes its true basis and foundation.[77] In "Overcoming Metaphysics,"[78] Heidegger wrote:

Metaphysics cannot be abolished like an opinion. One can by no means leave it behind as a doctrine no longer believed and represented. The fact that man as *animal rationale*, here meant in the sense of the working being, must wander through the desert of the earth's desolation could be a sign that metaphysics occurs in virtue of Being, and the overcoming of metaphysics occurs as the incorporation of Being. For labor (cf. Ernst Jünger, *Der Arbeiter*, 1932) is now reaching the metaphysical rank of the unconditioned objectification of everything present which is active in the will to will.[79]

And furthermore, in a lecture on Nietzsche, Heidegger makes it quite clear that his conception of the leaders by no means implies the glorification of totalitarianism.[80]

"In truth, the leaders represent the necessary consequence of the fact that has occurred in the mode of errancy, there where an emptiness extends itself which requires an order and a unique security of the beings. Thus this [state of affairs] is where the necessity of a direction comes from, i.e., of a calculation which makes the totality of beings secure through its plans."[81]

It is therefore clear that Schwan's claim that Heidegger's philosophy as a whole implies a glorification of totalitarianism, is without any ground.[82] On the same basis, I equally dismiss some fundamental assumptions of Reiner Schürmann's reflections on Heidegger's political thinking, although I agree with Bernard Dauenhauer that Schürmann's work on Heidegger's political philosophy cannot simply be dismissed.[83]

Schürmann states that Heidegger always remained deliberately and embarrassingly discreet and silent about the political dimension of his basic project to phenomenologically destroy classical metaphysics. In his opinion, that does not mean that the careful reader would have no idea at all where Heidegger stands as far as political philosophy is concerned. Schürmann endorses Harries's view that the fundamental themes of Heidegger's rectorial address of 1933 are rooted in *Being and Time* and continue to appear again in some of his later writings. He also shares Harries's opinion that these themes show a close affiliation of Heidegger's thought with basic ideas underlying National Socialism.[84] Schürmann feels that this safely established thesis makes careful reflection necessary. For "if before and after the 'turn' in his thinking Heidegger was, to be sure, a political thinker, and if his political standpoint does shine through several of his writings, what was that standpoint?"[85] In an effort to deal with this question, one can, according to Schürmann, take three different approaches. According to a first line of argument, one can simply identify the enduring political position behind Heidegger's thinking in general and his misled commitment in the early thirties to Nazism. This line, as we have seen already, was taken by Adorno, Lukács, and others. A second approach states that one must accept a development in Heidegger's thought on this point: Heidegger moved from a rather naive position, via a brief affiliation with National Socialism, to a position that was critical of that position. Schürmann finds both of these approaches inadequate and thus turns to a third line of argument, which rests on three assumptions: 1) Heidegger's thinking does contain a political dimension; 2) the political implications must be derived from his basic philosophical project, the question concerning the meaning of Being; and 3) Heidegger never developed a middle term between his ontology and a political thinking that might agree with it, so that it is understandable why one gropes in the dark if one tries to discover the basic elements of his political thought. Schürmann himself wishes to work out this missing link. He does so by reinterpreting Heidegger's conception of the ontological difference into a symbolic difference, in view of the fact that the domain of the symbol constitutes that domain among beings which explicitly thematizes the simultaneity of concealment and non-concealment.[86]

According to Schürmann, symbols constitute that area of the real whose understanding requires some way of ek-sisting; if one is to understand the full meaning of a symbol, one has to engage in a certain practice.[87] Now, if that is so, then it can be shown "how the practical a priori at work in the understanding of symbols provides a clue for the elaboration of categories of action in accordance with Heidegger's nonmetaphysical version of the ontological difference."[88] In Schürmann's view, Heidegger's interpretation of the ontological difference implies the "destruction of metaphysics and thus the very meaning which the tradition attaches to the notions of ground and origin"; and that is the reason why "in his project of raising anew the question of Being for itself and out of itself Heidegger henceforth deprives practical philosophy of its metaphysical ground, and at the same time suggests only by implication from what new ground action might become thinkable."[89] What is most important here is that for Heidegger "all attempts to ground political conduct on some unshakeable ultimate principle are invalidated. Action cannot be legitimated by referring it to a primordial ground or ultimate reason."[90] But that means that the very foundations of all metaphysical legitimations of the political order and of our political conduct are subverted.[91] Schürmann himself describes his position in this regard as follows:

> The question of the origin as it is raised by Heidegger . . . undercuts metaphysical constructions not only in thought but also in action. The phenomenological destruction, if it is thought of within *sumballein*, has concrete consequences that reverse the metaphysical way of grounding a practical philosophy. Such reversal becomes thinkable upon the condition that the origin of Being and language, their identical coming-forth, be not represented as the ultimate foundation of both theory and practice; that is, that the quest for an ultimate foundation be abandoned altogether. Then the essence of foundation

undergoes a reversal: it is not beings that call for a ground, but Being as the groundless ground calls upon ek-sistence. In this sense Heidegger's turn literally operates a subversion: the reversal of the essence of foundation is an overthrow *(vertere)* from the base or ground *(sub)*. The middle term that carries the phenomenological destruction into practical subversion is the symbolic difference. It translates the "turn" in thinking into an "overturn" in action. In a culture where philosophy has come to cooperate with the existing system to the point of radically abandoning its task of criticism, Heidegger's insistence on releasement and "life without why" as the practical a priori for the thought of Being opens an alternative way to think of life in society. The symbolic difference allows for the elaboration of an alternative type of political philosophy."[92]

Schürmann has tried to work out some of the basic elements toward such an alternative political philosophy, which in his view is in harmony with Heidegger's fundamental, "ontological" position. These elements can be summarized briefly as follows:

1) The abolition of the primacy of teleology in action.
2) The abolition of the primacy of responsibility in the legitimation of action.
3) Action is a protest against a (technologically) administered world.
4) There is a certain disinterest in the future of mankind due to a shift in the understanding of destiny.
5) Anarchy is the essence of the "memorable," which requires thought, and the essence of the "do-able," which requires action.[93]

According to Schürmann, these elements are to be understood in such a way that they mutually entail each other.

Heidegger's proper, although hidden, standpoint on a political philosophy which would agree with his thinking . . . entails the practical abolition of *archē* and *telos* in action, the transvaluation of responsibility and destiny, and the protest against a world reduced to functioning within the coordinates of causality. . . . To Leibniz's metaphysical tenet that everything has a "because" *(warum)* Heidegger opposes Meister Eckhart's "life without why" *(ohne warum)*. [94]

Contrary to what other authors have claimed, Schürmann maintains that this position is not a theory of the organization of man into collectivities; yet it is not the celebration of pure interiority, either. "Between a system of social constitution and its negation by spiritual individualism or apolitical solipsism there is a place for a thinking about society which refuses to restrict itself to the pragmatics of public administration as well as to romantic escapes from it."[95]

Dauenhauer has correctly observed that Schürmann's position gives rise to a host of questions.[96] I shall limit myself here to some questions which immediately pertain to Heidegger's own position in regard to the issues raised by Schürmann. It is indeed true that for Heidegger, once metaphysics is "overcome," one no longer can appeal to an ultimate *telos*, because we do not have access to such a *telos*. Yet that obviously does not entail that a man's actions could not be "goal-oriented." Heidegger takes here a position already taken earlier by Kant.[97] It most certainly is not the case that Heidegger ever advocated the abolition of the primacy of responsibility in the legitimation of action. When Schürmann tries to explain this claim and justify it on the grounds of statements made by Heidegger, he refers to *Der Satz vom Grund*,[98] where Heidegger writes that *Rechenschaft ablegen*, "to account for something," *rationem reddere*, etc. belong in the realm of calculative thinking, and adds that in all Western languages accountability has to do with accounting. I take Heidegger's observation to be correct, but I fail to see why E. Tugendhat and Schürmann derive from it that with such a concept of responsibility freedom gets lost, and why responsibility would not be essential in the legitimation of action.[99] It is the case that in virtually all legal frameworks of the West, accountability is defined with the help of some form of calculative thinking; that may not be the only way in which one can define accountability, but it certainly is an effective one for *merely legal* purposes. Be that as it may, in all reflections on moral issues it has been taken for granted that in the legitimation of moral action, responsibility is primary. As far as I know, no one has ever noticed a flagrant contradiction in these two claims. Thus I fail to see how Schürmann can construe Heidegger's observation concerning the meaning of the expression "to give an account for" to imply the abolition of the primacy of responsibility in the legitimation of action.

I do think that most people who live in a free and democratic society today have great difficulty with the bureaucratic manner in which our world is being administered technologically. Yet here again, making this observation does not imply promoting some form of anarchy. It is the case that our socio-political world has become so enormously complex that its administration appears to imply a bureaucracy, which all of us have great difficulty with and which we all nonetheless know that we ourselves created, because there does not seem to be an easy way of doing things in a better way.

The claim that in Heidegger's work there is a certain disinterest in the future of mankind is simply not true. It is true that Heidegger on several occasions has tried to explain that we often hold individual thinkers, scientists, politicians, etc., responsible for ideas, conceptions, and actions for which we should not hold them individually responsible.[100] It is the case that we live in an epoch in which Being itself is forgotten; it makes no sense to hold Kant responsible for that. We also live in an epoch which is dominated by atomic energy; in my opinion, it makes again little sense to hold Bohr or Heisenberg responsible for that. When we entered the world, we found a world and found ourselves in it in a manner for which (as such) we cannot yet be held responsible. This realization immediately leads to the idea that with respect to the future one should be fully aware of what one legitimately may still expect and hope for. There are many "things" taking place which in some sense "determine" the course of future events. Realizing these and similar "facts" has little to do with losing interest in the future of mankind.

I obviously agree with Schürmann that if one were to develop an explicit political philosophy on the basis of Heidegger's "ontology," it would have to be a political philosophy in which no appeal to a utopian *archē* or *telos* would be permissible, certainly not as long as the words *archē* and *telos* are understood as they have been in classical metaphysics. But instead of interpreting this fact to mean a subversion of ethics and political philosophy, I would like to interpret it in such a way that it becomes manifest as the condition of the possibility of a genuine ethics and a true political philosophy.

CONCLUSION

The critics of Heidegger's moral and political philosophy have obviously not been wrong in all the claims they have made. It is indeed true that Heidegger said many times that one of the basic intentions of his thinking was to overcome metaphysics, and that for that reason certain metaphysical assumptions will have to be eliminated in reflections on religion, natural theology, ethics, social and political philosophy, the arts, the sciences, and technology. Yet the destructive retrieve which is implicit in this effort to overcome metaphysics is not all negative, is not just destruction; it is also and equally essentially retrieve.

If that is so, it obviously will not do to accuse Heidegger of nihilism simply because he tries to overcome an appeal to "entities" which in principle cannot be known by man. Objecting to Platonism in ethics is not tantamount to defending nihilism. Rejecting the Platonic Form of the Good and the Platonic view of justice does not imply the rejection of the entire moral order; nor does it exclude that one maintains the "basic" obligation of justice, namely, to do good to others and to protect them from evil.[101] Heidegger's basic concern here is not to subvert the moral order but to find a "foundation" on the basis of which a meaningful discourse on ethical issues can take place. Also, it makes absolutely no sense to accuse him of having defended an extreme form of egoism and egocentrism. There have been critics who have tried to interpret *Being and Time* along these lines. Anyone who is willing and able to read the lecture courses which Heidegger taught in Marburg, before *Being and Time* was published, and in which the book was "prepared," so to speak, will see that such an interpretation is completely unwarranted.[102]

Similar remarks can be made for Heidegger's political philosophy. I agree with Schürmann that Heidegger indeed wished to overcome classical metaphysics and that that, as far as political philosophy is concerned, implies the radical elimination of a number of utopian assumptions suggested by many "leading" political theorists from Plato to Marx. Heidegger is not the only one and not even the first one to make this claim. One can turn to many political scientists whose works contain similar remarks. But again, overcoming metaphysics does not mean throwing all metaphysics away, and eliminating certain utopian and otherwise unwarranted political ideas is not tantamount to discarding all ideas about the political order. Here, too, "destruction" has to go hand in hand with retrieve.

It is peculiar that particularly as far as Heidegger's political ideas are concerned, he has been accused of two mutually exclusive theses. On the one hand, it has been argued that Heidegger's hermeneutic position forces him into maintaining the status quo and idealizing the past; on the other hand, he has been accused of having promoted some form of political "anarchy." I think that Schürmann was correct in arguing that Heidegger's conception of the history of Being and his "systematic" effort to overcome classical metaphysics forced him in political philosophy to a position in which access to some of the traditional *archai* is precluded in a definitive manner, and that his political philosophy for that reason could be called an-archic. Yet one should then also realize that the term *an-archic* now receives a meaning it usually does not have. Now it merely means that in the realm of the political and social, the human community has to constitute its social and political framework with its norms, laws, and institutions in such a manner that access to unknowable *archai* is excluded. Yet that does not mean that the constitution of such a framework should be arbitrary, unsocial, and inhumane. It merely means that one should realize that the constitution of such a framework is man's work, that it thus bears all the characteristics of being man's work, that it will be finite, temporal, historical, fallible, and imperfect, and that man himself can and must be held responsible for its implications and consequences.

The critic obviously will continue to maintain that by rejecting democracy, Heidegger clearly indicated, even toward the end of his life, that he was an ardent protagonist of National Socialism. When in the interview with *Der Spiegel* Heidegger wrote that he was not convinced that democracy can be coordinated with the technological age, this claim did not imply that he was convinced that National Socialism *could* be coordinated with this age. Rather, he had reasons to doubt whether democracy as we normally conceive of it indeed is relevant to the actual economic, social, and political framework with which we are now confronted in the atomic age. Recent empirical research into public opinion, lobbying practices, voting habits, and the manner in which political issues today are actually decided in the House and the Senate makes it abundantly clear that the concept of democracy is to be changed drastically to bring it into harmony with what in most "democratic" nations actually "lives" as democracy. We have always assumed that a politically conscious electorate is indispensable for a healthy democracy. We have equally assumed that the voting citizens constantly had to protect their rights and interests against the ever-present danger of tyranny and corruption. These assumptions appear now to be questionable, in view of the fact that the political systems which we took to be the paradigms of modern democracy appear not to satisfy these conditions. Thus we must now seriously ask whether the classical conception of democracy still has any relation to our actual political reality and whether it does not stipulate conditions which in practice appear to be incompatible.[103]

It seems to me to be in harmony with the ideas he developed in connection with Jünger's work that Heidegger questions whether democracy is still the adequate political framework for an atomic age. Let us not forget that democracy itself is no more than a human creation which time and again is to be adapted to the changing circumstances and situations. Secondly, the modern atomic world has become so complex that many aspects of our political life *factually* can be understood and evaluated only by a scientific elite group. The point here is not that social technocracy and "cybernetics" are ideals; the point is rather that it is not very clear how the classical idea of democracy is to be adapted to this overly complex world, and even whether that indeed can still be done at all.

Epilogue

In Heidegger's view, to philosophize means to engage in an effort to reflect critically on basic issues and to do so in such a way that the reflection persists in questioning. Questions are ways toward possible answers. If in philosophy such a reflection would ever be granted us, it would consist in a complete transformation of thinking and not in some statement about a certain state of affairs. In 1966 Heidegger published a brief essay, "The End of Philosophy and the Task of Thinking,"[1] later also incorporated in *Zur Sache des Denkens*,[2] in which he pursues this issue in greater detail in an effort to formulate the basic question, first raised in *Being and Time*, in a more primordial manner.

As we have seen, this question is the question of the meaning of Being, the question concerning the coming-to-pass of the truth of Being. This question must be asked now critically in such a way that it becomes clear "to what extent the critical question of what the matter of thinking is, necessarily and continually belongs to thinking" itself. In this overall perspective, two questions are considered here in particular: 1) What does it mean that in the present age philosophy has entered the final stage? 2) What task is still reserved for thinking now that philosophy has come to its end?[3]

I. PHILOSOPHY HAS ENTERED ITS FINAL STAGE. WHAT DOES THAT MEAN?
In the first part of the essay, Heidegger begins by stating that philosophy has become metaphysics. Metaphysics tries to think beings as such and as a whole; it tries to think the world, man, and God, insofar as they, as beings, belong together in Being. Metaphysics thinks beings as beings, and in so doing it posits, pro-poses, and gives reasons. Since the beginning of philosophy in the West, the Being of beings has shown itself as ground, *archē, aition,* principle. The ground is that from which beings, taken as beings, are what they are in their coming-to-be, passing-away, and abiding as the beings that can be known, handled, and acted upon. As

275

the ground, Being brings beings to their actual abiding presence. Thus the ground shows itself here as the presence which brings what is present in each case to presence. At one time the ground showed itself as that which is at the root of all ontic causation of what actually is (Descartes); later it showed itself as the transcendental which makes the objectivity of objects possible (Kant); still later it showed itself as the dialectical meditation of the movement of the absolute Spirit (Hegel), or as the historical process of production (Marx) and as the will to power that posits values (Nietzsche).

What is characteristic for metaphysical thinking is the fact that it starts from what is present and then posits and pro-poses that in its presence, thus exhibiting it as grounded by its ground. When we now speak of the end of philosophy, we do not take the end of metaphysics in a negative sense. Rather, it means the completion of metaphysics; yet that again does not mean the perfection, either, as if metaphysics would attain the highest perfection at its end. We have no criteria to make such claims and to argue that one epoch of metaphysics is more perfect than another. In philosophy, each epoch has its own necessity, and thus it is not for us to prefer one epoch over another, as we can do, for instance, with regard to different *Weltanschauungen*.

Heidegger then explains that the word *end* originally meant "place," *topos*. Thus the end of philosophy is *the* place, i.e., the place in which the entire history of philosophy is gathered in its most extreme possibility. It has often been said that throughout the history of philosophy, Plato's thinking has remained decisive, even though it has continually changed in form. Thus Nietzsche could say that metaphysics is Platonism and that his own philosophy is reversed Platonism. A similar remark can be made for Marx's philosophy; it too is a reversal of metaphysics. With this total reversal of philosophy, the most extreme possibility of philosophy is attained; philosophy has now entered its final stage. It is now capable only of attaining an epigonal renaissance and of bringing about variations of that renaissance. The variation which is dominant today is that of scientific realism.

We should not forget that the development of sciences within the field opened up by philosophy itself was already a decisive characteristic of Greek philosophy. Soon the sciences would become separated from philosophy and establish their complete independence. This process belongs to the completion of philosophy and is now in full swing in all regions of beings. This development looks like the dissolution of philosophy; in truth, however, it is its completion.[4]

If we look at the sciences of man, which have all become independent sciences, we see that today philosophy is turning into the empirical sciences of man and of all that can become the experiential object of his technology. The completion of philosophy is today the development of philosophy into independent sciences of man; philosophy has now found its place in the scientific attitude of a socially active humanity. This attitude is steered by cybernetics and, thus, is to be characterized by its technological character. The more technicity regulates and characterizes the appearance of the totality of the world and man's position in it, the less man seems to feel the need to pose the question concerning technicity.

The sciences interpret technologically everything that in their own structure is still reminiscent of their origin from philosophy. Furthermore, they understand as working hypotheses the categories upon which each science depends for the articulation of its domain of investigation. Finally, not only is their truth measured in terms of the effects which their applications bring about, but this truth is even equated with the efficiency of these effects.

Also, the sciences have taken over as their own task what in the course of its history philosophy, often inadequately, presented in regional ontologies. Their interest is thus oriented also toward the theory of the necessary structural concepts of the relevant areas of investigation. But "theory" now means merely the supposition of categories; the latter, furthermore, are denied all ontological meaning and given only a functional sense. The operational character of our pro-posing and calculating thinking, which, in addition, works with models, becomes dominant. Yet in the supposition of their categories, they continue to speak about the Being of beings. Thus even though the scientists often deny this, in the scientificity of the sciences itself the document of their origin from philosophy still speaks.

Heidegger concludes the first part of the essay by stating that the end of philosophy manifests itself as the triumph of the cybernetic organization of our scientific and technical world, and of the entire social order that is implied by it. It also means the beginning of a world civilization that is based on this Western way of thinking. Yet this end of philosophy is not the complete actualization of all the possibilities of philosophical thought. For it could very well be that there also is a first possibility from which philosophy's thinking started but which philosophy yet was unable to experience and adopt. In that case, the entire history of philosophy still conceals a task for thought which is accessible neither to philosophy as metaphysics nor to the sciences which developed from philosophy.[5]

II. WHAT TASK IS STILL RESERVED FOR THINKING AT THE END OF
PHILOSOPHY?

Heidegger begins part 2 of this essay by observing that one will say that a
thinking which is neither metaphysics nor science is almost unthinkable
and thus is a task which has concealed itself from philosophy since its
very beginning and throughout its various epochs. Furthermore, does
one, by making such a claim, not place oneself above all the great thinkers
of the past? The suspicion of arrogance indeed obtrudes; and yet one
must not forget that every attempt to say something about the supposed
task of philosophy begins by reviewing the entire history of philosophy.
In addition, this thinking must also think the historicity of that which
grants philosophy its history. That is the reason why the thinking whose
possibility we assume here must fall short of the philosophy of great
philosophers; thus this thinking is somehow less than philosophy. And
that is so also because of the fact that it obviously will have less influence
on people who are preoccupied with science and technicity than philosophy had in the preceding centuries. Finally, this kind of thinking is rather
modest in its aim, because of its merely preparatory character. Instead of
trying to give or lay a foundation, it merely attempts to awaken a readiness for a kind of thinking whose scope remains vague and whose coming
is still very uncertain. The first thing which this thinking must learn is
what task is still left for thinking at the end of philosophy.

Heidegger explains that he is thinking here about the possibility that
our world civilization one day might overcome the idea that the technical,
scientific, and industrial character is the only criterion of man's dwelling
on earth. It is obviously uncertain whether this civilization, which has
just begun, will soon be destroyed or whether it will be able to maintain
itself for a long time. Yet once the change to which we just alluded comes,
it will come because of the readiness of man for a determination which
always addresses itself to man in his destiny. This preparatory thinking
cannot predict the future. It merely says something to the present which
at the beginning of philosophy was already said but until now remained
unthought in an explicit manner. In the context of a lecture or a brief
essay, only a few remarks can be made about that which at the beginning
of philosophy was addressed to it; and in making them, we take our
guiding clue from that which philosophy itself offers as an aid in our
effort.[6]

If one asks what the task of thinking is, one asks about its matter, *die
Sache, to pragma auto*[7] of philosophy. In modern times this matter has
been indicated with the expression "the things themselves." We find this
expression in the preface of Hegel's *System of Science*, which Hegel has
placed before the introduction to the *Phenomenology of Spirit* and was

meant to be the first part of the system mentioned.[8] For Hegel the expression refers ultimately to the *Science of Logic.* In the expression "to the things themselves," Hegel places the stress on the *themselves,* so that the call criticizes the inadequate relations to the genuine matter of philosophy, which can never be the real totality of philosophy. This totality shows itself only in its own becoming. It occurs in the presentation of the matter as it develops; and in this presentation, theme and method coincide. Hegel calls this identity the *Gedanke,* and it is the thing itself of philosophy. Yet seen historically, this thing is subjectivity.

That is why Hegel in the same preface can state that the true in philosophy is to be understood as substance and as subject. The Being of beings or the presence of what is present is complete presence only when it becomes present as such for itself in the absolute Idea. But this coming to itself of Being occurs only in the speculative dialectic, so that the movement of the Idea, i.e., the method, is the matter itself. In other words, "to the thing itself" requires a philosophical method appropriate to it.[9] Yet what the matter of philosophy is, is decided from the very beginning: the matter of philosophy as metaphysics is the presence (= Being) of beings in the form of substantiality and subjectivity.

About one hundred years later, Husserl repeats the call "to the things themselves" in his *Logos* article of 1910–1911.[10] Here he rejects naturalistic psychology as well as historicism. The matter at stake in philosophy is again the subjectivity of consciousness, and the call "to the things themselves" determines again the development and the securing of a method as well as a criterion of truth (the principle of all principles). This criterion or principle requires that absolute subjectivity is the genuine matter of philosophy. The transcendental reduction to this absolute subjectivity gives a secure ground to the objectivity of all objects. Transcendental subjectivity is thus the sole absolute being.[11]

At the same time, the transcendental reduction which is the method of the "universal science" has the same mode of Being as this absolute being. That means again that the matter of philosophy and the method belong together; the method belongs to the matter, because it is the matter itself. But here, too, the matter of philosophy is determined from the very beginning; it is transcendental subjectivity. For Hegel, the speculative dialectic is the movement in which the matter as such of philosophy comes to itself, i.e., to its own presence. For Husserl, the transcendental method must bring the matter of philosophy to its ultimately originary self-givenness, i.e., to its own presence.[12] The two methods are as different as they can possibly be; yet the matter as such is the same, although it is obviously experienced in different ways.

We must now ask what it is that remains still unthought in this call "to the things themselves." By asking in this manner, we can come to see how that which is the matter of philosophy but which it is no longer capable of thinking conceals itself even where philosophy has brought its matter to absolute knowledge and to ultimate evidence. What remains unthought in the matter of philosophy as well as in its method is the *Lichtung*, the clearing, the opening, taken as primary phenomenon. That is true for both Hegel's dialectic and Husserl's originary intuition.[13]

We must realize here, Heidegger continues, that all philosophical thinking which somehow follows the call "to the things themselves," as far as its movement or method is concerned, is always already admitted to the free domain of the clearing. Yet philosophy appears to know nothing of this opening. Philosophy often speaks about the light of reason, but it does not pay any attention to the clearing of Being. One forgets here that man's light of reason, which was often called *lumen naturale*, can illuminate only that which is open. It does indeed concern the clearing, yet it does not at all form and constitute it; rather, it itself needs the clearing in order to be able to illuminate what comes-to-presence in the clearing. And that is true not only of the method of philosophy but also and even primarily of its subject matter, i.e., of the presence of what comes-to-presence. In whatever way that which comes-to-presence is presented, presence always remains dependent on the clearing's holding sway. Even that which is absent can as such not be, unless it comes-to-presence in the free space of the clearing.

All forms of traditional metaphysics, including its radical opponent, i.e., positivism, continue to speak the language of Plato. The basic word of his thinking, of his presentation of the Being of beings, is *eidos* or *idea*, the look or appearance in which the beings as such manifest themselves. But *eidos* taken in this manner is a mode of coming-to-presence. No being can look a certain way unless there is light. But there cannot be any openness and brightness without the clearing. And yet, the clearing which holds sway in Being and in presence continues to remain unthought in philosophy, even though it was spoken about at the very beginning of philosophy, where Parmenides reports about the goddess's claim that one must learn everything, "the untrembling heart of unconcealment, well-rounded, as well as the opinions of the mortals who lack the capacity to trust what is unconcealed."[14]

The goddess mentions *alētheia* here, non-concealment. It is said to be well-rounded because it is turned within the pure sphere of the circle, in which beginning and end are everywhere the same. In this turning there is no possibility of distortion. Every meditating human being is to experience "the untrembling heart of non-concealment," i.e., the essence of non-concealment, the place of stillness which gathers in itself what first grants non-concealment, the clearing of what is open.

Now, what prior to everything else first grants non-concealment is the way in which thinking pursues one thing and one thing only, namely, that coming-to-presence comes-to-presence *(dass anwest Anwesen)*. The clearing grants first of all the possibility of the way for the coming-to-presence, and grants the possible coming-to-presence of this presence itself. Thus we must think *alētheia,* non-concealment, as the opening which first grants Being and thinking as well as their coming-to-presence to and for each other. The quiet heart of the clearing is thus the place of stillness which first makes it possible that Being and thinking, coming-to-presence and accepting, can arise at all.[15] The possible claim to having a binding character of thinking is grounded in this belonging-together.

Heidegger remarks then that it was not for the sake of etymology that he translated *alētheia* as "non-concealment" but rather for the sake of the matter that is to be thought when one tries to think adequately what is called Being and thinking. Unconcealment is the element, so to speak, in which Being and thinking in their belonging-together must dwell and abide. *Alētheia* was already mentioned at the very beginning of philosophy; yet it has never been thought explicitly as such by philosophy. Nevertheless, we obviously have no right to "sit in judgment over philosophy, as though it left something unheeded, neglected it, and was thus marred by some essential deficiency."[16] What is asked for instead of criticism is that we all learn to listen to the silent address of Being. We all still need an education in thinking and, in addition, first of all the knowledge of what being educated in thinking truly means. But that can be decided in the final analysis only by the basic quality of that which above all else asks that it be admitted by us. But how can this quality make the decision possible for us, as long as we have not yet admitted it? In what circle are we moving here? It is the *eukukleos alētheiē,* the well-rounded non-concealment itself, thought as the clearing.[17] Thinking never reaches an end. Any place *(topos)* that in the reflection of the philosopher suggests itself as an end is really the place for a new beginning. For the one who thinks, there never will be a time in which he no longer has to learn. That is also the reason why this study ends where it began, and why each of us continuously has to begin again where it ended.

NOTES

When full bibliographical information is not given in the notes, the work is cited in full in the bibliography. Works by Heidegger are cited in full in the notes as well as listed chronologically in the bibliography.

Preface

1. William J. Richardson, *Heidegger: Through Phenomenology to Thought;* Otto Pöggeler, *Der Denkweg Martin Heideggers;* Walter Biemel, *Martin Heidegger in Selbstzeugnissen und Bilddokumenten dargestellt* (Reinbek: Rowohlt, 1973); J. L. Mehta, *Martin Heidegger. The Way and the Vision;* Arion L. Kelkel, *La légende de l'être. Langage et poésie chez Heidegger;* Jean-Michel Palmier, *Les écrits politiques de Heidegger;* Friedrich-Wilhelm von Herrmann, *Heideggers Philosophie der Kunst: Eine systematische Interpretation der Holzwege-Abhandlung 'Der Ursprung des Kunstwerkes';* Werner Marx, *Heidegger and the Tradition;* Henri Birault, *Heidegger et l'expérience de la pensée;* Vincent Vycinas, *Earth and Gods;* etc.

2. Otto Pöggeler, "Being as Appropriation," in *Philosophy Today* 19 (1975): 153.

3. Ibid.

4. Bernard Welte, "God in Heidegger's Thought," p. 85.

Chapter 1: Introduction: On the Essence of Truth

1. Walter Biemel, *Martin Heidegger,* p. 35. The translations of quotations from Heidegger's works are usually my own, although I have always consulted the existing English translations. The German word *Sein* has been translated as "Being," whereas *das Seiende* is translated as "being." Finally, the expression *das Seiende im Ganzen* has been rendered by "the beings as such and taken as a whole." Of the many "commentaries" on Heidegger's conception of truth, I wish to mention here at least the following: William J. Richardson, *Heidegger,* pp. 211–54; Henri Birault, "Existence et vérité d'après Heidegger," in *Phénoménologie—Existence.* Recueil d'études par H. Birault, H. L. van Breda, A. Gurwitsch, E. Levinas, P. Ricoeur, J. Wahl (Paris: Presses Universitaires de France, 1953), pp. 139–91; Jean Beaufret, "Heidegger et le problème de la vérité," pp. 758–85 (English translation in Heidegger's *Existential Analytic,* ed. F. Elliston [The Hague: Mouton, 1978], pp. 197–217); W. Bretschneider, *Sein und Wahrheit. Über die Zusammengehörigkeit von Sein und Wahrheit im Denken Martin Heideggers;* Carl Friedrich Gethmann, "Zu Heideggers Wahrheitsfrage," pp. 186–200; E. Tugendhat, "Heideggers Idee von Wahrheit," pp. 286–97; E. Tugendhat, *Der Wahrheitsbegriff bei Husserl und Heidegger;* Biemel, *Martin Heidegger,* pp. 61–78, 79–97.

2. Thomas Sheehan, "Heidegger's Early Years," p. 4.

3. Franz Brentano, *On the Several Senses of Being in Aristotle,* trans. Rolf George (Berkeley: University of California Press, 1975), pp. 3–5, 15–26.

4. Martin Heidegger, "Neuere Forschungen über Logik," in *Literarische Rundschau für das katholische Deutschland* 38 (1912): 466.

5. Martin Heidegger, *Logik: Die Frage nach der Wahrheit* (1925–1926), ed. Walter Biemel (Frankfurt: Klostermann, 1976).

6. Ibid., p. 26; cf. p. 417.

7. Ibid., pp. 197–269, 269–415.

8. Ibid., pp. 19–25, 127–61, 162–95.

9. Martin Heidegger, *Prolegomena zur Geschichte des Zeitbegriffs* (1925), ed. Petra Jaeger (Frankfurt: Klostermann, 1979).

10. Including secs. 42, 43, 45, and 46; note that sec. 44 (on truth) is missing. Cf. Martin Heidegger, *Sein und Zeit* (1927) (Tübingen: Niemeyer, 1953); trans. John Macquarrie and Edward Robinson (London: SCM Press, 1962); PGZ, pp. 293–306, 421–23, 424–31.

11. Aristotle, *Metaphysics, Gamma,* 1, 1003a21 and *alpha,* 1, 993b20.

12. SZ, p. 213 (256).

13. SZ, p. 214 (257).

14. SZ, pp. 214–15 (257–58).

15. SZ, p. 216 (259).

16. SZ, p. 217 (259).

17. SZ, p. 217 (260).

18. SZ, pp. 218 (261).

19. SZ, p. 218 (261) (with minor changes).

20. SZ, pp. 218–19 (261). *Dasein* is the technical expression which Heidegger uses to refer to man insofar as man is capable of understanding Being. Thus the term always refers to the questioner of Being and "suggests this unique privilege that distinguishes [him] from all other beings, sc. [his] comprehension of Being as such. . . ." (Cf. Richardson, *Heidegger,* p. 34 and n. 17.) The term never has an anthropological meaning; it is always used in a context which is strictly ontological. (Ibid.)

21. SZ, p. 219 (262) (with minor changes).

22. SZ, p. 219 (262). Cf. Biemel, *Martin Heidegger,* p. 63.

23. SZ, p. 220 (263).

24. SZ, p. 221 (263), with some minor changes.

25. SZ, pp. 220–23 (264–65).

26. Martin Heidegger, *Vom Wesen der Wahrheit* (1943) (Frankfurt: Klostermann, 1961); trans. John Sallis, in *Basic Writings,* ed. David Farrell Krell (New York: Harper & Row, 1977), pp. 117–41.

27. Richardson, *Heidegger,* p. 212. From the lecture course *On the Essence of Human Freedom* (1930), it is evident that the manner in which Heidegger's conception of truth developed between 1925 and 1930 may have been more complex than the preceding paragraph suggests. (Cf. Martin Heidegger, *Vom Wesen der menschlichen Freiheit. Einleitung in die Philosophie,* ed. Hartmut Tietjen [Frankfurt: Klostermann, 1982].) I have discussed some of the issues involved in a paper entitled "Being-True As the Fundamental and Basic Determination of Being," which was presented in 1983 during the seventeenth annual meeting of the Heidegger Circle (forthcoming). *On the Essence of Human Freedom* is concerned with the relationship between truth and freedom; it contains (among many other issues) Heidegger's interpretation of Aristotle's conception of ontological truth (*Metaphysica, Theta,* 10). Since the lecture course was delivered between April and July 1930, whereas the lecture "On the Essence of Truth" was presented in October and December of the same year (on different occasions), it is reasonable to assume that the lecture was formulated in its "definitive" form after the completion of the summer semester in which Heidegger lectured on human freedom. However, since Heidegger revised the lecture several times before he finally published it in 1943, it seems difficult at this time to solve all problems of chronology. Yet we do know that in 1943 Heidegger explicitly admitted to having left the

question of the truth of Being itself undeveloped and that the first paragraph of section 9 of the second edition was written in 1949.

28. Biemel, *Martin Heidegger*, p. 27; cf. pp. 26–27.

29. WW, pp. 5–6 (117–18).

30. WW, p. 8 (120). Cf. S. Thomas Aquinas, *Summa Theologiae*, I, 16, arts. 1–3.

31. WW, pp. 8–9 (121–22).

32. Richardson, *Heidegger*, p. 213; Biemel, *Martin Heidegger*, pp. 77–79.

33. WW, pp. 10–11 (123–24).

34. Richardson, *Heidegger*, pp. 213–14; for the close relationship between *das Seiende* ("being") and *das Offenbare* ("that which is open, the manifest"), cf. SZ, p. 28 (51).

35. WW, pp. 10–12 (122–25); Richardson, *Heidegger*, pp. 213–15; Biemel, *Martin Heidegger*, pp. 79–83.

36. WW, p. 12 (125); pp. 12–13 (125–26); Richardson, *Heidegger*, p. 215; Biemel, *Martin Heidegger*, pp. 83–84.

37. WW, p. 13 (126).

38. WW, p. 14 (127).

39. Biemel, *Martin Heidegger*, p. 84.

40. WW, pp. 14–15 (127–28).

41. WW, p. 14 (127).

42. Richardson, *Heidegger*, pp. 216–17.

43. WW, p. 15 (128).

44. WW, pp. 15–16 (128–29).

45. WW, p. 16 (129).

46. WW, p. 16 (129).

47. WW, p. 17 (130).

48. WW, p. 17 (130); Richardson, *Heidegger*, p. 218.

49. SZ, sec. 29; WW, p. 18 (130–31); Richardson, *Heidegger*, pp. 218–19.

50. WW, pp. 18–19 (131–32); Richardson, *Heidegger*, pp. 219–20.

51. Biemel, *Martin Heidegger*, p. 86; cf. also chap. 2 of this book.

52. WW, pp. 19–20 (132–34); Richardson, *Heidegger*, pp. 220–22.

53. Sec. 38.

54. WW, pp. 20–21 (134–35); Richardson, *Heidegger*, pp. 222–23; Biemel, *Martin Heidegger*, p. 88.

55. WW, pp. 21–22 (135–36); Richardson, *Heidegger*, pp. 224–25.

56. WW, pp. 22–23 (136); Richardson, *Heidegger*, pp. 224–25.

57. WW, p. 23 (136–37).

58. WW, p. 23 (137); Richardson, *Heidegger*, pp. 225–27.

59. WW, 25 (139); Richardson, *Heidegger*, pp. 228–29; Biemel, *Martin Heidegger*, pp. 89–90.

60. WW, p. 26 (140).

61. Biemel. *Martin Heidegger*, p. 77.

Chapter 2: The Thinking of Being

1. (Pfullingen: Neske, 1963). English translation by W. Kluback and J. T. Wilde, *What is Philosophy?* (New York: Twayne, 1958).

2. Martin Heidegger, *Platons Lehre von der Wahrheit. Mit einem Brief über den Humanismus* (Bern: Francke, 1947). English translation by Frank A. Capuzzi

and J. Glenn Gray (of the "Letter on Humanism" only), in *Basic Writings*, ed. David Farrell Krell (New York: Harper & Row, 1977), pp. 193–242.

3. In the concluding section of this chapter, I shall be concerned mainly with the relationship between "destruction," "retrieve," and "re-collection" in Heidegger's later works.

4. Martin Heidegger: *Was ist Metaphysik?* (1929) (Frankfurt: Klostermann, 1955); English translation of the 1929 lecture by David Farrell Krell, in *Basic Writings*, pp. 95–112; translation of the introduction to the 5th ed. (1949) by Walter Kaufmann, in *Existentialism From Dostoevsky to Sartre* (New York: Meridian Books, 1969), pp. 265–79; translation of the postscript to the 4th ed. (1943) by R. F. Hull and Alan Crick, in *Existence and Being*, ed. Werner Brock (Chicago: Regnery, 1949), pp. 349–61; *Einführung in die Metaphysik* (1935) (Tübingen: Niemeyer, 1957); English translation by Ralph Mannheim, *An Introduction to Metaphysics* (Garden City: Doubleday, 1961); *Was Heisst Denken?* (Tübingen: Niemeyer, 1961); English translation by Fred D. Wieck and J. Glenn Gray, *What Is Called Thinking?* (New York: Harper & Row, 1968); *Identität und Differenz* (Pfullingen: Neske, 1957); English translation by Joan Stambaugh, *Identity and Difference* (New York: Harper & Row, 1969); *Grundbegriffe* (1941), ed. Petra Jaeger (Frankfurt: Klostermann, 1981); *Vom Wesen der menschlichen Freiheit. Einführung in die Philosophie,* (1930) ed. Hartmut Tietjen (Frankfurt: Klostermann, 1982). Cf. also the "Letter on Humanism" and *Being and Time.*

5. Cf. *Oeuvres de Descartes,* ed. Charles Adam & Paul Tannery, vol. 6 (Paris: Vrin, 1956), p. 13; English translation by Lawrence J. Lafleur, *Discourse on Method and Meditations* (Indianapolis: Bobbs-Merrill, 1960), p. 12.

6. R. Descartes, *Discours,* p. 6 (6–7).

7. Ibid., p. 18 (15).

8. ID, pp. 35–75 (42–74).

9. ID, pp. 42–47 (46–51).

10. WP, pp. 7–8 (19–21).

11. WP, pp. 8–12 (21–29).

12. WP, pp. 12–15 (29–35).

13. WP, pp. 15–18 (35–41).

14. Martin Heidegger: "Der Spruch des Anaximander," in *Holzwege* (Frankfurt: Klostermann, 1963), pp. 296–343; "*Logos* (Heraklit, Fragment 50)," in *Vorträge und Aufsätze* (Pfullingen: Neske, 1954), pp. 207–229; "*Moira* (Parmenides, Fragment VIII, 34–41)," in VA, pp. 231–56; "*Alētheia* (Heraklit, Fragment 16)," in VA, pp. 257–82; English translation of these essays in *Early Greek Thinking,* trans. David Farrell Krell and Frank A. Capuzzi (New York: Harper & Row, 1975); *Die Grundprobleme der Phänomenologie* (Frankfurt: Klostermann, 1975); English translation by Albert Hofstadter, *The Basic Problems of Phenomenology* (Bloomington: Indiana University Press, 1982); this work contains reflections on Aristotle, medieval philosophy, Descartes, and Kant. Cf. also *Grundbegriffe; Die Kategorien- und Bedeutungslehre des Duns Scotus* (1916), in *Frühe Schriften,* ed. F.-W. von Herrmann (Frankfurt: Klostermann, 1978); *Kant und das Problem der Metaphysik* (1929) (Frankfurt: Klostermann, 1951); English translation by James S. Churchill, *Kant and the Problem of Metaphysics* (Bloomington: Indiana University Press, 1962); *Phänomenologische Interpretation von Kants Kritik der reinen Vernunft* (1927–1928), ed. Ingtraud Görland (Frankfurt: Klostermann, 1977); *Metaphysische Anfangsgründe der Logik im Ausgang von Leibniz,* (1928) ed. Klaus Held (Frankfurt: Klostermann, 1978); *Hegels*

Phänomenologie des Geistes (1930–1931), ed. Ingtraud Görland (Frankfurt: Klostermann, 1980); *Aristoteles: Metaphysik IX* (1931), ed. Heinrich Hüni (Frankfurt: Klostermann, 1981); *Schellings Abhandlung über das Wesen der menschlichen Freiheit* (1936), ed. H. Feick (Tübingen: Niemeyer, 1971); *Nietzsche*, 2 vols. (Pfullingen: Neske, 1961); English translation (incomplete) by David Farrell Krell and Frank A. Capuzzi (New York: Harper & Row, 1979ff.). Cf. for a brief discussion of the most important philosophers: Wiliam J. Richardson, *Heidegger,* pp. 106–160, 269–72, 299–382, 484–501, 514–26, 597–607, and passim.

15. HB, pp. 81–89 (215–21), 111–19 (236–42).
16. Cf. art. III of this chapter and the literature quoted there.
17. SZ, pp. 5–8 (24–28); cf. ibid., pp. 37–38 (62), 95–101 (128–34), 148–53 (188–95), 153–60 (195–203), 231–35 (274–78), 310–16 (358–64), 436 (487), and passim.
18. SZ, pp. 5–6 (25).
19. WP, pp. 18–20 (41–45). Cf. Arion L. Kelkel, *La légende de l'être,* pp. 483–84, 518–40.
20. ID, pp. 64–73 (66–74).
21. WP, pp. 21–22.
22. Aristotle, *Metaphysica,* Z, 1, 1028b2ff.
23. WP, pp. 22–25 (49–55).
24. WP, pp. 25–26 (55–58); cf. Richardson, *Heidegger,* p. 22.
25. WP, pp. 27–29 (59–63).
26. WP, pp. 29–31 (63–67); cf. Richardson, *Heidegger,* pp. 22–23.
27. WP, pp. 31–32 (67–69).
28. WP, pp. 33–34 (70–73); cf. SZ, sec. 6.
29. WP, pp. 34–35 (73–75).
30. WP, p. 36 (77).
31. Plato, *Theaetetus,* 155D.
32. Aristotle, *Metaphysica,* A, 2, 982b12f.
33. WP, pp. 36–40 (77–85).
34. WP, pp. 40–42 (85–89).
35. WP, pp. 42–43 (89–91).
36. WP, p. 20 (45); HW, p. 286 (132). Cf. VA, pp. 207–229 (59–78); WD, pp. 95–175 (148–244), passim.
37. WP, 43–45 (91–95); cf. chap. 7 below.
38. Cf. chap. 9 below.
39. WP, pp. 45–46 (95).
40. WP, p. 46 (95–97); cf. HW, p. 194 (54); SZ, sec. 7 b; *Der Satz vom Grund* (Pfullingen: Neske, 1957), p. 121.
41. Joseph J. Kockelmans, "Thanks-giving: The Completion of Thought," pp. 168–69; cf. SZ, pp. 212 (255), 226 (269); Richardson, *Heidegger,* p. 532.
42. Cf. the preface to this book and Otto Pöggeler, "Being As Appropriation," in *Philosophy Today* 19 (1975): 153; Friedrich-Wilhelm von Herrmann, *Heideggers Philosophie der Kunst,* p. xxiii.
43. Kockelmans, "Thanks-giving," p. 173 and 163; cf. Martin Heidegger, *Erläuterungen zu Hölderlins Dichtung* (Frankfurt: Klostermann, 1963), pp. 84 and 142; cf. also the epilogue to *What is Metaphysics?* passim.
44. HB, pp. 53–55 (193–195). Although Heidegger from 1914 on tried to overcome classical logic in strictly philosophical matters, at first he, too, still strongly stressed the scientificity of philosophy. That can be seen quite clearly in

Being and Time, secs. 1 through 7 and 32; *The Basic Problems of Phenomenology*, secs. 1 through 5 and passim; and most other early works and lecture courses.

45. HB, pp. 55–56 (195).
46. HB, pp. 56–58 (195–197); cf. GP, pp. 78–93 (55–57).
47. HB, pp. 58–61 (197–199).
48. HB, pp. 61–67 (199–204).
49. HB, pp. 67–71 (204–207); cf. VA, pp. 231–56 (79–101), HW, pp. 334–42 (48–57).
50. HB, pp. 71–74 (207–209).
51. Gray and Capuzzi translate *durch Sein* as "from Being," not as "by Being," presumably to avoid the language of causal thinking.
52. HB, pp. 74–76 (209–210).
53. Aristotle, *Metaphysica, Theta*, 10, 1051b22–25.
54. HB, pp. 76–77 (210–11).
55. HB, p. 77 (211–12).
56. HB, pp. 77–79 (212–13).
57. HB, pp. 79–80 (213–14).
58. HB, p. 80 (214).
59. HB, pp. 81–82 (215–16).
60. SZ, pp. 19–27 (41–49).
61. SZ, pp. 17–20 (38–42); pp. 372–404 (424–55).
62. SZ, pp. 20–23 (42–45).
63. KPM, p. 185 (211); Richardson, *Heidegger*, pp. 90–93; translation by Richardson.
64. GP, pp. 30–32 (22–23).
65. SZ, p. 153 (195).
66. GP, pp. 26–32 (19–23).
67. HB, pp. 81–82 (215–16).
68. SZ, p. 212 (255).
69. HB, p. 83 (216).
70. SZ, p. 38 (62).
71. HB, p. 83 (216–17).
72. HB, pp. 83–84 (217).
73. KPM, p. 182 (206).
74. KPM, p. 183 (207).
75. SZ, p. 22 (44); cf. pp. 19–27 (41–49).
76. SZ, p. 22 (44).
77. SZ, pp. 22–23 (44).
78. WM, p. 9 (266–67); KPM, pp. 8 (xxv), 185 (211).
79. VA, p. 260 (105); translation by Richardson (*Heidegger*, pp. 488–89).
80. Richardson, *Heidegger*, pp. 488–89; VA, pp. 260 (105), 279 (120–21), 261 (105–106).

Chapter 3: What Then Is Being?

1. H. Bergson, *Oeuvres*, ed. A. Robinet (Paris: Presses Universitaires de France, 1970), p. 1346; quoted by Thomas Sheehan in "Introduction: Heidegger, the Project and the Fulfillment," in *Heidegger: The Man and the Thinker* (Chicago: Precedent Publishing, 1981), p. vii. Cf Martin Heidegger, WD, p. 20 (50).

2. Sheehan, "Introduction: Heidegger," p. vii.

3. SZ, p. 1 (19).

4. "Towards the Topology of Dasein," in *Heidegger: The Man and the Thinker,* p. 95.

5. Ibid.

6. Sheehan, "Introduction: Heidegger," p. vii.

7. Ibid., pp. vii–viii.

8. Ibid., pp. viii–ix.

9. William J. Richardson, *Heidegger,* pp. 147–52. Cf. ibid., p. 167 n.

10. WG, p. 47 (111–13).

11. KPM, pp. 26 (22), 34 (33–34), 110 (122–23); SZ, pp. 212–30 (256–73); Richardson, *Heidegger,* p. 151.

12. WG, pp. 14–15 (23–27), 13 (21–22).

13. SZ, secs. 40, 53, 57, 62, and 68 b.

14. SZ, pp. 187–89 (232–34).

15. WM, pp. 34–40 (109–111); cf. WM, pp. 27–34 (98–104); Richardson, *Heidegger,* pp. 197–200; Bernard Welte, "God in Heidegger's Thought," p. 88.

16. WM, p. 41 (111–12); Richardson, *Heidegger,* pp. 200–201.

17. WM, p. 25 (139); Richardson, *Heidegger,* pp. 245–46; Richardson's translation.

18. EM, passim, particularly pts. 3 and 4.

19. Otto Pöggeler, "Heideggers Topologie des Seins," pp. 337–45; "Heidegger's Topology of Being," in *On Heidegger and Language,* ed. and trans. Joseph J. Kockelmans (Evanston: Northwestern University Press, 1972), pp. 116–26; cf. Martin Heidegger, ID, pp. 23–31 (31–39); cf. art. II below.

20. Richardson, *Heidegger,* pp. 698–704.

21. WM, p. 34 (105); Krell's translation with minor changes. For what follows, cf. Theodore J. Kisiel, "The Language of the Event: The Event of Language," pp. 85–104.

22. WM, p. 45 (352–53).

23. WM, p. 51 (360–61); SF, pp. 36–40; Richardson, *Heidegger,* p. 474.

24. Cf. chap. 4 below.

25. HB, p. 76 (210–11); Welte, "Heidegger's Thought," p. 89.

26. Richardson, *Heidegger,* p. 6.

27. WW, p. 20 (133–34); cf. the introduction to this book.

28. WW, p. 20 (133).

29. WW, pp. 21–23 (135–37); Richardson, *Heidegger,* pp. 220–27.

30. HW, pp. 42–43 (53–55); Richardson, *Heidegger,* pp. 405–406; cf. chap. 8 below.

31. HW, p. 244 (110).

32. Ibid.

33. Ibid.

34. HD, p. 23.

35. HD, pp. 104, 109, 138.

36. HD, p. 53.

37. HD, pp. 23–25, 138–39. Cf. Richardson, *Heidegger,* pp. 446–47, 452, 459, 468; however, also see ibid., p. 610 and pp. 638–40.

38. Cf. chap. 3 below; HW, p. 336 (50); Richardson, *Heidegger,* pp. 12–13.

39. VA, pp. 231–56 (79–101); WD, pp. 102–149 and 163–75 (163–244); ID, pp. 58–70 (60–71); cf. also chap. 3 below.

40. In ED, *Being* is uniformly used in the antiquated spelling of *Seyn* (Beon); cf. ED, pp. 7, 9, 19, 25.

41. Richardson, *Heidegger*, pp. 545, 556, 220–27; cf. WW, pp. 19–23 (132–37).

42. VA, pp. 70 (182), 220–21 (70–71); SG, pp. 107, 171, 184, 188; P, p. 156; G, p. 70 (89); US, pp. 103 (15), 197 (91); HW, p. 325 (39–40); FW, p. 4. Cf. Richardson, *Heidegger*, p. 640. That Being is nevertheless finite is shown in HW, pp. 339ff. (54ff.); cf. Richardson, *Heidegger*, pp. 523–24.

43. HD, pp. 18–19.

44. HD, pp. 17, 18, 108, 116, passim.

45. HD, p. 58.

46. HD, p. 61.

47. HD, p. 62.

48. HD, p. 71.

49. Ibid.; cf. Richardson, *Heidegger*, pp. 426–27.

50. Richardson, *Heidegger*, p. 8.

51. Ibid., p. 9; cf. pp. 8–9.

52. Sheehan, "Introduction: Heidegger," pp. x–xi.

53. HB, p. 77 (211); Welte, "Heidegger's Thought," pp. 90–91; cf. chap. 2 above.

54. Welte, "Heidegger's Thought," pp. 90–91; cf. the introduction to this book.

55. WM, p. 18 (274); SZ, p. 151 (192–93); H, p. 245 (110); HB, p. 84 (217); WM, p. 44 (351–52).

56. WM, pp. 19–20 (132–33); cf. WM, pp. 23 (136–37), 25 (139); Richardson, *Heidegger*, pp. 8–9.

57. WM, p. 20 (133–34).

58. Richardson, *Heidegger*, p. 245.

59. WM, pp. 15 (271–72), 11 (268), 25 (96–97).

60. WM, pp. 26–27 (97–98); Richardson, *Heidegger*, pp. 239–40.

61. Cf. Aristotle, *Metaphysica*, bks. *Gamma, E,* and *K.*

62. WM, p. 19 (275–76); cf. ID, pp. 45–73 (49–74).

63. Cf. SZ, p. 7 (26) and passim; WM, p. 15 (25–27).

64. WM, p. 23 (278–79); Richardson, *Heidegger*, pp. 165, 174, 246.

65. WD, pp. 2–3 (4–5), 85 (120–21), and passim; Richardson, *Heidegger*, p. 597; cf. pp. 413, 418.

66. WD, pp. 174–75 (226–27); Richardson, *Heidegger*, pp. 605–606.

67. WM, p. 46 (354); Richardson, *Heidegger*, pp. 520–21; cf. p. 476.

68. WM, p. 46 (354); Richardson, *Heidegger*, pp. 523, 562.

69. GP, pp. 321–469 (227–330).

70. HB, pp. 77 (211–12), 101 (229).

71. WW, pp. 11–12 (124–25).

72. SZ, p. 28 (51).

73. WW, p. 15 (27–28); Richardson, *Heidegger*, pp. 214–15, 217, 231.

74. G, pp. 41–42 (67–69).

75. G, p. 42 (68).

76. G, pp. 39–41 (65–67). Cf. Richardson, *Heidegger*, pp. 503–504.

77. WD, p. 153 (132–33); VA, p. 33 (25–26); WP, pp. 14–15 (33–35); cf. Richardson, *Heidegger*, pp. 618–19. Also see chap. 9 below.

78. "As When upon a Day of Rest," in HD, pp. 59–60; cf. Richardson, *Heidegger*, p. 424.

79. HD, p. 65.
80. HW, pp. 69–104 (115–54), p. 89 (137–38).
81. HD, pp. 57, 61. Cf Richardson, *Heidegger,* pp. 424–25.
82. WW, pp. 26–27 (140–41).
83. VA, p. 99 (110). Cf. for that and what follows also Otto Pöggeler, "Being as Appropriation," in *Philosophy Today* 19 (1975): 166–76.
84. Richardson, *Heidegger,* p. 614; ID, pp. 28–29 (36–38); VA, p. 278 (119–20). For what follows on the appropriating event, see Jean Greisch, "Identité et différence dans la pensée de Martin Heidegger. Le chemin de l'*Ereignis*," in *Revue des sciences philosophiques et théologiques* 57 (1973): 71–111.
85. VA, pp. 226–29 (76–78); cf. chap. 2 above.
86. WD, 147 (241); cf. Richardson, *Heidegger,* pp. 606–607.
87. ID, pp. 28–31 (35–39); Richardson, *Heidegger,* pp. 638–39.
88. ID, p. 63 (65–66).
89. US, p. 258 (127); trans. by Richardson (*Heidegger,* p. 639).
90. HB, p. 84 (216); cf. pp. 80–81 (214–15). The German word *Schickung* is often used in the sense of "Providence," as well as in the sense of "fate." In Heidegger it seldom has the meaning of "fate" or "destiny"; usually it has the meaning of ordering or arrangement (Moira), or even the "literal" meaning of "sending, mittence." I usually use "sending."
91. HB, p. 112 (237).
92. HB, pp. 82 (215–16), 86 (218–19); HW, p. 311 (26–27).
93. HB, pp. 73 (208), 65 (202–203), 118 (241).
94. ID, pp. 65–66 (67–68).
95. Richardson, *Heidegger,* pp. 638–39.
96. The term *Austrag* appears in US, pp. 24–25 (201–202), and is thematized in ID, pp. 63–68 (65–70). It is Heidegger's translation of the Greek *diaphora* and was used in 1944 for Heraclitus's *diapheromenon* (VA, p. 221 [71].) It may be translated as "dif-ference" (from the Latin *dif-ferre*). Richardson uses "issue" (in the sense of "dif-ference"). Heidegger himself uses the word in a sense which is distinct from the sense of *Unter-Schied* and *Differenz.* The latter stands for the ontological difference; the term *Unter-Schied* is difficult to translate into English (the "scission between"). Richardson suggests to use "dif-ference" in this case (*Heidegger,* p. 579 and n. 4).
97. N, Vol. 2, pp. 207–210 (153–57).
98. N, Vol. 2, p. 489 (82).
99. N, Vol. 2, p. 489 (82–83). This issue is discussed in greater detail in chap. 2 above.
100. ID, p. 67 (68–69).
101. Ibid.
102. Welte, "Heidegger's Thought," p. 91.
103. HW, pp. 310–11 (26–27).
104. Welte, "Heidegger's Thought," p. 92; HW, pp. 82–83 (129–31); cf. chaps. 10 and 11 below.
105. HW, p. 60 (72–73).
106. HW, p. 61 (73–74); cf. Richardson, *Heidegger,* p. 410.
107. WD, p. 85. Cf. chap. 7 below.
108. Richardson, *Heidegger,* pp. 292–93.
109. VA, p. 212 (63–64).
110. VA, pp. 214–18 (65–69).

111. VA, pp. 213–14 (64–65).
112. Richardson, *Heidegger*, pp. 496–98.
113. HB, p. 53 (193).
114. HB, p. 70 (206).
115. HB, p. 78 (212–13).
116. US, pp. 30–31 (208).
117. HB, pp. 116 (239–40), 119 (242); Richardson, *Heidegger*, p. 535.
118. Richardson, *Heidegger*, p. 609; cf. chap. 2 above.
119. WD, p. 119 (196–97); cf. 168 (192); cf. Richardson, *Heidegger*, p. 609.
120. SZ, pp. 334–50 (281–301).
121. Cf. US, pp. 210–16 (103–108).
122. Martin Heidegger, "Zeit und Sein," in *L'endurance de la pensée. Pour saluer Jean Beaufret*, ed. René Char (Paris: Plon, 1968), pp. 13–71; the essay also appeared in *Zur Sache des Denkens* (Tübingen: Niemeyer, 1969), pp. 1–25 (1–24).
123. SD, p. 2 (2).
124. SD, p. 36 (33–34).
125. SD, p. 35 (32–33).
126. SD, pp. 1–2 (1–3).
127. SD, p. 27 (25–26).
128. SD, pp. 2 (2), 27–28 (25–26).
129. SD, p. 3 (3). *Anwesen* is translated here as "Being-present"; usually it must be translated as "coming-to-presence."
130. SD, pp. 2–4 (2–4).
131. SD, pp. 4–5 (4–5).
132. SD, pp. 41–43 (37–40).
133. SD, pp. 5 (5), 39–41 (36–38).
134. SD, pp. 5–6 (5–6).
135. SD, pp. 6–8 (6–8).
136. SD, pp. 8–10 (9–10).
137. SD, pp. 10–11 (10–11); GP, pp. 327–62 (231–56).
138. SD, pp. 12–13 (12).
139. SD, pp. 6, 13–15 (12–14); cf. chaps. 5 and 7 below.
140. SD, pp. 15–16 (14–16).
141. SD, pp. 16–17 (16).
142. SD, pp. 17–18 (16–17).
143. SD, pp. 18–21 (17–20).
144. SD, pp. 21 23 (20–22). For other approaches to the event, cf. SD, pp. 44–45 (40–42).
145. SD, pp. 23–25 (22–24). For the preceding, see also: Greisch, "Identité et différence," pp. 71–111.

Chapter 4: Reflections on the Ontological Difference

1. William J. Richardson, *Heidegger*, pp. 3–15. Cf. A. Dondeyne, "La différence ontologique chez M. Heidegger," pp. 35–62, 251–93; Sam Ijsseling, "Het zijn en de zijnden. Een studie over de ontologische *Differenz* bij Martin Heidegger," pp. 3–51; Bruno Liebrucks, "Idee und ontologische Differenz," pp. 268–301; Sueo Oshima, "Barth's *Analogia Relationis* and Heidegger's Ontological Difference," pp. 176–94; Joseph J. Kockelmans, "Ontological Difference, Hermeneutics, and Language," pp. 195–234; Alberto Rosales,

Transzendenz und Differenz. Ein Beitrag zum Problem der ontologischen Differenz beim frühen Heidegger; John Sallis, "La différence ontologique et l'unité de la pensée de Heidegger," pp. 192–206; W. Beauthier, "Analogie des Seins und ontologische Differenz," in *Symposion* 4 (1955): 1–89; M. Loy Vail, *Heidegger and Ontological Difference* (University Park, Pa.: The Pennsylvania State University Press, 1972); Michael Theunissen, "Intentionaler Gegenstand und ontologische Differenz. Ansätze zur Fragestellung Heideggers in der Phänomenologie Husserls," pp. 344–62; Jean Greisch, "Identité et différence dans la pensée de Martin Heidegger. Le chemin de l'*Ereignis,*" in *Revue des sciences philosophiques et théologiques* 57 (1973): 71–111.

2. HW, p. 336 (50–51); KPM, p. 212 (243).

3. WM, p. 19 (257).

4. HW, pp. 161–62 (105–106), 317–18 (32–33); WM, p. 8 (266); WD, p. 175 (227–28); cf. especially WG, WM, and WW.

5. Richardson, *Heidegger,* pp. 6–10, 10–15; cf. EM, pp. 14–16 (14–16).

6. SZ, pp. 1–15 (19–35). Cf. SZ, pp. 56 (82), 92 (125), 132 (170), 436 (487), 437 (487); cf. also SZ, p. 212 (255); Richardson, *Heidegger,* pp. 103–104; John D. Caputo, "Fundamental Ontology and the Ontological Difference," pp. 28–35; Wolfgang Marx, "Die ontologische Differenz in der Perspektive der regionalen Ontologie des Daseins," pp. 176–97.

7. WG, pp. 15–16 (27–29); cf. pp. 9–18 (11–27).

8. KPM, p. 212 (243–44).

9. GP, sec. 22.

10. GP, p. 322 (227).

11. WG, pp. 15–16 (27–29); Richardson, *Heidegger,* pp. 174–75, 103–104, 163–64; Joseph J. Kockelmans, *On Heidegger and Language,* pp. 204–210.

12. SZ, pp. 350–66 (401–418); Otto Pöggeler, "Heideggers Topologie des Seins," pp. 331–57; for an English translation, cf. Kockelmans, *On Heidegger and Language,* pp. 107–35.

13. SZ, pp. 436–37 (486–88).

14. KPM, sec. 45.

15. GP, pp. 451–60 (318–24); WG, pp. 7–16 (5–29); KPM, p. 212 (243–44).

16. SZ, pp. 5–8 (24–28).

17. SZ, p. 152 (193–94); Carl Friedrich Gethmann, *Verstehen und Auslegung. Das Methodenproblem in der Philosophie Martin Heideggers,* pp. 32–45; Richardson, *Heidegger,* pp. 174–75; Joseph J. Kockelmans, "Destructive Retrieve and Hermeneutic Phenomenology in 'Being and Time,'" pp. 109–116; Kockelmans, *On Heidegger and Language,* pp. 206–10.

18. SZ, pp. 157–58 (199–210).

19. Richardson, *Heidegger,* p. 171.

20. US, p. 93 (7–8).

21. Ibid.

22. Richardson, *Heidegger,* pp. 174–75.

23. EM, pp. 1–39 (1–42); cf. in particular pp. 10–15 (9–16).

24. WD, p. 174 (227); cf. chap. 3.

25. WD, p. 174 (227); my translation.

26. N, vol. 2, pp. 203–213 (150–58).

27. N, vol. 2, pp. 206–209 (152–56).

28. N, vol. 2, pp. 207–208 (153–54); my translation.

29. US, pp. 24–25 (201–202); cf. ID, pp. 63–68 (65–70); VA, p. 221 (71).

30. N, vol. 2, p. 209 (155); my translation.
31. Ibid.; cf. Richardson, *Heidegger*, pp. 436–37.
32. Richardson, *Heidegger*, p. 501.
33. VA, pp. 227 (76–77), 225 (74–75).
34. Richardson, *Heidegger*, p. 501; cf. pp. 500–501.
35. Ibid., p. 517; cf. HW, p. 334 (48).
36. HW, p. 336 (50).
37. Ibid.
38. HW, p. 337 (51).
39. HW, p. 334 (49); partially my translation.
40. HW, p. 339 (54).
41. WM, p. 46 (354).
42. HW, p. 335 (50).
43. WM, p. 46 (354).
44. Richardson, *Heidegger*, p. 523; cf. p. 521.
45. WM, p. 46 (354).
46. Richardson, *Heidegger*, p. 475.
47. Ibid., pp. 475–76.
48. Ibid., pp. 476, 562–63.
49. Ibid., pp. 563–65.
50. WG, p. 5 (3).
51. WW, p. 26 (140).
52. Richardson, *Heidegger*, p. 565. Cf. chap. 3 above.
53. ID, p. 10 (21–22).
54. ID, pp. 37–73 (42–74).
55. ID, pp. 61–62 (63–65).
56. ID, pp. 72–73 (73–74).
57. ID, pp. 62–63 (65).
58. ID, pp. 61–62 (63–64).
59. ID, pp. 62–63 (64–65).
60. ID, pp. 64–65 (66–67).
61. EM, p. 98 (108–109); cf. Richardson, *Heidegger*, pp. 261–62.
62. VA, pp. 227–29 (76–78).
63. WD, pp. 82–83 (118–19).
64. US, pp. 30–32 (207–10).
65. US, pp. 21–22 (198–200), 24 (201–202), 25 (202–203). Cf. Richardson, *Heidegger*, pp. 578–79.
66. US, p. 26 (203–204).
67. US, p. 29 (206–207).
68. US, pp. 29–30 (207–208); Richardson, *Heidegger*, p. 579.
69. US, p. 30 (207–208).
70. WD, p. 147 (241); cf. chap. 3 above.
71. WD, p. 147 (241).
72. VA, p. 242 (88).
73. VA, p. 245 (91).
74. VA, p. 249 (95); cf. WD, p. 12 (30–31); EM, pp. 97–110 (107–122), 126–28 (138–40), 112–26 (123–38), 137–38 (150–52); cf. Richardson, *Heidegger*, pp. 606–607, 268. With respect to the last reference, it should be noted that Richardson believes that Heidegger refers here to what in EM, p. 47 (51) was called the original discord.

75. ID, pp. 18–23 (27–31); cf. chap. 2, where the implications are discussed in detail. Cf. VA, p. 225 (74–75); WD, p. 147 (240–41); ID, p. 29 (36).
76. ID, pp. 23–29 (31–36).
77. ID, p. 10 (21–22).
78. ID, p. 18 (27).
79. ID, p. 23 (31–32).
80. ID, p. 31 (39); cf. Greisch, "Identité et différence," pp. 71–111.
81. Kockelmans, *On Heidegger and Language*, p. 208, n. 34.
82. SD, p. 2.
83. VA, p. 74 (87).
84. VA, pp. 77–78 (90).
85. VA, p. 78 (91).
86. VA, p. 90 (102). For the reason why *Technik* is translated as "technicity," cf. Richardson, *Heidegger*, p. 326, and chap. 11 below.
87. SD, p. 25 (24).
88. SZ, pp. 35–36 (59–60).

Chapter 5: Reflections on the Fourfold

1. VA, pp. 170–72 (172–74), 176–77 (177–78).
2. VA, pp. 178 (179), 176–79 (177–80).
3. Martin Heidegger: *Erläuterungen zu Hölderlins Dichtung* (Frankfurt: Klostermann, 1944); Ibid., 2d enlarged ed., Frankfurt: Klostermann, 1951; Ibid., 4th enlarged ed., 1971; *Der Feldweg* (Frankfurt: Klostermann, 1953).
4. Otto Pöggeler, *Der Denkweg Martin Heideggers*, p. 248.
5. William J. Richardson, *Heidegger*, p. 572, cf. pp. 570–72.
6. Ibid., pp. 572, 625.
7. Pöggeler, *Denkweg*, pp. 247–67; Vincent Vycinas, *Earth and Gods*.
8. Richardson, *Heidegger*, pp. 570–73, 625, 406–407, 590, and passim.
9. For what follows, cf. Pöggeler, *Denkweg*, pp. 247–67; Vycinas, *Earth and Gods*, pp. 224–37, and passim.
10. Pöggeler, *Denkweg*, pp. 249–50; Richardson, *Heidegger*, pp. 36n, 167n, 406, and passim.
11. VA, pp. 176–77 (178–79).
12. Pöggeler, *Denkweg*, p. 248; cf. pp. 247–48; VA, p. 177 (179).
13. Plato, *Gorgias*, pp. 507–508.
14. Richardson, *Heidegger*, p. 571n.
15. Cf. Wang Pi, *Commentary on the Lao Tzu* (Hawaii: University of Hawaii Press, 1979), pp. 57–79; W. Bynner, *The Chinese Translations* (New York: Farrar, Straus, Giroux, 1978), pp. 360–61.
16. Pöggeler, *Denkweg*, pp. 248–49.
17. *Muthos* has the following significations: 1) anything delivered by mouth, word, speech; 2) conversation, talk; 3) purpose, plan; 4) story, legendary story, fable, myth.
18. WD, pp. 6–7 (10).
19. G, p. 37 (64).
20. ID, p. 51 (54–55).
21. VA, p. 276 (118); cf. pp. 275–79 (117–20).
22. US, p. 211 (104).
23. VA, pp. 195–96 (220–21).

24. G, pp. 40–43 (66–69).
25. US, pp. 197–98 (91–92).
26. US, pp. 213–14 (106–107); SG, pp. 143–44.
27. US, pp. 29 (206–207), 141–46 (43–48), 213–16 (106–108).
28. US, p. 213 (106); cf. chap. 3 above.
29. Pöggeler, *Denkweg*, pp. 250–51.
30. Aristotle, *Physics*, IV, 10–14, 217b29-224a17; cf. GP, pp. 327–61 (231–56).
31. WD, pp. 40–41 (100–101).
32. US, pp. 208–211 (101–104).
33. Pöggeler, *Denkweg*, pp. 251–52; cf. chap. 7 below.
34. VA, p. 178 (179); Pöggeler, *Denkweg*, pp. 252–53.
35. Pöggeler, *Denkweg*, pp. 253–55.
36. Pöggeler also gives a description of heaven and earth under the general heading of the animate and inanimate nature; for this description he makes use of unpublished manuscripts. I have decided not to follow him here, because such a description tends to suggest a concern for heaven and earth from an ontical rather than from an ontological point of view. I should like to stress, however, that this decision is not based on the assumption that Pöggeler's approach to the issue is unacceptable.
37. HW, pp. 7–68 (17–87); VA, pp. 145–204 (145–86, 213–29); US, pp. 24–32 (202–10), 204–16 (96–108).
38. Pöggeler, *Denkweg*, pp. 254–67 (passim).
39. H.-G. Gadamer, "Sein, Geist, Gott," in H.-G. Gadamer, W. Marx, and C. F. von Weizsäcker, *Heidegger. Freiburger Universitätsvorträge zu seinem Gedenken* (Freiburg: Karl Alber, 1977), pp. 55–57.
40. Richardson, *Heidegger*, pp. 406–407, 570–72, 625; Werner Marx, *Heidegger and the Tradition*, pp. 185–86; cf. pp. xxviii, 238–41, 189–91, 195–203, and passim.
41. Vycinas, *Earth and Gods*, p. 115; cf. p. 17.
42. Ibid., pp. 118–32, 133–73.
43. Ibid., p. 130n.
44. Ibid., p. 165n.
45. Pöggeler, *Denkweg*, pp. 249–56.
46. US, pp. 210–16 (103–108).
47. Martin Heidegger, *Beiträge zur Philosophie, 1936–1938*, ms. discussed by Pöggeler (*Denkweg*, p. 255).
48. Pöggeler, *Denkweg*, pp. 254–55.
49. Richardson, *Heidegger*, pp. 566–76, 403.
50. Friedrich-Wilhelm von Herrmann, *Heideggers Philosophie der Kunst*, pp. 111–23, 150–78, and passim.
51. HW, pp. 29–31 (39–42).
52. HW, pp. 31–34 (42–45).
53. HW, pp. 34–36 (45–48).
54. HW, pp. 36–38 (48–50).
55. HW, pp. 38–44 (50–55).
56. VA, pp. 163–85 (165–86).
57. VA, pp. 163–71 (165–72).
58. VA, pp. 171–72 (172–74).
59. VA, pp. 145–62 (145–61).
60. VA, pp. 145–52 (145–51).

61. VA, pp. 178–81 (179–82).

62. The terminology is confusing here, in that Kant and Heidegger use the terms *world* and *nature* in different senses; that is true particularly for the term *nature*. Cf. WG, pp. 27–37 (59–85), where Heidegger explains how his ontological conception of world is related to Kant's "idea in which the absolute totality of objects accessible in finite knowledge can be represented a priori," i.e., to "the transcendental (ontological) aggregate of things taken as appearances." For Kant's conception of nature, cf. WG, p. 32 (71) and Kant's *Critique of Pure Reason*, B 263 and B 446, note.

63. EM, pp. 88–149 (98–164).

64. EH, pp. 161–62.

65. Heidegger explains (ibid., p. 163) that this expression is to be thought here in the sense of the speculative dialectic of Schelling and Hegel. Freed from all finitude and every boundary, the regions belong in-finitely together.

66. EH, pp. 163–67.

67. EH, pp. 167–70.

68. EH, pp. 170–71.

69. EH, pp. 171–76.

70. EH, pp. 176–78.

71. EH, pp. 178–79. Cf. Heraclitus, Fragment B 54.

72. VA, p. 80 (92–93).

73. VA, p. 84 (96–97).

74. VA, p. 89 (101).

75. VA, pp. 90–91 (102–103).

76. VA, p. 92 (104).

77. VA, pp. 91–95 (103–106).

78. VA, pp. 95–97 (106–108).

79. VA, p. 97 (109).

80. Ibid.

81. VA, p. 99 (110).

82. Cf. Joseph J. Kockelmans, "Destructive Retrieve and Hermeneutic Phenomenology in 'Being and Time'," pp. 106–120 (passim).

83. Richardson, *Heidegger*, p. 572.

84. SD, pp. 61–80 (373–92).

85. SD, pp. 65–66 (377–78).

86. VA, p. 98 (109–110).

87. Marx, *Heidegger and the Tradition*, pp. 233–41, cf. also his "Die Sterblichen," pp. 160–75.

Chapter 6: The Fourfold: Gods and Mortals

1. HB, pp. 65–67 (202–204).

2. HB, pp. 58–62 (197–200).

3. Otto Pöggeler, *Der Denkweg Martin Heideggers*, pp. 259–60.

4. Ibid., pp. 259–60.

5. Thomas Sheehan, "Heidegger's Early Years," pp. 3–5.

6. Martin Heidegger, "A Recollection," in *Heidegger: The Man and the Thinker*, pp. 21–22.

7. US, pp. 95–99 (9–12).

8. Pöggeler, *Denkweg*, p. 261.

9. Cf. O. Schnübbe, *Der Existenzbegriff in der Theologie Bultmanns* (Göttingen: Vandenhoeck und Ruprecht, 1955); *Heidegger: Perspektiven zur Deutung seines Werks*, ed. Otto Pöggeler, pp. 11–54 (passim), 54–77, 169–78, 179–216; Heinz-Horst Schrey, "Die Bedeutung der Philosophie Martin Heideggers für die Theologie," pp. 9–21; Henri Birault, "La foi et la pensée d'après Heidegger," pp. 108–132; G. Noller, ed., *Heidegger und die Theologie. Beginn und Fortgang der Diskussion;* cf. PT, p. 7; Thomas F. O'Meara, "Tillich and Heidegger," pp. 249–61.

10. SZ, p. 229 (272).

11. SZ, p. 10 (30).

12. PT, p. 8.

13. Pöggeler, *Denkweg*, p. 261.

14. PGZ, pp. 109–110.

15. HW, pp. 193–247 (53–112). Cf. N, vol. 2, pp. 31–256 (vol. 4, pp. 1–196); N, vol. 2, pp. 335–98 (vol. 4, pp. 197–250).

16. Sass lists in his bibliography of Heidegger's philosophy almost one hundred items, many of them in Japanese. I list here only those which I take to be of importance for the issues raised in this chapter: H. Danner, *Das Göttliche und der Gott bei Heidegger;* J. Brechtken, "Geschichte und Transzendenz order die Gottesfrage am Ende der Metaphysik," pp. 587–609; F. Guibal, "Martin Heidegger et l'attente du 'Dieu divin'," pp. 594–624, 753–74; A. Jäger, *Gott;* Hans Jonas, "Gnosticism and Modern Nihilism," pp. 430–52; William J. Richardson, "Heidegger and God—and Prof. Jonas," pp. 13–40; H. Köchler, "Das Gottesproblem im Denken Heideggers," pp. 61–90; J. Paumen, "Heidegger et le thème nietzschéen de la mort de Dieu," pp. 238–62; K. Rosenthal, "Martin Heideggers Auffassung von Gott," pp. 212–29; W. Schulz, *Der Gott der neuzeitlichen Metaphysik;* F. Seven, *Die Ewigkeit Gottes und die Zeitlichkeit des Menschen;* G. Siewerth, "Martin Heidegger und die Frage nach Gott," pp. 516–26; Vincent Vycinas, *Search for Gods;* Bernard Welte, "God in Heidegger's Thought," pp. 85–100; J. Williams, "Heidegger, Death, and God," pp. 298–320. Cf. also n. 9 above.

17. *Philosophy Today*, 26 (1982): 85–100.

18. Welte, "Heidegger's Thought," p. 85.

19. Ibid.

20. Ibid., p. 98.

21. Ibid., pp. 87–92.

22. Ibid., pp. 87–88.

23. Ibid., pp. 88–89.

24. Ibid., p. 90.

25. HB, p. 76 (210).

26. Martin Heidegger, "Nietzsches Wort 'Gott ist Tod,' " in HW, pp. 193–247 (53–112).

27. F. Nietzsche, *Joyful Wisdom*, trans. K. F. Reinhardt (New York: Ungar Publ., 1960), pp. 167–69.

28. R. J. Hollingdale, "Introduction," to *Thus Spoke Zarathustra*, trans. R. J. Hollingdale (Baltimore: Penguin Books, 1961), pp. 9–12.

29. HW, p. 196 (57). For the meaning of the statement "God Is Dead," see particularly Martin Heidegger, "Das Rektorat 1933/34. Tatsachen und Gedanken," in the 1983 edition of *Die Selbstbehauptung der deutschen Universität* (Frankfurt: Klostermann, 1983), p. 25.

30. HW, pp. 202–204 (63–65).
31. HW, p. 197 (58).
32. HW, pp. 209–14 (70–75).
33. HW, pp. 235–43 (99–109).
34. HW, pp. 246–47 (111–12).
35. N, vol. 1, p. 322; cf. pp. 318–25.
36. ID, pp. 70–71 (72).
37. Pöggeler, *Denkweg*, pp. 261–62.
38. Welte, "Heidegger's Thought," pp. 92–98.
39. Pöggeler, *Denkweg*, pp. 261–67, passim.
40. Ibid., p. 262; cf. p. 318.
41. Ibid., pp. 262–63.
42. Ibid., p. 263.
43. Ibid., pp. 263–64.
44. Ibid., p. 264.
45. N, vol. 1, pp. 321ff.
46. SZ, p. 427n (499, xiii).
47. VA, p. 177 (178–79).
48. Pöggeler, *Denkweg*, pp. 265–66; 311n.
49. Ibid, p. 266.
50. Ibid., pp. 311–13n.
51. N, vol. 1, p. 254.
52. Sophocles, *Oedipus Rex*, 910: *errei de ta theia*, "and divine things are gone. . . ."
53. WM, p. 51 (361); cf. Sophocles. *Oed. Colon.*, 777–79: *pantōs gar echei tade kuros*, "for in every direction that which has come-to-pass keeps secure a decision concerning its own ending."
54. ID, pp. 70–71 (71–72).
55. ID, p. 70 (72).
56. HB, p. 103 (230).
57. Welte, "Heidegger's Thought," p. 93.
58. HW, pp. 246–47 (111–12).
59. VA, p. 183 (184).
60. Welte, "Heidegger's Thought," p. 94.
61. HB, p. 102 (230).
62. HW, pp. 250–51 (94–95).
63. HD, pp. 17–20 (249–54).
64. Welte, "Heidegger's Thought," p. 96.

Chapter 7: On the Essence of Language

1. Martin Heidegger, "Neuere Forschungen über Logik," in *Literarische Rundschau für das katholische Deutschland* 38 (1912): 466; Otto Pöggeler, *Der Denkweg Martin Heideggers*, p. 269. Cf. Martin Heidegger, *Die Lehre vom Urteil im Psychologismus*, in FS, pp. 1–130.
2. FS, p. ix.
3. Arion L. Kelkel, *La légende de l'être*, pp. 149–54.
4. Ibid., pp. 19–44 (passim).
5. Ibid., pp. 147–54; cf. Pöggeler, *Denkweg.*, pp. 269–80.
6. William J. Richardson, *Heidegger.*, p. 629n; cf. US, p. 91 (6).

7. US, p. 96 (9–10); cf. pp. 91–93 (5–8).
8. Pöggeler, *Denkweg*, p. 270.
9. SZ, p. 129 (166–67).
10. SZ, pp. 157–59 (199–202), 351–64 (412–15).
11. US, p. 93 (7).
12. SZ, sec. 7 b, pp. 132–34 (55–58).
13. SZ, sec. 7 c, pp. 34–39 (58–63).
14. SZ, sec. 17, pp. 76–83 (107–114), sec. 26–27, pp. 117–30 (153–68).
15. SZ, sec. 31–33, pp. 142–60 (182–203).
16. Cf. SZ, pp. 154–56 (196–99), 159–61 (201–204).
17. SZ, pp. 160–61 (203).
18. SZ, p. 161 (203–204).
19. SZ, p. 161 (204).
20. Ibid.
21. Ibid.
22. Ibid., pp. 162–63 (205–206); cf. Joseph J. Kockelmans, *On Heidegger and Language*, pp. 202–223; Kelkel, *Légende*, pp. 155–327.
23. Kelkel, *Légende*, pp. 335–36.
24. SZ, p. 161 (204).
25. Kelkel, *Légende*, pp. 329–36; cf. N, vol. 1, p. 29; EM, pp. 62 (68–69), 141 (154–55); HB, pp. 89–93 (221–24).
26. SZ, pp. 160–61 (203–204).
27. SZ, pp. 32–33 (55–56).
28. Richardson, *Heidegger*, pp. 66, 171, 628. For what follows, cf. John Sallis, "Language and Reversal," pp. 381–97.
29. EM, pp. 104–108 (114–19). Cf. Richardson, *Heidegger*, pp. 268–70.
30. EM, p. 131 (144).
31. Ibid.
32. EM, p. 11 (11–12); WD, p. 85 (120).
33. EM, pp. 62–63 (69), 131 (144), 120 (131).
34. US, p. 185 (80).
35. Ibid.; Richardson, *Heidegger*, p. 609.
36. WD, p. 119 (196); Richardson, *Heidegger*, p. 609.
37. WD, p. 119 (196).
38. WD, p. 83 (118–19).
39. Richardson, *Heidegger*, p. 610; WD, p. 83 (118–19).
40. EM, p. 120 (131–32), 131–33 (144–46), 141 (154–55), 101 (111–12); cf. Richardson, *Heidegger*, pp. 292–95.
41. EM, p. 131 (144–45); WD, p. 90 (131); Richardson, *Heidegger*, p. 611.
42. VA, pp. 207–229 (59–78).
43. VA, pp. 212–13 (63–64); WD, pp. 117–25 and 170–73 (194–207).
44. VA, pp. 212–13 (63–64); Richardson, *Heidegger*, p. 495.
45. Richardson, *Heidegger*, p. 496.
46. Ibid., p. 497.
47. VA, pp. 213–16 (64–67).
48. VA, p. 228 (77).
49. Richardson, *Heidegger*, p. 543.
50. Ibid.
51. HB, p. 116 (239); Richardson, *Heidegger*, p. 543.
52. HB, p. 115 (239); cf. p. 116 (239–40).

53. HB, p. 116 (239).
54. HW, p. 286 (132).
55. "Das Wesen der Sprache," in US, pp. 159–216 (57–108).
56. "Die Sprache," in US, pp. 1–33 (189–210).
57. US, p. 145 (47).
58. US, pp. 11 (189), 145 (47), 179–81 (75–76), 198–202 (92–96).
59. US, pp. 11–15 (189–93), 145–49 (47–51), 199–202 (93–96), 252–55 (121–24).
60. US, pp. 21–26 (199–203).
61. US, pp. 20–22 (198–200), 198–202 (92–96); HB, pp. 68–80 (205–214). Cf. Kockelmans, *Heidegger and Language,* pp. 23–25.
62. US, p. 22 (199); cf. chap. 5. For the translation of *dingen,* cf. n. 68 below.
63. US, p. 22 (199–200).
64. SZ, pp. 64–65 (93); WG, pp. 23–29 (47–91).
65. US, pp. 21–25 (199–202).
66. Cf. chap. 4 of this book; US, pp. 25–26 (202–203).
67. US, pp. 26–28 (203–205).
68. The German word *dingen* which Heidegger uses here has several meanings: "to take someone in one's service, to try a case in court, to bargain, to hire, to beg, to bid, to invite," etc.; cf. the Swedish *tinga.* Although Heidegger seems to use it here in the sense of "to do what things are 'supposed' to do as things," I prefer to translate *dingen* as "begging," in view of the fact that there is no English verb "to thing." As for *welten,* Heidegger seems to be using this verb also in the sense of "to do what a world is 'supposed' to do as a world." The verb *welten* is no longer used in modern high German; yet there still is a Swabian verb *welten,* which has the meaning of the high German *walten,* "to hold sway." In view of the fact that there is no English verb "to world," I prefer to translate *welten* in "die Welt weltet" as "to govern" or "to hold sway." Cf. Benecke, Müller, und Zarnche, *Mittelhochdeutsches Wörterbuch* (Hildesheim: Olms, 1963), vol. 3, p. 563.
69. US, p. 29 (206–207).
70. US, p. 26 (203–204).
71. US, p. 29 (206–207).
72. US, p. 29 (206–207); trans. by Richardson (*Heidegger,* p. 580).
73. US, p. 30 (207–208).
74. Richardson, *Heidegger,* p. 580.
75. US, pp. 31–32 (208–209).
76. US, pp. 31–32 (208–209); Richardson, *Heidegger,* pp. 579–81.
77. ID, p. 30 (37–38); Kockelmans, *Heidegger and Language,* pp. 218–20.
78. US, p. 178 (74). Cf. John Sallis, "Towards the Showing of Language," in *The Southwestern Journal of Philosophy* 3 (1973): 75–83.
79. US, pp. 159 (57), 177 (73), 196–97 (90–91).
80. US, pp. 161 (59), 179 (75), 199 (93).
81. US, p. 159 (57).
82. US, pp. 159–60 (57–58).
83. US, pp. 160–61 (58–59). In passing, Heidegger defines *metalinguistics* as "the metaphysics of the thoroughgoing technicalization of all languages into the sole operative instrument of interplanetary information exchange." US, p. 160 (58).
84. US, pp. 160–61 (58–59).

85. US, pp. 161–63 (59–61).
86. US, pp. 163–66 (61–63).
87. US, pp. 168–69 (65–66).
88. US, pp. 169 (67).
89. US, pp. 169–70 (66–67).
90. US, pp. 170–73 (67–69).
91. US, p. 173 (69).
92. US, p. 175 (70); cf. chap. 9 below.
93. US, pp. 174–75 (70–72). The word *Frömmigkeit* is usually translated as "piety." In modern high German the word indeed means "piety, devoutness, godliness," etc. The original meaning of the word, however, was "ability, solidity, excellence, proficiency (=*Tüchtigkeit*), or bravery *(Tapferkeit)*." *Fromm* originally had the meaning of *nützlich* ("useful"), *brauchbar* ("serviceable"), *tüchtig* ("fit, able, strong, proficient"), *trefflich* ("excellent"), *tapfer* ("brave"), *rechtschaffen* ("righteous, upright"), or *fügsam* ("adaptive, supple, docile, obedient," etc.) Heidegger indicates that he uses the noun *Frömmigkeit* here in the sense of "docility" or even "submission."
94. US, pp. 175–77 (70–73).
95. US, pp. 177–78 (73–74).
96. US, pp. 178–79 (74–75); cf. SZ, sec. 69 b.
97. US, pp. 180–81 (75–76).
98. US, pp. 181–84 (76–80).
99. US, pp. 188–91 (83).
100. US, p. 190 (85).
101. US, pp. 190–91 (85).
102. US, pp. 191–92 (86–87).
103. US, pp. 192–93 (87).
104. US, pp. 193–95 (88–89). For the meaning of *Es gibt* . . . ("It grants . . ." instead of the common "There is . . ."), see chap. 2 above.
105. US, p. 195 (90).
106. US, pp. 196–99 (90–93).
107. US, p. 199 (93).
108. US, pp. 199–202 (93–95).
109. US, p. 202 (95).
110. US, pp. 202–205 (95–99).
111. US, p. 208 (101).
112. US, pp. 208–211 (101–104).
113. US, p. 211 (104).
114. US, pp. 211–13 (104–106). It should be stressed here that *zeitigen* and *räumen* are common German verbs. *Zeitigen* means "to bring to maturity," whereas *räumen* means "to make room for."
115. US, p. 213 (105–106).
116. US, pp. 213–14 (106–107).
117. US, p. 215 (107).
118. US, pp. 215–16 (107–108).

Chapter 8: On Art and Art Works

1. HW., p. 344 (xxiii–xxiv).
2. N, vol. 1, pp. 11–254 (vol. 1, 1–220).

3. (Munich: Langan, 1937). This essay was later included in *Erläuterungen zu Hölderlins Dichting* (Frankfurt: Klostermann, 1963), pp. 31–46 (270–91).

4. Cf. chap. 7 above.

5. Cf. *Poetry, Language, Thought,* pp. xxiii–xxiv.

6. HW, pp. 66–68 (79–81).

7. HW, p. 344. In the 1960 Reclam edition, Heidegger added that the *Addendum* was written in 1956. (PLT, p. xxiv.) Cf. Jacques Taminiaux, "Le dépassement heideggérien de l'esthétique et l'héritage de Hegel," in *Recoupements,* pp. 175–182 and passim.

8. HW, p. 66 (79). Cf. Calvin O. Schrag, "The Transvaluation of Aesthetics and the Work of Art," pp. 109–124; Jacques Taminiaux, "Entre l'attitude esthétique et la mort de l'art," in *Recoupements,* pp. 150–74; H.-G. Gadamer, "On the Problematic Character of Aesthetic Consciousness," in *Graduate Faculty Philosophy Journal* 9 (1982): 31–40. For the remark on "great art," see H, pp. 29–30 (40–41); cf. also Taminiaux, "Le dépassement," pp. 199–201.

9. Hegel, *Werke,* X, 1, pp. 134–35; 16. Cf. Taminiaux, "Le dépassement," pp. 177–78.

10. HW, pp. 66–67 (79–80).

11. HW, pp. 67–68 (81). Cf. Taminiaux, "Le dépassement," p. 178.

12. HW, pp. 67–68 (81). Cf. Friederich-Wilhelm von Herrmann, *Heideggers Philosophie der Kunst,* pp. xvii–xxi; Otto Pöggeler, *Der Denkweg Martin Heideggers,* p. 207; Otto Pöggeler, *Philosophie und Politik bei Heidegger,* p. 122; Taminiaux, "Le dépassement," pp. 177–81, 206–208; Albert Hofstadter, "How to Escape from Hegel's Aesthetics!" in *Graduate Faculty Philosophy Journal* 9 (1982): 5–30.

13. HW, pp. 7–8 (17-18); cf. von Herrmann, *Heideggers Philosophie,* pp. 1–5; H.-G. Gadamer, "Zur Einführung," in Martin Heidegger, *Der Ursprung des Kunstwerkes* (1960), (Stuttgart: Reclam, 1970), pp. 107–109.

14. HW, p. 8 (18); cf. Walter Biemel, *Martin Heidegger,* p. 93; von Herrmann, *Heideggers Philosophie,* pp. 5–13.

15. HW, pp. 9–10 (19–20); cf. von Herrmann, *Heideggers Philosophie,* pp. 13–19.

16. HW, pp. 10–11 (20–21); for what follows, cf. von Herrmann, *Heideggers Philosophie,* pp. 21–64.

17. HW, p. 11 (21).

18. HW, pp. 10–11 (20–21). Cf. SZ, pp. 200–212, 42–45, 59–62, 356–64 (244–56, 67–71, 86–90, 408–415).

19. HW, pp. 11–12 (21–22).

20. HW, pp. 12–13 (23).

21. HW, pp. 13–14 (23–24). For this common source, which consists in the manner in which in each case the ontological difference comes-to-pass, cf. chap. 4 above. See also Jean Greisch, "Identité et différence dans la pensée de Martin Heidegger. Le chemin de l'*Ereignis,*" in *Revue des sciences philosophiques et théologiques* 57 (1973): 71–111.

22. HW, pp. 13–14 (24). Cf. VA, pp. 163–81 (165–86).

23. HW, pp. 14 (24–25).

24. HW, pp. 15–16 (25–26).

25. HW, pp. 15–16 (26).

26. HW, pp. 16–19 (26–30). For Heidegger's position on the "true" conception

of the thingness of things, cf. chap. 7 above; cf. also Martin Heidegger, *What is A Thing?* and the lecture "The Thing," in VA, pp. 163–85 (165–86).

27. HW, p. 23 (34).

28. HW, p. 25 (36). For the preceding, see von Herrmann, *Heideggers Philosophie,* pp. 65–90. Cf. also Meyer Schapiro, "The Still Life of a Personal Object—A Note on Heidegger and van Gogh," in *The Reach of Mind,* ed. M. L. Simmer (New York: Springer, 1968), pp. 203–209. Cf. Jacques Derrida, *La vérité en peinture* (Paris: Flammarion, 1978). It seems to me that Derrida has effectively dealt with Schapiro's criticism in so far as it is without sufficient ground; yet Derrida also shows that Heidegger's example has its own typical presuppositions.

29. HW, pp. 25 (36). For the relationship between *alētheia* and *energeia,* cf. Taminiaux, "Le dépassement," pp. 181–82. Also note the indirect reference to Plato's *ekphanestaton* (*Phaedrus,* 250 D).

30. HW, pp. 25–27 (36–38).

31. PLT, pp. 86–87; HW, pp. 59 (71), 64 (77). For the relationship between Being and man referred to here, see chap. 2 above and chap. 9 below.

32. HW, pp. 20–21 (30–32).

33. HW, p. 28 (39).

34. HW, pp. 29–30 (39–41); for what follows, cf. von Herrmann, *Heideggers Philosophie,* pp. 105–111; Taminiaux, "Le dépassement," pp. 199–201.

35. HW, pp. 30–31 (41–42). Cf. chap. 5 above; von Herrmann, *Heideggers Philosophie,* pp. 111–23.

36. HW, p. 33 (44). Cf. von Herrmann, *Heideggers Philosophie,* pp. 124–50,

37. For the meaning of the verb *welten* in Heidegger's later works, cf. chap. 7, no. 68 above.

38. HW, pp. 33–34 (44–45). Cf. SZ, pp. 63–92 (91–125); WG, pp. 23–42 (47–99); Biemel, *Martin Heidegger,* pp. 97–98; von Herrmann, *Heideggers Philosophie,* pp. 150–66.

39. HW, pp. 34–35 (45–46). Note that there is no earth conception in Hegel; cf. Taminiaux, "Le dépassement," pp. 201–203.

40. HW, pp. 35–36 (46–48); cf. Biemel *Martin Heidegger,* pp. 98–99.

41. HW, p. 37 (48). Cf. chap. 9.

42. HW, p. 37 (49); cf. pp. 37–38 (48–49).

43. HW, p. 38 (49); cf. Biemel, *Martin Heidegger,* pp. 99–101; von Herrmann, *Heideggers Philosophie,* pp. 166–78.

44. HW, pp. 38–39 (50). For what is said about truth, see chap. 1 above; cf. also Biemel, *Martin Heidegger,* pp. 101–105, and von Herrmann, *Heideggers Philosophie,* pp. 179–221.

45. HW, pp. 39–40 (50–51); cf. Martin Heidegger, *Vom Wesen der menschlichen Freiheit. Einleitung in die Philosophie,* ed. Hartmut Tietjen (Frankfurt: Klostermann, 1982), pp. 66–109.

46. HW, pp. 40–41 (51–52).

47. HW, p. 41 (52).

48. HW, pp. 41–42 (52–53).

49. HW, pp. 42–43 (53–54).

50. William J. Richardson, *Heidegger,* pp. 405–406. Note that there is no double concealment in Hegel's conception of truth; cf. Taminiaux, "Le dépassement," pp. 203–204.

51. HW, p. 43 (55); Richardson, *Heidegger,* p. 406.

52. HW, p. 44 (55).

53. HW, p. 44 (56).

54. HW, p. 45 (56); cf. Biemel, *Martin Heidegger*, pp. 106–107.

55. HW, p. 45 (56–57).

56. HW, pp. 45–46 (57–58); for what follows, cf. von Herrmann, *Heideggers Philosophie*, pp. 227–83.

57. Cf. the remarks on *technē* and *technitēs* made in N, vol. 1, pp. 95–98 (vol. 1, pp. 80–83); cf. also HW, pp. 46–48 (57–60). In order to be able to avoid suggesting ideas not meant by Heidegger, I have not used the expressions "creating," "creation," and "the creative process," because they have become part and parcel of modern aesthetics, where they are used in another sense.

58. HW, p. 48 (60).

59. HW, p. 49 (60).

60. HW, p. 49 (61); cf. PLT, pp. 82–83.

61. PLT, p. 83; cf. pp. 85–86; SZ, sec. 44.

62. Cf. ID, pp. 59–64 (62–69); von Herrmann, *Heideggers Philosophie*, p. 241. For the negativity of Being, cf. chaps. 3 and 4 above; WW, passim; and Richardson, *Heidegger*, pp. 211–54.

63. HW, pp. 49–50 (61); PLT, p. 85.

64. HW, p. 50 (62); WG, pp. 20–41 (39–95), passim; Biemel, *Martin Heidegger*, pp. 107–108.

65. HW, pp. 50–51 (62).

66. HW, p. 51 (63).

67. HW, pp. 51–52 (63–64).

68. HW, p. 52 (65); cf. Richardson, *Heidegger*, p. 407; Biemel, *Martin Heidegger*, p. 109.

69. PLT, p. 84; cf. HW, p. 52 (64); cf. chap. 9 below.

70. HW, p. 52 (64); cf. von Herrmann, *Heideggers Philosophie*, pp. 254–70.

71. HW, pp. 52–53 (64–65).

72. HW, p. 53 (66); Biemel, *Martin Heidegger*, p. 109; von Herrmann, *Heideggers Philosophie*, pp. 271–83.

73. HW, p. 54 (66).

74. HW, p. 54 (66).

75. HW, p. 55 (67). For what follows, cf. von Herrmann, *Heideggers Philosophie*, pp. 284–302.

76. HW, p. 55 (67); cf. SZ, pp. 295–310 (341–58), 316–31 (364–80), and passim.

77. HW, pp. 55–56 (68).

78. HW, p. 56 (68); cf. Biemel *Martin Heidegger*, pp. 109–111.

79. HW, pp. 56–57 (69); cf. von Herrmann, *Heideggers Philosophie*, pp. 303–310.

80. HW, p. 57 (69).

81. HW, p. 57 (69–70).

82. HW, p. 58 (70).

83. HW, p. 58 (70–71); cf. von Herrmann, *Heideggers Philosophie*, pp. 311–15.

84. HW, p. 59 (71); Biemel, *Martin Heidegger*, pp. 111–12.

85. PLT, pp. 86–87.

86. PLT, pp. 86–87; cf. chaps. 3 and 4 above.

87. HW, p. 59 (72); cf. von Herrmann, *Heideggers Philosophie*, pp. 315–36.

88. HW, pp. 59–60 (72); PLT, p. 86; cf. chap. 9 below.

89. HW, p. 60 (73).
90. HW, pp. 60–62 (73–75); cf. chaps. 7 and 9 of this book.
91. HW, p. 62 (75); cf. von Herrmann, *Heideggers Philosophie*, pp. 336–46.
92. HW, p. 62 (75).
93. HW, pp. 62–63 (75–76).
94. HW, p. 63 (76).
95. Ibid.
96. HW, p. 64 (77).
97. HW, p. 64 (77); cf. von Herrmann, *Heideggers Philosophie*, pp. 346–58.
98. HW, p. 65 (78); Biemel, *Martin Heidegger,* p. 113.
99. HW, p. 65 (78).
100. For important problems connected with Heidegger's effort to think the essence of art from the perspective of Hegel's aesthetics, cf. Taminiaux, "Le dépassement," pp. 175–81 and 206–208; Hofstadter, "Escape from Hegel!" passim. Yet also see Martin Heidegger, "Die Herkunft der Kunst und die Bestimmung des Denkens (1967)," in *Distanz und Nähe. Reflexionen und Analysen zur Kunst der Gegenwart,* ed. Petra Jaeger und Rudolf Lüthe (Festschrift for Walter Biemel), (Würzburg; Königshausen & Neumann, 1983), pp. 18–22.

Chapter 9: Thinking and Poetizing

1. HW, pp. 59–62 (71–75); Friedrich-Wilhelm von Herrmann, *Heideggers Philosophie der Kunst,* pp. 314–45; chap. 2 above. For what follows, see also: Walter Biemel, "Poetry and Language," pp. 65–105; Henri Birault, "Thinking and Poetizing in Heidegger," pp. 147–68; Else Buddeberg, *Heidegger und die Dichtung,* passim; Else Buddeberg, *Denken und Dichten des Seins;* E. F. Hirsch, "Heidegger und die Dichtung," pp. 271–83; David Rasmussen, *Poetry and Truth,* passim; O. Ugirashebuja, *Dialogue entre la poésie et la pensée d'après l'oeuvre de Heidegger;* Werner Marx, *Heidegger and the Tradition,* pp. 135–241; Werner Marx, "The World in Another Beginning: Poetic Dwelling and the Role of the Poet," pp. 235–59; Beda Alleman, *Hölderlin und Heidegger;* Jean Beaufret, *Dialogue avec Heidegger;* Arion L. Kelkel, *La légende de l'être,* pp. 339–610; William J. Richardson, *Heidegger,* passim.
2. Richardson, *Heidegger,* p. 635.
3. Kelkel, *Légende,* pp. 607–10.
4. EM, pp. 88–149 (98–164).
5. Richardson, *Heidegger,* pp. 295–96, 291–95, 397; cf. EM, pp. 11 (11–12), 20 (20–21), 101 (111–12), 110 (121–22), 121 (143–44), 141 (154–55), and passim.
6. HD, p. 66, and passim.
7. HW, pp. 296–343 (13–58).
8. HW, p. 303 (19); cf. Richardson, *Heidegger,* p. 522; Kelkel, *Légende,* pp. 501–503, 544–45.
9. Emil Steiger, *Zu einem Vers von Mörike. Ein Briefwechsel mit Martin Heidegger,* p. 8.
10. Martin Heidegger, *Hölderlins Hymnen 'Germanien' und 'Der Rhein'* (Frankfurt: Klostermann, 1980).
11. Ibid., pp. 29–33. For the threefold meaning of *founding (stiften),* cf. HW, pp. 62–64 (75–77); also see chap. 8.
12. WM, p. 51 (360–61).
13. US, p. 38 (160).

14. US, p. 195 (89–90).
15. US, p. 196 (90).
16. US, p. 196 (90).
17. WD, p. 8 (12 and 19); cf. Beaufret, *Dialogue*, vol. 3, pp. 70–89.
18. ED, pp. 23, 15; HB, pp. 116–17 (240).
19. HW, p. 252 (95–96).
20. WD, p. 155 (134–35); VA, p. 188 (214).
21. US, p. 237 (155–56).
22. US, pp. 237 (155–56), 196 (90); cf. Kelkel, *Légende*, pp. 504–507.
23. HW, pp. 247 (112), 303 (19); EM, pp. 19 (20–21), 144 (158), 69–70 (96–97); VA, pp. 163–81 (165–81); cf. Kelkel, *Légende*, pp. 507–508.
24. VA, pp. 13–44 (287–317); TuK, pp. 37–47 (36–49); SD, pp. 61–80 (373–92); cf. Beaufret, *Dialogue*, vol. 3, pp. 155–82, 217–29; cf. chap. 8 and the epilogue of this book.
25. Carl Friedrich Gethmann, *Verstehen und Auslegung*, pp. 275–334.
26. WD, pp. 6–8 (10–12); VA, pp. 136–43; Kelkel, *Légende*, pp. 528–39; W, p. 78.
27. HB, pp. 80–89 (214–21); SD, pp. 53–58 (49–54); 1–25 (1–25). Cf. chap. 7 above.
28. SZ, p. 384 (435–36).
29. Martin Heidegger, *Die Selbstbehauptung der deutschen Universität* (Breslau: Korn, 1933), pp. 18–21.
30. EM, pp. 116–17 (127–29); cf. chap. 12, art. II below.
31. EM, pp. 145–46 (159–60); cf. Marx, *Heidegger and the Tradition*, pp. 233–41; Otto Pöggeler, *Philosophie und Politik bei Heidegger*, pp. 43–67.
32. WD, pp. 6–10 (10–12, 19–21); VA, pp. 187–204 (213–29); cf. Beaufret, *Dialogue*, vol. 1, pp. 85–86, and passim.
33. HB, pp. 85–86 (218–19).
34. Cf. Kelkel, *Légende*, pp. 594–607.
35. Richardson, *Heidegger*, p. 558.
36. Ibid., p. 635.
37. US, pp. 21–22 (198–200).
38. HW, p. 54 (66); HD, pp. 29–30, 140; cf. chap. 8 above.
39. US, pp. 159–216 (57–108).
40. US, pp. 162–63 (59–61), and US, p. 216 (108).
41. WM, p. 51 (360–61).
42. Ibid.
43. HB, p. 86 (218–19).
44. Richardson, *Heidegger*, pp. 636–37.
45. Heidegger, *Hölderlins Hymnen*, p. 33.
46. Ibid., p. 36.
47. HD, pp. 29–30; cf. Kelkel, *Légende*, pp. 607–610.
48. Martin Heidegger, *Hebel—Der Hausfreund* (Pfullingen: Neske, 1958), pp. 33–35.
49. HD, p. 41.
50. Heidegger, *Hebel*, p. 25.
51. Ibid., p. 33.
52. ED, p. 19.
53. Ibid., p. 120.

Chapter 10: On Science

1. Martin Heidegger, *Die Lehre vom Urteil im Psychologismus* (Leipzig: Barth, 1914), p. 111; Carl F. von Weizsäcker, *Der Garten des Menschlichen* (Munich: Carl Henser, 1977).

2. SZ, pp. 356–64 (408–15), 392–404 (444–55); WM, pp. 24–27 (95–98); FD, pp. 49–83 (65–108); HW, pp. 69–104 (115–54); VA, pp. 45–70 (155–82); G, pp. 17–28 (48–57); WD, pp. 10–19 (28–32, 37–44), 56–61 (32–36, 44–47); N, vol. 1, pp. 473–658; N, vol. 2, pp. 31–256.

3. Cf. Joseph J. Kockelmans, "Heidegger on the Essential Difference and Necessary Relationship between Philosophy and Science," pp. 147–66; Theodore J. Kisiel, "Science, Phenomenology, and the Thinking of Being," pp. 167–83; Joseph J. Kockelmans, "The Era of the World-as-Picture," pp. 184–201; William J. Richardson, "Heidegger's Critique of Science," pp. 11–36; Karlfried Gründer, "Heidegger's Critique of Science," pp. 15–32; John C. Sallis, "Towards the Movement of Reversal," pp. 138–68; Theodore J. Kisiel, "Heidegger and the New Images of Science," pp. 162–81; P. Chiodi, *Heideggers Einfluss auf die Wissenschaften;* P. Chiodi, *Martin Heideggers Einfluss auf die Wissenschaften* (Bern: Francke, 1969). Cf. HW, pp. 69–70.

4. The original title of the essay was "Die Begründung des neuzeitlichen Weltbildes durch die Metaphysik"; it was later, in 1950, published in *Holzwege* under the title: "Die Zeit des Weltbildes" [The era of the world-as-picture]. Cf. HW, pp. 69–104 (115–54).

5. HW, pp. 69 (116), 89–90 (137–38).

6. VA, p. 45 (155); cf. chap. 8 above.

7. HW, p. 70 (116–17).

8. HW, p. 70 (117); VA, pp. 45–70; FD, pp. 49–83 (65–108).

9. HW, pp. 70–71 (117–118).

10. FD, pp. 50–53 (66–69).

11. FD, pp. 50–51 (66–67).

12. FD, pp. 51–52 (67–68).

13. FD, p. 52 (68).

14. FD, p. 52 (68). Cf. Immanuel Kant, Preface to *Metaphysical Foundations of Natural Science*, trans. Belfort Bax (London: Bell and Sons, 1883), p. 140.

15. FD, pp. 52–53 (68–69).

16. FD, pp. 53–59 (69–76).

17. Kockelmans, "The Era," pp. 187–89.

18. HW, p. 71 (118).

19. HW, pp. 71–72 (118–19); Kockelmans, "The Era," p. 188.

20. FD, p. 59 (76).

21. FD, pp. 59–60 (76–77).

22. FD, p. 60 (77–78).

23. Cf. Isaac Newton, *Mathematical Principles of Natural Philosophy and his System of the World*, trans. A. Motte (1729), revised trans. by Florian Cajori (Berkeley: University of California Press, 1946), p. 13.

24. Ibid., p. xxii.

25. FD, pp. 60–61 (78–79).

26. FD, p. 69 (89).

27. FD, pp. 69–70 (90).

28. FD, p. 70 (90).
29. FD, p. 70 (91).
30. FD, pp. 70–71 (91).
31. FD, p. 71 (91–92).
32. Aristotle, *Physics*, II, 1, 192b21–22.
33. HW, pp. 72–73 (118–20).
34. FD, pp. 71 (92).
35. FD, p. 71 (92–93).
36. Cf. sec. III of this chapter.
37. HW, pp. 74–76 (120–23); cf. Kockelmans, "The Era," pp. 189–192.
38. FD, pp. 71–72 (93–94).
39. HW, pp. 76–77 (123–24); VA, p. 59 (170–71). Kockelmans, "The Era," pp. 192–96.
40. HW, p. 90 (138–39).
41. HW, pp. 77–78 (124).
42. HW, pp. 78–80 (124–27).
43. HW, p. 80 (127).
44. HW, pp. 80–81 (127–28).
45. HW, pp. 82–84 (128–32).
46. HW, pp. 85–87 (132–35).
47. HW, pp. 93–94 (141–43).
48. FD, pp. 74–76 (96–98).
49. FD, pp. 76–77 (98–99).
50. FD, p. 77 (99).
51. FD, p. 78 (100).
52. FD, p. 78 (100).
53. FD, p. 77–78 (99–100).
54. FD, p. 78 (101).
55. FD, pp. 78–79 (101–102). Cf. R. Descartes, *Oeuvres*, vol. 10, p. 501; *Rules for the Direction of the Mind*, trans. F. P. Lafleur (Indianapolis: Bobbs-Merrill, 1961), p. 8.
56. FD, p. 80 (103).
57. FD, pp. 80–81 (103–104).
58. FD, pp. 81–82 (105–106).
59. FD, pp. 82–83 (106–108).

Chapter 11: Technicity

1. N, vol. 2, pp. 7–29.
2. Published in "Die Überwindung der Metaphysik," in VA, pp. 91–97 (103–109).
3. HW, pp. 248–95 (91–142).
4. Published in VA, pp. 13–44, and later in *Die Technik und die Kehre* (Pfullingen: Neske, 1962), pp. 5–36. The lecture was published for the first time in *Die Künste im technischen Zeitalter* (Dritte Folge des Jahrbuchs "Gestalt und Gedanke", herausgegeben von der Bayerischen Akademie der schönen Künste), ed. Clemens Graf Podewils (Munich: Oldenbourg, 1954), pp. 70–108.
5. Friedrich Dessauer: *Philosophie der Technik: Das Problem der Realisierung* (Bonn: Cohen, 1927); *Streit um die Technik* (Frankfurt: Knecht, 1958²); Ernst Jünger: *Der Arbeiter: Herrschaft und Gestalt* (Hamburg: Hanseatische Verlagsan-

stalt, 1932); "Vom Ende des geschichtlichen Zeitalters," in Jean Beaufret et al., *Martin Heidegger zum siebzigsten Geburtstag* (Pfullingen: Neske, 1959), pp. 309–41.

6. Norbert Wiener: *Cybernetics or Control and Communication in the Animal and the Machine* (New York: John Wiley and Sons, 1950[8]); *The Human Use of Human Beings: Cybernetics and Society* (Cambridge: The Riverside Press, 1950); *Selected Papers of Norbert Wiener* (Cambridge: The MIT Press, 1964); "Some Moral and Technical Consequences of Automation," in *Science* 131 (1960): 1355–58.

7. Jacques Ellul: "The Technological Order," in *Technology and Culture* 3 (1962): 394–463; *The Technological Society*, trans. J. Wilkinson (London: Cape, 1965); Georg Klaus: *Kybernetik und Erkenntnistheorie* (Berlin: VEB Deutscher Verlag der Wissenschaften, 1969[3]); *Kybernetik und Gesellschaft* (Berlin: VEB Deutscher Verlag der Wissenschaften, 1964); *Kybernetik in philosophischer Sicht* (Berlin: Dietz Verlag, 1961); *Spieltheorie in philosophischer Sicht* (Berlin: VEB Deutscher Verlag der Wissenschaften, 1968); Karl Steinbuch: *Automat und Mensch: Über menschliche und maschinelle Intelligenz* (Berlin: Springer, 1965[3]); *Falsch Programmiert: Über das Versagen unserer Gesellschaft in der Gegenwart und vor der Zukunft, und was eigentlich geschehen müsste* (Stuttgart: Deutsche Verlagsanstalt, 1968); *Die informierte Gesellschaft: Geschichte und Zukunft der Nachrichtentechnik* (Stuttgart: Deutsche Verlagsanstalt, 1966); *Ja zur Wirklichkeit* (Stuttgart: Seewald Verlag, 1975); Jürgen Habermas, *Technik und Wissenschaft als 'Ideologie'* (Frankfurt: Suhrkamp, 1969[3]); for an important critical discussion of these works, see Egbert Schuurman, *Technology and the Future;* for a more elaborated bibliography, see Schuurman, *Technology*, pp. 409–420; *Bibliography for the Philosophy of Technology*, ed. C. Mitcham and R. Mackey (Chicago: University of Chicago Press, 1973).

8. Cf. Schuurman, *Technology*, pp. 102–108, and passim.

9. K. Tuchel, *Die Philosophie der Technik bei Friedrich Dessauer: Ihre Entwicklung, Motive und Grenzen* (Frankfurt: Knecht, 1964), p. 60.

10. "Martin Heidegger über die Technik" (in *Streit um die Technik*, pp. 348–68), which is part of "Die Technik in existenzialphilosophischer Schau" (ibid., pp. 311–68).

11. Cf. ibid., p. 355ff.

12. Schuurman, *Technology*, pp. 103–104, 104–108.

13. TuK, p. 21 (302); cf. Schuurman, *Technology*, pp. 102–108.

14. Schuurman, *Technology*, p. 55.

15. Ibid., pp. 55–56.

16. Friedrich Georg Jünger, *Die Perfektion der Technik* (Frankfurt: Klostermann, 1953[4]), p. 10. Cf. his *The Failure of Technology* (Chicago; Regnery, 1956); *Maschine und Eigentum* (Frankfurt: Klostermann, 1953[2]); *Sprache und Kalkül* (Frankfurt: Klostermann, 1956); and *Die vollkommene Schöpfung* (Frankfurt: Klostermann, 1966).

17. Schuurman, *Technology*, pp. 55–57.

18. Ibid., p. 70.

19. Jünger, *Sprache*.

20. Schuurman, *Technology*, p. 70.

21. Jünger, *Sprache*, p. 13.

22. Ibid., p. 12.

23. Ibid., p. 27; cf. Schuurman, *Technology*, pp. 70–72.

24. Heidegger does refer to Ernst Jünger in *Zur Seinsfrage* (1956); cf. *Wegmarken* (Frankfurt: Klostermann, 1976), p. 395.

25. Schuurman, *Technology*, p. 100.

26. TuK, p. 3 (ix–x).

27. VA, pp. 13–44 (287–317). However, also see n. 53.

28. (Munich: Oldenbourg, 1954), pp. 70–108.

29. (Pfullingen: Neske, 1962). "The Question of Technology" was translated by William Lovitt in *The Question of Technology and Other Essays* (New York: Harper and Row, 1977). "The Turning," on the other hand, was translated by Kenneth R. Maly and appeared first in *Research in Phenomenology* 1 (1971): 3–16. In this chapter I shall quote both essays from *The Question of Technology and Other Essays*, although "The Question of Technology" also appears in *Basic Writings* (pp. 287–317).

30. Cf. J. Loscerbo, "M. Heidegger: Remarks concerning Some Early Texts on Modern Technology," in *Tijdschrift voor Filosofie* 39 (1977): 106–112. Loscerbo gives here a justification for these translations of *Gestell* and *Bestand*.

31. TuK, p. 5 (4).

32. Schuurman, *Technology*, p. 87; cf. William Lovitt, "A *Gespräch* with Heidegger on Technology," in *Man and World* 6 (1973): 44; Langan, pp. 191–200.

33. WW, pp. 10–12 (112–25).

34. TuK, pp. 5–7 (4–6).

35. Schuurman, *Technology*, p. 88.

36. TuK, p. 9 (8).

37. Lovitt, "*Gespräch*," p. 46.

38. Plato, *Symposium*, 205 B.

39. TuK, pp. 7–11 (6–10).

40. TuK, p. 11 (10–11).

41. TuK, pp. 11–12 (11–12); cf. introduction of this book and chap. 8 above.

42. Schuurman, *Technology*, p. 89.

43. TuK, p. 12 (12–13).

44. Aristotle, *Ethica Nicomachea*, VI, 3 & 4, 1139b14–17.

45. TuK, pp. 12–13 (13).

46. TuK, pp. 13–17 (13–17). For the translation of the term *Bestand*, see Lovitt, "*Gespräch*," pp. 49–50.

47. HW, pp. 265–66 (109–110).

48. HW, p. 289 (135).

49. HW, p. 265 (110).

50. HW, p. 266 (110).

51. HW, p. 267 (111–12). For the term *raw material*, cf. VA, pp. 92 (104), 95 (106).

52. HW, p. 272 (116).

53. HW, p. 272 (117).

54. HW, pp. 272–74 (117).

55. TuK, p. 21 (22).

56. TuK, pp. 17–18 (18).

57. TuK, pp. 18–19 (18–19).

58. For reasons why *Enframing* is not a good English word for *Ge-stell*, see Loscerbo, "M. Heidegger," p. 107n; cf. pp. 106–110.

59. TuK, pp. 20–22 (21–23); WD, p. 155 (135–36).

60. TuK, p. 22 (22).

61. TuK, p. 23 (23); Lovitt, *"Gespräch,"* pp. 52–53; Schuurman, *Technology,* pp. 91–92.
62. TuK, p. 24 (24).
63. TuK, pp. 23–24 (23–24).
64. TuK, p. 24 (25).
65. ID, pp. 25–26 (33–34).
66. ID, pp. 26–27 (34–35).
67. ID, pp. 27–29 (35–37).
68. ID, p. 30 (38).
69. TuK, pp. 23–24 (24).
70. TuK, p. 26 (27). Cf. Lovitt, *"Gespräch,"* p. 53.
71. Lovitt, *"Gespräch,"* p. 54.
72. TuK, pp. 24–25 (25).
73. TuK, p. 25 (25–26).
74. TuK, p. 26 (26).
75. Lovitt, *"Gespräch,"* p. 55.
76. TuK, p. 26 (26).
77. TuK, pp. 26–27 (26–27).
78. G, pp. 11–28 (43–57).
79. G, pp. 20–21 (50–51).
80. G, p. 21 (51).
81. G, pp. 21–22 (51–52).
82. G, pp. 22–23 (52–53). Cf. "Nur noch ein Gott kann uns retten," in *Der Spiegel,* 1976, no. 23, p. 209; English trans. by M. P. Alter and John D. Caputo, "Only a God Can Save Us: Der Spiegel's Interview with Martin Heidegger," in *Philosophy Today* 20 (1976): 277.
83. G, pp. 23–24 (53–54).
84. G, p. 26 (55).
85. G, p. 27 (56).
86. G, pp. 27–28 (56).
87. TuK, pp. 27–28 (27–28).
88. TuK, pp. 28–29 (28–29); Lovitt, *"Gespräch,"* pp. 55–56.
89. TuK, pp. 30–31 (30).
90. TuK, p. 31 (30–31); cf. Lovitt, *"Gespräch,"* 56–57.
91. TuK, p. 32 (32).
92. TuK, p. 32 (32).
93. TuK, pp. 32–33 (32–33).
94. TuK, p. 33 (33).
95. TuK, p. 33 (33).
96. TuK, p. 34 (34).
97. TuK, p. 35 (35).
98. TuK, pp. 34–35 (34–35).
99. TuK, pp. 35–36 (35). For the meaning of *Frömmigkeit,* see chap. 6, n. 93.
100. TuK, p. 37 (36–37).
101. TuK, pp. 38–39 (38–39).
102. TuK, pp. 39–40 (39–40).
103. TuK, pp. 40–41 (40–42).
104. TuK, pp. 41–42 (42–43).
105. TuK, pp. 42–43 (43–44).
106. TuK, pp. 43–44 (44–45).

107. TuK, pp. 44–45 (46–47).
108. TuK, pp. 45–46 (47–48).
109. TuK, pp. 46–47 (48–49).
110. TuK, p. 47 (49).

Chapter 12: On Ethics and Politics

1. For Heidegger's conception of ethics and basic ethical issues, cf. Bernard Boelen, "The Question of Ethics in the Thought of Martin Heidegger," pp. 76–105; Otto F. Bolnow, "Existenzialismus und Ethik, in *Die Sammlung* 4 (1949): 321–335; H. Mongis, *Heidegger et la critique de la notion de valeur;* Luk Boeckaert, "Ontology and Ethics," pp. 402–419; Robert G. Butkus, *Heidegger's Thought and Ethics;* I. Fetscher, G.-G Grau, K.-H. Ilting, and O. Pöggeler, *Probleme der Ethik zur Diskussion Gestellt;* B. Sitter, *Dasein und Ethik;* Anthony Camele, "Heideggerian Ethics," pp. 284–93; John D. Caputo, "Heidegger's Original Ethics," pp. 127–138; R. H. Cousineau, *Humanism and Ethics;* Helmut Kuhn, *Begegnung mit dem Sein. Meditationen zur Metaphysik des Gewissens;* G. Morra, "Martino Heidegger," pp. 205–220; H. Oyen, "Fundamentalontologie und Ethik," vol. 2, pp. 107–121; C. A. van Peursen, "Ethik und Ontologie in der heutigen Existenzphilosophie," in *Zeitschrift f. evang. Ethik,* 2 (1958): 98–112; L. Ferry & A. Renaut, "La dimension éthique dans la pensée de Heidegger," pp. 36–54. For Heidegger and politics, cf. Beda Alleman, "Martin Heidegger und die Politik," pp. 962–76; P. Bourdieu, *Die politische Ontologie Martin Heideggers;* Otto Pöggeler, *Philosophie und Politik bei Heidegger;* Reiner Schürmann, *Le principe d'anarchie;* F. Fédier, "Trois attaques contre Heidegger," pp. 893–904; M. Buber, "Geltung und Grenzen des politischen Prinzips," in *Hinweise,* 1953, pp. 339–46; Karsten Harries, "Heidegger as a Political Thinker," pp. 642–69; Bernard Dauenhauer, "Renovating the Problem of Politics," pp. 624–41; Karl Löwith, "Les implications politiques de la philosophie de l'existence chez Heidegger," pp. 343–60; Jean-Michel Palmier, *Les écrits politiques de Heidegger;* etc.

2. Cf. Heidegger's "Letter on Humanism" and "A Letter to a Young Student," in VA, pp. 182–85 (183–86); cf. also the interview with *Der Spiegel.*

3. Cf. T. Adorno, *Jargon der Uneigentlichkeit* (Frankfurt: Suhrkamp, 1965); Alexander Schwan, *Politische Philosophie im Denken Heideggers;* P. Hühnerfeld, *In Sachen Heidegger;* Eric Weil, "Philosophie politique, théorie politique," in *Revue française de science politique* 11 (1961): 267–94; also see the publications by Harries, Schürmann, Nicholson, Löwith, Buber et al.

4. SZ, pp. 270–316 (315–64); 320n (496–97); HB, pp. 93–117 (224–40); *Die metaphysische Anfangsgründe der Logik im Ausgang von Leibniz* (1928), ed. Klaus Held (Frankfurt: Klostermann, 1978), secs. 11 and 13 (passim).

5. Otto Pöggeler, "Die ethisch-politische Dimension der hermeneutischen Philosophie," in *Probleme der Ethik,* pp. 45–81.

6. Joachim Ritter, *Metaphysik und Politik. Studien zu Aristoteles und Hegel* (Frankfurt: Suhrkamp, 1969), pp. 77ff.

7. Pöggeler, "Ethisch-politische Dimension," pp. 61–63.

8. Ibid., pp. 63–65.

9. H.-G. Gadamer, "Über die Möglichkeit einer philosophischen Ethik," in *Kleine Schriften,* vol. 1: *Philosophie—Hermeneutik* (Tübingen: Mohr, 1976), pp. 179–91; "Rhetorik, Hermeneutik und Ideologiekritik," in *Kleine Schriften,*

vol. 1, pp. 113–30; cf. R. Buber, "Theory and Practice in the Light of the Hermeneutic-Criticist Controversy," in *Cultural Hermeneutics* 2 (1975): 337–52.

10. Pöggeler, "Ethisch-politische Dimension," pp. 78–81.

11. Cf. for instance: R. Weber, "A Critique of Heidegger's Concept of Solicitude," in *The New Scholasticism* 45 (1971): 127–38; F. A. Olafson, *Principles and Persons. An Ethical Interpretation of Existentialism* (Baltimore: Johns Hopkins University Press, 1967); cf. B. Sitter, " 'Sein und Zeit' als Theorie der Ethik," in *Philosophische Rundschau* 16 (1969): 273–81.

12. Cf. E. Levinas, *Totality and Infinity*, trans. A. Lingis (The Hague: Nijhoff, 1976); Boeckaert, "Ontology and Ethics," pp. 402–419; Steven Gans, "Ethics or Ontology," pp. 117–21.

13. Boelen, "Ethics," pp. 76–105.

14. Cf. for instance the publications by Gadamer, Pöggeler, and Caputo mentioned above (n. 1).

15. SZ, p. 16 (37).

16. Ibid.

17. SZ, secs, 54–60, 62, 64, and passim.

18. Heidegger, *Metaphysische Anfangsgründe*.

19. ML, p. 199.

20. Boelen, "Ethics," p. 78.

21. EM, pp. 149–52 (164–67).

22. EM, pp. 149–50 (164–65).

23. EM, pp. 150–51 (165).

24. EM, p. 151 (165).

25. EM, pp. 151–52 (165–66).

26. EM, pp. 151–52 (166).

27. EM, p. 152 (166).

28. EM, p. 152 (167).

29. Cf. for instance Mongis, *Heidegger et la critique;* H.-G. Gadamer, "Das ontologische Problem des Wertes," in *Kleine Schriften*, vol. 4: *Variationen* (Tübingen: Mohr, 1977), pp. 205–217; cf. Joseph J. Kockelmans, "Hermeneutik und Ethik," in *Kommunikation und Reflexion*, ed. W. Kuhlmann (Frankfurt: Suhrkamp, 1982), pp. 649–84.

30. Cf. chap. 5 above.

31. HB, pp. 93–117 (224–40).

32. HB, pp. 97–98 (226–27); cf. pp. 93–98 (224–27).

33. HB, p. 99 (228).

34. HB, pp. 99–100 (228).

35. HB, p. 101 (229).

36. HB, p. 104 (231).

37. WD, p. 73 (79).

38. HB, pp. 104–105 (231–32).

39. HB, p. 105 (232).

40. Ibid.

41. HB, pp. 105–106 (232).

42. HB, p. 106 (232).

43. HB, p. 106 (232–33).

44. Aristotle, *De Partibus Animalium*, I, 5, 645a17ff.

45. HB, pp. 106–107 (233).

46. HB, p. 109 (234–35).

47. HB, p. 111 (236).
48. HB, pp. 114–15 (238–39).
49. HB, p. 115 (239).
50. HB, p. 115 (239).
51. HB, pp. 116–17 (240).
52. EM, pp. 151–52 (165–67).
53. Pöggeler, "Ethisch-politische Dimension," p. 45.
54. Cf. E. Tugendhat, *Der Wahrheitsbegriff bei Husserl und Heidegger.* Cf. Pöggeler's review of this book in *Philosophisches Jahrbuch,* 76 (1969): 376–85; cf. also Reinhard Maurer, "Von Heidegger zur praktischen Philosophie," Pöggeler, "Ethisch-politische Dimension," 46n.
55. SD, pp. 61–80 (373–92); cf. the postscript of this book.
56. Martin Heidegger, *Phänomenologie und Theologie,* p. 38.
57. Cf. the bibliographical information in the works by Palmier, Schürmann, and Pöggeler mentioned above. According to Palmier, in East Germany alone there are well over one hundred attacks on Heidegger's political philosophy which have appeared thus far (*Écrits politiques,* p. 341).
58. F. Fédier, "Trois attaques contre Heidegger," pp. 883–904; cf. also "À propos de Heidegger: une lecture dénoncée" (in *Critique,* no. 242) and "À propos de Heidegger" (in *Critique,* no. 252). See also the article by Alleman mentioned by Pöggeler (*Politik bei Heidegger,* pp. 105–106).
59. "Nur noch ein Gott kann uns retten," interview with M. Heidegger by R. Augstein and G. Wolff, in *Der Spiegel* 30 (1976): 193–219; trans. M. P. Alter and John D. Caputo ("Only a God Can Save Us"), in *Philosophy Today* 20 (1976); 267–84. Cf. also "Das Rektorat 1933/34," pp. 21–43.
60. Cf. n. 1 above. For a critique of Schwan's position, see Palmier, *Écrits politiques,* pp. 150–59, and Pöggeler, *Politik bei Heidegger,* pp. 121–25.
61. Cf. n. 1 above; see also Karl A. Moehling, "Heidegger and the Nazis," in *Heidegger: The Man and the Thinker,* pp. 31–43.
62. In addition to the publications mentioned in n. 1 above, see: T. Cassirer, *Aus meinem Leben mit Ernst Cassirer* (New York: Scribner's, 1950), pp. 165–67; J. P. Faye: "Heidegger et la 'revolution'," pp. 151–59; "Attaques nazies contre Heidegger," pp. 137–54; "La lecture et l'énoncé," pp. 288–95; G. Lukács, *Existentialisme ou Marxisme,* trans. E. Kelernen (Paris: Nagel, 1961); Graeme Nicholson, "The Commune of *Being and Time,*" pp. 708–726; Graeme Nicholson, "Camus and Heidegger: Anarchists," pp. 14–23; M. de Gandillac, "Entretiens avec Martin Heidegger," pp. 713–24.
63. Martin Heidegger, *Die Selbstbehauptung der deutschen Universität* (Breslau: Korn, 1933). For the short essays mentioned, see G. Schneeberger, *Nachlese zu Heidegger* (Bern: no publisher mentioned, 1962).
64. *Philosophy Today* 20 (1976): 271. Cf. Heidegger, "Das Rektorat," pp. 21–39.
65. Cf. Palmier, *Écrits politiques,* pp. 146–64, 267–93, and passim.
66. Ibid., pp. 45–145. Cf. Heidegger, "Das Rektorat," pp. 40–43.
67. EM, p. 117 (138).
68. *Philosophy Today,* 28 (1976): 276.
69. Cf. EM, p. 152 (166); VA, pp. 91–97 (103–109), 13–44 (287–317); HW, p. 62 (75); N, Vols. 1 and 2, passim.
70. Gregory Schufreider, "Heidegger on Community," in *Man and World* 14 (1981); 25–54.

71. Ibid., p. 49.

72. Ibid., pp. 41–42.

73. EM, p. 152 (166).

74. Schufreider, "Heidegger on Community," pp. 25–26, 47–51, passim.

75. Palmier, *Écrits politiques*, pp. 169–293.

76. Ernst Jünger, *Der Arbeiter: Herrschaft und Gestalt* (Hamburg: Hanseatische Verlagsanstalt, 1932).

77. Palmier, *Écrits politiques*, p. 286, cf. pp. 278–93. Cf. Heidegger, "Das Rektorat," pp. 24–25.

78. Cf. VA, pp. 71–99 (84–110).

79. VA, p. 72 (85).

80. VA, p. 110.

81. Palmier, *Écrits politiques*, pp. 291, 286–87.

82. Ibid., p. 291.

83. Bernard Dauenhauer, "Does Anarchy Make Political Sense?" pp. 369–75.

84. Reiner Schürmann, "Political Thinking in Heidegger," p. 191.

85. Ibid., p. 193.

86. Ibid., pp. 193–95; cf. Dauenhauer, "Anarchy," p. 369.

87. Reiner Schürmann, "The Ontological Difference and Political Philosophy," p. 99.

88. Ibid., p. 99.

89. Ibid., p. 100.

90. Dauenhauer, "Anarchy," pp. 369–70.

91. Ibid.

92. Schürmann, "Ontological Difference," pp. 121–22.

93. Reiner Schürmann, "Questioning the Foundations of Practical Philosophy," pp. 361–67; cf. "Ontological Difference," p. 122n.

94. Schürmann, "Questioning the Foundations," p. 370.

95. Schürmann, "Ontological Difference,", p. 122.

96. Dauenhauer, "Anarchy," p. 370.

97. Immanuel Kant, *Grundlegung zur Metaphysik der Sitten*, in *Gesammelte Schriften*, ed. by the Prussian Academy of the Sciences, 22 vols. (Berlin: Reimer, 1910–1942), vol. 4, pp. 428–30.

98. SG, pp. 167–69.

99. Schürmann, "Questioning the Foundations," pp. 362–64; Tugendhat, *Wahrheitsbegriff*, p. 383.

100. Schürmann, "Questioning the Foundations," pp. 365–66. As for Heidegger's position, cf. all passages in which Heidegger attributes the primacy to Being in the coming-to-pass of the process of the truth of Being.

101. Cf. Thomas Aquinas, *Summa Theologiae*, II II, q. 79, art. 1.

102. Martin Heidegger, *Logik. Die Frage nach der Wahrheit*, ed. Walter Biemel (Frankfurt: Klostermann, 1976); *Grundprobleme der Phänomenologie; Prolegomena zur Geschichte des Zeitbegriffs; etc.*

103. Cf. G. Védel, *La Dépolitisation, mythe ou réalité* (Paris: Presses Universitaires de France, 1962); R. Remond, *La démocratie à refaire* (Paris: Colin, 1963).

Epilogue

1. The essay first appeared in a French translation by J. Beaufret and D. Fédier in *Kierkegaard Vivant* (Paris: Gallimard, 1966), pp. 165–204.

2. Martin Heidegger, *Zur Sache des Denkens* (Tübingen: Niemeyer, 1969), pp. 61–80; English by Joan Stambaugh in *Basic Writings*, pp. 373–92.

3. SD, p. 61 (373).

4. SD, pp. 61–63 (374–76).

5. SD, pp. 63–65 (376–78).

6. SD, pp. 66–67 (378–79).

7. Plato, *The Seventh Letter*, 341 C.

8. Cf. G. W. F. Hegel, *Phenomenology of Spirit*, trans. A. V. Miller (Oxford: Clarendon Press, 1977), pp. 1–45.

9. SD, pp. 67–68 (379–81); cf. Hegel, *Phenomenology of Spirit*, p. 27.

10. Edmund Husserl, "Philosophie als strenge Wissenschaft," in *Logos* 1 (1910–1911): p. 301; cf. p. 340.

11. Edmund Husserl, *Ideen zu einer reinen Phänomenologie und phänomenologischen Philosophie*, vol. 1, ed. Walter Biemel (The Hague: Nijhoff, 1950), secs. 24 and 49; cf. *Formale und transzendentale Logik* (Halle: Niemeyer, 1929), p. 240.

12. SD, pp. 69–70 (381–83).

13. SD, pp. 70–73 (383–85).

14. Parmenides, Fragment I, 28–30.

15. SD, pp. 73–75 (385–87).

16. SD, p. 76 (388).

17. SD, p. 80 (392).

BIBLIOGRAPHY

There are several excellent bibliographies of works by Heidegger and of publications on his thought. The most extensive one is that prepared by Hans-Martin Sass: *Martin-Heidegger: Bibliography* (Bowling Green: Philosophy Documentation Center, 1982).

There is a much shorter, but very helpful, bibliography of English translations of Heidegger's works and of English books and articles on Heidegger's thinking by H. Miles Groth, in Thomas Sheehan, ed., *Heidegger: The Man and the Thinker* (Chicago: Precedent Publishing, Inc., 1981), pp. 281–347.

I have decided to limit myself here to a list of all the works by Heidegger and of those publications on his thought which I have used in writing this book. This bibliography is divided into three sections:
I. Works by Heidegger in chronological order with English translations.
II. Books and articles on Heidegger's thinking.
III. Collections of essays on Heidegger's thought.

I. Works by Heidegger in Chronological Order with English Translations

"Das Realitätsproblem in der modernen Philosophie." In *Philosophisches Jahrbuch* 25 (1912): 353–63. (Cf. FS, pp. 1–15.)
"Neuere Forschungen über Logik." In *Literarische Rundschau für das katholische Deutschland* 38 (1912): 465–72, 517–24, 565–70. (Cf. FS, pp. 17–43.)
Die Lehre vom Urteil im Psychologismus. Ein kritisch-positiver Beitrag zur Logik. Leipzig: Barth, 1914. (Cf. FS, pp. 59–188.)
Die Kategorien- und Bedeutungslehre des Duns Scotus. Tübingen: Mohr, 1916. (Cf. FS, pp. 189–411.)
"Der Zeitbegriff in der Geschichtswissenschaft." In *Zeitschrift für Philosophie und philosophische Kritik* 161 (1916): 173–88. (Cf. FS, pp. 413–33.)
   "The Concept of Time in the Science of History." Translated by H. S. Taylor and H. W. Uffelmann. *The Journal of the British Society for Phenomenology* 9 (1978): 3–10.
Sein und Zeit (1927). Tübingen: Niemeyer, 1953.
   Being and Time. Translated by John Macquarrie and Edward Robinson. London: SCM Press, 1962.
Kant und das Problem der Metaphysik (1927). Frankfurt: Klostermann, 1951.
   Kant and the Problem of Metaphysics. Translated by James S. Churchill. Bloomington: Indiana University Press, 1962.
Vom Wesen des Grundes (1928). Frankfurt: Klostermann, 1928.
   The Essence of Reasons. Translated by Terrence Malick. Evanston: Northwestern University Press, 1969.
Was ist Metaphysik? (1929). Frankfurt: Klostermann, 1955.
   (Postscript added to 4th edition in 1943; introduction added to 5th edition in 1949.)
   What is Metaphysics? Translated by David Farrell Krell. In Martin Heidegger, *Basic Writings,* edited by David Farrell Krell, pp. 95–116. New York: Harper & Row, 1977.

"Postscript" to *What is Metaphysics?* Translated by R. F. C. Hull and Alan Crick. In Werner Brock, *Existence and Being*, pp. 349–61. Chicago: Regnery, 1949.

"Introduction" to *What is Metaphysics?* Translated by W. Kaufmann. In W. Kaufmann, ed., *Existentialism from Dostoevsky to Sartre*, pp. 265–79. New York: New American Library, 1975.

Vom Wesen der Wahrheit (1930, 1943). Frankfurt: Klostermann, 1961.

On the Essence of Truth. Translated by John Sallis. In *Basic Writings*, pp. 117–41.

Die Selbstbehauptung der deutschen Universität (1933). Breslau: Korn, 1933.

Einführung in die Metaphysik (1935). Tübingen: Niemeyer, 1953.

An Introduction to Metaphysics. Translated by Ralph Manheim. New Haven: Yale University Press, 1959.

Erläuterungen zu Hölderlins Dichtung (1936, 1944). Frankfurt: Klostermann, 1953.

Translation of the second essay (pp. 31–45 of the German edition) by Douglas Scott: "Hölderlin and the Essence of Poetry," in Werner Brock, ed., *Existence and Being*, pp. 270–91.

Holzwege (1936–1946). Frankfurt: Klostermann, 1950.

The book contains six essays, whose English translations appeared in different collections:

"Der Ursprung des Kunstwerkes." In *Holzwege*, pp. 1–68.

"The Origin of the Work of Art." In Martin Heidegger, *Poetry, Language, Thought*, trans. Albert Hofstadter, pp. 7–87. New York: Harper and Row, 1971.

"Die Zeit des Weltbildes." In *Holzwege*, pp. 69–104.

"The Age of the World Picture." In Martin Heidegger, *The Question Concerning Technology and Other Essays*, trans. William Lovitt, pp. 115–54. New York: Harper & Row, 1977.

"Hegels Begriff der Erfahrung." In *Holzwege*, pp. 105–192.

Hegel's Concept of Experience. Translated by J. Glenn Gray. New York: Harper & Row, 1970.

"Nietzsches Wort 'Gott ist tot.'" In *Holzwege*, pp. 193–247.

"The Word of Nietzsche: 'God Is Dead.'" In Martin Heidegger, *The Question concerning Technology and Other Essays*, trans. William Lovitt, pp. 53–112.

"Wozu Dichter?" In *Holzwege*, pp. 248–95.

"What Are Poets For?" In Martin Heidegger, *Poetry, Language, Thought*, trans. Albert Hofstadter, pp. 91–142.

"Der Spruch des Anaximander." In *Holzwege*, pp. 296–343.

"The Anaximander Fragment." In Martin Heidegger, *Early Greek Thinking*, trans. David Farrell Krell and Frank A. Capuzzi, pp. 13–58. New York: Harper & Row, 1975.

Nietzsche (1936–1946). 2 vols. Pfullingen: Neske, 1961.

Nietzsche, vol. 1: *The Will to Power As Art.* Translated by David Farrell Krell. New York: Harper & Row, 1979.

Nietzsche, vol. 4: *Nihilism.* Translated by Frank A. Capuzzi and David Farrell Krell. New York: Harper & Row, 1982.

Vorträge und Aufsätze (1943–1954). Pfullingen: Neske, 1961.

The collection contains eleven essays, which were translated by different people for different occasions:

"Die Frage nach der Technik." In VA, pp. 13–44.

"The Question concerning Technology." In Martin Heidegger, *The Question concerning Technology and Other Essays*, trans. William Lovitt, pp. 3–35.

"Wissenschaft und Besinnung." In VA, pp. 45–70.

"Science and Reflection." In Martin Heidegger, *The Question concerning Technology and Other Essays*, trans. William Lovitt, pp. 155–82.

"Überwindung der Metaphysik." In VA, pp. 71–99.

"Overcoming Metaphysics." In Martin Heidegger, *The End of Philosophy*, trans. Joan Stambaugh, pp. 84–110. New York: Harper & Row, 1973.

"Wer ist Nietzsches Zarathustra?" In VA, pp. 101–126.

"Who Is Nietzsche's Zarathustra?" Translated by Bernd Magnus. In *Review of Metaphysics* 20 (1967): 411–31.

"Was heisst Denken?" In VA, pp. 129–43.

This lecture is, practically speaking, identical with the first two lectures of the lecture series with the same title; cf. below.

"Bauen, Wohnen, Denken." In VA, pp. 145–62.

"Building Dwelling Thinking." Translated by Albert Hofstadter. In *Basic Writings*, pp. 323–39.

"Das Ding." In VA, pp. 163–85.

"The Thing." in Martin Heidegger, *Poetry, Language, Thought*, trans. Albert Hofstadter, pp. 165–86.

". . . dichterisch wohnet der Mensch. . . ." In VA, pp. 187–204.

". . . Poetically Man Dwells. . . ." In Martin Heidegger, *Poetry, Language, Thought*, trans. Albert Hofstadter, pp. 213–29.

"*Logos* (Heraklit, Fragment 50)." In VA, pp. 207–229.

"*Logos* (Heraclitus, Fragment B 50)." In Martin Heidegger, *Early Greek Thinking*, trans. David Farrell Krell, pp. 59–78.

"*Moira* (Parmenides VIII, 34–41)." In VA, pp. 231–56.

"*Moira* (Parmenides VIII, 34–41)." In Martin Heidegger, *Early Greek Thinking*, trans. Frank A. Capuzzi, pp. 79–101.

"*Alētheia* (Heraklit, Fragment 16)." In VA, pp. 257–82.

"*Alētheia* (Heraclitus, Fragment B 16)." In Martin Heidegger, *Early Greek Thinking*, trans. Frank A. Capuzzi, pp. 102–123.

Platons Lehre von der Wahrheit (1942). *Mit einem Brief über den "Humanismus"* (1946). Bern: Francke, 1947.

"Plato's Doctrine of Truth." Translated by John Barlow. In *Philosophy in the Twentieth Century II*, W. Barrett et al., eds., pp. 251–70. New York: Random House, 1962.

"Letter on Humanism." Translated by Frank A. Capuzzi and J. Glenn Gray. In *Basic Writings*, pp. 193–242.

Was heisst Denken? (1951–1952). Tübingen: Niemeyer, 1954.

What Is Called Thinking? Translated by Fred D. Wieck and J. Glenn Gray. New York: Harper & Row, 1968.

Der Feldweg (1953). Frankfurt: Klostermann, 1953.

"The Pathway." Translated by Thomas Sheehan. In Thomas Sheehan, ed., *Heidegger: The Man and the Thinker*, pp. 69–71. Chicago: Precedent Publishing, Inc., 1981.

Aus der Erfahrung des Denkens (1954). Pfullingen: Neske, 1954.

"The Thinker As Poet." In Martin Heidegger, *Poetry, Language, Thought*, trans. Albert Hofstadter, pp. 3–14.

Was ist das—die Philosophie? (1955). Pfullingen: Neske, 1956.
    What Is Philosophy? Translated by Jean T. Wilde and William Kluback. New
    Haven: College & University Press, 1968.
Zur Seinsfrage (1955). Frankfurt: Klostermann, 1956.
    The Question of Being. Translated by William Kluback and Jean T. Wilde.
    New York: Twayne, 1958.
Der Satz vom Grund (1955–1956). Pfullingen: Neske, 1957.
Identität und Differenz (1957). Pfullingen: Neske, 1957.
    Identity and Difference. Translated by Joan Stambaugh. New York: Harper
    & Row, 1969.
Hebel—Der Hausfreund (1957). Pfullingen: Neske, 1958.
    Hebel--Friend of the House. Translated by Bruce V. Foltz and Michael
    Heim. In *Contemporary German Philosophy* 3 (1983): 89–101.
Unterwegs zur Sprache (1950–1959). Pfullingen: Neske, 1957.
    On the Way to Language. Translated by Peter D. Hertz and Joan Stambaugh.
    New York: Harper & Row, 1966.
    The first essay of US, namely, "Die Sprache," was translated by Albert
    Hofstadter and appeared in *Poetry, Language, Thought,* pp. 189–210.
"Vom Wesen und Begriff der *Phusis.* Aristoteles, Physik B, 1" (1958). In *Wegmar-*
    ken, pp. 239–301 (Frankfurt: Klostermann, 1976).
    "On the Being and Conception of *Phusis* in Aristotle's Physics B, 1."
    Translated by Thomas Sheehan. In *Man and World* 9 (1976): 219–70.
Gelassenheit (1959). Pfullingen: Neske, 1959.
    Discourse on Thinking. Translated by John M. Anderson and E. Hans
    Freund. New York: Harper & Row, 1966.
Kants These über das Sein (1962). Tübingen: Niemeyer, 1962.
    "Kant's Thesis about Being." Translated by Ted E. Klein and William E.
    Pohl. In *The Southwestern Journal of Philosophy* 4 (1973): 7–33.
Die Frage nach dem Ding (1962). Pfullingen: Neske, 1962.
    What Is A Thing? Translated by W. Barton and Vera Deutsch. Chicago:
    Regnery, 1969. The translation of part of this book (namely, FD, pp. 66–108)
    was reprinted in *Basic Writings,* pp. 247–82.
Die Technik und die Kehre (1962). Pfullingen: Neske, 1962.
    "The Question concerning Technology." Translated by William Lovitt. In
    The Question concerning Technology and Other Essays, pp. 3–35. "The Turn-
    ing." Translated by William Lovitt. In *The Question,* pp. 36–49.
Wegmarken (1967). Frankfurt: Klostermann, 1978.
Zur Sache des Denkens (1969). Tübingen: Niemeyer, 1969.
    On Time and Being. Translated by Joan Stambaugh. New York: Harper &
    Row, 1972.
Phänomenologie und Theologie (1927, 1964). Frankfurt: Klostermann, 1972.
    "Phenomenology and Theology." Translated by James Hart and John
    Maraldo. In *The Piety of Thinking,* pp. 3–21. Bloomington: Indiana Univer-
    sity Press, 1976.
Schellings Abhandlung über das Wesen der menschlichen Freiheit (1936). Edited
    by H. Feick. Tübingen: Niemeyer, 1971.
Die Grundprobleme der Phänomenologie (1927). Edited by F.-W. von Herrmann.
    Frankfurt: Klostermann, 1975.
    The Basic Problems of Phenomenology. Translated by Albert Hofstadter.
    Bloomington: Indiana University Press, 1982.

Logik. Die Frage nach der Wahrheit (1925–1926). Edited by Walter Biemel. Frankfurt: Klostermann, 1976.

Phänomenologische Interpretation von Kants Kritik der reinen Vernunft (1927–1928). Edited by Ingtraud Görland. Frankfurt: Klostermann, 1977.

Metaphysische Anfangsgründe der Logik im Ausgang von Leibniz. Edited by Klaus Held. Frankfurt: Klostermann, 1978.

Prolegomena zur Geschichte des Zeitbegriffs (1925). Edited by Petra Jaeger. Frankfurt: Klostermann, 1979.

Hölderlins Hymnen 'Germanien' und 'Der Rhein' (1934–1935). Edited by Suzanne Ziegler. Frankfurt: Klostermann, 1980.

Hegels Phänomenologie des Geistes (1930–1931). Edited by Ingtraud Görland. Frankfurt: Klostermann, 1980.

Aristoteles: Metaphysik IX (1931). Edited by Heinrich Hüni. Frankfurt: Klostermann, 1981.

Grundbegriffe (1941). Edited by Petra Jaeger. Frankfurt: Klostermann, 1981.

Vom Wesen der menschlichen Freiheit (1930). Edited by Hartmut Tietjen. Frankfurt: Klostermann, 1982.

Frühe Schriften (1912–1916). Edited by Friedrich-Wilhelm von Herrmann. Frankfurt: Klostermann, 1978.

II. Books and Articles on Heidegger's Thinking

Adamczewski, Zygmunt. "On the Way to Being." In *Heidegger and the Path of Thinking*, ed. J. Sallis, pp. 12–36. Pittsburgh: Duquesne University Press, 1970.

Alderman, Harold G. "Heidegger's Critique of Science and Technology." In *Heidegger and Modern Philosophy. Critical Essays*, ed. Michael Murray, pp. 35–50. New Haven: Yale University Press, 1971.

——— "The Work of Art and Other Things." In *Martin Heidegger: In Europe and America*, ed. E. G. Ballard and Ch. E. Scott, pp. 157–69. The Hague: Nijhoff, 1973.

Alleman, Beda. *Hölderlin und Heidegger.* Zurich: Atlantis, 1954.

——— "Martin Heidegger und die Politik." In *Merkur* 21 (1967): 962–76.

Anderson, John M. "Truth, Process and Creature in Heidegger's Thought." In *Heidegger and the Quest for Truth*, ed. Manfred S. Frings, pp. 28–61. Chicago: Quadrangle Books, 1968.

Aubenque, Pierre. "Travail et 'Gelassenheit' chez Heidegger." In *Études Germaniques* 32 (1977): 259–67.

Ballard, Edward G. "Heidegger's View and Evaluation of Nature and Natural Science." In *Heidegger and the Path of Thinking*, ed. John C. Sallis, pp. 37–64. Pittsburgh: Duquesne University Press, 1970.

Bartky, Sandra Lee. "Heidegger's Philosophy of Art." In *Heidegger: The Man and the Thinker*, ed. Thomas Sheehan, pp. 257–74. Chicago: Precedent Publishing, Inc., 1981.

Beaufret, Jean. *Dialogue avec Heidegger.* 3 vols. Paris: Minuit, 1973–1974.

———. "Heidegger et le problème de la vérité." In *Fontaine* 63 (1947): 758–85.

Biemel, Walter. "Heidegger and Metaphysics." In *Heidegger: The Man and the Thinker*, ed. Thomas Sheehan, pp. 163–172. Chicago: Precedent Publishing, Inc., 1981.

——— *Le concept du monde chez Heidegger.* Louvain: Nauwelaerts, 1950.

——— *Martin Heidegger: An Illustrated Study.* New York: Harcourt, Brace, Jovanovich, 1976.

——— "Poetry and Language." In *On Heidegger and Language*, ed. Joseph J. Kockelmans, pp. 65–105. Evanston: Northwestern University Press, 1972.

Birault, Henri. "Existence et vérité d'après Heidegger." In *Revue de Métaphysique et de Morale* 56 (1950): 35–87.

——— "La foi et la pensée d'après Heidegger." In *Recherches et Débats* 10 (1955): 108–132.

——— *Heidegger et l'expérience de la pensée.* Paris: Gallimard, 1978.

——— "Thinking and Poetizing in Heidegger." In *On Heidegger and Language*, ed. Joseph J. Kockelmans, pp. 147–68. Evanston: Northwestern University Press, 1972.

Boeckaert, Luk. "Ontology and Ethics: Reflections on Levinas' Critique of Heidegger." In *International Philosophical Quarterly* 10 (1970): 402–419.

Boelen, Bernard. "The Question of Ethics in the Thought of Martin Heidegger." In *Heidegger and the Quest for Truth*, ed. Manfred S. Frings, pp. 76–105. Chicago: Quadrangle Books, 1968.

Bourdieu, P. *Die politische Ontologie Martin Heideggers.* Frankfurt: Syndikat, 1976.

Brechtken, J. "Geschichte und Transzendenz oder die Gottesfrage am Ende der Metaphysik." In *Tijdschrift voor Filosofie* 39 (1977): 587–609.

Bretschneider, W. *Sein und Wahrheit. Über die Zusammengehörigkeit von Sein und Wahrheit im Denken Martin Heideggers.* Meisenheim: Hain, 1965.

Buddeberg, Else. *Denken und Dichten des Seins.* Stuttgart: Metzler, 1956.

——— *Heidegger und die Dichtung.* Stuttgart: Metzler, 1953.

Butkus, Robert G. *Heidegger's Thought and Ethics.* Dissertation, University of Waterloo, 1957.

Camele, Anthony. "Heideggerian Ethics." In *Philosophy Today* 21 (1977): 284–93.

Caputo, John D. "Fundamental Ontology and the Ontological Difference." In *Proceedings of the Catholic Philosophical Association* 51 (1977): 28–35.

——— "Heidegger's Original Ethics." In *The New Scholasticism* 45 (1971): 127–38.

——— "The Poverty of Thought: A Reflection on Heidegger and Eckhart." In *Heidegger: The Man and the Thinker*, ed. Thomas Sheehan, pp. 209–216. Chicago: Precedent Publishing, Inc., 1981.

——— *The Way Back into the Ground. An Interpretation of the Path of Heidegger's Thought.* Dissertation, Brynn Mawr College, 1968.

Chiodi, P. *Heideggers Einfluss auf die Wissenchaften.* Bern: Francke, 1949.

Cousineau, R. H. *Humanism and Ethics. An Introduction to Heidegger's Letter on Humanism, with a Critical Bibliography.* Louvain: Nauwelaerts, 1972.

Danner, H. *Das Göttliche und der Gott bei Heidegger.* Meisenheim: Hain, 1971.

Dauenhauer, Bernard. "Does Anarchy Make Political Sense? A Response to Schürmann." In *Human Studies* 1 (1978): 369–75.

——— "Renovating the Problem of Politics." In *The Review of Metaphysics* 29 (1976): 624–41.

Deely, John N. *The Tradition via Heidegger: An Essay on the Meaning of Being in the Philosophy of Martin Heidegger.* New York: Humanities Press, 1972.

Dondeyne, A. "La différence ontologique chez M. Heidegger." in *Revue Philosophique de Louvain* 56 (1958): 35–62, 251–93.

Faye, J. P. "Attaques nazies contre Heidegger." In *Meditations* 5 (1962): 137–54.
———— "Heidegger et la 'révolution'." In *Meditations* 3 (1961): 151–59.
———— "La lecture et l'énouncé." In *Critique* 237 (1967): 288–95.
Fedier, F. "Trois attaques contre Heidegger." In *Critique* 234 (1966): 893–904.
Ferry, L. and Renaut, A. "La dimension éthique dans la pensée de Heidegger." In *Nachdenken über Heidegger*, ed. Ute Guzzoni, pp. 36–54. Hildesheim: Gerstenberg Verlag, 1980.
Fetscher, I.; Grau, G.-G.; Ilting, K.-H.; and Pöggeler, O. *Probleme der Ethik zur Diskussion gestellt.* Munich: Alber, 1972.
Gandillac, M. de. "Entretiens avec Martin Heidegger." In *Les temps modernes* 1 (1946): 713–24.
Gans, Steven. "Ethics or Ontology: Levinas and Heidegger." In *Philosophy Today* 16 (1972): 117–21.
Gethmann, Carl Friedrich. *Verstehen und Auslegung. Das Methodenproblem in der Philosophie Martin Heideggers.* Bonn: Bouvier, 1974.
———— "Zu Heideggers Wahrheitsfrage." In *Kantstudien* 65 (1974): 186–200.
Gethmann-Siefert, Annemarie. *Das Verhältnis von Philosophie und Theologie im Denken Martin Heideggers.* Munich: Alber, 1974.
Gründer, Karlfried. "Heidegger's Critique of Science." In *Philosophy Today* 7 (1963): 15–32.
Guibal, F. "Martin Heidegger et l'attendu du 'Dieu divin'." In *Études* 334 (1971): 594–624, 753–74.
Harries, Karsten. "Heidegger As a Political Thinker." In *The Review of Metaphysics* 29 (1975–1976): 642–69.
Herrmann, Friedrich-Wilhelm von. *Heideggers Philosophie der Kunst: Eine systematische Interpretation der Holzwege-Abhandlung 'Der Ursprung des Kunstwerkes'.* Frankfurt: Klostermann, 1980.
Hirsch, E. F. "Heidegger und die Dichtung." In *Journal of the History of Philosophy* 6 (1968): 271–83.
Hühnerfeld, P. *In Sachen Heidegger.* Hamburg: Hoffman & Campe, 1961.
Ijsseling, Sam. "Het zijn en de zijnden. Een studie over de ontologische *Differenz* bij Martin Heidegger." in *Tijdschrift voor Filosofie* 28 (1966): 3–51.
Jäger, A. *Gott: Nochmals Martin Heidegger.* Tübingen: Mohr, 1978.
Jonas, Hans. "Gnosticism and Modern Nihilism." In *Social Research* 19 (1952): 430–52.
Kelkel, Arion L. *La légende de l'être. Langage et poésie chez Heidegger.* Paris: Vrin, 1980.
Kisiel, Theodore J. "Heidegger and the New Images of Science." In *Research in Phenomenology* 7 (1977): 162–81.
———— "The Language of the Event: The Event of Language." In *Heidegger and the Path of Thinking*, ed. John C. Sallis, pp. 85–104. Pittsburgh: Duquesne University Press, 1970.
———— "Science, Phenomenology, and the Thinking of Being." In *Phenomenology and the Natural Sciences*, ed. Joseph J. Kockelmans and Theodore J. Kisiel, pp. 167–83. Evanston: Northwestern University Press, 1970.
———— "Towards the Topology of Dasein." In *Heidegger: The Man and the Thinker*, ed. Thomas Sheehan, pp. 95–105. Chicago: Precedent Publishing, Inc., 1981.
Köchler, H. "Das Gottesproblem im Denken Heideggers." In *Zeitschrift für katholische Theologie* 95 (1973): 61–90.

Kockelmans, Joseph J. "Destructive Retrieve and Hermeneutic Phenomenology in 'Being and Time'." In *Research in Phenomenology* 7 (1977): 106–137.

———— "The Era of the World-as-Picture." In *Phenomenology and the Natural Sciences,* ed. Joseph J. Kockelmans and Theodore J. Kisiel, pp. 184–201. Evanston: Northwestern University Press, 1970.

———— "Heidegger on the Essential Difference and Necessary Relationship between Philosophy and Science." In *Phenomenology and the Natural Sciences,* ed. Joseph J. Kockelmans and Theodore J. Kisiel, pp. 147–66. Evanston: Northwestern University Press, 1970.

———— "Heidegger on Theology." In *The Southwestern Journal of Philosophy* 4 (1973): 86–108.

———— "Heidegger on Time and Being." In *Martin Heidegger: In Europe and America,* ed. E. G. Ballard and Ch. E. Scott, pp. 55–76. The Hague: Nijhoff, 1973.

———— "Ontological Difference, Hermeneutics, and Language." In *On Heidegger and Language,* ed. Joseph J. Kockelmans, pp. 195–234. Evanston: Northwestern University Press, 1972.

———— "Thanks-giving: The Completion of Thought." In *Heidegger and the Quest for Truth,* ed. Manfred S. Frings, pp. 163–83. Chicago: Quadrangle Books, 1968.

Kuhn, Helmut. *Begegnung mit dem Sein. Meditationen zur Metaphysik des Gewissens.* Tübingen: Mohr, 1953.

Liebrucks, Bruno. "Idee und ontologische Differenz." In *Kant-Studien* 48 (1956): 268–301.

Lingis, Alphonso F. "On the Essence of Technique." In *Heidegger and the Quest for Truth,* ed. Manfred S. Frings, pp. 126–38. Chicago: Quadrangle Books, 1968.

Lohmann, Johannes. "M. Heidegger's 'Ontological Difference' and Language." In *On Heidegger and Language,* ed. Joseph J. Kockelmans, pp. 303–363. Evanston: Northwestern University Press, 1972.

Löwith, Karl. "Les implications politiques de la philosophie de l'existence chez Heidegger." In *Les temps modernes* 2 (1946–1947): 343–60.

Marx, Werner. *Heidegger and the Tradition.* Translated by Theodore J. Kisiel and Murray Greene. Evanston: Northwestern University Press, 1971.

———— "Die Sterblichen." In *Nachdenken über Heidegger,* ed. Ute Guzzoni, pp. 160–75. Hildesheim: Gerstenberg Verlag, 1980.

———— "The World in Another Beginning: Poetic Dwelling and the Role of the Poet." In *On Heidegger and Language,* ed. Joseph J. Kockelmans, pp. 235–59. Evanston: Northwestern University Press, 1972.

Marx, Wolfgang. "Die ontologische Differenz in der Perspektive der regionalen Ontologie des Daseins." In *Nachdenken über Heidegger,* ed. Ute Guzzoni, pp. 176–97. Hildesheim: Gerstenberg Verlag, 1980.

Maurer, Reinhard. "Von Heidegger zur praktischen Philosophie." In *Rehabilitierung der praktischen Philosophie,* ed. M. Riedel, pp. 415–54. Freiburg: Alber, 1972.

Mehta, J. L. *Martin Heidegger. The Way and the Vision.* Honolulu: University of Hawaii Press, 1976.

———— *The Philosophy of Martin Heidegger.* New York: Harper & Row, 1971.

Mongis, H. *Heidegger et la critique de la notion de valeur.* The Hague: Nijhoff, 1976.

Morra, G. "Martino Heidegger: la morale come abitazione nel'essere." In *Etica* 3 (1964): 205–220.

Nicholson, Graeme. "Camus and Heidegger: Anarchists." In *University of Toronto Quarterly* 1971, pp. 14–23.

——— "The Commune of *Being and Time.*" In *Dialogue* 10 (1971): 708–726.

Noller, G., ed. *Heidegger und die Theologie. Beginn und Fortgang der Diskussion.* Munich: Karl Alber, 1967.

O'Meara, Thomas F. "Tillich and Heidegger: A Structural Relationship." In *The Harvard Theological Review* 61 (1969): 249–61.

Oshima, Sueo. "Barth's *Analogia Relationis* and Heidegger's Ontological Difference." *The Journal of Religion* 53 (1973): 176–94.

Ott, Heinrich. *Denken und Sein. Der Weg Martin Heideggers und der Weg der Theologie.* Zollikon: Evangelischer Verlag, 1959.

Oyen, H. "Fundamentalontologie und Ethik." In *Library of the Xth International Congress of Philosophy,* vol. 2, pp. 107–121. Amsterdam, 1948.

Palmier, Jean-Michel. *Les écrits politiques de Heidegger.* Paris: L'Herne, 1968.

Paumen, J. "Heidegger et le thème nietzschéen de la mort de Dieu." In *Revue Internationale de Philosophie* 14 (1960): 238–62.

——— "Heidegger et le sens du chemin." In *Revue de l'Université de Bruxelles* 17 (1964–1965): 384–425.

Perotti, James L. *Heidegger and the Divine: The Thinker, the Poet, and God.* Athens: Ohio University Press, 1974.

Pöggeler, Otto. *Der Denkweg Martin Heideggers.* Pfullingen: Neske, 1963.

——— "Heidegger's Topologie des Seins." In *Man and World,* 2 (1969): 331–57. (English in *On Heidegger and Language,* ed. Joseph J. Kockelmans, pp. 107–135. Evanston: Northwestern University Press, 1972.)

——— "Metaphysics and the Topology of Being in Heidegger." In *Heidegger: The Man and the Thinker,* ed. Thomas Sheehan, pp. 173–85. Chicago: Precedent Publishing, Inc., 1981.

——— *Philosophie und Politik bei Heidegger.* Freiburg: Alber, 1972.

——— "Sein als Ereignis." In *Zeitschrift für philosophische Forschung* 13 (1959): 597–632. (English in *Philosophy Today* 9 [1975]:152–78.)

Pugliese, Orlando. "Vermittlung und Kehre. Grundzüge des Geschichtsdenkens bei Martin Heidegger." In *Symposion* 18 (1965): 1–226.

Rasmussen, David. *Poetry and Truth.* The Hague: Mouton, 1974.

Richardson, William J. "Heidegger and God—and Prof. Jonas." In *Thought* 40 (1965): 13–40.

——— "Heidegger's Critique of Science." In *The New Scholasticism* 42 (1968): 511–36.

——— *Heidegger: Through Phenomenology to Thought.* The Hague: Nijhoff, 1963.

Richardson, William J. "Heidegger's Way through Phenomenology to the Thinking of Being." In *Heidegger: The Man and the Thinker,* ed. Thomas Sheehan, pp. 79–93. Chicago: Precedent Publishing, Inc., 1981.

Ricoeur, Paul. "The Critique of Subjectivity and *Cogito* in the Philosophy of Heidegger." In *Heidegger and the Quest for Truth,* ed. Manfred S. Frings, pp. 62–75. Chicago: Quadrangle Books, 1968.

Rosales, Alberto. *Transzendenz und Differenz. Ein Beitrag zum Problem der ontologischen Differenz beim frühen Heidegger.* The Hague: Nijhoff, 1970.

Rosenthal, K. "Martin Heideggers Auffassung von Gott." In *Kerygma und Dogma* 13 (1967): 212–29.

Sallis, John. "Into the Clearing." In *Heidegger: The Man and the Thinker,* ed. Thomas Sheehan, pp. 107–115. Chicago: Precedent Publishing, Inc., 1981.

———— "Language and Reversal." In *Southern Journal of Philosophy* 8 (1970): 381–97.

———— "La différence ontologique et l'unité de la pensée de Heidegger." In *Revue Philosophique de Louvain* 65 (1967): 192–206.

———— "Towards the Movement of Reversal: Science, Technology, and the Language of Homecoming." in *Heidegger and the Path of Thinking,* ed. John C. Sallis, pp. 138–68. Pittsburgh: Duquesne University Press, 1970.

Schöfer, Erasmus. *Die Sprache Heideggers.* Pfullingen: Neske, 1962.

Schrag, Calvin O. "Re-thinking Metaphysics." In *Heidegger and the Quest for Truth,* ed. Manfred S. Frings, pp. 106–125. Chicago: Quadrangle Books, 1968.

———— "The Transvaluation of Aesthetics and the Work of Art." In *The Southwestern Journal of Philosophy* 4 (1973): 109–124.

Schrey, Heinz-Horst. "Die Bedeutung der Philosophie Martin Heideggers für die Theologie." In *Martin Heideggers Einfluss auf die Wissenschaften,* pp. 9–21. Bern: Francke, 1969.

Schulz, W. *Der Gott der neuzeitlichen Metaphysik.* Pfullingen: Neske, 1957.

Schürmann, Reiner. *Le principe d'anarchie. Heidegger et la question de l'agir.* Paris: Seuil, 1982.

———— "The Ontological Difference and Political Philosophy." In *Philosophy and Phenomenological Research* 40 (1979): 99–122.

———— "Political Thinking in Heidegger." In *Social Research* 45 (1978): 191–221.

———— "Questioning the Foundations of Practical Philosophy." In *Human Studies* 1 (1978): 357–68.

Schuurman, Egbert. *Technology and the Future,* pp. 80–125. Toronto: Wedge Publishing Company, 1980.

Schwan, Alexander. *Politische Philosophie im Denken Heideggers.* Cologne: Westdeutscher Verlag, 1965.

Seven, F. *Die Ewigkeit Gottes und die Zeitlichkeit des Menschen.* Göttingen: Vandenhoeck und Ruprecht, 1979.

Sheehan, Thomas. "Heidegger's Early Years: Fragment for a Philosophical Biography." In *Heidegger: The Man and the Thinker,* ed. Thomas Sheehan, pp. 3–19. Chicago: Precedent Publishing, Inc., 1981.

Siewerth, G. "Martin Heidegger und die Frage nach Gott." In *Hochland* 53 (1960–1961): 516–26.

Sitter, B. *Dasein und Ethik.* Munich: Alber, 1975.

Steiger, Emil. *Zu einem Vers von Möricke. Ein Briefwechsel mit Martin Heidegger.* Zurich: Artemis, 1951.

Taminiaux, Jacques. *Recoupements.* Bruxelles: Ousia, 1982.

———— "Finitude and the Absolute: Remarks on Hegel and Heidegger." In *Heidegger: The Man and the Thinker,* ed. Thomas Sheehan, pp. 187–208. Chicago: Precedent Publishing, Inc., 1981.

Theunissen, Michael. "Intentionaler Gegenstand und ontologische Differenz. Ansätze zur Fragestellung Heideggers in der Phänomenologie Husserls." In *Philosophisches Jahrbuch* 70 (1962–1963): 344–62.

Tugendhat, E. "Heideggers Idee von Wahrheit." In *Heidegger. Perspektiven zur Deutung seines Werkes,* ed. Otto Pöggeler, pp. 286–97. Cologne: Kiepenheuer und Witsch, 1969.

———— *Der Wahrheitsbegriff bei Husserl und Heidegger* (Berlin: de Gruyter, 1967).

Ugirashebuja, O. *Dialogue entre la poésie et la pensée d'après l'oeuvre de Heidegger.* Bruxelles: Lumen Vitae, 1977.

Veauthier, W. "Analogie des Seins und ontologische Differenz." In *Symposion* 4 (1955): 1–89.

Vietta, Egon. *Die Seinsfrage bei Martin Heidegger.* Stuttgart: Schwab, 1950.

Vycinas, Vincent. *Earth and Gods.* The Hague: Nijhoff, 1961.

———— *Search for Gods.* The Hague: Nijhoff, 1972.

Waelhens, Alphonse de. *La philosophie de Martin Heidegger.* Louvain: Nauwelaerts, 1941.

Welte, Bernard. "God in Heidegger's Thought." In *Philosophy Today* 26 (1982): 85–100.

———— "Seeking and Finding: The Speech at Heidegger's Burial." In *Heidegger: The Man and the Thinker,* ed. Thomas Sheehan, pp. 73–75. Chicago: Precedent Publishing, Inc., 1981.

Williams, J. "Heidegger, Death, and God." In *Studies in Religion* 1 (1972): 298–320.

III. Collections of Essays on Heidegger

Ballard, Edward G., and Scott, Charles E., eds. *Martin Heidegger: In Europe and America.* The Hague: Nijhoff, 1973.

Elliston, Frederick, ed. *Heidegger's Existential Analytic.* The Hague: Mouton, 1978.

Frings, Manfred S., ed. *Heidegger and the Quest for Truth.* Chicago: Quadrangle Books, 1968.

Gadamer, H. G.; Marx, W.; and Weizsäcker, C. F. von, eds. *Heidegger: Freiburger Universitätsvorträge zu seinem Gedenken.* Freiburg: Alber, 1977.

Guzzoni, Ute, ed. *Nachdenken über Heidegger.* Hildesheim: Gerstenberg Verlag, 1980.

Kockelmans, Joseph J., ed. *On Heidegger and Language.* Evanston: Northwestern University Press, 1972.

Murray, Michael, ed. *Heidegger and Modern Philosophy: Critical Essays.* New Haven: Yale University Press, 1978.

Pöggeler, Otto, ed. *Heidegger: Perspektiven zur Deutung seines Werkes.* Cologne: Kiepenheuer und Witsch, 1969.

Robinson, J. M., and Cobb, B. J., eds. *The Later Heidegger and Theology.* New York: Harper and Row, 1962.

Sallis, John C., ed. *Heidegger and the Path of Thinking.* Pittsburgh: Duquesne University Press, 1970.

Sheehan, Thomas, ed. *Heidegger: The Man and the Thinker.* Chicago: Precedent Publishing, Inc., 1981.

Anteile. Martin Heidegger zum 60. Geburtstag. Frankfurt: Klostermann, 1959.

Durchblicke. Martin Heidegger zum 80. Geburtstag. Frankfurt: Klostermann, 1970.

Martin Heideggers Einfluss auf die Wissenschaften. Bern: Francke Verlag, 1969.

Martin Heidegger zum siebzigsten Geburtstag. Pfullingen: Neske, 1959.

INDEX

Index of Names

Index of Subjects